THE BIOPSYCHOLOGY OF MOOD AND AROUSAL

The Biopsychology
of Mood and Arousal

Robert E. Thayer

New York   Oxford
OXFORD UNIVERSITY PRESS
1989

Oxford University Press

Oxford   New York   Toronto
Delhi   Bombay   Calcutta   Madras   Karachi
Petaling Jaya   Singapore   Hong Kong   Tokyo
Nairobi   Dar es Salaam   Cape Town
Melbourne   Auckland

and associated companies in
Berlin   Ibadan

Copyright © 1989 by Oxford University Press, Inc.

Published by Oxford University Press, Inc.,
200 Madison Avenue, New York, New York 10016

Oxford is a registered trademark of Oxford University Press

Library of Congress Cataloging-in-Publication Data
Thayer, Robert E.
The biopsychology of mood and arousal / by Robert E. Thayer.
p.   cm.   Bibliography: p.   Includes index.
ISBN 0-19-505162-9
1. Mood (Psychology)—Physiological aspects.
2. Arousal (Physiology)
3. Psychobiology.   I. Title.
[DNLM: 1. Affective Symptoms—psychology.
2. Arousal—physiology.
3. Psychophysiology.   WM 171 T372b]
QP401.T42 1989   152.4′54—dc19   DNLM/DLC   for Library of Congress
89-2914   CIP

9 8 7 6 5 4 3 2 1
Printed in the United States of America
on acid-free paper

To Elsie, Daniel, Leah, and Kara,
four loved ones in two generations who have given me much.

PREFACE

This book presents a broad analysis of nonpathological mood states and reviews the scientific research on mood that has taken place over the past decade. Although most of this research has a psychological basis, I have attempted to demonstrate that the central concepts have clear biological underpinnings, and that the best current understanding of mood occurs in this context.

The complex model for conceptualizing mood outlined in these pages is the product of over two decades of empirical research that has led me to a theory of naturally occurring arousal states and their manifestations in conscious awareness. My research began with detailed psychometric analyses of core mood states and a variety of construct-validation studies incorporating psychophysiological assessments and predictions taken from general biopsychological theory. I have been encouraged by colleagues to draw much of this work together and to relate it to current research on mood, because many of my more important early findings have since been validated and extended by others working in laboratories on diverse scientific problems.

The kind of biopsychological analysis of mood offered here is currently quite popular, but this was not always the case. American psychology has moved from behaviorist models in the 1960s that almost entirely neglected mood as important to influential cognitive paradigms in the 1970s that neglected affect and mood variables as well. Only now have scientists from many orientations begun to recognize that moods are natural biological processes. It is increasingly clear from expanding research programs, or at least from theoretical comment, that behavioral and biological scientists regularly think of moods and emotions as significantly affected by basic biological influences such as sleep-wake rhythms and other biological cycles, by psychomotor activity, and nutritional substances, and in the larger sense by biologically fixed temperaments that set limits to the mood changes an individual can experience. There is also increasing recognition that affective states themselves significantly influence a variety of cognitive and motivational processes.

Writing this book has offered some special degrees of difficulty. In addition to researchers concerned with mood-related topics, the book is intended for scientists and professionals from diverse backgrounds. For example, I have attempted to make the work accessible to exercise physiologists, nutrition scientists, psychotherapists, and biologists concerned with human behavior. This represents a wide variety of disciplines, and although each field employs scientific methods, each has its own technical language, and to some extent its own empirical approach. Consequently, in writing the book I often found myself dealing with a technical concept by focusing on the underlying logic and, not infrequently, the reader will encounter explanatory passages where I have avoided the use of a technical term that would have made the discussion considerably more difficult for some readers.

As a second point about intended audience, I should indicate that my work has never been concerned primarily with self-help applications. The concepts under discussion, however, are so immediate to most people's experience that questions of application inevitably arise. In my experience it is clear that individual differences are very important and, therefore, the first step in applying these ideas is usually systematic self-observation. Over the years of teaching upper-division university classes on research methodology, I have developed procedures for longitudinal self-studies of mood that are both didactically valuable, and that students find quite personally beneficial. Thus, I have included several detailed appendixes with measurement materials and procedures (both technical and simplified) so readers can carry out sound self-observational studies.

My work on mood owes much to the pioneering ideas of early biopsychologists such as Donald Hebb, Elizabeth Duffy, and Robert Malmo. These broad thinkers recognized that superseding the great complexities of the body there are general variations that provide understanding that is lost if the intricacies become too much the focus. Furthermore, their recognition of the close association of physiological and psychological processes appears to be accepted without question today, but their work did much to set the stage for that understanding. My work also owes much to Vincent Nowlis, my professor of many years ago who oversaw my doctoral dissertation and who pioneered most of the multivariate methods for the study of mood that are in wide use today.

A large number of individuals have been of great immediate help in the writing of this book. They gave their time and efforts to carefully read and critique various chapters, and in several cases the whole book. I am very thankful for their efforts, and their criticisms were extraordinarily valuable, but these colleagues cannot be blamed for any shortcomings of this book since in many cases I chose not to follow all their suggestions.

Martin Fiebert, Kirby Gilliland, and Auke Tellegen read the whole book and provided systematic comments on each chapter. Martin Fiebert was particularly helpful because his prompt and insightful feedback about each chapter was provided as the book was being written. Colleagues who read large portions or individual chapters of the book and who provided valuable feedback include Alexander Beckman, Hans Eysenck, Kenneth Green, Raphael Hanson, Ralph Hupka, Jeanne Kohl, Kevin MacDonald, Ruth Stewart, Nancy Voils, and Sharon Wolf. I am also thankful for the help of various editors at Oxford University Press, and particularly for the invaluable assistance of Joan Bossert and Linda Grossman.

July 1988   R.E.T.
Long Beach, California

CONTENTS

1 Introduction, 3

The Resurgence of Interest in Mood and Affect, 4
Mood as a Biopsychological Concept, 4
Energetic and Tense Arousal, 6
Mood, Perception of Personal Problems, and Self, 8
Consciousness and Self-Observation, 9
Mood, Self-Management, and Self-Help, 11

2 Modern Perspectives on Mood, 13

Dimensions and Assessments of Mood, 15
Methods of Experimentally Manipulating Mood States, 20
Mood, Biology, and Physiology, 25
Mood, Memory, and Other Cognitive Processes, 32
Mood and Illness, 37
Food and Mood, 38
Weather, Geophysical Phenomena, and Mood, 39
Naturally Occurring Antecedents of Mood, 41
Other Mood-Related Topic Areas, 43
Analytic Retrospective and Future Orientation, 44

3 Arousal: A Basic Element of Mood and Behavior, 46

Energetic Arousal, 48
Tense Arousal, 50
The Moods of Interacting Arousal Reactions, 52
Evidence that Arousal Reactions Are Registered
in Conscious Awareness, 54
The Language of Arousal Feelings, 59
Evolutionary Biology Issues, 62
Biopsychological Overview of Arousal, 65

4   Daily Rhythms of Subjective Energy
        and Other Biopsychological Cycles, 67

Circadian Rhythms of Energetic Arousal, 68
Endogenous Control of Energetic Arousal, 71
Arousal Rhythms and Psychological Perspective Changes:
Problem Perception and Optimism, 73
Individual Differences in Daily Rhythms, 78
Other Rhythms of Energetic and Tense Arousal, 83
Speculations and Applications, 86

5   Determinants of Energetic and Tense Arousal,
        Including Cognitive–Mood Interactions, 88

Exercise and Energetic Arousal: Experimental Demonstrations, 88
Biological Considerations, 93
Other Determinants of Energetic Arousal, 95
Interactions of Cognition and Energetic Arousal, 98
Requirements Versus Resources Imbalances:
Basic Antecedents of Tense Arousal, 101
Cognitive-Affective Interactions Involving Subtle
but Persistent Negative Mood States, 104
Bioevolutionary Analyses of Tense Arousal, 106

6   The Natural Interaction of Energetic and Tense Moods:
        A Multidimensional Arousal Model, 110

Summary of Mood Interactions, 111
Early Experimental Evidence, 112
The Covariation of Energy and Tension, 113
High Tension and Low Energy, 115
Low Energy and Vulnerability to Tension, 117
High Energy and Low Tension, 119
Exhaustion, 122
Selected Physiological Mechanisms, 124
Mood and Biology, 128
Other Arousal Models in Comparison, 129
Summary of a Multidimensional Arousal Model, 134

7   Issues Relating to Formal and Informal Research on Mood, 137

Reliability of Mood Measurements Through Data Aggregation, 137
The Value of Naturalistic Versus Laboratory Test Conditions
in the Study of Mood, 139
Self-Study for the Understanding of Mood Dynamics, 144

8 Toward an Understanding of Nonpathological Mood States:
Evidence, Speculations, and Applications, 147

Essential Features of Mood, 147

An Understanding of Mood Based on Energy and Tension, 149

Hypothetical Scenario Regarding the Mood States
of a Person Under Stress, 152

Self-Determined Mood Modulation: Use of Sugar Snacks,
Caffeine, Tobacco, and Other Drugs, 157

Unanswered Questions About Mood, 163

Applications: Systematic Self-Observation, 168

Applications: Projects, Measurement Materials,
and Designs for Systematic Self-Observation, 170

Applications: Moderate Exercise for Short-Term
Mood Modulation, 171

Applications: Recognition and Accommodation
to Time of Day Mood Effects, 174

Applications: Enhancing Mood Through
Increasing Long-Term Energetic Arousal
and Decreasing Tense Arousal, 176

Appendix I The Activation-Deactivation Adjective Check List
(AD ACL), 178

Appendix II Self-Study Designs to Determine Diurnal Rhythms
of Energetic Arousal, 181

Appendix III Correlational Analyses of Energy, Tension, and Various
Other Mood and Behavioral Processes, 184

Appendix IV Experimental Studies of Antecedents of Energy
and Tension, 187

Notes, 191

References, 195

Author Index, 223

Subject Index, 231

THE BIOPSYCHOLOGY OF MOOD AND AROUSAL

1

Introduction

For laypeople, moods are background feelings that last for a time and that often have no particular cause. Usually a mood is identified simply as "good" or "bad." Sometimes moods are invoked as explanations for someone else's unusual behavior. They may account for the fact that the individual is acting differently than expected in a given situation. Moods are so much a part of everyday life that much of the time little thought is given to them, and yet most people consider them to be important. From time to time, powerful moods appear to be more significant in controlling one's life than events. At these times it seems that they not only influence feelings but most thoughts as well.

The scientific study of mood has a respectable, although not extensive, history. Philosophical analyses have shown that moods predispose other behaviors (Nowlis, 1965; Ryle, 1949). Medical analyses have identified some of the biochemical bases of disordered states of mood (Green & Nutt, 1983; Post & Ballenger, 1984; McNeal & Cimbolic, 1986). Measurement studies have shown that moods can be reliably assessed (Purcell, 1982; Watson & Tellegen, 1985; Thayer, 1967). And psychological analyses have given a picture of wide-ranging antecedents and consequences of a variety of mood states (see Chapter 2).

Mood studies were not always welcomed by the scientific community, however. For example, the behavioral and cognitive paradigms so prevalent in the 1960s and 1970s often tended to devalue the significance of moods. Frequently, mood and affect went without mention in prominent analyses of behavior (Zajonc, 1980). As will be clear in the pages that follow, however, this devaluation is changing in recent times. Most behavioral analyses today include significant affective components (cf. Tomkins, 1981).

An individual's moods are sometimes characterized by extremes, or pathological deviations. But most of the time, people fall within a middle range of feelings that occur periodically during daily life patterns. These middle range feelings, which are the main focus of this book, have important biological significance, and represent essential information about personal transactions with the world. As I shall attempt to demonstrate in Chapter 3 and elsewhere, certain core mood states give vital signals about one's readiness for action and need for rest and recuperation. Feelings of energy and tiredness are the subjective signal

3

systems of these crucial conditions of life. Other important core moods carry information about danger and safety. Here, the subjective states, or signal systems, range from fear, tension, and anxiety to feelings of calmness and quietness.

The Resurgence of Interest in Mood and Affect

Although mood always was of vital interest to laypeople, and although there has been a substantial scientific research effort to uncover therapeutic methods for dealing with pathological mood states, experimental psychologists have paid relatively little attention to mood until the last decade or so. In the past ten years, however, close to 1,000 scientific papers were published that dealt directly or indirectly with mood and affect. They ranged from careful studies of measurement to analyses of a wide variety of mood antecedents, as well as studies of mood consequences or manifestations.

The physiological and other biological bases of mood are highlighted in much of this research, although the exact mechanisms of operation have not been clarified (Mason, 1984; McNeal & Cimbolic, 1986). What has emerged, however, is the necessity for coordinated physiological and psychological studies to understand these relationships. In addition, the association of mood with all manner of bodily functioning has been amply documented. From the research literature it is apparent that mood is related to illness (e.g., Stone et al., 1987), sleep (e.g., Johnson, 1982; Kleitman, 1963; Taub, 1977), physical activity (Folkins & Sime, 1981), and nutrition (Spring, Chiodo & Bowen, 1987; Thayer, 1987a). There is also excellent evidence that mood and cognition are interrelated in many respects (Isen, 1984), and that mood and memory are integrally associated with each other (Blaney, 1986). Mood as a general bodily phenomenon and the importance of cognitive-affective interaction are central themes of this book.

Although not all the published research on mood and affect has supported the theoretical position presented here, I have tried to review relevant research and theory that both supports and does not support my position. With certain exceptions, the current status of scientific work on mood and affect across the field is surveyed. However, various areas are not fully represented in proportion to the available published material. In particular, the vast literature on pathological mood states, including theories of depression, is not fully reviewed. Instead, the focus is on normal (nonpathological) mood states, especially on the antecedents and measurement questions associated with them. Nor have I attempted to deal in detail with the large amount of technical work on the subjective effects of various drugs, or with the social-psychological work on mood and social behavior.

Mood as a Biopsychological Concept

Mood is primarily a psychological manifestation. Most that is known about it comes directly or indirectly from self-report. Thus, controlled introspections of affect, together with cognitive processes and external life events, provide the most reliable immediate understanding of this general affective condition. However, even though subjective feelings and psychological processes supply the most basic evidence in any scientific or personal analysis of mood, it is also clear that mood has integrally related psychophysiological and biochemical components. Moreover, elemental biological processes are important influences on mood. Clearly mood is a biopsychological process that involves the whole individual. In other words, moods would not occur without biochemical, psychophysiological, and cognitive components, as well as subjective reactions.

The importance of these nonsubjective components must not be overemphasized, however. It is not uncommon to encounter the implicit assumption that mood is nothing more than a response caused by cognitive, physiological, and/or biochemical events. In other words, subjective feelings are somehow regarded as the last processes in a chain of more important physiological changes. In my view, however, subjective feelings, thoughts, and psychophysiological and biochemical processes all interact together, and each has its own necessary function in ongoing behavior. Therefore, one process is no more influential than the others, and all are necessary for moods to occur.

Since a mood occurs over time, it may be reasonable to consider initiating events (e.g., biochemical changes produced by cognitive interpretations), but once the mood is occurring the interaction of many bodily systems contributes to its full nature. Thus, if a person is experiencing a powerful mood, the biochemical processes that occurred early in the affective reaction will not provide a complete understanding of the continuing mood. For such an understanding it is necessary to view the ongoing interactions among the full range of bodily systems. Furthermore, these reactions do not occur independently of ongoing life events. Understanding the mood must entail reviewing these life events together with all of the multilevel bodily processes.

This also applies to dysphoric mood states. It may be true that a set of events was interpreted as dangerous, which somehow led to complex biochemical changes, and finally to a negative mood state. But even though a cognitive interpretation may have initiated the sequence, the negative mood is an ongoing process that has gone far past the initial interpretations. The initial cognitive reaction becomes much less important as the mood is occurring. Nor does modifying the cognitive reactions ensure mood control. The issue of control is very complicated, and even the most complete studies still do not provide a good understanding of it. It seems likely that cognitive shifts sometimes effectively modify mood states, but other bodily changes may prove more effective. Probably it is a combination of processes that eventually will be found to be most effective in controlling moods.

Considering mood as a biopsychological response has other implications as well. For example, if moods are part of a general biological system, one of the primary implications is that this system has emerged through evolutionary development. In the millions of years in which *Homo sapiens* evolved, probably no major element of the body developed without having a survival function. Therefore, the presence of mood states today indicates that our ancestors were somehow selected for the capability to have these bodily experiences. At some point in the evolutionary process, moods must have had a genuine functional utility, even though that may not be clear, or perhaps even germane, at the present time. But one can be fairly certain that this usefulness existed, or the biological system would not now be present. Thus, an understanding of moods will be greatly enhanced if this functional significance can be seen more clearly.

Energetic and Tense Arousal

Perhaps the central theme in this book concerns the interactions of two broadly inclusive mood systems. They are called *systems* because it is likely that each includes the simultaneous interactions of a number of mechanisms of bodily arousal. These systems are *broadly inclusive* because they probably extend from the biochemical and cellular levels of function to activation of various subsystems of the brain, and finally to conscious awareness. It is at this highest level of integration—the awareness of bodily sensations and of related subjective feelings—that the most evidence exists for these two systems (Thayer, 1967, 1970). Even at the psychophysiological and biochemical levels of analysis, the evidence for the existence of these systems is still mixed, perhaps because of the complexities involved. Because the evidence is much more clear at the level of conscious awareness, the most attention will be focused on it.

As shall be discussed further in Chapter 3 (also see Thayer, 1967, 1978a, 1986), the first system—energetic arousal—is recognizable by subjective sensations of energy, vigor, or peppiness. The second system—tense arousal—is associated with feelings of tension, anxiety, or fearfulness. These labels are somewhat imprecise, because their meaning depends on a person's social and linguistic background. That is, two self-observers of different cultures or with different language training would undoubtedly give different names to the same feelings. In fact, there is a sufficient diversity of background even among educated, middle-class American adults to make their self-ratings using these adjectives only crude indexes of the two arousal states.

Although subjective feelings of energy and tension may be measured in a variety of ways, in my research I have usually employed the Activation-Deactivation Adjective Check List (AD ACL) for this purpose (Thayer, 1967, 1978a, 1986). This is a short test that I developed some years ago to serve as a very general indication of momentary levels of different arousal states (see Chapter 3 and Appendix I). The AD ACL is one of the more widely used self-rating tests for assessing mood, but it is particularly popular when psychophysiologically related arousal states are of interest (Mackay, 1980).

Energetic arousal and tense arousal, as I call the two major mood systems, represent two very basic mood-behavior orientations. In the first case, feelings of energy predispose a person to move, to act, to be physically active. Declines in these feelings, together with feelings of tiredness, generally impel rest or inaction. On the other hand, in relation to the second system, when some real or imagined danger is present, feelings of tension, anxiety, or fearfulness also predispose preparation for action. With activation of the tense arousal system, however, there is not only preparation for action, but also restraint or inhibition. The idea that these inhibitory responses act together with actions that prepare for bodily readiness seems inconsistent with certain elements of the long-standing biological theory of the "fight or flight" syndrome. But, as I shall argue in Chapter 5, a careful analysis of original work on this theory indicates that this inhibitory process, coupled with preparation for action, is quite consistent with that long-standing concept (Arnold, 1945; Cannon, 1929/1963).

In a sense, these two mood systems are represented in consciousness as two kinds of subjective energy. One of them is called "tense-energy" and the other "calm-energy." It is often difficult to explain the difference, as many people associate tension with energy. This is understandable in a society inundated and inured by stressors, where many people are tense most of the time. Thus, when low-level chronic tension becomes the norm, the tension feelings may go unnoticed.

The feeling of calm-energy is often recognized by persons who have regularly practiced relaxation or have mastered stress-management techniques. People with extensive athletic training often understand this state as well. These groups may possibly be more attuned to the differences because they have sufficiently often experienced a rapid change from tense-energy to calm-energy, and thus the two states are distinguishable to them.

Energetic and tense arousal are at the core of many other commonly identified moods (see Chapter 8). For example, low energy and high tension are basic components of depression, particularly agitated depression (Amer. Psychiatric Assoc., 1980). Optimism is closely associated with high energy and low tension, as are happiness and pleasurable bodily feelings (Thayer, 1987b). Finally, calm-energy is a pleasurable feeling that might be identified simply as a good mood, while tense-tiredness is unpleasant and might be identified as a bad mood.

As will become apparent in Chapter 6, one of the most far-reaching implications arising from the separation of the energetic and tense arousal systems is that there is a predictable relationship between feelings of energy and tension at different levels of intensity. For example, it appears that a moderate amount of tension raises energy feelings, as when an upcoming deadline is remembered and an individual is motivated to get to work. However, as many people realize, *reduced* energy is the result of substantial amounts of tension, or long-standing debilitating tension. On the other hand, *increasing* energy often has a tension-reducing effect.

This complex relationship between energy and tension feelings is important theoretically because it makes understandable certain otherwise confusing everyday life occurrences. Some of the immediate implications considered most extensively in this book relate to the rhythmic increase or decrease of tension within a circadian energy cycle. For example, tension is often greatest at the times of day, such as late afternoon, when energy is low. But tension is reduced when energetic arousal is increasing or at the times of day, such as late morning, when energy is high.

Tension reduction is also considered extensively in relation to the energy variations that occur with gross voluntary motor activity. This can explain the familiar positive effects of physical activity, particularly moderate exercise. It is increasingly evident that many sorts of moods are modulated to a substantial degree by complex interactions of energy and tension as these states are affected by exercise.

There are a number of other examples of apparently anomalous relations among arousal states that at least bear examination in the context of this assumed complex relationship between energy and tension. For example, consider the differential effects on energy and tension of various psychoactive drugs such as caffeine, cocaine, and tranquilizers (see Chapters 6 and 8). When caffeine works optimally, it increases energy and alertness while decreasing tension (Sawyer, Julia, & Turin, 1982). The street use of cocaine often produces the same affect for its users (Grinspoon & Bakalar, 1985). Tranquilizers, on the other hand, work optimally when they decrease anxiety or tension and leave energy unaffected or increased (Iversen & Iversen, 1975). In each case, these apparently anomalous effects might be understood within the complex relationship described between energetic and tense arousal.

It is possible that the motives behind sugar-snacking are also based in this complex relationship (Thayer, 1987a; also see Chapters 5 and 8). The amount of research on food and mood is surprisingly small, but there is some evidence that one important reason for snacking on simple carbohydrate foods may be to raise energy, a motive quite unnoticed by most. Instead, if self-analyses are made, the snack is seen as somehow causing a person to feel better, and in particular, less tense. There is evidence, however, that the short-term energy boost derived from the food not only provides positive feelings, but may also be instrumental in whatever tension reduction occurs. In these ways as well as a variety of others, the complex relationship between energy and tension could be the basis of significant daily behavior patterns.

Mood, Perception of Personal Problems, and Self

Basic perceptual processes regarding self and the world are probably affected by mood (Bower, 1981; Isen, 1984). As an example, consider long-term personal problems, the kind that most people have to a greater or lesser degree. A commonsense view of mood as related to personal difficulties and troubles is that circumstances in a person's life are positive and negative in nature, and that at any particular time the individual's moods are good and bad because of the problems (McArthur, 1972). A strict cognitive-behavioral analysis of this view would stress interpretations of external events as affecting mood. They are certainly important, but they are not the only important aspect in the perception of personal problems.

As will be argued in Chapters 4 and 5, a very interesting and largely overlooked element is that naturally occurring moods, particularly energy and tension, may subtly color the reality of the personal problems (Thayer, 1987b). In other words, *interpretations* of personal problems at any one time appear to be only partially influenced by what is actually happening in the external environment. Also important is how energetic or tired one is at the moment, together with the degree of tension or calmness. While these differences are not large, over time they can be important.

This is quite a fundamental idea, particularly in light of the transitory nature of energy feelings. A normal person's general energy state shifts each day in a predictable cycle that appears to be largely endogenously controlled (Thayer, 1967, 1978b; Thayer, Takahashi, & Pauli, 1988). Therefore, the same personal problems appear different at ten o'clock in the morning—the high-energy time— than they do at four in the afternoon or eleven at night—the low-energy times (Thayer, 1987b). Evidence will be presented in Chapter 4 that these subtle but measurable differences in problem perception are due to an internally shifting biological cycle of energy and the interaction of this cycle with tension.

The fundamental nature of this view of personal problems is further emphasized when one considers that even moderate exercise significantly raises energy feelings (Thayer, 1978b, 1987a, 1987b), and therefore the perceptions of problems may also change in this process. Similarly, within minutes of ingestion, common substances like sugar and caffeine affect energy (Sawyer et al., 1982; Thayer 1987a). Here the evidence is not definitive, but it is quite possible that these substances also subtly affect problem perception. Thus, as one's energy state is continuously changing, important elements of perceptual reality may also be changing.

The immediate theoretical extensions of these ideas regarding moods, personal problems, and even optimism are quite important, and the implications arising from this viewpoint are wide-ranging indeed. For example, one can consider mood-cognition relationships as similar to the memory associations that occur with drug conditions. In this state-dependency paradigm, learned responses seem to be closely associated with artificially induced states. Thus, each time those states are reintroduced, the same learned responses are consciously produced (Blaney, 1986; Bower, 1981). This may have something to do with the way information is stored within the brain or it may be simply a result of the context of the situation.

There may be a similar kind of cognitive-affective state association related to naturally occurring moods (Thayer, 1987b). For example, when an individual feels highly energetic, and at the same time is relatively calm, his or her perceptions of both self and the world are distinctly different from when that person is tired and at the same time tense. Not only are memories of past successes and failures likely to be different, but perceived likelihoods of future successes and failures are also probably different. In one case self-esteem is high, and in the other, it is low (Rubadeau, 1976; Rubadeau & Thayer, 1976).

Consciousness and Self-Observation

Another important theme in this book concerns consciousness and systematic self-observation. Much of behavioral science for most of this century has been distinctly unfriendly to the concept of consciousness, which never quite fit into the hard science that was sought (Boring, 1953; Lyons, 1986; Natsoulas, 1970). Consciousness can't be directly observed, even with the most sophisticated physiological instruments, but must be described by a fallible observer. Many seem to feel implicitly that an adequate science cannot exist on such a soft substrate.

This book presents the view that the psychology of mood not only must take account of consciousness, but at this point in scientific understanding of the person, this psychology must be largely based on systematic self-observation of states of consciousness. There is little doubt that moods have biochemical elements or that physiological processes are important parts of mood states. But even with the current understanding of these complex processes, the vital dependent variable is still how a person feels.

With all that, a reasonable question still remains: Can systematic self-observation of states of consciousness really provide a science of mood? Is it not hopeless to expect that at a psychological level one can understand the complex biosystem of a person, with its intricate neural interconnections and wide-ranging biochemical processes? In my view, the answer to these questions is that it is not a matter of using one level of analysis *or* another. Moods are probably biochemically mediated, and the brain is probably the locus of their control. What is called consciousness is probably the highest of many interacting systems (Thayer, 1967, 1970, 1986). It is a manifestation of integrated processes that are occurring at a number of levels simultaneously.

From the point of view of the investigator, consciousness can provide a more wide-ranging, and in one sense, more easily interpretable, picture of mood than lower-level physiological processes. An analysis of mood, going from the more basic biochemical level up through molar physiological levels and to the level of conscious awareness, is somewhat analogous to looking at an object through a microscope while changing powers. At the highest power of resolution, elements of the object can be seen that are lost at other levels, but conversely, more general patterns can only be viewed at lower levels of resolution (cf. Peele, 1983). In the case of mood, the more easily interpretable mood-behavior relationships can be viewed only at the level of conscious awareness. These general patterns are easily lost as one moves toward precise biochemical analyses. Valuable and unique insights into mood can be gained at each level, however.

The importance of consciously experienced mood states is even greater when one considers their probable biological function. As indicated earlier, these subjective states are not likely to be accidents of biology. Instead, they serve as signal systems about general bodily conditions. Because they exist at the highest level in the hierarchy from cellular to cerebrocortical processes, moods represent a summation about what is happening in the body at any moment. In ways that are not as yet fully understood, elemental moods probably provide information that the individual can use to modify immediate behavior, make plans for the future, and communicate to others in social settings (Burghardt, 1985; Hilgard, 1977; Schwartz & Clore, 1983; Underwood, 1982).

Mood, Self-Management, and Self-Help

Various other themes, somewhat less developed, are also expounded in this book. For example, the methods by which people manage their own moods of energy and tension in everyday life circumstances are considered. Most adults have devised methods for handling energy supply and anxiety control, but many of these strategies have not received a great deal of attention by researchers. It is clear, however, that in individual cases the strategies are often ill-considered and the results frequently quite unfortunate.

One sees, for example, a high school student who is going to take a very important SAT exam, but who has had very little sleep for the past few nights. Or one finds people arguing or making decisions about important life issues when they are extremely tired or are under stress. Exercise is often avoided at the very times when it might be most beneficial. In addition, negative long-term effects often develop from some of the most common methods people use to manage energy and tension: using drugs such as caffeine, nicotine, or alcohol. Illicit drugs are also used, but less commonly. And it may be true that the most common "drug" of all used for managing energy and tension is food, particularly sugar (see Chapter 8).

Still another theme in these pages concerns the applications of theoretical and empirical findings to everyday life. Although this is not a self-help book, and no lists of methods to elevate mood are readily provided, this point must be addressed because the topics raised have immediate implications for self-functioning. Years of research and teaching in this area have made it clear to me that an understanding of the dynamics of mood states is an essential first step in alleviating the unpleasantness of negative moods. And the first step in this understanding is systematic self-observation.

If a person realizes that his or her mood is low, while a few hours earlier it was high and there was little change in external circumstances to cause the shift, it is easy to be seduced by the idea that random biochemical factors produced the change. But it may be much more fruitful to look at matters such as one's diurnal energy cycle, amount of previous energy expenditure, amount and type of previous night's sleep, and food recently eaten. Unfortunately, this analysis isn't easy. It is first necessary to have conducted self-observations, probably over sufficient time to assure their reliability. Mood-affecting factors are often very subtle and usually are separated by time from the first appearance of the problem.

This kind of self-analysis is also necessitated by the wide differences among people. For example, it is possible to describe the endogenous energy curve as low upon awakening, rising to a peak at late morning and a subpeak in early evening, and as having low points in late afternoon and just before sleep (Thayer, 1978b; Thayer et al., 1988). But even though this curve reflects most people's energy cycle, it does not capture the important individual differences represented among various cycles—for example, morning and evening types. Similarly, one can cite data which clearly indicate that for most people a mere ten-minute walk measurably raises energy for one to two hours, but these observations probably would not apply to an aerobics instructor in superb physical condition, and the observations may not apply equally at all times of the day.

What this means for purposes of practical application is that each person must be his or her own expert, and systematic self-observation is an essential tool in that process. To this end, the appendixes of this book provide the measuring instruments and guidelines for a number of self-experiments. None of these is easy, but each offers invaluable information about subtle mood influences and about one's own idiosyncratic reactions to different conditions and circumstances.

In the following chapters, the above ideas will be discussed much more fully. Chapter 2 provides a broad general review of research on mood, particularly that published in the past ten years. Chapter 3 discusses the two central mood systems of energetic and tense arousal much more completely, including their measurement and some of their most important biological and physiological associations. Chapters 4 and 5 deal with important antecedents of energetic and tense arousal, such as biological cycles, exercise, and cognitive-mood interactions. Chapter 6 provides a thorough description of the interactions that occur between energetic and tense arousal, including the conditions under which energy and tension are positively correlated and under which a negative correlation exists.

Chapter 7 systematically analyzes strategies for self-observation, including issues of validity, research design, and the value of self-analyses. The last chapter, 8, is both integrative and somewhat speculative. It discusses common mood states and their relationship with energetic and tense arousal, and also covers the methods that people use to manage energy and tension. In particular, a theoretical analysis is provided of sugar ingestion and of common and illicit drug use. Finally, applications in everyday life of these ideas are extensively considered. The appendixes provide measurement materials and procedures for systematic self-studies.

2

Modern Perspectives on Mood

To the radical behaviorists of the 1960s, behavioral processes were the central focus of experimental psychology. Moods often were regarded as curious spillovers, or just aftereffects.[1] Moods were hardly of greater interest to the scientific psychologists of the 1970s, when cognitive processes received the greatest focus (Zajonc, 1980). But in the 1980s, mood has been rediscovered. Writing at the beginning of this decade, Sylvan Tomkins may have been prophetic in stating that "the next decade or so belongs to affect" (Tomkins, 1981). The field is now rich with investigations and speculations about mood and general affect. In the past ten years, more than 500 scientific articles with "mood" or "moods" in the title have been published in English. This does not include dissertations, of which there were more than 500. Furthermore, since the *Psychological Abstracts* does not carry mood as a major descriptor, one must look under "Emotional states" to find many mood-related articles. Under this category, there have been more than 700 published references in the past ten years, in addition to the 500 plus mentioned above. Not all of these references to emotional states dealt with mood, of course, but in my judgment at least a fifth and perhaps half of them were mood-related. Thus, depending on how one evaluates them, there were close to 1,000 published articles relating to mood in the past ten years.

Not all of these 1,000 or so papers dealt with mood as the central element, but if it wasn't central, at least it was important. Over two-thirds of the articles were concerned primarily with the antecedents of mood. For example, there were more than 100 published articles on the effects that drugs and pharmacological agents, including alcohol, tobacco, and caffeine, have on mood. There were more than 100 references dealing with cognitive determinants of mood, and more than 50 papers on affective disorders. Physiological (including brain) connections to mood were discussed in more than 50 papers. And methods used for experimentally inducing mood states for study were covered by from 25 to 50 papers, depending on how one classifies various articles. There were many other categories in this subdivision of antecedents, a few of the more researched were biological rhythms (including menstrual cycles), illness (not including elation-depression), sleep, exercise, and food.

A little less than a quarter of the references in this ten-year period dealt primarily with the consequences or manifestations of mood. More than 100 papers were concerned with the effect of mood on cognition or information processing. Perhaps the most widely researched area in this group, represented by more than 50 papers, involved the relationship between mood and memory. Over 10 percent of the papers in this period dealt with issues of measurement (almost 50 papers) and mood conceptualization, including papers concerned with the dimensions or component parts of mood (more than 25) and those dealing with moods and personality traits (almost 50).

In the pages that follow, I shall attempt some general review of the articles published on mood, taking as my guide references in the *Psychological Abstracts*. Because of the number, this must be a limited coverage, but it will at least note trends and some representative research. In addition to this review, I will briefly comment in a number of sections about material relevant to this book.

Common Uses of Mood-Related Terms

Before reviewing these research areas, however, let us consider common uses of the terms "mood," "affect," "emotion," and "feeling." These words are often used interchangeably in both technical and popular language. Although some differences among them can be detected, there is a great deal of overlap, and because there is no consensus about these terms, perhaps the best that is possible is to recognize some of the similarities and differences that have been suggested.

Mood is related to emotion, but when the term "mood" is used, it usually implies a longer course of time, which is probably the central distinction between the two. For example, Nowlis (1965) has referred to a continuum of time including temperaments, moods, and emotions. Another difference between the two is that the antecedents of emotions can often be identified, but moods come and go, seemingly without identifiable cause. For example, a dog rapidly approaching may result in an emotion of fear, but if the feeling lasts for hours or days, and the dog is no longer present, we could speak of a fearful or anxious mood.[2]

A third difference sometimes described between the two is that emotion can be more intense and variable than mood. Often, mood is a subtle background state that is difficult to identify, but emotion is more likely to be both easily identifiable and also quite changeable. A similarity between emotions and moods is that usually both are states of feeling as opposed to thinking. However, mood is sometimes used to refer to an apparent cognitive reaction (e.g., concentration from Mood Adjective Check List, Nowlis, 1965; confusion-bewilderment from Profile of Mood States, McNair, Lorr, & Droppleman, 1971) where thought processes appear to have a central part.

Although mood is primarily a subjective state and is usually associated with feelings, in clinical settings it is often inferred from behavior (e.g., slumped shoulders, slow movements) as well as subjective reports. This partially objective characteristic of mood is sometimes used to distinguish it from affect. However, mood and affect are quite similar (Owens & Maxmen, 1979), and in the general psychological literature, the two are often used synonymously. In addition to the objective-subjective distinction, another difference occasionally claimed concerns the immediacy of affect (much like emotion), as opposed to the more lengthy history associated with a particular mood (Ketai, 1975). Mood may be inferred from a pattern of behavior over time to a greater degree than affect. Thus, mood generally includes affect, but affect is not always equivalent to mood.

Mood is often used to refer to a disposition, and in this respect it is not a concrete set of behaviors, but instead an assumed tendency or inclination to act (Ryle, 1949). Nowlis speaks of the dispositional character of moods in the sense that they are "temporary tendencies to show certain characteristics under certain specified circumstances or to show them with greater or lesser likelihood under those circumstances" (Nowlis, 1965, pp. 352–53). Although these circumstances are not fully known for any particular mood, it is still meaningful to employ moods in cause and effect reasoning. Thus, in causal terms one may infer that a person in a particular mood will act a certain way. Of course, sometimes a person does not act that way when experiencing that mood, but the knowledge that an individual is in a particular mood provides an increased degree of prediction.

Defining mood as a *tendency* to act a particular way under certain circumstances is especially useful in understanding one of the important characteristics of this subjective condition. Moods are influential, but they do not always control behavior. Moreover, as I shall argue elsewhere, the tendency of subtle moods to influence behavior may be most apparent when they have been present for a lengthy period of time (see Chapter 5). Initially, the mood may be disregarded and overridden, but over time it can control a person's behavior.

Considering this matter in another way, a particular situation may affect behavior differently, depending on the mood of the individual. For example, someone who is experiencing a very positive mood may react differently to a minor irritation than he or she would if in a negative mood. Here, mood has an effect on behavior, but one that is secondary to the immediate situational determinants of the behavior. In this case, mood would be a moderator variable.

The vernacular use of mood takes at least three forms. One usage is, "I'm in the mood for *x*" (meaning the individual is predisposed for some kind of activity). A second is, "I'm in an *x* mood" (referring to a variety of affective, and sometimes cognitive, states). Finally, "I'm in a good (bad) mood" (a state undifferentiated except that it is hedonically positive or negative). Each of these usages has been employed, either directly or indirectly, by scientific investigators. The last usage (good-bad mood) is probably the most common form employed by laypeople, but until the last several years it was used infrequently by scientists. Now, however, it is often used by scientists.

Dimensions and Assessments of Mood

One of the most persistent and theoretically troublesome questions regarding mood concerns its dimensions or component parts. People often speak simply of being in a "good mood" or "bad mood," which implies general undifferentiated affect. But it is not uncommon to hear references to an angry or a sexy mood, which connote particular kinds of affect. Also, as indicated earlier, people may speak of contemplative or thoughtful moods, here referring to a cognitive reaction.

Not surprisingly, scientific analyses have mirrored these various common usages. For example, most modern analyses of mood owe a great deal to Nowlis and his associates (Nowlis, 1965), who were the first to define and analyze mood using statistical methods in which many variables were considered simultaneously (primarily factor analysis). The Nowlis Mood Adjective Check List (MACL) includes the dimensions of aggression, anxiety, surgency, elation, concentration, fatigue, social affection, sadness, skepticism, egotism, vigor, and nonchalance. For Nowlis, these dimensions include all moods. Although each of these dimensions may be hedonically positive or negative, the hedonic characteristic of each is not the central characteristic of mood.

It is clear from Nowlis's research, as well as other published studies, that the dimensions of mood usually cannot be separated from mood assessments. Thus, the hypothetical mood dimensions are often tied to particular systems of measurement. For example, another measure of mood is the Profile of Mood States (POMS; McNair, Lorr, & Droppleman, 1971). Although no count has been made, this measure may be the one most often used in research today. Developing it in part from the Nowlis checklist as well as other sources, the authors of this test included the dimensions of tension-anxiety, depression-dejection, anger-hostility, vigor, fatigue, and confusion-bewilderment in mood. Still another general mood measure that is widely used is the Curran and Cattell Eight State Questionnaire (8SQ; Curran & Cattell, 1976). This measure includes anxiety, stress, depression, regression, fatigue, guilt, extraversion, and arousal (alertness).

The MACL, POMS, and the 8SQ all portray mood as multidimensional, without describing it as primarily positive or negative (good-bad) in character. However, these checklists include a large number of factors, and without sufficient theoretical guidance many investigators employing one of these ACLs have simply grouped the many factors together in seemingly meaningful categories. For example, although the original designers of the tests probably would not have used such categorizations, it is very common to read reports by investigators who used the full checklists, but drew conclusions based on changes among the various "positive" and "negative" factors. This approach is understandable, because the grouping of mood factors into positive and negative categories is easily comprehended, and such groupings appear to be theoretically useful. It is quite confusing to maintain distinctions among mood dimensions if theoretical models are not provided for the ways in which these factors interact.

Thus, it is not surprising that some current theoretical conceptions have focused mainly on the two categories of positive and negative affect or mood. Tellegen and Watson (Tellegen, 1985; Watson & Tellegen, 1985; Zevon & Tellegen, 1982) reanalyzed a number of studies conducted with diverse mood adjective checklists and extracted the two major factors they considered meaningful in these studies. They concluded that on a descriptive level, affect should be conceptualized in two general dimensions—positive and negative.

The best mathematical description of the relationship between these two factors was found to be an orthogonal, or independent, relationship. It should be borne in mind that this is a descriptive relationship indicating the way these dimensions of affect relate to each other in broad cross-sectional studies, and it does not necessarily indicate that when levels of affect are changed the dimensions would maintain this independence. However, it remains uncertain exactly what the relationship between these dimensions is in a variety of everyday situations.[3] If this relationship is orthogonal, one of the most problematic implications would seem to be that an individual may be in both a positive and negative mood at the same time.

Diener, Emmons, and their associates have argued that positive and negative affect are bipolar (Diener & Emmons, 1985; Diener & Iran-Nejad, 1986). A person in a positive mood experiences less negative affect, and vice versa. They provided evidence that over time, positive and negative affect do appear to be independent, but in assessments of mood on the same day, and particularly in very emotional circumstances, positive and negative affect form an inverse relationship. These investigators attempted to clarify this relationship by pointing out that over time mood may be viewed in terms of separate frequency and intensity dimensions (Diener et al., 1985; Larsen & Diener, 1985; Larsen, Diener, & Emmons, 1986).

Some reconciliation between the concepts of orthogonal versus bipolar dimensions of positive and negative affect may be found with a widely used multidimensional measure of mood, the Activation-Deactivation Adjective Check List (AD ACL; Thayer, 1967, 1986). This measure was developed some years ago, and its use subsequently made clear that most mood states (not necessarily including angry and sexual moods) may be subsumed under two bipolar dimensions. Moreover, these two dimensions are associated with positive and negative affective tone (Thayer, 1978a). This point is especially clear when examining the two dimensions of Watson and Tellegen (1985), because many of their marker adjectives are the same ones that identify the AD ACL dimensions of energetic and tense arousal (i.e., high-low positive affect = active, peppy, drowsy, sleepy, sluggish. High-low negative affect = fearful, jittery, at rest, calm, placid).

Energetic and tense arousal appear to be factor analytically orthogonal just as Watson and Tellegen found positive and negative affect to be. However, this apparent independence of the two types of arousal conceals a complex relationship between the dimensions. They are positively correlated from low to moderate levels and negatively correlated from moderate to high levels. For example, a moderate degree of tension may increase subjective energy (tense-energy), but a high degree of tension reduces energy (tense-tiredness). Therefore, when the moods are low in intensity the dimensions may be uncorrelated or have a positive relationship. But with high-intensity circumstances (e.g., Diener et al., 1985, high emotion), the two dimensions are negatively correlated, and they appear to be bipolar. These relations will be discussed more fully later, particularly in Chapter 6.

Other models and measures have also been suggested. For example, Matthews and his associates (Matthews, Jones, & Chamberlain, ms. in preparation) analyzed the factors on the AD ACL and confirmed the dimensions of energetic and tense arousal, but by adding other mood-descriptive adjectives they were able to identify a third dimension specifically related to positive and negative affect. A pleasure dimension was obtained by Russell and Mehrabian (Russell, 1978, 1980; Russell & Mehrabian, 1977) as well as other related, but slightly different dimensions.

These studies provide evidence about mood dimensionality. But, unfortunately, the findings from factor analyses, including those of Watson and Tellegen, are not definitive. With factor analysis, the number of dimensions obtained depends on the number and composition of mood-descriptive adjectives used as measures. Another variable is the method for extracting the number of factors. And even if these methods were standardized, the moods being experienced by participants completing the ACLs will affect the relative strength of the factors under study and quite possibly their relationship with other factors. Thus, in establishing dimensionality, factor analyses must be supplemented with other kinds of evidence.

There are many models of mood and associated measurements of more limited domain. One example in wide general use is the Multiple Affect Adjective Check List (MAACL; Zuckerman & Lubin, 1965), which was designed to assess three clinically relevant negative affects, and it includes the dimensions of anxiety, depression, and hostility. Thus, unlike the previously discussed tests the MAACL was not designed to conceptualize affect in general, at least not until a recent reanalysis (Zuckerman & Lubin, 1985; cf. Gotlib & Meyer, 1986). Instead, it dealt with important clinical dimensions of affect.

Still other widely used limited-domain measurements assess such aspects of mood as depression and anxiety. Examples are the Beck Depression Inventory (Beck et al., 1961), the Global Bunney-Hamburg Scale (Bunney & Hamburg, 1963), and the State-Trait Anxiety Inventory (Spielberger, Gorsuch, & Lushene, 1970). A wide variety of other adjective checklists and mood measures have also been developed, and a number of the more widely used mood measures have been translated for other language cultures (e.g., Bohlin & Kjellberg, 1973; Mackay et al., 1978; Mackay, 1980), shortened or factor analytically reorganized (Gotlib & Meyer, 1986; Shacham, 1983), or have been adapted for low-vocabulary subjects (Cruickshank, 1984).

Other ways of assessing mood have also been employed, with greater or lesser success. Examples here include simple visual analogue scales, in which participants merely indicate where they perceive themselves to be on a linear scale (Eastwood, Whitton, & Kramer, 1984; Folstein & Luria, 1973). Various expressive characteristics associated with mood have also been widely investigated (Scherer, 1986), and the content of tape-recorded statements have been analyzed for mood variations (Taub & Berger, 1974). Mood has even been assessed by expert judgments of paintings (Heine & Steiner, 1986).

As a final point on matters of measurement, it is clear from the literature on mood that not everyone agrees that mood assessments based on self-ratings are valid (Nisbett & Wilson, 1977; Wilson, Hull, & Johnson, 1981; Wilson, Laser, & Stone, 1982). However, the preponderance of research studies continue to employ successfully one form or another of self-report. Moreover, a distinction must be made between the validity of self-reports by people about reasons for their behaviors versus the validity of people's ratings of their current bodily states. In any event, many persuasive arguments support the use of self-report (e.g., Quattrone, 1985), and supportive research evidence for its use continues to be published (e.g., Caplan, 1983; Slavney & Pauker, 1981; Thayer, 1970; Watson, 1988b).

In order to adequately conceptualize mood, it is important to understand the theoretical relationship between this subjective condition and personality traits. (Although according to Allen and Potkay [1981], this distinction may be more apparent than real.) Studies of the relationship usually hold that the broad personality types, traits, or dispositions act somehow as parameters, or boundaries, of the more limited mood dispositions. Many studies have related mood to such broad personality traits and types, particularly Eysenck's three-dimensional typology of extraversion, neuroticism, and psychoticism. For example, in one such study assessing university students over several days, those students high on Eysenck Personality Questionnaire neuroticism showed more negative mood states (Williams, 1981). These finding were confirmed in part by one of my studies (Thayer, Takahashi, & Pauli, 1988), in which tense arousal, measured each waking hour over six representative days, correlated significantly with EPI-assessed neuroticism. Relations between Eysenck's types and mood have been obtained in other studies as well (Costa & McCrae, 1980; Emmons & Diener, 1986; Kendell et al., 1984; Kirkcaldy, 1984).

Another example of the relationship between personality trait and mood state (trait-state interaction) that has inspired much research is Ellis's model, which predicts a relationship between irrational thoughts and depression. For instance, in one study, persons scoring high on the Irrational Beliefs Test proved more susceptible to negative mood manipulation, while low scorers were more susceptible to positive manipulation (Cash, Rimm, & MacKinnon, 1986). These results were quite compatible with an earlier study showing that persons with high levels of irrational thinking demonstrated greater intensity and variability of depressed mood, as measured over a number of days by a depression checklist (Vestre, 1984).

Other personality traits that have commonly been associated with moods are internal-external control (e.g., Benassi, Sweeney, & Defour, 1988; Lefcourt et al., 1981), and Type A personality (e.g., Strube et al., 1983). In each of these studies, relationships were observed between more fixed or long-term elements of personality and short-term dispositions.

As a final note, a particularly promising area of study is the relationship between mood *variability* and personality type (Eysenck & Eysenck, 1985; Eysenck & Hepburn, 1987; Munte et al., 1984; Underwood & Froming, 1980; Williams, 1981). It is likely, in my view, that there are general constants in behavior that predispose mood variability, and which may indicate biological constraints on mood changes. I believe that the Eysenck studies regarding extraversion, neuroticism, and psychoticism (Eysenck, 1967; Eysenck & Eysenck, 1985) are the most logical place to focus this research, because the theoretical underpinnings of these types clearly suggest mood states. This is undoubtedly why so much mood-related research has already been conducted on these types of personality. However, other personality traits that have been the focus of research (Ellis & Internal–External Control) show strong correlations with mood states. It is clear that there is much room left for further research in this area, particularly in relation to combinations of trait characteristics and mood dimensions.

Methods of Experimentally Manipulating Mood States

Experimental studies in which mood is manipulated appear to offer the best way to understand the cause and effect relationships involving this affective state. But as ethical constraints limit substantial manipulations of mood states, critics can argue that experimental studies result only in small changes that are not representative of natural life experiences. Nevertheless, many experimental studies have been published, usually with results that are consistent with theoretical expectations. By revealing a cross-section of important mood antecedents, the various experimental methods employed demonstrate that mood is probably affected in multiple ways.

Autosuggestion and Hypnosis Manipulations

Perhaps the most frequently used experimental manipulation in the past ten years was developed by Velten in his doctoral research (Velten, 1967, 1968). Although Velten's procedure is often modified, in the original research, participants in the experiment read aloud or to themselves a series of statements designed to produce either elation, depression, or a neutral mood. They were instructed to be responsive and receptive to the idea of the statement. In many ways this manipulation is similar to hypnotic suggestions.

A wide variety of studies have employed the Velten procedure to produce depression and elation, and generally the results have been consistent with predictions.[4] Also, various behaviors consistent with predictions have been unobtrusively observed following this kind of mood manipulation. For example, Natale and Bolan (1980) used videorecordings during a standardized interview of persons who were given the depression manipulation, and they found a significant decrease in the use of hand gestures and a marginal increase in lowered head postures, indicative of depression. Matheny and Blue (1977), using a similar procedure, found the reaction time differences among persons responding to elation, neutral, and depression manipulations (see D. M. Clark [1983] for a review of other related research). Although this induction procedure probably has only a weak effect (Frost & Green, 1982; Isen & Gorgoglione, 1983), the evidence does suggest that it is at least moderately efficacious.

Although the Velten procedure apparently produces mood change, alternative explanations for the results are possible, particularly those relating to expectation effects or "demand characteristics" (Buchwald, Strack, & Coyne, 1981; Isen, 1984). But even though the observed changes in mood may be due to the subject's expectations, these changes could still be quite consistent with the purposes of the experimenter. To illustrate this point, Polivy and Doyle (1980) subjected participants to a "demand characteristics" condition with instructions to pretend to experience moods that they were not really feeling. Slightly more than half of these people later reported actually feeling the appropriate mood, even though they had been instructed only to pretend (see also Coleman, 1975).

Many of the Velten mood manipulation statements appear to be direct manipulations of what I call energetic arousal.[5] For example, in the depression manipulation, between 28 and 38 percent of the statements can be interpreted as suggesting decreases in energetic arousal (e.g., "I want to go to sleep—I feel like just closing my eyes and going to sleep right here." "Just a little bit of effort tires me out." "I'm getting so tired out I can feel my body getting exhausted and heavy."). Similarly, in the elation manipulation, between 12 and 18 percent of the statements may be interpreted as increasing energetic arousal (e.g., "I'm full of energy." "I've certainly got energy and self-confidence to spare." "I'm full of energy and ambition—I feel like I could go a long time without sleep."). Therefore, the experimental effects produced by the Velten procedure might also be interpreted as due to changes in energetic arousal.

This issue has been the subject of a number of experiments associated with different types of Velten statements. Frost, Graf, and Becker (1979) divided manipulation statements into those dealing with somatic suggestions (e.g., fatigue and exhaustion) and those concerning self-evaluations (e.g., low self-worth). Using regular induction procedures with these two types, as well as with the standard groupings, resulted in greater self-reported depression with the somatic statements than with the self-devaluation ones. Kirchenbaum, Tomarken, and Humphrey (1985) also found that somatic statements were more potent than self-evaluative ones, both in self-evaluation measures and on performance (math problem-solving). In particular, enhanced performance was found with the positive somatic statement group. In my view, the use of suggestions for enhanced energy, as opposed to suggestions of depression or low energy, is a potentially rich area for future research.

In other experiments, somatic inductions also resulted in significant effects on mood, but in these studies inductions involving self-evaluative statements had a greater effect on ' memory (Rholes, Riskind, & Lane, 1987; Riskind, Rholes, & Eggers, 1982) and on the perception of common problems (Riskind & Rholes, 1983) than did the somatic statements. These two kinds of results are difficult to reconcile on the basis of current evidence, but it is likely that affective response (particularly depression) is quite complex. Mood and cognitive reaction could be somewhat independent.

Apparently moods are quite manipulable, judging from some of the techniques that have been successfully employed. For example, in two experiments Laird and his associates developed an elaborate story designed to induce experimental participants to frown or smile (Laird et al., 1982). Significant mood changes were obtained on mood measurements taken a few minutes later. A similar method was successfully used by Riskind (1983), but in addition to manipulated facial expression, his experimental participants also assumed postures consistent with happiness or sadness (chest expanded with body upright and erect versus neck bowed, body stooped and slumped).

Hypnosis is still another popular method in which the subject cooperates in achieving mood change. Bower (1981) and his associates have effectively used hypnosis to produce moods of happiness and sadness, and to study various aspects of information processing relative to these states. In several experiments this procedure involved using hypnotically susceptible persons (the top 15 percent of those tested for such susceptibility), who were hypnotized and then asked to develop a specific mood by recalling a particular experience in which that mood occurred (Gilligan & Bower, 1984). Subjects were then instructed to intensify the emotional state and to maintain it until given further instructions.

Another method similar to hypnosis was successfully employed by Gage and Safer (1985). These experimenters used tapes that started with quasi-hypnotic suggestions involving relaxation and internal focus. Next, participants were instructed to imagine either a very close friend who becomes increasingly ill or to imagine vacationing on an island with a friend. And finally, participants were instructed to maintain the mood after the end of the tape. These tapes were similar to ones used by Rosenhan, Salovey, and Hargis (1981) to manipulate mood.

Obviously, these various methods of mood induction, in which the participant "cooperates" in achieving the desired affective state, leave open the possibility that participant expectations or demand characteristics can explain the results (Isen, 1984). However, the fact that participants have been unobtrusively observed to behave consistently with the desired states indicates that probably the simplest form of demand characteristics cannot alone explain these results (e.g., Matheny & Blue, 1977; Natale & Bolan, 1980; Polivy & Doyle, 1980; see also Gilligan & Bower, 1984, regarding hypnosis manipulations). Even more convincing evidence concerning this point is the fact that the obtained behavioral changes in a variety of areas were consistent with complex theoretical predictions about mood relations (Blaney, 1986; Gilligan & Bower, 1984; Teasdale, 1983). Thus, a kind of construct validation of the procedure has been at least partially demonstrated.

It may appear improbable that any significant mood shift could occur by using techniques that so obviously rely on participant cooperation in achieving the effect. On the other hand, perhaps this is not surprising because we have known for some time that thoughts exert powerful controls on behavior. Virtually every theory of cognitive psychology holds that thoughts influence emotions, and successful clinical techniques and methods of stress management regularly employ procedures in which thought processes control anxiety or tension.

Film and Music Manipulations

Not only have manipulation techniques, in which demand characteristics could play a significant role, been used, but a number of more disguised methods of influencing mood have been successfully employed. For example, films have long been useful in this regard (cf. Nowlis, 1965). Movie fans who have experienced great mood changes following a powerful film are probably aware of this effect. Rooijen and Vlaander (1984) recently employed a documentary of "grief therapy" to effectively induce depression. Isen and Gorgoglione (1983) successfully employed a comedy film to induce a somewhat protracted affective change, but another film that was employed to induce a negative mood had less effect. The success of this kind of manipulation undoubtedly is highly dependent on the quality of the film, the group under study, and probably on the temporal cultural period (i.e., powerful films of the 1950s may have little effect in the 1980s).

An informal survey that I once conducted indicated that more than 10 percent of the adult respondents found music to be the best way of alleviating their bad moods, so I find it quite reasonable that this manipulation has been successfully employed in mood research. Pignatiello, Camp, and Rasar (1986) manipulated elation and depression with twenty-minute tapes of selections of instrumental classical, popular, and musical score soundtracks. These tapes had been previously judged as depressing or elating by musical therapy interns and others. Also, Teasdale, Clark, and their associates successfully employed music in connection with their studies of cognitive relationships to elation and depression (D. M. Clark, 1983).

Disguised Manipulations of Natural Settings

Isen and her associates have used a number of ingenious methods that were assumed to affect mood on the basis of observed behaviors (initially prosocial or helping behaviors, but also various cognitive reactions). These methods of mood manipulation are probably among the least contaminated by demand characteristics as participants were generally unaware that an experiment was occurring, and they appear to be quite valid because they involve natural situations that people encounter every day. In some of these experiments, participants "found" a dime in the coin return slot of a telephone or were offered a cookie while studying in the library (Isen & Levin, 1972), or they received free samples (Isen, Clark, & Schwartz, 1976). However, because mood was not directly measured in several of these experiments, but instead was indirectly inferred from stimulus conditions and related behaviors, it is not clear to what degree the affective state actually was changed.

If these various methods of manipulating mood are valid, as they appear to be, they suggest, interestingly, that moods can be easily changed. There are extremely important applications to the idea that mood can be changed by merely thinking of positive or negative statements, or placing one's face in a frown or a smile, or even just pretending to act consistently with a particular mood. Popular admonitions to "whistle a happy tune" or smile at ten people or think about feeling good may be more valuable in practical mood management than many scientists recognize. On the other hand, one must balance findings that employed these techniques against the possibility that these mood changes may be only transitory and of little significance in the face of strong physiological and biochemical processes.

Stress, Exercise, and Drug Manipulations

Methods that are probably more powerful in manipulating mood have been employed, using a variety of stressors to produce anxiety, fear, and other negative mood states. The personality literature of the 1950s and 1960s is replete with such studies involving noise, threatened electric shock, exams, verbal attack, and other similar manipulations (e.g., Polivy, 1981). These mood antecedents generally affect bodily arousal, and as shall be discussed further in later chapters, this arousal may be the basis of fundamental mood variations. In recent times this kind of mood manipulation has not been widely employed, however, probably due to university ethics review boards.

There have been a number of studies, though, in which less controversial arousal manipulations were quite successfully employed to affect mood. For example, in my own work moderate exercise (a short brisk walk) proved to be one of the most reliable mood manipulators. In several studies, subjective energy was enhanced and tension decreased by this manipulation (Thayer, 1978b, 1987a, 1987b). Moreover, moods of optimism and related states were also influenced this way (Thayer, 1987b; see also Chapter 5). Clark and her associates effectively employed arousal manipulations to influence mood-related memory and information processing (Clark, Milberg, & Erber, 1984; Clark, Milberg, & Ross, 1983).

Other arousal manipulations are also commonly employed in studies of mood. For example, circadian and ultradian rhythms were extensively studied in relation to energy, tension, and other mood states (see Chapter 4 and discussion below concerning mood and menstrual cycles). Other moods, such as optimism, happiness, and physical well-being, have been studied in relation to circadian arousal rhythms (Thayer, 1987b).

There is a vast literature concerning the effects of drugs on mood, but ethical constraints have probably limited the use of these chemical substances for systematic studies of mood states. There is, however, good potential for utilizing common substances in experimental manipulations, if the research volunteers already use these substances and if the amount of the substance to be employed is small. The most likely candidate for this kind of research is caffeine. Even relatively low doses appear to affect mood (Gilliland & Andress, 1981; Gilliland & Bullock, 1983–84; Sawyer, Julia, & Turin, 1982). Revelle, Gilliland, Anderson, and their associates (Anderson, 1987; Gilliland, 1980; Revelle et al., 1980) have successfully employed caffeine in a number of interesting studies of mood.

Some recent research in my laboratory suggests that sugar ingestion (Thayer, 1987a) and cigarette smoking may also be used to induce either energetic or tense arousal. And finally, arousal-affecting manipulations of sleep states have been extensively studied in relation to moods. A later chapter will concentrate more fully on these kinds of studies.

Mood, Biology, and Physiology

Virtually every knowledgeable person assumes that mood is based on physiological, and in particular, neurochemical substrates. Moreover, there is little question that the brain is the central mediator of mood states. Therefore, research in the past several decades has attempted to delineate these important relationships. This research has been accompanied by a rich body of speculative information that has opened the door to a number of important theoretical possibilities. Unfortunately, these abundant speculations are limited by a lack of hard data.

Biochemical Correlates of Mood

It is assumed, for example, that the brain amines play a central role in an individual's moods. These substances function at the level of the synapse, selectively enhancing and reducing neural transmission. The three monoamines most associated with mood are norepinephrine, dopamine, and serotonin. (Norepinephrine and epinephrine, together with their precursor, dopamine, are catecholamines, and serotonin is an indolamine.) Other neurotransmitters, including acetylcholine, may also be important in mediating mood.

Problems in understanding their role is partly due to the fact that evidence about neurotransmitters and mood derives mainly from studies based on indirect measures of aminergic activity together with assumptions about abnormal states (mostly complex forms of depression). For example, many studies have shown differential levels of catecholamine metabolites in the urine and cerebrospinal fluids of persons with various degrees of affective disorders (e.g., see Mason, 1984; see also Mendels & Amsterdam, 1981). One problem here is that cause and effect are difficult to establish. At best, one can observe time-lagged correlations between neurotransmitters and mood at a number of different periods, but even these studies are rare. Another problem about understanding the role of the brain in mood dysfunction is the uncertainty, particularly in urine analyses, concerning the degree to which relevant metabolic end products represent central versus peripheral functioning of any particular neurotransmitter.

An important source of evidence relating mood and neurotransmitters comes from studies on drugs believed to influence aminergic activity and affective disorders (Green & Nutt, 1983; McNeal & Cimbolic, 1986). This kind of evidence has been quite valuable theoretically; nonetheless, applying it is highly complicated, as it involves relationships among unknowns, such as the exact physiological impact of the pharmacological agents. Some of these questions have been partially clarified with research on animals, but there are obvious limitations in these kinds of studies for understanding mood.

Early findings led a number of investigators to propose theories of affective disorder on the basis of aminergic activity. The best known of these theories held that depression was due to low levels of brain catecholamines, particularly norepinephrine (Bunney & Davis, 1965; Schildkraut, 1965). However, serotonin has also been proposed as the important element in these disorders (Glassman,

1969). Similarly, acetylcholine (Gershon & Shaw, 1961; Janowsky, 1980) was suggested, as were interactions of amine systems (Mendels et al., 1975).

The catecholamine hypothesis that was so promising in the 1960s and 1970s proved less tenable as more data were gathered. This theory was particularly persuasive because of the effectiveness of such drugs as monoamine oxidase inhibitors and tricyclic antidepressants, which increase noradrenergic activity by decreasing the breakdown of norepinephrine as well as blocking its uptake. However, newer antidepressant agents are effective even though they do not appear to work primarily on noradrenergic systems of the brain. This is not certain, however, since recent work has focused—profitably—on the effects of various antidepressant drugs over time on the density and sensitivity of amine receptor systems (Mason, 1984; McNeal & Cimbolic, 1986). Still another reason that the amine hypothesis cannot be discarded is that it may be useful in understanding subtypes of depression (Schildkraut et al., 1984). Finally, an interesting possibility related to the original catecholamine theory arises from the fact that the newer antidepressants have an effect on the dopaminergic systems, which means dopamine could be the central neurotransmitter involved in depression (Mason, 1984).

Indirect evidence that amines are important in mood comes from research which suggests that exercise, an important antidepressant (McCann & Holmes, 1984; see also Chapter 5) and general mood elevator (see Chapter 8), increases monoaminergic activity (Ransford, 1982). Other research indicates that stress affects noradrenergic function and is also likely to affect mood (e.g., Edmondson, Roscoe, & Vickers, 1972; Jones, Bridges, & Leak, 1968; Rubin et al., 1970; see also review by Frankenhaeuser, 1978). Additional indirect evidence of the effects of brain amines on mood comes from sleep studies that implicate such neurotransmitters as serotonin in this process (e.g., Hartmann, 1982–83). And, as I shall argue in Chapter 5, sleep is probably an important element of mood modulation. Finally, studies on arousal-related drugs such as amphetamines, barbiturates, and tranquilizers directly implicate a number of neurotransmitter systems (Iversen & Iversen, 1975).

At the present time, it is most probable that neurotransmitters affect mood, but the exact mechanisms of action as well as the most important transmitters are unclear. The present state of knowledge has led recent reviewers of the research literature to state that "no global conclusion on the neurochemical cause of depression is warranted" (Mason, 1984, p. 427) and "that we still have little knowledge about the etiology of depression or, more specifically, about the various pathways to depression" (McCann & Holmes, 1984, pp. 371–72). Even less certainty can be maintained about the relationship between neurotransmitters and nonpathological mood states as they affect people in daily functioning.

An understanding of these relationships would be greatly enhanced by studies of covariations between mood and biochemical variables over time. Of course, such studies would be descriptive and therefore not as useful for understanding cause and effect relationships as manipulative studies, but nevertheless, this kind of research would provide a more complete picture than is now available of these important interactions.

One study recently published by Fibiger and his associates represents a promising beginning for research of this type (Fibiger et al., 1984). These investigators took mood measurements from six graduate students over a one-week period, with accompanying urine samples. From these samples, they were able to demonstrate significant covariations between mood and each of the three catecholamines—norepinephrine, epinephrine, and dopamine—as well as the ratios of these amines. They also correlated mood with cortisol levels. Although interpreting the various mood scales was somewhat unclear, some promising findings emerged from this study. Regression analyses indicated that high levels of epinephrine, norepinephrine, and dopamine in the urine all predicted tiredness, irritability, and tension as well as alertness. This mood state is similar to the tense-tired state that will be described later in the book.

Although this study was very promising, certain questions remain unanswered and await further theoretical development. For example, at each measurement period, the mood was presumably assessed according to feelings at the moment, but the urinary excretions represented physiological functions that occurred some time before. Moreover, since these measurements were made at various points in each individual's diurnal cycle, it is unclear whether the obtained correlations represented well-known circadian cyclical variations of each of the variables, as opposed to cause and effect relationships. Nevertheless, the study at least suggests that mood states do not exist independently of biochemical events. As more research is conducted, better models may be constructed for simultaneously assessing mood and biochemical functioning.

Fibiger and his associates (Fibiger et al., 1984) also found a significant correlation between cortisol and alertness. This relationship is consistent with other research indicating that cortisol level maintains a circadian rhythm that roughly corresponds to the rhythm of energetic arousal (see Chapter 4).[6] The rhythmicity of alertness is not the only possible correlate of cortisol. It has long been known that dysregulation of the hypothalamic-pituitary-adrenal system is a prime biological indicator of affective disorder (Pepper & Krieger, 1984). This dysregulation is manifested through excessive secretion of cortisol from the adrenal gland and resistance to feedback inhibition (e.g., abnormalities in the dexamethasone suppression test).

Brain Opioid Systems

In certain respects, the same kind of speculation that exists regarding biogenic amines and mood also exists for the currently "hot" area of neuropeptides and behavior. A good deal of this informed speculation about possible relationships has filtered to the lay public, where the belief seems to be firmly held that endorphins underlie all the pleasurable states that people experience. By extension, positive mood states are usually included in these beliefs. But these speculations are supported only by indirect evidence.

The discovery in the early 1970s of opiate receptors in the brain and the subsequent isolation of endogenous, opiatelike substances in the body (see reviews by Akil & Watson, 1983; R. J. Miller, 1983) led to a great deal of research on a variety of aspects of behavior and inevitably to research on relationships between these substances and mood (e.g., Post et al., 1984). This was a natural development, since exogenous opiate compounds have substantial influences on mood and related affective states. Moreover, the idea of such a relationship was enhanced by discoveries of relationships between opioid peptide function and important mood-related phenomena such as pain (Foley et al., 1979; Luttinger et al., 1984) and stress (Panksepp, 1986).

At the present time it is clear that beta endorphin and related compounds do have something to do with mood, but exactly how they function in this context is still unclear. Part of this uncertainty has to do with the complexity of mood states themselves, and the fact that most research on opioid peptides takes place on animal models. Even if direct brain research on humans were possible, relevant mood variables are by no means understood.

In my view, on the basis of recent findings the most likely areas in which relationships might be found between mood and opioid peptides comes from research on threat, stress, and exercise. A number of studies have indicated that situations involving direct or indirect threat—and anxiety as a reaction—result in increased activity of the opioid peptide system (e.g., Morley & Levine, 1980; Panksepp, Siviy, & Normansell, 1985; Post et al., 1984). This has led Panksepp to the provocative and quite plausible conclusion that "a unitary functional principle underlying opioid function in the brain is the homeostatic reestablishment of baseline conditions in many types of neuronal circuits following stressful perturbations" (Panksepp, 1986, p. 82). Other studies relating strenuous exercise to opioid peptide function (Carr et al., 1981; Colt, Wardlaw, & Frantz, 1981; Markoff, Ryan, & Young, 1982) also suggest an association with mood, and these findings are probably consistent with Panksepp's conclusions.

A review of two recent studies relating, in different ways, endogenous opioids to mood will illustrate both the promise and the limitations of research in this area. In the first study,[7] Post and his associates drew cerebrospinal fluid from thirty-seven normal volunteers after having administered MAACLs immediately prior to the spinal taps. The participants experienced varying degrees of anxiety about the procedure necessary to draw fluids, and these self-rated levels were correlated with assays of all biologically active opioid substances in the cerebrospinal fluid.

The obtained correlation was a significant −.40, indicating that the least anxious persons had the highest levels of circulating opioids, and vice versa. This would suggest that the opioids reduced anxiety, although such a causal sequence is impossible to prove with this research. This negative correlation for normal participants contrasted with a +.47 correlation of anxiety in unmedicated depressed patients (as rated by nurses) with opioid activity in these individuals. Apparently different processes affected the normal and clinical groups. Even this conclusion is uncertain, however, since the relationships were small in comparison with the large number of correlational tests completed in this study.

A second recent study has employed the opioid antagonist naloxone (Janal et al., 1984). Utilizing a double-blind procedure on two occasions, twelve long-distance runners were administered either naloxone or a saline solution following 6.3-mile runs done at near maximal effort. At varying time periods after that (twenty to fifty minutes), visual analogue mood tests as well as other measurements were taken. The runners who were administered naloxone had considerably lower self-ratings of joy and euphoria thirty and forty minutes after the run as compared to those who had received the saline, but other mood ratings were not affected. This finding appears to indicate that the endogenous opioids influence the joy and euphoria that occurs following strenuous exercise. But caution must be maintained in such an interpretation because naloxone may have other physiological effects than the assumed opioid antagonism (R. J. Miller, 1983).

Brain Lateralization and Mood

Other indications that mood is closely associated with neural processes come from research on lateralization of brain function and depression. In the past ten years, a number of studies have been published describing a relationship between left hemispheric brain damage and a depressed mood. For example, in several studies (Robinson, 1983; Robinson et al., 1985; Robinson et al., 1986) Robinson and his associates found statistically significant differences in self- and staff-rated depression among stroke patients with left hemispheric brain damage. This was apparently independent of hemispheric dominance as judged by handedness (Robinson et al., 1986). These investigators also found that the closer to the frontal pole of the left hemisphere that the brain damage occurred, the more likely that depression would result. There was also intriguing evidence that damage to the right hemisphere may produce undue cheerfulness.

These findings and others (for reviews, see Davidson, 1984; Leventhal & Tomarken, 1986; Tucker, 1981; cf. Gage & Safer, 1985) have generated theories that the brain is organized not only with regional mediation of affect, but also with reciprocal or balancing affective reactions. For example, Fox and Davidson (1984) have argued that the two hemispheres of the brain mediate approach and avoidance reactions, and that these tendencies are represented in positive and negative emotions. In a model similar to that of Pribram and McGuinness (1975), Tucker and Williamson (1984) recently proposed a different theory, in which the right hemisphere and its lateralized noradrenergic substrate mediates an arousal system that responds to input from the external environment. Balancing this is the activation system of the left hemisphere, which, with its dopaminergic substrate, mediates vigilance and motor readiness. Anxiety and related states are associated with activation of the left hemisphere, while more positive emotional states are presumably the conscious representation of the arousal system.

Mood and Biological Rhythms, Including PMS

Sleep and biological rhythms as important variables in relation to mood have received considerable attention in recent years. But the mood variables associated with these functions were generally limited to measures of arousal and alertness. These will be discussed further in subsequent chapters.

Other studies of biological rhythms were conducted on female menstrual cycles, particularly premenstrual tension. In the past ten years dozens of studies have been published concerning this phenomenon. About three-fourths of these investigations indicated increased tension in the premenstrual period (e.g., Collins, Eneroth, & Landgren, 1985; Sanders et al., 1983), but about a fourth of these studies showed no increase (e.g., Golub, 1981). Clearly, this is a problematic area in which some investigators suspect that reports of premenstrual tension are due to expectation effects (e.g., Slade, 1984).

However, studies in which the possible effects of expectation have been indirectly controlled do show premenstrual tension exists. For example, in one study somatic symptoms persisted premenstrually even though placebos reduced mood effects (Metcalf & Hudson, 1985). This suggests that the mood reports may be suppressed by experimental manipulation, but the underlying physical determinants of the mood resisted such manipulation. Another study showed that depression was more easily induced premenstrually than at other cycle times (Boyle, 1985). And, in another indirect indication of increased tension, there were observations of more alcohol consumption premenstrually (Sutker et al., 1983).

This kind of research is difficult and time-consuming to complete. Repeated-measurement research designs, which are likely to be most sensitive to these subtle mood effects, require lengthy periods of study for the multiple observations across cycles necessary to achieve reliable measurements (see Chapter 7). Thus, studies that show no premenstrual tension do not necessarily indicate that this tension is due simply to expectation. The lack of effect may be due to inaccurate mood measurements or experimental procedures in which the measurements are not taken in sufficient numbers to detect the subtle mood effects.

Also, the existence of expectation effects may not necessarily indicate that premenstrual tension is imaginary, because very subtle mood changes that persist over a number of days may eventually have a strong effect due to cognitive-mood interactions (see Chapter 5). Finally, the often obtained negative effects could occur because of strong individual differences (Biro & Stukovsky, 1985; Dejonc et al., 1985). In other words, premenstrual tension may not represent a typical experience in the general population, but instead the experience only of certain women. If this is true, population sampling would be an important consideration in this kind of research.

In addition to premenstrual tension, a number of investigators have observed menstrual midcycle variations in mood states, associated with increased energy and positive moods in general (e.g., Backstrom et al., 1983; Sanders et al., 1983). These findings are less likely to be based on expectation effects than findings of premenstrual tension, yet they support the tension results in the sense that biologically meaningful cycles may underlie both kinds of mood effects. Although the biological utility of premenstrual tension is not as clear as the utility of midcycle positive mood variations, the existence of one makes the existence of the other more plausible. These two mood-biological rhythm relations will be discussed more fully in Chapter 4.

General Arousal States and Mood

In addition to the relationship of biological cycles, brain, and biochemical substrates to mood, more general variations in the autonomic nervous system and the skeletal-muscular system are probably related to mood (cf. Levenson, 1983). Research demonstrating this relationship has been done, but not to any great extent. Two studies of interest in this regard were conducted by Levenson and Gottman (1983, 1985). These investigators asked married couples to discuss a variety of marital situations on videotape while being monitored with physiological sensors (cardiovascular, skin conductance, and somatic activity). Next, these couples separately viewed the videotapes, and continuously adjusted a rating dial representing a scale from very negative to very positive feelings as different segments appeared. From these data, it was possible to predict marital satisfaction, but only on the basis of broad composites of the physiological and affective data taken across situations. Greater general arousal of the couples while viewing these discussions predicted marital dissatisfaction three years later. Marital dissatisfaction was also predicted when husbands did not match their wives' negative affect while viewing the tape, and when wives *did* match their husbands' negative affect. This research indirectly indicates the association of physiological and affective reactions. In particular, it indicates that both variables are important in predicting significant behavioral relations.

The specific predictiveness of Levenson and Gottman's global measurements of physiological and affective cross-situational reactions, as opposed to individual measurements related to specific marital situations, illustrates the utility of viewing psychophysiological responses as elements of general arousal. General arousal appears to be an excellent bridge between psychology and physiology. Arousal is sometimes defined by behavioral responses, but usually it refers to a general psychophysiological response. And moods are natural manifestations of these general bodily reactions. Thus, arousal is a kind of simultaneous activation of many physiological and psychological systems in response to a variety of kinds of stimulation (see Chapter 3).

Two recent studies of mine considered arousal and mood relationships in a different way (Thayer, 1987b). Over a period of several weeks, participants completed self-ratings of energy, tension, and optimism, as well as other kinds of mood, at various fixed times in their circadian arousal cycles, and also following moderate exercise. Previous research indicated that arousal would be high or low in these various periods and conditions. Moods were found to covary with the circadian and exercise-produced arousal changes. The high arousal state of late morning and following moderate exercise was associated with heightened energy, optimism, and other related states. Tension was also reduced in these periods. Low arousal periods, such as late afternoon, were associated with reduced energy, less optimism and increased tension. Moreover, across arousal periods, low energy and high tension ratings usually predicted substantially reduced optimism. In a later study (Thayer, Takahashi & Pauli, 1988), similar relationships between circadian cycle and mood were obtained.

An interesting new development in the literature on mood is the association between arousal and state-dependent memory. It is now increasingly clear that the nervous system is organized in such a way that there is a linkage between various moodlike states and cognitive material that has been associated with those states. For example, there is excellent experimental evidence that when an individual is experiencing various kinds of affect, cognitive content maintains a meaningful consistency with the affect. Let us consider here some research that is particularly appropriate to the association between memory and moodlike states of arousal. This research suggests that arousal cues can form important bases of this state dependency.

In two experiments, Clark and her associates (Clark, Milberg, & Ross, 1983) required experimental participants to memorize material in either high or normal arousal conditions. Subsequent recall tests indicated that memory was best when there was a match between the arousal state at learning and at recall. Thus, the material learned during exercise was recalled more fully immediately following other exercise than it was in a normal state of arousal, and vice versa. This learning and recall consistency as a function of arousal level was demonstrated both for recall following physical exercise and for recall following the kind of arousal generated by an erotic film.

In a third experiment (Clark, Milberg, & Ross, 1983), these investigators also provided evidence that the kind of arousal generated by feedback of good performance was more likely to result in a positive outlook when accompanied by exercise-generated arousal than if it was associated with a lower state of arousal. These results suggest interesting relations among arousal, mood, and cognition, particularly because they bring together conceptually the mood and state-dependent memory literature with the experimental psychology literature that links cognition, information processing, and arousal (e.g., Broadbent, 1971; M. W. Eysenck, 1982; Hockey, 1983). In the next section, mood and state-dependent memory will be considered more fully.

Mood, Memory, and Other Cognitive Processes

The evidence presented in the previous section suggests that biochemical processes, psychophysiological activity, and subjective moods are all interconnected, consistent with the theory advanced in this book that bodily processes often operate as an integrated whole in relation to general arousal reactions. This consistency is particularly apparent with regard to affective and cognitive states. As I indicated above, the nervous system appears to be organized in such a way as to make thoughts consistent in tone with mood states—a widely documented, but as yet not fully understood, phenomenon.

State-Dependent and Congruent Memory Processes

The association between tone of thinking and mood state has important practical implications. For instance, it may be the reason why such debilitating moods as depression include not only components of strong emotion (e.g., sadness) but also thoughts about self and the future that appear to reinforce and continue the debilitating condition (e.g., Beck, 1967). Furthermore, this association is not just limited to depressive mood states. Moods of elation, and quite possibly other moods as well, are often associated with a consistent tone of thought. Thus, when we are depressed we appear to have negative thoughts, and when we are elated, the tone of our thoughts is positive.

This research area is one of the most active in the current literature on mood. Dozens of papers have been published on the topic in the past ten years. There is too much material for anything like complete coverage in this chapter of their empirical and theoretical contributions (recent reviews include Blaney, 1986; Gilligan & Bower, 1984; Isen, 1984; Teasdale, 1983), but let me summarize certain important aspects of the topic.

First, state-dependent learning has frequently been demonstrated with animals as well as with humans (Overton, 1984). In such research, drugs that act on the central nervous system are employed to demonstrate that if learning occurs or attention given during a particular drug state, when the subjects are reintroduced to that same drug state later, they will have a better memory of what was learned than if recall is attempted in a nondrugged or a different drug state. This state-dependent memory retrieval has been demonstrated with such well-known drugs as alcohol and marijuana, as well as with a wide range of others, including various anesthetics, narcotics, anxiolytics, and stimulants. Even nicotine was recently employed to show state dependency (Peters & McGee, 1982). Early theorizing about this phenomenon centered on particular brain mechanisms, but more recent ideas have focused on the conditioning of stimulus contextual cues (cf. Tulving & Thompson, 1973) arising from the distinctive effects of various drugs (Overton, 1984).

Moods can produce states similar to those produced by drugs, so it is not surprising that attempts were made to demonstrate state-dependent memory with moods as well. In the previous section, I described research in which an association was drawn between states of arousal and state-dependent memory, with the implication that arousal may be a basis of mood-related state dependency (Clark, Milberg, & Ross, 1983). Another experiment designed to assess the relationship between mood-related state and memory was conducted by Weingartner and his associates, who utilized regularly occurring state changes of eight patients with bipolar mood disorders (Weingartner, Miller, & Murphy, 1977). From eight to twenty weeks, these patients were regularly subjected to word association tests, and at a later time they attempted to recall the associations. Recall was better if they were in a mood state similar to the one they were in when the test was given than in a different state. More evidence for this was provided by Clark and Teasdale, who used naturally occurring biological cycles among clinical depressives to demonstrate greater accessibility in memory for mood congruent material (Clark & Teasdale, 1982).

There have been a number of other demonstrations of the state dependency effect in normal persons, using the kinds of experiments described earlier. For example, Bower (1981) and his associates used hypnosis to place subjects in either a happy or sad mood while they learned different lists of words. Subsequently, in similar hypnotically induced happy or sad moods, greater recall was found for the words learned in the same mood than those learned in the opposite mood. All these results appear to demonstrate that learning is state dependent, with moods as the state variables.

However, there have been some failures to reproduce these results with moods and state-dependent learning (see review by Blaney, 1986). Thus, at the present time, the evidence suggests that state dependency may be only weakly related to moods (Blaney, 1986; Isen, 1984). But these failures could be due to inaccurate representations of intense and naturally occurring mood states. It is possible that the experimental manipulations that were employed, with their inherent limitations due to ethical constraints, were simply not strong enough to reproduce the effects of natural mood states. If this is the case, results such as those of Weingartner, Miller, and Murphy (1977) may be more representative of real life than the results from studies that failed to show state dependency. And even if this argument proves invalid, another relevant point is that quite substantial behavioral effects could arise out of weak state dependencies if one assumes that subtle moods can have inordinate behavioral effects when they are persistent over time (see Chapter 5).

Mood congruence, generally exemplified by individuals having greater accessibility to thoughts and memories that hold the same affective tone as the particular mood the subjects are in, is another example of cognitive-affective consistency, and compared to state dependency this phenomenon has received much more experimental support (Blaney, 1986). Mood congruence is also exemplified by the enhanced learning of verbal material that is consistent in tone with an existing mood state.

Teasdale and Fogarty (1979) conducted an experiment that demonstrates mood congruence. These investigators caused subjects to feel elation or depression using a Velten-type mood induction procedure. In each state, neutral cue words were presented with the request that subjects recall memories of real life experiences that were either pleasant or unpleasant. Measures of the time necessary for recall in each state indicated that it took significantly longer to retrieve pleasant memories in the depressed state. Two other experiments indicated that remembering unpleasant experiences was easier when depressed, and recalling positive memories was easier in the elated state (Teasdale & Taylor, 1981; Teasdale, Taylor, & Fogarty, 1980).

An experiment exemplifying another kind of mood congruence was conducted by Brown and Taylor (1986). Using Velten-type mood induction to produce happy and sad mood states, these investigators next exposed subjects to positive and negative adjectives regarding personality traits. Later they reestablished moods by the use of guided imagery and autobiographical recollections, and then unexpectedly asked subjects to recall as many of the original adjectives as they could. Although state dependency of recall was not apparent in this experiment, mood congruence did occur, since those individuals who received sad mood induction prior to adjective exposure recalled more negatively charged adjectives.

In addition to the experiments described above, Blaney (1986) has provided an excellent review of many other experimental procedures aimed at demonstrating state dependency and mood congruence, including studies that involved individual differences and those based on manipulated effects. This is a complex area, and in this limited coverage I have been unable to comment on such potentially important matters as the apparent asymmetry of cognitive reactions to positive and negative mood states, or the possible relevance of automatic versus controlled processes in this regard (cf. Isen, 1984). Nor was it possible to discuss findings that mood congruence effects were obtainable only with self-reference sets (Blaney [1986] reviews the evidence on this matter).

No single existing theory so far accounts for all the phenomena described above, but of the various conceptualizations that have been offered to understand state dependency and mood congruence effects, the most elaborated and best known is that of Bower and his associates (Bower, 1981; Gilligan & Bower, 1984; Singer & Salovey, 1988). Let me present an overly simplified form of this theory. As they see it, moods are part of an associative network that represents memory and that includes a wide range of concepts, schemata, and events. In a state dependency paradigm, induction of a mood results in the development of an associative network that includes not only the activated mood but also concepts and related stimuli that were learned and paid attention to in that particular mood. Therefore, the next time that the mood is activated, related elements of the associative network are also activated. The net result is enhanced memory for all elements of the associative network when the mood is again present. Similarly, in a mood congruence paradigm, the induction of a mood state activates a network related to that mood based on past experience. In this situation, the material presented can be much more elaborated because of the large number of associative connections that can be made. And these additional associations serve to enhance memory. This theory accounts for why a particular mood state produces greater accessibility to mood congruent material. Again, the associative network that is activated with the mood increases the congruent material that was previously memorized, learned or experienced.

Thus, this theory accounts for most of the observed findings regarding state dependent and mood congruent phenomena. However, there are certain empirical and logical problems the theory does not clarify. For example, if a network is based on past associations with a particular mood, one assumes that reactivation of the mood would also activate the associated connections. But this may involve an extremely large number of connections, which would lead to a kind of retrieval-cue overload. The theory also does not handle well the different intensities of moods and their influence on the associative network. It seems clear that different associations may occur for low-intensity moods than high-intensity moods, for instance. And the network concept may not be able to account for recent empirical findings that show similar and dissimilar concepts can be held within the same associative network (Johnson & Tversky, 1983).

Other Cognitive Processes and Mood

In addition to experiments on mood and memory, or mood and cognitive congruence, the literature is replete with research showing the influence of mood on a variety of other cognitive processes. To note a few of these studies, there is research indicating that positive moods enhance creative responses (Isen, Daubman, & Nowicki, 1987), and negative moods increase irrational thinking (Madigan & Bollenbach, 1986). Moreover, moods influence immediate self-perceptions. In one study, depressed patients viewing videotapes of themselves saw twice as many negative as positive behaviors in comparison with judgments by neutral observers who saw an equal number of these behaviors (Roth & Rehm, 1980). And in another study, subjects hypnotically induced to be in a mood of social well-being and success saw more positive behaviors in videotapes of themselves and others, but those induced to feel social failure and rejection saw more negative behaviors (Forgas, Bower, & Krantz, 1984). In still another study, depressed females who were of normal weight overestimated their body size compared to less depressed persons (Taylor & Cooper, 1986).

Recent research has shown that thinking about the future is influenced by positive and negative moods (Alloy & Ahrens, 1987; Brown, 1984; Thayer, 1987b; Wright & Bower, 1981). As one would expect, good moods lead to optimism about the future and expectations of success, and bad moods lead to the opposite. Thus, it is not surprising that happy and sad moods influence feelings of self-efficacy (Kavanagh & Bower, 1985). Also, subjects in a negative mood appeared more likely to rate the risks of having various kinds of fatal and nonfatal accidents higher, while positive mood reduced the amount of risk one saw (Johnson & Tversky, 1983). Research has also shown that subjects in a positive mood were more willing to risk a medical operation than those in a negative mood (Deldin & Levin, 1986). However, risk-taking behavior may be more complicated than it appears. One study indicated that when stakes were high, those in a positive mood required a higher probability of winning in order to take a risk, but when stakes were low, positive affect increased risk-taking (Isen & Nehemia, 1987).

Recently, Johnson and Magaro (1987) reviewed a large body of evidence about cognitive deficits in states of psychopathology, particularly in affective disorders. They presented a conceptualization that accounts nicely for this evidence, and which suggests that the cognitive deficits apparent in psychopathology are produced in part by low levels of effort (cf. Cohen et al., 1982). These effort reductions are indirectly related to the severity of illness and are believed to retard the storage and encoding of information. The cognitive deficits are also related to the disorganizing effect of the illness. (This model is quite relevant to the multidimensional arousal model presented in this book, as variations in effort are probably directly related to energetic arousal and indirectly related to tense arousal. See Chapter 6.) Johnson and Magaro also believe that specific deficits related to mood disorders can be traced to problems in encoding and retrieving information congruent with the current mood and to activating memories associated with a particular mood.

Mood and Illness

One of the central theses of this book is that moods have biological functions; part of these functions are that moods can serve as indicators of the body's readiness for action, or of its need for rest and recuperation. Moods may serve as signals of danger or as indications of safety. If this thesis is correct, major moods should reflect general illness as well as psychopathologies. Recently, a number of studies that correlated mood with general medical assessments suggest that this relationship does exist.

One of the best indications of the relationship between mood and illness comes from an extensive study that was conducted in a large primary care general medical facility. In this research, 37 percent of the patients studied reported that they had experienced severe tiredness and fatigue prior to their illness, often for many months before seeking treatment (Buchwald, Sullivan, & Komaroff, 1987; also see Kroenke et al., 1988). Specific illnesses have also been linked to moods. For example, in one study conducted by Harrigan et al. (1984) seventeen middle-aged people who suffered periodic migraine headaches completed mood measurements three times daily for twenty-one to seventy-five days. Headache periods were correlated with negative mood shifts as expected, but it was also possible to predict headaches from twelve to thirty-six hours prior to the headache. Feelings of constraint and fatigue were the best predictors, particularly in the afternoon.

Blanchet and Frommer (1986) conducted a study of epileptic seizures in which twenty-seven adults suffering from diverse forms of epilepsy completed ratings of a number of types of mood for a period of more than fifty days. Seizures could be predicted by ratings of negative mood on the same day or the day prior to when the seizure occurred. Also, analyses of written verbal comments of the participants revealed more negative affect. In addition, ratings of energy dropped significantly on seizure days. Thirty allergy patients took part in still another study of mood-illness relationships. Using a double-blind procedure, investigators found that mood varied as a function of sublingual exposure to allergens (King, 1981).

Studies relating mood to immune system response represent one of the most interesting developments in this area, and a good deal of indirect evidence exists for such a relationship (see review by Baker, 1987. Also note McClelland et al., 1980; McClelland, Ross, & Patel, 1985; Monjan, 1984). More direct evidence comes from research by Linn and her associates, who studied the immune responses of ninety-eight men who had experienced a recent family death or serious illness (Linn, Linn, & Jensen, 1984). These individuals were asked to fill out a depression checklist, and those scoring highest on the depression measure showed significantly less lymphocyte responsiveness, although no significant difference was observed as a function of recent death or illness.

In another study, Dillon and Baker (1985–86) employed salivary immunoglobulin A (IgA), a substance that reflects more transitory changes of the immune system as a mood indicator. They measured IgA levels both before and after a humorous videotape and a control tape were shown. The investigators found significant increases in immune responses after the humorous film was shown as compared to the control. Moreover, there were indications of individual differences in this regard because pre-IgA concentrations correlated significantly with scores on the Coping Humor Questionnaire administered to participants. This study suggests that positive affect (humor) is an antecedent of immune system response.

In one of the most complete studies of mood and immune response published to date, Stone and his associates (Stone et al., 1987) tested for IgA concentrations as well as for positive and negative mood from dental students three times weekly for eight weeks. On each occasion, students rated their mood on the basis of reactions for the whole day. Immune system response was found to be lower on days of strongly negative mood and higher on days of strong positive mood. These studies and others suggest a close relationship exists between mood and illness.

Food and Mood

Although the relationship between eating and mood is of intense interest in the general culture, this area of study is highly underrepresented in the scientific literature. Popular science writers commonly assume that mood is directly affected by certain food groups (Dufty, 1975; Fredericks & Goodman, 1969), but there is a surprisingly small amount of data to support this. For example, sugar consumption is widely believed to result in tension, but recently, biochemical studies have suggested that, contrary to belief, the primary effect of sugar ingestion may be tiredness (Spinweber, 1981; Wurtman, Hefti, & Malemed, 1981; see also review by Spring, Chiodo, & Bowen, 1987). In a recent study of mine, however, sugar ingestion was immediately followed by an increase in energy, and by tiredness and increased tension after an hour (Thayer, 1987a). I have argued that tiredness could be the primary biological effect of sugar ingestion, but that observed tension increases could be a secondary effect that occurs when a tired person is forced to continue ongoing activities.

The physiological mechanisms that account for the effects of sugar on mood are by no means understood. If in fact there is a relationship, blood glucose levels may well be involved, but there is little evidence indicating the association between them and mood change (Horton & Yates, 1987). Other possibilities linking sugar and mood may involve insulin (Christie & McBrearty, 1979) or tryptophan and serotonin (Hartmann, 1982–83; Wurtman & Wurtman, 1986).

More studies are needed, such as the one conducted by Christensen and his associates (Christensen et al., 1985) in which a single-subject research design was employed to determine the effects of dietary change. Four subjects were selected for this study on the basis of metabolic imbalance, and they were placed on a high-protein low-carbohydrate diet that was void of sucrose and caffeine. After two weeks on this diet, MMPI and POMS mood measurements indicated more stability and less distress as compared to baseline measurements.

Clearly, this area needs special research designs for adequate data. Because the effects of food on mood are probably quite subtle, single-subject designs such as the one above and methods of data aggregation in natural settings (Thayer, 1987a) may be essential for adequate research. Even then, however, there is the possibility of expectancy effects with such longitudinal designs.[8]

Other kinds of research involving food and mood are more common in the scientific literature. For example, there is now evidence that personality characteristics are related to eating behaviors (Mehrabian, 1987), and particularly to poor eating habits under certain conditions. For instance, restrainers (dieters) have been found to eat more when in an anxious or depressed mood (e.g., Baucom & Aiken, 1981; Cooper & Bowskill, 1986; Ruderman, 1985; see also review by Ruderman, 1986). In one of these studies, Ruderman (1985) manipulated mood by requiring subjects to complete solvable or unsolvable math problems. After this, subjects were required to take a "taste test," which actually allowed the investigator to assess the amount of crackers consumed. In the dysphoric mood condition, those who tended to diet ate more crackers.

Still another area associated with food that has received some attention is the effect of diet regimens on mood. Although there was some early evidence of negative mood reactions from such programs (see Wadden, 1984; Smoller, Wadden, & Stunkard, 1987), more recent studies suggest positive mood effects. This situation is complex, however, as indicated by the research of Wadden, Stunkard, and Smoller (1986). They studied twenty-eight obese women who lost an average of 19.2 kilograms in six months. For these individuals, mood improved from the pre-diet state to the post-diet state, but over half of them experienced a worsening of mood for one or more weeks. The study further indicated that retrospective mood measurements versus those taken concurrently, as well as type of measurement, may influence conclusions about the mood effects of such programs.

Weather, Geophysical Phenomena, and Mood

Once while visiting Sweden, I was told by one person at a lively dinner party that if I came again at midwinter I would be unlikely to encounter the same high-spirited atmosphere. This observation seemed to corroborate anecdotal reports that people in northern climates experience negative moods during the weather extremes, and it suggests weather has some kind of biophysical effect on mood. But such conclusions may be incorrect, because even if weather-mood correlations are observed, inconveniences or social advantages associated with the climate changes may be the reason for mood variations, not direct geophysical effects on bodily processes. For example, in climates with lots of snow and ice there are considerable problems connected with clothing, vehicle maintenance, and so forth. And in humid weather there are also difficulties with clothing and other aspects of self-maintenance (cf. Persinger, 1983).

Nonetheless, a number of studies indicate that a relationship exists between mood and weather. For example, in one interesting study relating weather, mood, and helping behavior, Cunningham (1979) correlated measures of the willingness of participants to respond to questions with weather readings obtained from the National Weather Service (NWS) in the Minneapolis, Minnesota, area over thirty-six weekday periods. The amount of sunshine was the best weather predictor of willingness to help. Cunningham then correlated weather with the amount of tips that customers left in a restaurant and mood states as recorded by waitresses. Once again, amount of sunshine was the best predictor, although, as in the first study, temperature and humidity also showed significant correlations.

In another study conducted in the Maryland area, Sanders and Brizzolara (1982) collected mood measurements at the beginning of each class period over a five-week summer session. The three significant weather predictors of mood were temperature, barometric pressure, and humidity. In particular, humidity correlated negatively with vigor and other positive moods. Still another study, conducted in Canada during November and December by Howarth and Hoffman (1984), showed that the weather variables which best predicted mood were humidity (negative), temperature, and hours of sunshine.

Other geophysical factors may be implicated in mood variations as well. There are several recent experiments concerning the association between positive and negative ions and mood. These studies are particularly convincing because they were carried out with "blind" experimental designs. Positive ionic concentrations tend to be associated with pollution as well as with such weather conditions as the warm dry winds of the Santa Anas in southern California, the chinook of Canada, and the foehn of Switzerland and central Europe. Negative ionic concentrations often occur after rainstorms or around bodies of circulating water (e.g., waterfalls and seashores), and they may even be associated with running shower water (Soyka & Edwards, 1976).

Charry and Hawkinshire (1981) subjected research participants to positive ionic concentrations and found increased tension and irritability. Tom et al. (1981) found that negative ionic concentrations increased energetic feelings as well as improved reaction time. Similarly, Buckalew and Rizzuto (1982) found that negative ions produced increases in positive mood states and decreases in negative states. Finally, Baron, Russell, and Arms (1985) also found that negative ions produced significant positive mood shifts.

Another geophysical phenomenon that has recently received a good deal of popular attention through a television series on the brain is so-called winter depression. Some people may have affective disorders with seasonal variations, in which depression is most pronounced in winter (Lewy, 1984). In one interesting experiment (Rosenthal et al., 1985), thirteen patients with seasonal affective disorder were treated for two one-week periods with 2,500 lux of light (this is approximately the amount of illumination given by sunlight from a window on a clear spring day). The treatment had a marked antidepressant effect. Much more evidence is necessary before conclusions can be drawn about seasonal disorders and light therapy, however, because there are a number of other possible explanations for these phenomena.

One other geophysical phenomenon that deserves comment because of the widely held beliefs associated with it is the relationship between cycles of the moon and mood-related behaviors. In the weather, helping, and tipping studies mentioned above (Cunningham, 1979), the lunar phase showed small but significant correlations with helping and with the amount of tips left (full moon = less helping and more tipping), although for various methodological reasons Cunningham noted that these correlations may be spurious. Since there is a good deal of controversy about the proper interpretation of existing evidence concerning lunar phase and behavior (e.g., Campbell, 1982; Garzino, 1982), Rotton and Kelly (1985) systematically combined the results of published studies about this phenomenon. Their conclusions suggest that there is little evidence for any relationship. In their words, "Although a few statistically significant relations emerged, effect size estimates indicated that phases of the moon accounted for no more than 1% of the variance in activities usually termed lunacy. Alleged relations between phases of the moon and behavior can be traced to inappropriate analyses, a failure to take other (e.g., weekly) cycles into account, and a willingness to accept any departure from chance as evidence for a *lunar effect*."

Naturally Occurring Antecedents of Mood

In recent times a good deal of attention has been paid to the kinds of naturally occurring events that affect moods, and a variety of influences have been tentatively identified. None of the findings was entirely unexpected, but nevertheless, the actual empirical data provide greater understanding than is possible from simple casual observations. As examples of research, Kirchler used a diary method to study thirty unemployed workers over a six-month period (Kirchler, 1985). Feelings of well-being decreased during unemployment, and bad moods were often attributed to internal factors and family members as well as to the economic situation. In another longitudinal study, of youths leaving high school, those not employed after six months experienced relatively greater negative moods, more depression, as well as lower self-esteem (Tiggemann & Winefield, 1984).

Lesser events also affect mood. For example, in two longitudinal studies conducted by Metalsky and his associates (Metalsky et al., 1982; Metalsky, Halberstadt, & Abramson, 1987), low midsemester grades were found to result in greater depression. Indeed, as might be expected, the kinds of small but unpleasant events that can occur daily clearly result in negative moods. Lewinsohn and his associates have produced various kinds of evidence of this in connection with a theory of depression. For example, in one study the expected relationships were found among unpleasant events, pleasant events, and depression reactions in a group of subjects who made self-ratings daily (Lewinsohn & Amenson, 1978).

A number of longitudinal studies conducted in natural settings over several-week periods have been used to assess influences on mood. Although these studies are difficult to complete, and they can often be faulted on the basis of possible subject expectation effects, in my view their results are frequently more meaningful in the long run than those obtained from artificial laboratory studies. In one such study by Eckenrode (1984), ninety-six women completed daily diaries for one month. Eckenrode found that the most important direct determinants of mood were daily stressors and physical symptoms as opposed to more long-term life events and chronic stressors. In another, somewhat similar longitudinal study by Stone (1987), desirable family leisure events were the most predictive of positive moods. Undesirable work events were highly predictive of negative moods. Other longitudinal research recently published has shown relationships between daily mood reports and descriptions of social interactions, frequency of exercise, health problems, and perceived stress (Clark & Watson, 1988; Watson, 1988a). In one attempt to determine the extent of influence from life events, Stone and Neale (1984) found that negative events affected mood on the same day, but had no effect on the following day.

Still other research relating to common perceptions about mood found that the "Blue Monday" phenomenon was unsupportable. There was no evidence that moods were any worse on Mondays than on other weekdays (Stone et al., 1985). Weekends, on the other hand, were associated with better mood states. Other evidence of this positive weekend effect was obtained by Rossi and Rossi (1977), who collected daily mood ratings over a forty-day period and found that positive moods peaked on weekends.

As might be expected, these daily influences on mood do not affect everyone in the same way and under all circumstances. Mood is influenced by a number of other factors as well as by various individual differences. For example, the data of Eckenrode described above were further analyzed in a recent paper (Caspi, Bolger, & Eckenrode, 1987), and the authors indicated that chronic ecological stress (perceived threats in the neighborhood of residence) increased the likelihood of stressors immediately affecting mood as well as having the effects persist to the next day. Social support systems tended to reduce the enduring effects, although not the immediate ones. These researchers also found the unexpected result that previous exposure to major life events decreased the impact of stressful daily events (perhaps due to a kind of habituation effect or the effect of learning coping skills). Viney (1986) also found that social support systems were important in reducing the negative moods of hospitalized patients.

Important individual differences have also been observed to affect the impact of daily events on moods. In the research described above regarding midterm college exams, Metalsky et al. (1982, 1987) found evidence for a diathesis stress model in their reformulated theory of human helplessness and depression. Those students identified as having depressogenic attributional styles were not only affected immediately by a low grade, but they showed that the effect persisted. Larsen and his associates (Larsen, Diener, & Emmons, 1986) have provided evidence that certain individuals have a predisposition for strong affective response to diverse kinds of stimulation as compared to others, who show relatively weak affective responses. This individual difference measure is similar to the very interesting Pavlovian concept of Strength of Nervous System (Teplov, 1972. See also Eliasz, 1985; Klonowicz, Ignatowska–Switalska, &

Wocial, 1986; Strelau, 1983). And finally, an individual difference often suspected was empirically identified by Larson, Czikszentmihalyi, and Graef (1980), who used a new time-sampling method to determine that adolescents experience wider and quicker mood swings than other age groups.

Other Mood-Related Topic Areas

A large number of papers have been published on mood as related to helping behavior. In general, this research shows that both positive and negative moods affect tendencies to help in a variety of circumstances (e.g., Isen, Clark, & Schwartz, 1976). However, at least one early analysis suggested that these effects of mood are weak and that the evidence for a relationship is meager (Wispe, 1980). Nonetheless, reliable relationships have been reported in a large number of studies (see reviews by Carlson & Miller, 1987; Isen, 1984), and recent research continues to suggest an association between mood and helping (e.g., Berkowitz, 1987; Cramer et al., 1986; Manucia, Baumann, & Cialdini, 1984).

Mood disorders, particularly depression, comprises one of the most, if not the most, active research areas concerning mood. There are many excellent recent reviews, and, reflecting the fact that affective disorders are still not understood, important theoretical models continue to be offered (Barnett & Gotlib, 1988; Belsher & Costello, 1988; Healy & Williams, 1988; Hinz & Williamson, 1987; Hollon, DeRubeis, & Evans, 1987; Hyland, 1987; Ingram, 1984; Post & Ballenger, 1984; Pyszczynski & Greenberg, 1987; Romano & Turner, 1985; Whybrow, Akiskal, & McKinney, 1984).

The effects of drugs on mood is another topic that has generated a large amount of published research. In the past ten years, the greatest number of studies has concerned the effects of alcohol on mood, but a number of studies were also published concerning the effects of benzodiazepines (e.g., Valium), amphetamines, caffeine, and nicotine on mood. The multivolume edited work, *Handbook of Psychopharmacology,* is an excellent reference for much of this research (Iversen, Iversen, & Snyder, multiyear).

Finally, the relationship of cognition to affect is an area that has received a good deal of attention, much of it in response to the interchange between Zajonc (1980, 1984) and Lazarus (1982, 1984). There are a number of recent reviews and new theoretical analyses of this area (e.g., Brewin, 1985; Coyne & Gotlib, 1983; Peterson & Seligman, 1984; Pittman & Heller, 1987; Weiner, 1985). From them, it is clear that no consensus of opinion has been achieved about the primacy of either cognition or affect, except perhaps that the two interact continuously.

Analytic Retrospective and Future Orientation

As I indicated at the beginning of this chapter, the earlier neglect of mood as an important aspect of personality has given way to a new and widespread interest.

The field is now rich with investigations and speculations about this general affective state, as can be observed by the lively literature on mood dimensionality and—integrally related—by the numerous studies of mood measurement. Investigators are fashioning their own measuring instruments in the context of a particular theoretical focus, and by doing so are discovering new information about mood. Yet issues of mood dimensionality remain among the most problematic in the field. The current tendency for many to simply categorize a variety of moods as positive or negative may be too simplistic. Although at one level, this approach has been undeniably useful, more precise studies would likely yield a picture of much greater complexity and provide more real understanding.

As research across the board indicates, moods are as interrelated with biological phenomena as with social experiences. Much evidence exists that biochemical and psychophysiological events are related to moods, perhaps as precursors but more likely as elements of larger psychological and physiological systems having rich patterns of interaction. The relationship of moods to general bodily functioning is clearly evident, for example, in studies that show these affective states to be influenced by a variety of illnesses, and perhaps by all systemic illness.

An association certainly exists between mood and cognition. The vigorous area of study concerning state-dependent memory and mood congruence is one of the most productive. Its implications are substantial, including an opportunity to gain a much better understanding of depression and also of various positive mood states. Other elements of cognition and social behavior have also been found to be closely associated with mood. Important questions about the primacy of affect versus cognition have greatly stimulated thinking about these relationships, and as is true for biochemical and psychophysiological relationships, the emerging picture shows affect, cognition, and social behavior to be inextricably intertwined.

The great variety of mood antecedents is clearly reflected in the many ways that have been devised to manipulate moods for experimental study. The ease with which such manipulations can be accomplished clearly indicates that moods are not inexorably fixed, but that social and cognitive events readily affect them. Studies of natural events also make this clear.

Studies of the relationships between natural events and mood represent some of the most interesting developments in the whole field, because they make much more credible the use of longitudinal research carried out in natural settings and often utilizing data aggregation. Researchers are gradually recognizing that the complexities of mood associations cannot be entirely determined by traditional laboratory and nomothetic methods. Future research on mood will probably verify the existence of a rich interrelationship of variables ranging from biological cycles to complex social interactions. In addition to direct effects on mood, we are likely to find that mood is influenced by these variables acting as moderators of many cognitive and social elements of daily experience. Moreover, since many of these variables are in continuous change, a genuine understanding will probably require a kind of calculus for mood-behavior interactions.

Certain blind spots still exist in our understanding of mood, however. If I had to pick one area in which the most significant blind spot exists, it would concern the genetic basis of moods. This is not to suggest that no work is going on in this area, but considering the likely importance of genetic factors in any complete understanding, the research efforts here are clearly underrepresented. H. J. Eysenck, perhaps the leading biologically oriented personality authority in the world, believes that two-thirds of the real measurement variance of personality is genetically determined (personal communication, September 29, 1987; see also Brody, 1988; Eaves, Eysenck, & Martin, 1988; Pedersen, et al., Tellegen et al., 1988). This percentage may not be correct, but most knowledgeable people working in this area recognize that at least a large portion of personality variance is likely to be genetically controlled. And if this is true of general personality, can moods, with their probable physiological associations, be much less affected by genetic determinants?

In a related way, there is entirely too little recognition of the biological underpinnings of many mood states. Of course, this generalization does not hold for moods associated with affective disorders (e.g., depression), because medical researchers are well aware of these underpinnings. But frequently, those who deal with normal moods pay little or no attention to these probable relationships. And yet, so much evidence now indicates a close association of physiological and psychological variables with mood that virtually every discussion of mood research should consider the biological implications. Furthermore, a rich area of theory concerning the functional nature of moods from an evolutionary perspective is greatly neglected in most publications.

The effects on mood of exercise and food is another topic in which less research exists than might be expected. It is possible that the lay public is ahead of the scientists regarding these likely antecedents of mood. People appear to recognize that in their own lives important relationships exist among these variables, and there are rapidly increasing applications of these beliefs in clinical practice. Nevertheless, the amount of scientific research is very limited. Up until now, serious scientists apparently have been hesitant to venture into some of these overly popularized areas, but the likelihood of important relationships among mood, exercise, and food is so strong that this neglect should not continue.

The remaining chapters present a number of conceptualizations that may provide remedies for some of the shortcomings mentioned above. These ideas are a kind of wedding of biological and social interactions with mood. They are necessarily crude because there are still too many unanswered questions for any real certainty to exist, and yet a model is offered that is logical and that may provide some guidance for future investigations.

3

Arousal: A Basic Element
of Mood and Behavior

The concept of arousal as a general bodily process is both necessary and controversial in the biological and behavioral sciences—particularly psychology and
physiology (e.g., Andrew, 1974; Duffy, 1962; Eason & Dudley, 1971; Levenson,
1983; Thayer, 1978b; Thayer, 1985). The controversy surrounding this concept
derives mainly from the complexity of bodily processes, a complexity that seems
to defy classification on a single arousal continuum. Yet the fact that one or
more of these continua exists seems undeniable. It is clear that on most days we
move from quiescence to activity, and back again to quiescence. Thus a continuum of integrated bodily changes occurs between sedentary rest and intense
exercise, and from mild to intense emotions.

Does one common process represent all these variations in bodily intensity
or are the processes entirely different? Does a general type of arousal occur at all
levels of bodily functioning or are these responses quite specific? Is it possible
to employ a general arousal concept to analyze mood and cognition, or is behavior simply too complex for one to assume integrated arousal-related patterns?
Together with an analysis of the nature of arousal, these are some of the questions to be addressed in this chapter.

Usually arousal refers to bodily reactivity or to reactivity within subsystems
of the body. Arousal can be quite specific, as with brain activation in relation to
changes in electrophysiological frequency and amplitude, or in the case of cardiovascular arousal, when increased or decreased physical demand leads to
changes in heart rate and blood pressure. But often arousal, or activation, is
more general, referring to the changes occurring in the whole body as emotions
shift from quiescence to high activation, or referring to the general bodily
changes associated with exercise, sleep, and wakefulness. It is the latter case that
I shall focus on.

Practically every broad psychological theory has employed some variation of
an arousal model. In early psychological history, variations of arousal concepts
were employed by Wundt (1896) in his tridimensional theory of emotions and
by Freud (1953–55) in his conceptions of psychosexual tension. Arousal, or acti-

46

vation, was given a more solid foundation empirically by Elizabeth Duffy's (1962) psychophysiological analyses of the activation of behavior, and activation theories were strengthened by research on the reticular activating system (Lindsley, 1951), an integrated series of brain structures in the mesencephalon and thalamus found to be associated with sleep, wakefulness, and general behavioral intensity.

In an early, quite influential theoretical analysis, the relationship of psychophysiological, neuroanatomical, and behavioral conceptualizations of arousal was persuasively argued by Malmo (1959). In recent times, as more is learned about the great complexity of the body, broad psychological theories have generally been eschewed, but arousal concepts have retained their attractiveness, particularly in relation to theories of emotion (e.g., Mandler, 1984), personality (e.g., Eysenck, 1967; Eysenck & Eysenck, 1985), and temperament (e.g., Buss & Plomin, 1984; MacDonald, 1988), and also in more limited analyses of exercise (e.g., Thayer, 1987a, 1987b), sleep-wakefulness (e.g., Horne, 1983), and cognitive functioning (e.g., M. W. Eysenck, 1982; Humphreys & Revelle, 1984).

Criticisms of general arousal concepts have probably limited wider use of these concepts. Usually these criticisms are based on the extreme complexity of the central and peripheral nervous systems; conceptions of arousal that hypothesize that many bodily subsystems are directly and integrally related on a single intensity continuum can be criticized if the various subsystems do not show correlations (e.g., Vanderwolf & Robinson, 1981) or if the arousal construct is too broad (Neiss, 1988). For example, some years ago Lacey (1967) described low correlations among three subsystems, each of which are thought to reflect arousal. He concluded that there appear to be three kinds of arousal: behavioral, cortical, and autonomic.

The kind of criticism that cites low intercorrelation of arousal among bodily systems can itself be criticized on methodological grounds. A more complex research design than has yet been provided is necessary before demonstrating conclusively that there is no correlation among subsystems of general arousal. However, criticizing the criticisms does not prove the general concept. So far, theoretical and design problems have precluded entirely convincing demonstrations of general arousal theories based on a single arousal dimension which underlies all behavior.

A more telling argument against Lacey's kind of criticism of general arousal is that it makes little sense evolutionarily. Why would natural selection favor animals that had dissociations among behavioral, cortical, and autonomic arousal reactions? Given the elemental and adaptive nature of the arousal reaction, such dissociations would appear to carry distinct survival disadvantages. Criticisms of a single arousal continuum are more likely to have validity if the concept of multiple arousal systems is based on biologically meaningful divisions and interaction patterns among arousal dimensions (e.g., Thayer, 1978b).[1]

My concept of arousal is based on such a multidimensional system. This approach retains the traditional psychophysiological leaning, but I have primarily employed psychological evidence supplemented by biological and physiological data. To exemplify the two kinds of arousal concepts that are combined in my approach, I will use the following hypothetical examples.

Energetic Arousal

A young man is sitting quietly under a tree on a warm summer day. After resting, soon he will mow the lawn, a demanding—albeit not unpleasant—task. When he is sitting, his body's physiological processes are in a pattern of quiescence; energy-conserving and recuperative functions dominate.

As he rises and begins to mow, however, his whole body is changed from the quiescent state to one of mobilization for vigorous action. As the activity progresses, a pattern of bodily activation or arousal occurs that encompasses all physiological systems at once (cf. Brooks & Fahey, 1984; Duffy, 1962; Kalat, 1984). Moreover, as will become more apparent below, important psychological systems are involved simultaneously in this wide-ranging arousal reaction.

Involved in this psychophysiological shift is his brainstem reticular activating system with its forward projection areas—the most important arousal system of the brain (Andrew, 1974; Mountcastle, 1980; Kalat, 1984). Large portions of his midbrain and cerebral cortex are involved in mediating sensory information, using it to plan and execute action through the form of complex motor sequences, adding refinements to performance, and in executing further actions. Integrally involved in this process are systemic changes in neurotransmitters (e.g., acetylcholine, norepinephrine, dopamine, and serotonin), which act as central nervous system (CNS) modulators, selectively enhancing and inhibiting synaptic transmission of appropriate electrochemical impulses (Kalat, 1984).

With the exertion necessary for the activity, the autonomic branch of his peripheral nervous system shifts from a parasympathetic pattern, involving the vegetative functions of body maintenance, rest, and recuperation, into a sympathetic pattern associated with mobilization for action—in this case nonemergency action (Andreassi, 1980; Sternbach, 1966). There are significant changes in his endocrine system, including the release of such hormones as adrenaline (epinephrine), which increases metabolic and cardiac arousal (Galbo, 1983; Frankenhaeuser, 1975).

As he pushes the mower, his heart pumps faster to circulate greater amounts of glucose and oxygen, and to carry away metabolic end products (Karpman, 1987; Rowell, 1974). His blood pressure rises due to the constriction of the peripheral blood vessels as the blood flows to more needed areas, and due to the increased heart activity necessary to supply active muscle and nervous tissue with oxygen (Karpman, 1987). At the same time, his respiratory system is also activated, thus providing the necessary gas exchange (Dejours, 1964; West, 1974). Breathing becomes not only faster but also deeper to enable greater infusion of oxygen, the necessary substance of metabolic activity, and to expel the increased concentrations of carbon dioxide that occur with arousal.

As the mowing progresses, the arousal reaction affects all physical levels, even cellular. For example, while he moves rapidly about his work, there is an increase in his general metabolism, the biochemical link between demand and action (Galbo, 1983; Saltin, 1973). Insulin concentrations in his blood are decreased, thus enabling glycogen stored in the liver to be more readily available for the metabolic requirements of active muscles, nerves, and brain (Shephard, 1982). As he settles into mowing, the initial anaerobic chemical processes in the cells are replaced by aerobic glycolysis. And with exercise adenosine triphosphate (ATP), the basic energy unit of cell metabolism, is rapidly converted (Shephard, 1982).

The young man's skeletal-muscular system is clearly in a state of activation throughout this activity (deVries, 1986). As he strains to push the mower forward, for example, the large extensor muscles of his legs alternatively contract with each push and then relax. Reciprocally acting flexor muscles bring the leg into place for the next push. For maximum efficiency, muscles of his face not necessary for this activity relax, but contractions of other muscles of the back, shoulders, and arms are integrated with leg muscle activity.

These are only a portion of the changes occurring in this hypothetical example, however. Such an arousal pattern probably encompasses the whole individual, and all systems interact for optimal mobilization of resources and execution of physical activity. A casual observer might not be aware of the young man's internal changes, but on a gross level, arousal would be apparent through the man's orientation to the lawn mower and his movements. As the young man scrutinizes the area in front of the mower to avoid rocks, a good observer might note dilation of his pupils. Perspiration and skin color changes would also denote arousal (Brooks & Fahey, 1984; Shephard, 1982).

Although these psychophysiological changes are highly complicated, this process is fairly well-known, mainly from the work of exercise physiologists (e.g., Brooks & Fahey, 1984; deVries, 1986; Shephard, 1982). Usually what is not fully appreciated is the degree of interconnectedness between psychological processes with physiological arousal. For this general arousal reaction, it is highly likely that there is an integrated response that incorporates all major bodily systems, including psychological systems.

An important part of the psychological processes of arousal is the often scientifically overlooked phenomenon of conscious awareness. Consciousness provides highly integrated information from many parts of the body, in this case about arousal. The function of this information is not presently agreed upon—in fact it has hardly been discussed—but quite possibly there is a connection with a kind of executive mechanism and the cognitive control of behavior (cf. Hilgard, 1977).

This young man might be aware, for example, of a wide variety of bodily arousal sensations, ranging from sweat on his hands to increases in body heat. Even the unpracticed self-observer is aware in a general way of his or her muscle, heart, and respiratory action. Most adults and even small children can name and describe the sensations that are the likely bases of arousal-related feelings. The names of these feelings—energy, tiredness, fatigue—are common parts of language probably because they are so useful.

For our hypothetical young man, the feeling of drowsiness as he sat under the tree was a conscious awareness of a particular state of arousal. And as he continued to work on the lawn, arousal would be apparent through slowly developing feelings of energy, vigor, and peppiness. Through these various feelings, the internal arousal processes could be gauged.

If an internal view of the young man's body were possible, particularly with appropriate integration of patterns of systemic change, the intricate relationship between physiology and subjective feelings would undoubtedly be better appreciated. Just as his cardiovascular system was in a quiescent state while he sat under the tree and became activated when he began mowing, so his feelings would change from a tired and sleepy state to one of energy and vigor.

Naturally, this change in subjective feelings would be influenced by such important factors as physical conditioning, degree of effort, amount of rest, food previously eaten, and so on. The physiological changes would be similarly influenced by these factors. If, as I propose, physiological and psychological arousal processes maintain a close and functional interaction, it is highly likely that the body reacts as a whole to generalized arousal.

My name for this very broad reaction that incorporates seemingly diverse physiological and psychological processes is "energetic arousal." I use this name to place major emphasis on the conscious awareness component of the system. Although the complexity of central and peripheral physiological systems has so far defied clear demonstrations of this general arousal continuum, evidence derived from conscious awareness makes its existence quite clear. And it is this level of conscious awareness that is the main subject matter of this book.

Energetic arousal ranges from bodily quiescence to activation, and it is closely associated with gross motor activity. This kind of arousal also probably underlies the sleep-wake cycle in a general way. Although the physiological arousal processes associated with gross motor activity are mostly understood, the processes underlying wakefulness and sleep are still not agreed upon. Moreover, the relationship between the physiology and conscious awareness for both these elemental biological actions is still a matter of controversy. Yet the evidence that I shall present, mainly of a psychological nature, strongly suggests an underlying bodily system such as energetic arousal for both physical activity and the sleep-wake cycle. For example, in both exercise-related arousal and the more subtle changes associated with the sleep-wakefulness cycle, roughly the same arousal-related feelings are present.

Tense Arousal

Now let us consider the same hypothetical young man in a different situation. He is working slowly at his desk in a quiet office. It is late afternoon, and he is feeling rather drowsy. His physiological and psychological state is one of quiescence, or low arousal.

The telephone rings, and his boss, speaking in a loud voice, orders the young man to come to his office immediately. The sound of the boss's voice suggests anger, and the young man is immediately alarmed. As he walks hesitatingly down the hall, he remembers his almost forgotten doubts that his work is satisfactory, and he remembers his previous well-founded fears about keeping his job. In an agitated attempt to discover in advance what the problem might be, his mind races over his many mistakes, the undeniable inadequacies in his past performance.

At this point, the low-arousal condition would have changed to high arousal, a state apparently very similar to that described when mowing a lawn. They both have much the same function—bodily mobilization for physical activity—but in the latter case it is mobilization for a potential emergency, not for a simple and somewhat pleasant physical task. As in the other example, it is likely that the pattern of this mobilization is evolutionarily determined, and it occurs naturally, without consideration or planning.

If one compared common psychophysiological responses that might occur in an "emergency" situation such as this, and those occurring during an activity like mowing a lawn, the two would largely overlap (Mandler, 1984), mostly because they are both associated with gross motor activity. In one case it is the activity necessary to mow a lawn, and in the other case it is the nonconscious preparation for the effort that *may* be necessary in the face of danger. (This danger-associated arousal reaction is popularly known through the fight or flight concept originated by Cannon [1929/1963] and later, through the alarm reaction to stress as described by Selye [1956]).

As the young man walks down the hall, his central and peripheral nervous systems, the cardiovascular and respiratory systems, and the various neurochemical systems of his body would be activated (Asterita, 1985; Frankenhaeuser, 1975; Panksepp, 1986; Ursin, Baade, & Levine, 1978). The endocrine system, including adrenaline secretion, would have much the same metabolic and cardiovascular activating function in this case as it had when physical activity was involved. And the activation of all these bodily systems would depend on the necessary fuel obtained through increased metabolic activity at the cellular level.

Although these arousal changes in the two situations may be similar, there are at least three kinds of distinguishable differences between the energetic and tense arousal reactions described. Two of these differences are associated with skeletal-muscular reactions and patterns of attention. And although they are obviously important for a complete analysis of the matter, these two differences are outside the focus of this discussion; therefore, only passing comment will be provided. The third difference, however, concerns feelings of arousal, the focus throughout this book.

Let us first consider differences in skeletal-muscular reactions and attention. In the lawn mowing experience, the muscles of the young man would have served to propel the mower forward in a fairly uninterrupted and directed fashion. Smooth, ongoing bodily movement would be evident by the muscle activity. But in walking down the hall to meet the boss, a different muscular pattern would probably occur. Muscles in the back, shoulders, and neck would be activated in both cases, but in the emergency reaction they would be tight, and the resulting movements would be jerky and uneven.

This pattern appears to be one of preparation for directed motor activity, but not execution. One biological interpretation of the emergency-generated muscular pattern could be that the skeletal muscles bind or inhibit action. Perhaps in evolutionary history this was a means of avoiding detection by predators until action decisions were made or until some sort of fight or flight reaction was forced. Preparatory arousal, coupled with motor inhibition, is the apparent muscular pattern for emergency response.

A second important difference in the arousal reactions would be in the focus of attention. When mowing the lawn, the young man's focus would be on the job, enabling him to avoid rocks and cut more efficiently. His attention would be task-directed, with little deviation. In contrast, while walking down the hall to encounter the danger represented in the wrath of the boss, his mind would race. In seconds, he would probably consider many hypotheses to explain the danger. His attention might be described as distracted. And yet the term "distracted" suggests some kind of reduction of attention, which would be inappropriate here.

A better interpretation of this apparent distraction is that in the presence of danger his attention would be wholly directed to the danger stimulus. From an evolutionary perspective, this would be the most adaptive response. But in the present case, and any time that anxiety is present,[2] the real danger would not be known. Thus, his attention would seem to shift rapidly from thought to thought, as if the correct interpretation of danger could be made with sufficient scanning of relevant information. If the young man were engaged in some task not related to his perceived danger, his attention would not be completely on the task, thus giving the appearance of distracted attention.

A third difference, and for purposes of this book the most important one, concerns the young man's subjective experiences while walking down the hall. Energy, vigor, and peppiness—the feelings of high energetic arousal—probably would not be present. Instead, there might well be a "sinking feeling" or even a feeling of profound fatigue. Subjective tiredness could well describe this state. Even more salient than tiredness or fatigue would be feelings of fearfulness, anxiety, and tension. These feelings also indicate bodily arousal, but in this case the arousal reaction appears different. As in the lawn mowing experience, the arousal reaction described here ranges from bodily quiescence or calmness to intense activation. But there are certain differences, particularly in regard to the subjective component. In my view, as this arousal system probably mediates danger-related activities, the conscious components facilitate this function. To emphasize the differences between conscious awareness in the two arousal reactions, I call this type of activation "tense arousal."

The Moods of Interacting Arousal Reactions

From my perspective, the differences between the two kinds of arousal are best seen in subjective mood reactions. Since they may be experienced daily, these moods provide the best simple validation of the arousal concepts. For example, moderately high tense arousal, together with a similar level of energetic arousal, produce "tense-energy." "Tense-tiredness" represents high tense arousal and low energetic arousal. The other two combinations are "calm-energy" and "calm-tiredness."

The first of these moods, tense-energy, is well-known to most achievement-oriented individuals who live moderately stressful lifestyles. Based on the theory of "Type A personalities" (Matthews, 1982), it would be reasonable to assume that tense-energy is frequently experienced by this type of individual. The energy feelings that are part of this mood indicate adequate personal resources to deal with life circumstances, but the feeling of tension also implies stress, and in a more general sense, danger. The effects of this danger would, of course, be subject to cognitive interpretation; the danger might be immediate and apparent, but in most modern circumstances it is likely to be only vaguely perceived.

As will be discussed more in Chapter 4, the tense-energy mood has a certain daily variability for those with stressful lifestyles. The mood is usually present during the first third of the day, and periodically thereafter if the person had a reasonably good night's sleep. When the tense-energy mood is present, physical resources are high, even though the stress from pressing and overly ambitious work schedules may be substantial. Thus, the feelings of energy that result from rest previously obtained are mixed with relatively high levels of stress-related subjective tension.

It is interesting that this tense-energetic mood state is perceived as moderately positive by many adults in this present-day culture. While in this state, a good deal of work is accomplished, and there can be an almost pleasant kind of excitement associated with the daily activities. Some of my students have characterized this state as being "pleasantly wired" or "supercharged," which I believe are merely alternatives for such expressions as "energy" and "tension" in combination.

A related mood state is tense-tiredness. This condition indicates declining physical resources together with subjective tension. Tense-tiredness intermixed with tense-energy might well be the most prevalent mood pattern of Type A personalities. Following tense-energy, the fatigue and loss of vigor associated with tense-tiredness would be a natural function of human biological cycles. And yet the stress-produced tension present in the first part of the day would probably remain high, as there is still much to be done and physical resources decline. Thus, tense-energy would gradually be replaced by tense-tiredness.

At least some types of depression include a strong component of tense-tiredness (Becker, 1974; Wheeler et al., 1950). One of the most salient characteristics of depression is subjective fatigue or the absence of energy. In the lives of persons experiencing this negative mood, all but the required tasks go unattended. Subjectively, they are always tired. Depressed single people sit home and watch T.V. instead of going out and meeting others. Married people don't talk much to their family. There is no interest in sex. Exercise, even walking, is avoided. Even such basic activities as brushing teeth or getting out of bed are neglected.

Although depressed people appear overtly to be in a state of very low arousal, I believe it is primarily energetic arousal that is low. There is some difference of opinion on this matter, but many clinical analyses indicate that chronic anxiety is part of depression, or at least that anxiety is part of some kinds of depression (American Psychiatric Association, 1980; Becker, 1974). My own experimental work with self-reported depression (see Chapter 8) among nonclinical adult cases has shown clear patterns of low energy and high tension associated with the condition (Bassin & Thayer, 1986).

Insomnia is another condition in which tense-tiredness can be noted. This is particularly true of the kind of insomnia that occurs with a genuine need of sleep as opposed to the condition in which a person overestimates the amount of sleep required and attempts to sleep without being really tired. Tiredness is a common experience for the insomniac, and yet sleep is difficult to achieve. Prevalent scientific opinion about this condition often identifies anxiety or tension as one of the factors responsible for the continued wakefulness (e.g., Kales & Kales, 1984). Thus, an individual with insomnia experiences tense-tiredness while attempting to sleep.

Comparisons between tense-tiredness and tense-energy provide particularly good examples of the interactions and distinctions between the energetic arousal and tense arousal systems. Without these kinds of examples, however, tension, energy, and the associated conditions of physiological arousal might be seen as variations of the same psychophysiological system, perhaps differentiated only in terms of subjective labeling.[3] But juxtaposing tense-tiredness and tense-energy makes the distinction quite clear.

A similar opportunity for differentiation is provided by the last two mood states associated with energetic and tense arousal—calm-energy and calm-tiredness. These states are often unrecognized by modern, stress-plagued persons. For them, chronic low-level tension is so prevalent that it seems normal and goes unnoticed. There are indications, however, that those who have meditated extensively or practiced other kinds of relaxation techniques in the past have greater familiarity with these calm moods. For others, these moods are only experienced during vacations or times of extended leisure.

Calm-energy denotes high bodily resources and an absence of tension or anxiety. Like tense-energy, it has a certain periodicity, and it is enhanced by health, good sleep, and proper nutrition. It is a quite pleasant state, and it may be associated with great productivity (see Chapter 8).

In calm-tiredness, bodily resources are low, but danger is absent. The person experiencing calm-tiredness is completely relaxed, and recuperative processes may occur without interruption. It may be a necessary antecedent to deep and untroubled sleep. Like calm-energy, this state is also very pleasant, and in my view the two states in cyclical pattern represent optimal mood conditions.

Evidence that Arousal Reactions Are Registered in Conscious Awareness

Generalized arousal operates simultaneously at many levels of bodily functioning. Arousing circumstances and naturally changing conditions not only generate physiological reactions but they are also registered in conscious awareness. These feelings of arousal can be studied for scientific purposes.

The evidence for asserting that people are consciously aware of arousal is varied. A good deal of it comes from viewing arousal as a psychophysiological phenomenon, particularly from the perspective of feelings associated with arousal. Another level of evidence occurs through self-evident personal experience. For instance, in the two hypothetical examples described at the beginning of this chapter, most would agree that the person was likely aware of many of the bodily changes occurring between quiescence and high activation.

Still another kind of evidence could be provided through examples in natural life circumstances in which there is a change in physiological processes accompanied by a related change in feelings of arousal. Shifts from wakefulness to pre-sleep states (see Chapter 4) or differences between health and serious illness (see Chapter 5) are clear examples of this. In both cases there are general metabolic declines accompanied by feelings of tiredness and loss of energy.

As one specific example, a carefully controlled scientific study of covariation between physiological and psychological arousal reactions can be found in the famous starvation experiment conducted in 1944 by the Selective Service System and the University of Minnesota (Keys et al., 1950). Its participants were conscientious objectors who voluntarily submitted to nine months of severe food restriction to provide data needed for the war effort. These conditions resulted in chronic states of low bodily arousal. As indicated by Keys et al. (1950, pp. 827–28), the physical effects of starvation were quite striking. For example, "both face and body (of the participants) showed marked emaciation." There were "marked decreases in pulse rate and basal metabolism," which may be regarded as "critical indicators of lowering of speed in the automatic functions of the body. . . . Voluntary movements also became noticeably slower, and energy output was in general markedly reduced. . . . The marked reduction in strength and endurance was paralleled by a general curtailment of self-initiated, spontaneous activities."

What is of interest for the present discussion is that during this time of starvation there were corresponding psychological changes. The greatest change occurred in self-rated feelings of energetic arousal. Of the extensive data that were obtained daily from the participants, feelings of tiredness showed the most change between control and starvation periods (Keys et al., 1950, pp. 825, 912). In comparison with the normal food intake period, participants felt much more tired during the starvation period. A typical reaction of one of the participants was, "I no longer cared to do anything that required energy." Thus, as the various participants suffered a general decline in physical function, subjectively they experienced a distinct loss of energy and increased tiredness.

Other psychological changes also occurred, as will be discussed further elsewhere. Among these changes, irritability and depression increased significantly. And, of course, thoughts of food dominated the consciousness of these men. They thought about it, talked about it, and daydreamed about it. The latter point is a good example of the way that elemental bodily processes—in this case, hunger—can influence basic perceptual and motivational processes.

This evidence about general covariations between physiological and psychological states of arousal in natural settings adds greatly to the plausibility of the arousal construct. However, controlled laboratory studies employing point by point comparisons of physiological and psychological variables in limited time frames provide a different kind of support. Unfortunately, that evidence is not complete enough to provide clear scientific proof. Researchers have only begun to deal with this matter seriously, and in my view the research that already has been done—including my own—suffers from some significant methodological problems.

It would seem like a relatively simple matter to systematically study covariations among various physiological and psychological reactions concurrently with controlled manipulations of arousal, and thus to determine the exact correspondence among the various bodily systems. There are many problems with this type of research design, however, some of them underlying the controversies that have existed about arousal as a valid general concept.

One major problem concerns measuring the delicate psychological reactions that usually reflect arousal states. For example, such arousal feelings as energy, tiredness, tension, or calmness may be quite apparent under natural life circumstances to the person experiencing them, but in an artificially controlled laboratory setting these subtle feelings can easily be masked by more prepotent states of consciousness. A feeling of energy is noticeable and most articulate adults can identify it. However, if a subject is placed in a strange laboratory in which she or he is being monitored continuously by an array of physiological sensors, and if that person is asked to rate his or her current energy state, the measures obtained may be unrelated to the physiological state. Other psychological factors will be so influential that the subtle energy feelings can easily escape attention.

It is possible, of course, to adapt a person to the laboratory situation so that more natural feelings could be accurately ascertained. This might involve such a process as training expert self-observers. But such a research procedure is almost never done. Although such research would be quite valuable, for various reasons the dominant research paradigms of our time never include this sort of procedure.

Still another problem concerns the types of feelings to be measured in the research. When seeking reliable self-analyses of arousal, it is not sufficient simply to ask participants in an experiment what they feel, with no other focus imposed. It is much more appropriate to request specific kinds of ratings.

These are only some of the problems with this research, however. Another substantial problem concerns the method of assessing and combining physiological measures that could be correlated with the self-reports of arousal feelings. In order to assess such an all-encompassing state as generalized arousal, more than one physiological system should be measured. But with multiple measures, questions immediately arise about how to combine them. And combining physiological systems to index arousal is not simple, because each individual system maintains bodily homeostasis in a different way. Therefore, any one system is unlikely to be a perfect index of the more general arousal state. The complexity of this problem is further raised because each physiological system has its own latency of response and point of maximal action prior to compensatory reaction and rebound (Duffy, 1972). These problems could be mitigated somewhat if measurement were carried out over many occasions (cf. Schnore, 1959), but this is seldom done, and even if it is, these problems are not entirely solved.

Another related point, particularly when dealing with energetic arousal, is that at any one time some physiological systems may not correlate with energetic feelings as well as other systems do. Feelings of energy and vigor probably reflect general activation of a wide variety of psychophysiological systems when viewed over time. However, in some situations it is likely that energy feelings reflect the *potential* for arousal instead of the actual arousal that is occurring in many physiological systems. This would be especially true if natural activity patterns do not occur.

This point can be illustrated with the example of activity patterns common to a small child. Children move and are active when they feel energetic, and they rest when feelings of tiredness occur. They have not yet learned the necessity to restrain themselves when they feel like being active, and they aren't as subject to the pressures that most adults feel to be active in times of tiredness. For these little people, an analysis over time probably would yield a better match between feelings of energy and a wide variety of psychophysiological systems than occurs for adults.

With typical adult behavior, an individual may feel energetic, but remain quiescent for social reasons. In this case, the correlation would probably be low between energetic feelings and a number of physiological systems that are closely related to motor activity. Similarly, people may feel tired, but force themselves to be physically active, again for similar reasons. These circumstances might also result in low correlations. Although adults may manifest substantial correlations over time among these psychological and physiological systems, due to forced or restrained activity a better physiological indication of energetic arousal may exist in conjunction with such slowly changing bodily rhythms as diurnal and circadian patterns (see Chapter 4).

The fact that energy feelings reflect potential as well as actual arousal of some systems leaves the experimental demonstration of physiological-psychological covariations quite complicted. Nevertheless, if care is exercised to control some of the more substantial error sources mentioned above, experiments concurrently measuring physiological and self-report indexes of arousal are at least feasible. This research would be much more conclusive, however, if certain questions could be satisfactorily addressed. For example, since energy feelings undoubtedly are associated with some physiological substrate, deciding which physiological systems are the best indicators of arousal potential in various activities is important. This issue has received relatively little research attention, nor have such likely candidate systems as basal metabolic rate or blood glucose levels.

Even with these various methodological problems, however, two of my early studies in this area (Thayer, 1967, 1970) were quite successful in demonstrating substantial correlations between self-report and physiological indexes of arousal. The general approach was to bring people into a psychophysiological laboratory in which a number of measures of arousal, including self-ratings, could be collected simultaneously. In this controlled setting, arousal was manipulated by situational promptings to ensure sufficient variability for statistical analyses. Thus, physiological and self-report measures of arousal could be compared and correlated as changes in arousal occurred.

The physiological measurements taken in this experiment included heart rate, finger blood volume, skin conductance (finger), and muscle action potentials (forearm flexors). Self-ratings of arousal were made with such self-descriptive adjectives as energetic, tired, jittery, and calm. The experimental conditions employed to manipulate arousal included requiring participants to sit quietly and relax for a period of time, and then engage in an arousing task of counting backwards from 100 by sixes or sevens while a loud buzzer was sounded, during which time they were repeatedly urged to count faster. With this procedure, arousal changes could be observed in the physiological and psychological systems, and differences in measures could be calculated and correlated.

Changes in degree of arousal were exactly as expected between the deactivation and activation conditions. In one study of forty-one female college students (Thayer, 1970), skin conductance and heart rate changed as expected in 85 and 93 percent of the cases, respectively. Finger blood volume and muscle action potentials showed the expected changes in 68 and 62 percent of the cases, respectively. Self-ratings of arousal also changed as expected, thus indicating a clear relationship between the physiological and self-report measures. Of the four self-report indexes employed, a shift toward greater arousal occurred in 75 to 100 percent of the cases.

Consistent with other research on psychophysiological measures (Lacey, 1967), intercorrelations of these physiological functions among experimental participants were very low. However, when physiological measures were combined to form a single general arousal index, and this index was correlated with self-report measurements, the resulting correlations increased substantially. This was particularly true when combinations of skin conductance and heart rate were correlated with self-ratings of arousal (Thayer, 1970).

The fact that self-report measures correlated substantially higher with combinations of physiological measures than the physiological measures correlated among themselves is of considerable theoretical interest. It not only suggests that general bodily arousal must be evaluated with multiple physiological systems, but it also suggests that self-report may be a better index of arousal than any single physiological measure. The potential superiority of self-report is further indicated because the most sensitive of the self-report measures recorded the expected change in 100 percent of the cases, and the best of the physiological measures (heart rate) showed change in 95 percent of the cases (and other physiological measures ranged to only 62 percent change).

Considering how common mistrust of self-report is, assertions about the relative superiority of this assessment of arousal compared to physiological measurements may appear questionable. However, when viewed in the context of the hierarchical organization of the nervous system, these assertions make good sense. The nervous system is organized with increasing levels of integration

(Sherrington, 1947), and the cortex stands at the highest level of this hierarchy. Self-report is largely a cerebrocortical function, and as such it represents a high level of integration.

Both conscious awareness and self-report provide indications about arousal that is related to heart rate, respiration, and muscular tension, just to name a few systems that can be sensed and reported on. One can be aware of potential energetic arousal as well as actual arousal. Thus, self-report is likely to include even the most basic information about bodily resources. It is true that self-report is subject to shortcomings related to honesty, attentional focus, and linguistic interpretation, but these problems can be overcome under appropriate experimental conditions. Because of the integrative nature of the information that awareness can provide, self-report remains a highly valid index of arousal.

The Language of Arousal Feelings

The exact nature of language in referring to arousal feelings is very important for several reasons. First of all, from a psycholinguistic perspective the descriptive language about these feelings could provide information on the basic dimensionality of arousal. According to this perspective, as language evolves to reflect fundamental biological and social structures, a linguistic analysis of common arousal descriptors and how they relate to each other might provide important understanding about arousal.

On a more practical but nonetheless important level, an exact determination of the language used to describe arousal feelings would greatly enhance scientific measurement, especially if self-ratings are being employed to assess this biopsychological condition. Asking people to describe their state in an open-ended format is obviously inefficient and rife with potential for measurement error. But asking for self-ratings on the basis of a set of descriptive adjectives that exactly reflects the possible variations in arousal states clearly enhances the measurement process.

Some years ago, when the need for arousal descriptors that could be used for self-ratings became clear, I set out to develop a set of adjectives that exactly described all possible nondirective arousal states. I borrowed extensively from the earlier pioneering research of Nowlis (1965) and his associates concerning the wider dimensions of mood. Adjectives previously used by Nowlis, as well as other descriptive adjectives and their synonyms, were systematically gathered. In addition to searches of previous lists of mood adjectives and of thesauri, possible resource persons were asked for suggestions. And finally, a systematic search was made of the literature on arousal to determine appropriate descriptors.

Adjectives were retained in the list if they described various levels of general nondirectional arousal. Omitted from this list were such adjectives as "hungry" and "thirsty," which implied directed states of arousal. Also omitted were adjectives relating to aggression, anger, or sexual arousal, which also implied directional elements. What was left, therefore, were adjectives that described feelings that ranged from alert, energetic, and jittery states to fatigued, tired, and calm states. As much as possible, this list represented all levels of general nondirectional arousal.

At the time this list was constructed, prevailing opinion in certain scientific circles held that arousal was a single dimension underlying all behavior (Duffy, 1962). However, there were differences of opinion about this matter. Thus, one of the important questions to be investigated with the list of adjectives concerned the dimensionality of arousal. Would self-ratings of arousal represent simple differences in levels of a single arousal continuum, or would analyses of usage indicate qualitatively different kinds of arousal? Also, from the psycholinguistic perspective, a usage determination might provide valuable information about the nature of arousal.

To study arousal dimensionality through language usage, the adjective list was placed in a format with which respondents could describe their momentary feelings by rating each of the adjectives on a four-point scale (Thayer [1986] provided empirical analyses of this rating scale). Since the existence of varied arousal feelings was crucial to this analysis, groups of respondents were solicited who might be expected to be experiencing different arousal states. For example, people completed these self-ratings at various times of the day and just before sleep, during athletic activities, and just prior to college exams, which were probably anxiety-inducing. Respondents included college students and university staff and faculty. All were verbally skilled adults.

These various sets of self-ratings were then repeatedly factor analyzed to determine if a smaller number of factors (statistically derived dimensions) could account for a larger group of variables (adjective ratings). After many factor analyses, the results have been surprisingly similar (Thayer, 1986). Instead of one general factor, four separate factors have consistently emerged, and all arousal-descriptive adjectives are grouped with these four factors. The first factor includes such adjectives as energetic, lively, active, vigorous, and full of pep (named General Activation or Energy). The second factor includes sleepy, drowsy, tired, wide-awake, and wakeful (named Deactivation-Sleep or Tiredness). A third factor includes such adjectives as tense, clutched-up, fearful, jittery, and intense (named High Activation or Tension). And finally, a fourth factor includes adjectives such as still, at rest, calm, quiet, and placid (named General Deactivation or Calmness; see review in Thayer, 1986).

Because orthogonal rotations (mathematical requirements for independent relationships among factors) were employed in the original factor analyses, the results indicated four independent arousal dimensions. This finding was subsequently interpreted as supporting the single arousal concept, and the factors were thought to represent different levels of one arousal continuum (Thayer, 1967). This turned out to be an oversimplification, however.

Later analyses of the relationship among these dimensions (using oblique factor rotations and second order analyses) indicated instead that the first two factors were negatively correlated, and thus they seemed to represent two poles of a single bipolar dimension (Thayer, 1978a, 1978b). Moreover, these same analyses suggested that the second two factors were independent of the first two, and were themselves negatively correlated. Thus, they apparently formed two poles of a second bipolar dimension.

This last interpetation now appears to be the correct one. From this we can see that nondirective arousal is not characterized as a single intensity dimension, but instead as two interacting dimensions. One of them, energetic arousal, is clearly related to alertness and readiness for action, and conversely, to fatigue and tiredness. It is bounded on one pole by subjective feelings relating to energy, vigor, liveliness, and wakefulness, and on the other pole by feelings such as tiredness, fatigue, drowsiness, and sleepiness. The second dimension, tense arousal, is also bipolar, and it clearly relates to the presence or absence of danger or emergency reactions. It can be characterized by feelings of tension, jitteriness, fearfulness, calmness, quietness, and placidity.

There is now some scientific consensus that the language of arousal feelings forms two dimensions. A number of other studies in this domain have been conducted with varying arousal descriptors, and factor analyses usually show two dimensions (Mackay et al., 1978; Purcell, 1982; Thayer, 1986; Watson & Tellegen, 1985). These dimensions have been given different names by others (e.g., Watson & Tellegen, 1985), but the dimensions themselves are descriptively very similar to energetic and tense arousal.

Still, even with the factor analytic evidence, uncertainties exist about whether the two dimensions are actually composites of a number of lesser dimensions. For example, is it too simplistic to assume a dimension bounded on one side by subjective energy and on the other by tiredness? Instead, is it possible that there are different kinds of subjective energy, such as mental energy and physical energy? The same kind of differentiation might be made with regard to tiredness, and it might also be made for various states of anxiety or tension, and for states of calmness.

Such distinctions are quite possible. But an even greater possibility is that the four factors described above really represent four arousal dimensions, and not just two pairs of reciprocal factors. In fact, the oblique factor rotations and second order analyses that were completed only approximated the two-dimensional model that was described (Thayer, 1978a, 1978b).

Of course, this less than perfect fit to the model could be due to measurement errors. But another point to consider is that in experimental work, the two pairs of factors do not always covary exactly as expected (see review in Thayer, 1978b). Thus, the current interpretation of two arousal dimensions must remain somewhat tentative. It is possible that when more is known we will find that there are actually four separate dimensions of nondirectional arousal, and the four factors representing them usually act as two reciprocal pairs, but not always.

Even with the possibility of multiple dimensions, I have chosen to interpret the data as indicating there are only two—tense and energetic arousal. If the finer differentiations are valid, this would not preclude the validity of the two-dimensional model—particularly if these additional subdivisions did not behave in qualitatively different ways from the two dimensions. This is particularly true with regard to the assumed positive correlation of the two general dimensions from low to moderate levels and the negative correlation from moderate to high. It may be that there are actually a greater number of arousal dimensions than two, but if the others are roughly associated with the two general ones, and if they all behave consistently with the complex covariation pattern described above, the two-dimensional model would still be valid.

Finally, another relevant issue that remains unsettled is the possibility that pleasurable and unpleasant affect are somehow different from energetic and tense arousal. I previously found that energetic arousal has a positive affective tone, and tense arousal, a negative tone (Thayer, 1978a). Moreover, because of the complex relationship between the two dimensions (see Chapter 6), in their full range these dimensions are largely orthogonal, just as some theorists argue mood to be (Watson & Tellegen, 1985). However, in high arousal conditions the tense-tiredness or calm-energy feelings that occur would place the two dimensions in a negative correlation, just as some have found positive and negative affect to be negatively correlated (Diener & Emmons, 1985; Diener & Iran-Nejad, 1986).

Evolutionary Biology Issues

I have presented some of the case for the existence of energetic and tense arousal systems, and psychological evidence presented elsewhere in this book provides a kind of validation of these biopsychological concepts. If it were possible to prove the adaptive function of the two arousal systems in evolutionary development, the case would be greatly strengthened. But such proof is outside the intended scope of this book, and in any event, it is not really possible. Unlike the strongly supported empirical evidence for the two arousal dimensions, proof of evolutionary function must remain largely theoretical and speculative. Nevertheless, it is useful to consider briefly the two arousal systems in relation to their possible functional utility or adaptiveness in evolutionary history.

There is little dispute about the adaptive function of elemental arousal mechanisms that enable movement, rest, recuperation, sleep, wakefulness, and danger orientation. These are certainly among the most basic processes of animal life. It is not obvious, however, that these elemental processes are mediated by two arousal systems. Although many would agree that there is a certain logic in this division, particularly considering the psychological evidence, certainly it would be more difficult to present convincing evidence that these are the only arousal systems of the body. Partly for that reason, other variations in arousal (e.g., those related to hunger, thirst, sex, anger) are not included in the two-dimensional model presented. Later, it may be found that these kinds of arousal are related to the hypothesized two dimensions, but at this point the evidence in that regard is very weak.

Let us take a biological-evolutionary perspective and consider the likelihood that the arousal variations outlined in the previous pages indicate a division into two systems instead of only one. I would argue for this division in the following way. As humans evolved, there would certainly have been a necessity for efficient recognition of and reaction to danger, especially in a predatory environment. However, the adaptive function of danger recognition, with the subsequent physical preparation and execution of action patterns, would certainly not have occurred without biological costs. These costs—related to scanning the environment, preparing for the danger, and reacting—probably would have reduced the effectiveness of nondanger-related life functions while any threat existed.

These points are significant because it must be assumed that in the evolutionary past, potential personal threat was constantly present. Thus, food-gathering, procreational, and recreational (stress-reducing) functions would be inhibited to the extent that danger-related action patterns were occurring. Assuming that both these functions (danger- and nondanger-related) are biologically important, human ancestors who could efficiently carry them out would probably have had some survival advantage. This advantage may have been slight or substantial; it is hard to judge. However, it would have had to be sufficient for natural selection processes to result in genetically fixed differences in arousal reactions.

Since psychomotor activity or the preparation for activity would be central both in danger- and nondanger-related behaviors, it is not unreasonable to assume a certain amount of overlap between bodily mechanisms of arousal in the two general functions. For example, the cardiovascular, respiratory, endocrine, and general metabolic processes could easily be the same for both functions, which would account for the difficulty in establishing clear differences between bodily reactions associated with mere physical activation and those relating to danger and stress (Lazarus & Folkman, 1984; Mandler, 1984).

There are certain demonstrable bodily differences in reactions to dangerous and nondangerous environments, however. These fixed patterns of bodily function do not overlap, and yet each may have had an adaptive advantage. The clearest difference, it seems to me, exists in conscious awareness. The arousal feelings in a dangerous environment are distinctly different from those in a safe environment in which physical activity is occurring. In one case, tension, fearfulness, and anxiety predominate, while in the other, energy, vigor, and peppiness are the conscious feelings.

The preponderance of evidence suggests that these distinctive states of consciousness are not just subjective interpretations of what otherwise would be the same feelings. That is, the interpretations are not different because an individual evaluates one environment as dangerous and another as benign. Instead, they are very real manifestations of two kinds of arousal reaction.

The differences in arousal feelings are especially clear when one observes the interaction of the two kinds of subjective reactions at different levels of intensity. This matter will be discussed much more fully in Chapter 6, but to describe it briefly, there appears to be a curvilinear relationship between the two arousal dimensions. During periods of potential danger, self-ratings of energy and tension exhibit a positive correlation from low to moderate levels. That is, as tension feelings change from low to higher levels, energy feelings also increase up to a point, and vice versa. But from moderate to high levels, self-ratings of the two feelings are negatively correlated. As tension feelings change from moderate to high, energy feelings decrease, and vice versa. There are numerous examples of this curvilinear relationship. Primarily, they can be seen in arousal changes associated with stress and in biological cycles of energetic arousal. The effects of certain psychoactive drugs also provide persuasive corroborative evidence.[4]

The possible adaptive function of these differences in arousal feelings and the interaction pattern between arousal feelings is an interesting matter. I view the subjective states as signal systems of resources or depletions, and of danger or safety. They register in conscious awareness the state of the whole body at any point in time and provide a continuing indication of readiness for action or of the need for rest and recuperation. Moreover, in the case of danger, the unpleasantness of the associated feelings is likely to produce behavioral avoidance, thus reducing the danger.

Such signal systems would appear, on the face, to be highly adaptive. One interpretation of the mechanism by which this adaptation could occur is that within the higher levels of the nervous system, perhaps the cerebral cortex, there exists a kind of executive or planning function (Hilgard, 1977; Miller, Galanter, & Pribram, 1960). This executive or planning function would be facilitated by the ongoing registration of information concerning the state of the body, especially resources and depletions. These would be used to plan activities and to make related decisions. One might argue that awareness of arousal enables an individual to examine the bodily state much more carefully over time than would be the case if immediate reactivity were required. The feelings related to arousal tend to be remembered (for further discussions about the function of consciousness, see Burghardt, 1985; Hilgard, 1977; Miller, Galanter, & Pribram, 1960; Schwarz & Clore, 1983; Underwood, 1982; Wyer & Carlston, 1979), and thus access to these subjective reactions would be particularly useful. They would enable the individual to make careful examinations. Therefore, natural selection would favor cognitive awareness of arousal.

Another possible basis for the adaptiveness of conscious awareness of arousal is related to the associated human capacity for language. The ability to describe states of arousal clearly facilitates communication about resources and depletions. Humans are very social animals, and the language system supports this sociability. For example, because it is possible to describe to another the state of one's readiness for action or need for rest, group decisions can be made concerning activity or rest.

In speculating about the adaptiveness of the positive and negative correlations at different intensity levels of arousal, it seems to me that it is necessary to consider another difference between activation patterns in dangerous and benign situations. This is the difference in skeletal-muscular reactions. Here ethologists offer some relevant observations on behavior. Many animals react initially to the possible presence of a predator by attending carefully or by rapidly scanning cues in the environment. Once the predator is located, the animal reacts by freezing until an action decision is made. It is here that the differences in skeletal-muscular reactions are apparent.

Ethologists have studied this phenomenon quite carefully, and they have even proposed terms to describe the behavior (e.g., McBride, 1971). The "flight distance," for example, is the point at which flight occurs when skeletal-muscular inhibition or freezing will not suffice. But prior to that flight, or "fight" as the case may warrant, there is overt inactivity. This inactivity, of course, should not be thought of as low arousal. An animal in the presence of a predator is in a state of high physiological and psychological arousal. Its body rapidly mobilizes for whatever action is necessary, but at the same time there is muscular inhibition.

It is interesting to note, and perhaps not too great a speculative leap to suggest, that the curvilinear reactions between arousal measurements at different intensity levels is quite consistent with the behavior patterns of an animal in a predatory environment. The mere existence of a potential predator increases fearfulness and tension (the positive correlation). These feelings ensure that the danger will not go unattended. Energy is raised to enable response. And if the predator is not in the immediate vicinity, the response may be increased, or at least continued, psychomotor activity.

However, if the predator is near, and the fear or tension is appropriately high, then a freeze response is most adaptive until it is no longer tenable. This state of high tension would correspond to feelings of low energy (the negative correlation), and these feelings could be associated with the behavioral freeze response. Conversely, when the danger requires immediate physical activity, it may be most adaptive to have no fear. Thus, the suddenly heightened physical activity (energetic arousal) would be associated with reduced tense arousal (again, the negative correlation).

This discussion of evolutionary mechanisms is quite speculative. And yet some such basis for evolutionary development was probably present. Given the economy of bodily processes for accomplishing elemental functions, it is highly unlikely that capacities for conscious awareness of arousal states, or interaction patterns among those states, would have evolved in their present form without some adaptive basis.

Biopsychological Overview of Arousal

Energetic and tense arousal systems, or at least systems very similar to these, are evident at many levels of bodily functioning. Certainty about these matters varies with the clarity of the evidence at each level, of course. For example, from the perspective of evolutionary biology, it is evident that systems such as these could easily have evolved as highly adaptive mechanisms for interacting with nonhostile and hostile environments. However, this is a largely speculative analysis that is mainly useful in its logical support of the concepts. At the level of brain functioning, there is evidence of multiple arousal systems, but the neural processes are very complex, and therefore this evidence, while supportive, is still tentative. Focusing on peripheral bodily mechanisms, particularly those associated with exercise, an energetic arousal system such as that described is quite identifiable, but the identification of two arousal systems is not certain.

The psychological evidence offers the best understanding of these distinctive arousal systems. And it is for this reason that I refer to arousal as biopsychological—a concept with biological underpinnings but the most clear interpretation at the psychological level. Arousal responses represent integrations of physiological and psychological processes, but at the present time these responses are most easily identified in the context of consciousness and feeling.

Feelings that range from energy to tiredness and from tension to calmness commonly exist in everyday experience. Moreover, the two kinds of arousal feelings, when carefully monitored, yield identifiable relationships at different levels of intensity. In benign settings involving exercise, or in settings representing varying degrees of danger, there are complex and changing mixtures of energy and tension feelings. Depending on the intensity of reaction, consciousness is often dominated by one or the other subjective state.

Interpreted in this framework, mixtures of energy and tension can be identified in moods that emanate from stress or from the opposite experience. Even such well-known conditions as depression and insomnia include these core feelings. By using these feelings as markers of arousal, one can identify a variety of antecedents (such as exercise, nutrition, sleep, and time of day) and wider manifestations, such as moods, self-perceptual processes, and probably many elements of cognition.

4

Daily Rhythms of Subjective Energy and Other Biopsychological Cycles

The newly emerging area of chronobiology, or perhaps more appropriately for this chapter, "chronopsychology," can provide extremely important insights into mood. There is an extended history of research on biological cycles, including empirical observations and some theory (see reviews by Brown, 1982; Colquhoun, 1982), but until the last half of this century scientists have not really captured the full significance of these natural cycles in relation to mind and behavior (Aschoff, 1965; Colquhoun, 1971; Halberg, 1969). And even in much of the science as it is now developing, the full range of rhythmicities has hardly been investigated and assimilated. This deficiency is particularly apparent with regards to psychological concepts.

It is clear that virtually every system of the body which has been investigated exhibits its own rhythmicity, usually circadian (about 24 hrs.), or ultradian (less than 24 hrs.), but most of the systems so far documented have been relatively basic physiologically or biologically. For instance, it is now known that the metabolic and neuroendocrine systems, as well as more general psychophysiological systems, show variation over predictable time courses, and probably with endogenous (self-sustaining and internally controlled) rhythms. But I believe similar endogenous rhythms probably characterize our most basic moods as well.

This chapter is about some of these important rhythmicites as they apply to mood. It deals with the circadian rhythmicity of such subjective states as energy, alertness, tiredness, and fatigue. Multiday periods as well as cycles of one to two hours are considered. The relationship of predictable diurnal (daily) rhythms to fundamental self-perceptual processes is also discussed. In particular, it appears that circadian rhythms of energetic arousal may be key components to the subtle daily shifts in the way that people perceive the apparent seriousness of personal problems, and to variable states of optimism. Individual differences in arousal rhythms in relation to personality characteristics such as morningness-eveningness and introversion-extraversion are discussed here as well. Finally, this chapter provides some speculations about the possible applications concerning the chronobiology of energetic and tense arousal to social interaction.

Circadian Rhythms of Energetic Arousal

Although moods of energy and tiredness are influenced by many factors, each day these moods form a natural rhythm with predictable high and low points. The change in these states is so gradual and subtle that the rhythm is often over-looked unless it is subjected to systematic observation. Thus, from moment to moment, little difference is usually noticed, but ratings taken three hours apart often show a considerable change.

The natural cyclical variation of subjective energy is probably an endogenous circadian rhythm that, once established, maintains its cyclical form over time and resists change. Exciting events, physical activity, and substances that are eaten or drunk may substantially affect energetic moods at any particular time, but such variations occur on top of a slowly changing cycle that repeats itself each twenty-four hours. It is clear, therefore, that all mood-affecting factors must be evaluated in relation to this background rhythm.[1]

The overall shape of this energetic arousal cycle was first observed in the middle 1960s (Thayer, 1967). In that study, fifty male and female college students each completed four AD ACLs (see Chapter 3 and Appendix I) at different times representing the full waking day: just after morning awakening, and just before lunch, dinner, and night sleep. The results indicated clear diurnal or daily rhythms for all AD ACL measurements, with energetic arousal showing the greatest degree of diurnal rhythmicity. Peaks of arousal were found in the period just before lunch.

This early study provided a useful indication of rhythmicity and some infor-mation about the peak of the diurnal arousal cycle, but it contained a number of methodological problems. A particularly important limitation was that only four periods were sampled in the day, and therefore the exact shape of the dirunal cycle could not be ascertained.

Another study by Clements, Hafer, and Vermillion (1976) provided mea-sures of two additional periods in the day. These investigators obtained AD ACL ratings from six separate groups of experimental participants at hours ranging from 8:00 A.M to 9:00 P.M. In their study, peak energetic arousal was found at 2:10 P.M., as opposed to 12:30 P.M. in the 1967 study. However, a possible source of error in the later study was that a number of different groups were used at different times of day, and each participant provided self-ratings only once. Thus random differences between groups could have affected the diurnal pattern obtained.

In 1978 I published the results of a more complete study that corrected some of the deficiencies of previous research (Thayer, 1978b). This study involved twenty-five male and female college students who completed AD ACLs imme-diately after morning awakening, just before night sleep, and at two-hour periods throughout the day for two full days. In addition to the self-report measurements of arousal, participants took their temperature and pulse rate at each assessment period.

In this study, measurements of energetic arousal showed much greater diurnal rhythmicity than the measurements of physiological activity, yet another indication of the potential superiority of consciously aware self-ratings in assessing global arousal states (see Chapter 3). Figure 4–1 indicates some of these results, and the diurnal pattern represented is generally the same as that obtained in later studies. From the figure, it is apparent that these experimental participants experienced relatively low subjective energy on awakening, and that energy rose slowly to a peak at around noon. This high point was followed by a drop in the afternoon and a small subpeak in the early evening. Finally, energy fell slowly to a low point just before sleep.

It is noteworthy that energy was not at its highest daily point immediately after a full night of sleep. The gradual rise in energy in the morning has now been observed across individuals and conditions many times, providing clear evidence that subjective energy is usually low after awakening in the morning even if the previous night's sleep has been lengthy and refreshing. This observation often appears counterintuitive to persons not familiar with circadian rhythms. However, it is the nature of this subtle background rhythm to change slowly and to reach peaks and troughs at certain times of the day.

The exact daily peak of energetic arousal is of some theoretical interest in determining physiological mechanisms underlying its endogenous rhythm, and in discovering the relationship between arousal and related behavior (e.g., Eysenck & Folkard, 1980; Revelle et al., 1980). The 1978 study placed the peak at late morning, but a subsequent study involving eighteen participants who used the AD ACL to rate themselves each hour of the day for six full days (Thayer, Takahashi, & Pauli, 1988) found the peak to be in the early afternoon

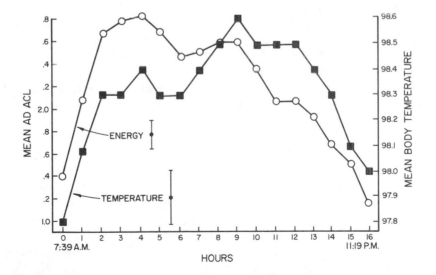

FIGURE 4–1. Mean self-report and body temperature scores for daily periods from awakening to sleep (brackets indicate median variability $\pm$ 1 σ_M).

(between 1:00 and 2:00 P.M.). This slightly later peak is consistent with findings by Folkard and his associates (Folkard et al., 1976; Folkard, Monk, & Lobban, 1978; Monk et al., 1983) regarding self-ratings of alertness.[2]

To some extent, this issue of rhythm peak must be understood in relation to principles of sampling because there are individual differences in peaks of energy. Some people become maximally energetic soon after arising, and others reach their peak relatively late in the day. Therefore, the sampling of these different types of individuals in any particular study will determine the maximum arousal point for the group as a whole. Results of research on cycles are much more meaningful when other physiological or performance measurements are included in the same study. Nevertheless, it is of some interest to note that in my research the largest number of persons reached their daily peak of energy in the first third of the day compared to those peaking in the second or third tri-period of the day.

A later acrophase, or peak, of self-rated arousal was obtained in an excellent study by Dermer and Berscheid (1972), and this difference in peak times may illustrate the variations in cycles of energetic and tense arousal. These investigators obtained hourly self-ratings from fifty-four college students over a four-day period. To rate themselves, students used a scale ranging from −10 (extreme tiredness, boredom, or fatigue) to +10 (extreme alertness, hypersensitivity, or excitement). In order to give the participants some indication of how to use the scale, the experimenters told these students that a number close to −10 might be used just after they had gotten up in the morning, and—significantly—that a number close to +10 might be used if they had just been in a car accident. With this procedure, the acrophase (5:39 P.M.) was somewhat later than the maximum arousal point obtained in most other self-rating studies.

Although these differences in peaks of arousal may have been due to sampling variations, another possible reason for the difference is that Dermer and Berscheid's experimental participants included both energetic and tense arousal in their ratings. Tiredness would represent low energetic arousal, but a car accident or related experiences would probably represent high *tense* arousal. This point is particularly significant because my research has shown that tense arousal also follows a diurnal rhythm, but its peak is usually later than the peak of energetic arousal.[3] I have found that the most common pattern involves daily peaks of energy at late morning or early afternoon, and during this peak, tension is relatively low. It is also typical for individuals to feel most tense late in the afternoon or early in the evening as energy declines (see Chapter 6). Considering this pattern, it is clear that Dermer and Berscheid's possible inclusion within a single rating of the two kinds of arousal could have produced an acrophase later in the day.

The relationship of cycles of energetic arousal to other elements of psychological functioning is certainly of interest, and I shall deal with that further in other sections, but for now let me comment on its relation to biological functioning. Figure 4–1 includes the subjects' temperature levels, which were taken each time self-ratings of arousal were taken in the 1978 study. The peak of this bodily function—about 5:00 P.M.—is consistent with many studies previously done on body temperature. Following the early theory of Kleitman (1963) and others, body temperature was often thought to be a good measure of performance, if not the basis itself of circadian performance differences. Many psychomotor tasks show diurnal rhythms that peak late in the day, at similar times to the usual temperature peak (Blake, 1967b; Colquhoun, 1982). However, this matter has recently been investigated more fully, and there are indications that mental tasks, particularly those involving memory (Colquhoun, 1982; Folkard, 1982), may peak early in the day, at a time more consistent with peaks of energetic arousal.

Endogenous Control of Energetic Arousal

Crossing multiple time zones rapidly when traveling by airplane offers a good opportunity to observe the resistance to change that occurs with established patterns of energy, tiredness, and alertness. Although there might be individual differences in this regard (Graeber, 1982), most people who travel this way find themselves unable to immediately adapt to the new time culture after crossing as few as two time zones. This disruption can also be observed in individuals whose work shifts are frequently changed, and it is particularly apparent in those who go from a typical day shift to night work. There may even be a significant personal disruption caused by changing back and forth two times a year between daylight savings and standard time (Monk & Folkard, 1983).

This disruption in patterns of energy and tiredness does eventually diminish, however, and new cycles are established. It is not known exactly which synchronizing agents (also called zeitgebers or time-givers) most affect this mood rhythm, but new sleeping and waking patterns,[4] and changes in times of meals, are obvious possibilities. And as will become more apparent in the next chapter, the most important influence on arousal rhythms may be physical activity.[5]

Evidence about the resistance of energetic arousal patterns to rapid change may be found in several studies. For example, English researchers systematically gathered data concerning individuals crossing multiple time zones. In one study (Fort, 1968), a person flying from Manchester to Chicago, and experiencing a six-hour time shift, retained the phase pattern of energetic arousal for four days following the shift, although tense arousal became largely adapted to the change after the first day. The subject also retained peak performance measurements according to Manchester time. In a second study (Conroy et al., 1969) of an individual traveling home from Delhi to Manchester, energetic arousal patterns shifted immediately to the new English time, but overall arousal remained low for two days, and increased sleepiness was reported for three days. Various physiological and performance measurements also showed disruption. The differences between the two studies reflect the fact that individuals vary in their adaptation to time zone travel, but both studies suggest that patterns of arousal are disrupted by rapid time shift.

Swedish researchers have provided more complete evidence about the endogenous nature of energetic arousal. In one study (Patkai, Åkerstedt, & Pettersson, 1977), twenty-four permanent night workers in the printing department of a Swedish newspaper completed AD ACLs at various working times and at other periods of their waking day. Physiological and performance data were also gathered for the first, third, and fifth nights of their weekly shift (six nights work and three nights off). Energetic arousal peaked at around 10:00 P.M., and this peak did not change significantly throughout the days of their shift. The amount of catecholamines in the bloodstream, as measured by urine tests, peaked at about the same time as energy, while body temperature and reaction-time performance peaked slightly later. In this study, it is clear that energetic arousal peaked at a considerably later time than it does for typical day workers (see previous section), and this different peak is just what might be expected for persons who have inverted their waking and activity patterns, but who attempt to rejoin the day culture on their days off. The later peak times probably represented a combination of night and some day influences.

These researchers also performed a study on individuals who worked a mixed night and day schedule, and thus for part of the time were forced to accommodate to the physical and mental requirements of day work (Åkerstedt, Patkai, & Dahlgren, 1977). In this case, thirteen male typesetters of a Swedish newspaper worked seven consecutive nights, followed by a day off. They then worked two days from morning to midafternoon, followed by four days off. As one might expect from the varied activity pattern of these workers, on their first night of the seven-night shift, peak energetic arousal occurred early in the evening and before the period of work began. But by the fourth night of that shift, there had been a phase shift in energetic arousal, so the peak was slightly after midnight, during the period of work.

Thus, for these workers, one activity pattern for seven days was probably day-oriented, and the peak energy time (early evening) reflected that pattern. But going into their seven-day night shift, the energy cycle slowly changed to accommodate the new night pattern. This is an excellent demonstration of an endogenous cycle that resists change, but that does change slowly as external requirements vary. It is not clear from this study which external requirements exerted the major influence, but I believe that physical activity patterns probably played an important role.

Other evidence of endogenous energetic arousal patterns was gathered by Swedish researchers studying sleep deprivation, using a variant of the AD ACL. Bohlin and Kjellberg (1973) found significant decreases in measurements of factors related to energetic arousal after one night of sleep deprivation. And even more convincing was the research of Froberg (1977), who showed that during a seventy-two-hour period of sleep deprivation, the rhythmicity of alertness (an aspect of energetic arousal, Thayer 1967) continued to correspond to waking periods, even though there was an overall decrease in arousal. These studies and various others with similar methodology provide a considerable amount of evidence that energetic arousal forms an endogenous circadian rhythm.

Arousal Rhythms and Psychological Perspective Changes:
Problem Perception and Optimism

Circadian arousal rhythms appear to be core elements of other secondary moods and general psychological reactions. There is evidence that each day, as energetic arousal rises and falls in a predictable rhythm, it subtly influences an individual's general perspectives about self, personal issues, and social interactions. Indeed, these effects may be so pervasive that an individual's basic sense of optimism or pessimism is influenced. Although these general cognitive changes have received very little scientific attention, it is here that arousal rhythms could have their most important impact on behavior.

The significance of these rhythms in relation to cognitive perspectives and secondary feelings may remain largely unrecognized because the nature of this influence is extremely subtle. Rhythmic changes in energy are background states that can be disregarded and overridden on any single occasion if motivation is strong enough. As such, their effects are difficult to capture in scientific analyses, particularly if research, as is usually conducted by behavioral scientists, focuses on the effects of manipulations during a single occasion as opposed to analyzing effects over more lengthy periods of time (see Chapter 7). Therefore, rhythmic changes appear to be of little significance.

Rhythmic mood changes have a minimal influence on any one occasion, but the long-term effect on behavior of repeatedly occurring patterns can be quite substantial. These background states probably exert little influence in comparison to a strong resolve to overcome them or in comparison with potent situational influences. A vague feeling that occurs day after day can be disregarded at first, and with strong self-discipline it might be disregarded for quite some time. But eventually it will have an influence. I believe that as we understand this phenomenon better, we will find that over time the cognitive and motivational influence of these subtle states is likely to be weighted by their persistence (see Chapter 5).

Some kinds of circadian mood effects are relatively well-known in the general culture. Consider, for example, the common experience of late-night worry about problems, which, when considered at another time, appear to be much less serious. Obstacles and difficulties in one's life often seem overwhelming in a tired state, and yet the same problems appear much more manageable when one is feeling strong and vigorous. The problems themselves do not change; the mood of the individual considering them changes.

A student of mine related exactly such a case after hearing a lecture about this matter. He described a problem that had been worrying him for weeks, and he indicated that late one evening, at 11:00 P.M., while he thought about the issues he became increasingly agitated. The more he considered the problem, the more agitated he became. Finally, he was convinced that the problem was insoluble. Eventually the young man went to sleep, and although his rest was not as lengthy and deep as it might have been, it was somewhat refreshing. In the morning as he considered the problem, it appeared quite manageable and not nearly so serious. He realized that there were actions he could take and possible solutions, and he felt much more calm and relaxed than he had the night before. This example is quite interpretable in the context of circadian arousal rhythms.

To illustrate this point, consider a series of experiments recently conducted with the aim of carefully investigating the relationship between arousal rhythms and a wide variety of psychological functions. The first experiment (Thayer, 1987b) was designed to study the variability of perceptions about a personal problem at various times of day. Times were chosen to represent high and low points of the known diurnal cycle of energetic arousal. The rating periods occurred just after awakening in the morning, mid to late morning, late afternoon, and just before night sleep. A fifth time—immediately following a brisk ten-minute walk—was also included to assess the effects of moderate exercise.

In order to capture the subtle mood effects that might occur, participants were required to make self-ratings about the apparent seriousness of personal problems on ten days over a three-week period. With this procedure, it was possible to capture the effects associated with a particular time of day and to reduce or cancel out the effects of uncontrollable events that might influence participants on any one day (cf. Rushton, Brainerd, & Pressley, 1983).

The eight experimental participants were selected on the basis of referrals from the university counseling center and from volunteers who heard about the research in various classes. Each was an individual who was experiencing the kind of unremitting problem that could be expected to continue in more or less the same degree of severity over the three weeks of the experiment. For example, one woman was going through a painful marital separation, another was experiencing an unyielding weight problem, and a third had problems with severe parental discord.

The experimental procedure involved first completing an AD ACL, then thinking about the problem for a minute or so, and finally rating its seriousness, its difficulty of solution, and the likelihood that it would be solved. The experiment was carried out wherever the person happened to be at the prearranged times of day.

The results of this experiment clearly indicate the degree to which time of day subtly interacts with perception of personal problems. On any one day the problem was sometimes perceived as more serious, sometimes less, but when the ratings of all days were combined, seven of the eight participants rated the problem as more serious and less likely to be solved at late afternoon than in the late morning. And even with the small numbers involved, this was a statistically significant effect. Also, problems were perceived as more serious at late night and early morning times than mid morning, but these differences did not reach statistical significance.

A dynamic relationship between energetic and tense arousal may account for the fact that the perceived seriousness of the problems varied significantly from late morning to late afternoon, but did not reach statistical significance in the low energy periods of early morning and late night. This relationship will be more fully discussed in Chapter 6, but in short, I have hypothesized that energy and tension in interaction have extremely powerful effects on behavior. Thus, problems can be expected to be perceived as most serious when there is low energy and high tension, and least serious when there is high energy and low tension. In this research, energy was highest during the comparison period of mid to late morning. But tension was highest at late afternoon, and it was relatively lower at early morning and late night. Therefore, for these participants this afternoon period of low energy and high tension was the particular time when problems might be expected to appear most serious.

According to the underlying theory, however, problems should seem especially serious at any time of day when energy is low and tension is high, and that is exactly what the data showed. Irrespective of time of day, the rating period when each participant felt least energetic and most tense was the period that the problem appeared most serious—a highly reliable effect.

To summarize, the apparent seriousness of the personal problems varied with the naturally occurring diurnal energy level of the experimental participants. When energy was low, the problems appeared more serious. In contrast, daily peaks in energy were associated with a more positive view of the problems. The naturally occurring mood conditions that predisposed the *most* serious perception of the problems were low energy and high tension together. In comparison, the problems were perceived in the most positive light when the participants felt low tension and high energy.

To determine how general these effects were, the previous experiment was replicated in a second study involving ratings of optimism and various other moods (Thayer, 1987b). In this case, twelve college students made self-ratings of optimism, physical well-being, and happiness, in addition to completing AD ACLs. In order to obtain the greatest differences between high and low arousal periods, ratings were made at late morning, late afternoon, and at another time following a brisk walk. (The results of the exercise condition in this and the previous experiment will be discussed in Chapter 5.) Participants completed these ratings on six days distributed over several weeks. At each testing session, participants filled out an AD ACL, and then spent a minute or two considering their life circumstances. Following this period of general reflection, they rated their overall optimism, happiness, and physical well-being.

The results were strikingly similar to those of the first experiment. As was true with perceptions of personal problems, optimism ratings varied on individual days, but when the six days were averaged, all twelve participants reported being more optimistic at late morning than late afternoon. This morning period also produced feelings of greater physical well-being and happiness, but these differences were not as great as were those for optimism. As was similar to the previous experiment, optimism was greatest when the participant felt the most energy and least tension, and lowest when the individual felt least energetic and most tense.

A third experiment investigated similar issues, but using a different methodology (Thayer, Takahashi, & Pauli, 1988). In this study, experimental participants were first interviewed and asked to judge which hours of the day in their usual life patterns were best and worst for various psychological processes. They answered questions concerning the time of day that problems appeared most and least serious, the times that they felt most and least optimistic, and the times that they were most and least likely to experience depression. These participants were also asked about the most and least likely times for conflict with significant others, and the best and poorest hours for accomplishing various intellectual tasks.

Following the interview, and during the next four weeks, the eighteen participants in this experiment conducted self-ratings of their current arousal states at each hour for six complete days. AD ACLs were completed just after awakening in the morning and at the top of each hour thereafter until just before sleep. The average participant rated their current energy and tension levels about 100 times in the four weeks of the study.

From the results of the first interview, it was possible to determine the arousal state of the times that the subjects had designated as best and worst for the various functions. It is important to note that in the interviews, the participants indicated many different best times of day as well as many different worst times of day for the various functions. In other words, there was not a single best or worst time across participants or across functions.

The results were quite clear. Self-rated energy was found to be significantly higher at the hours when participants had reported that problems were usually least serious. Energy was also significantly higher at the hours when interviews indicated a usual pattern of highest optimism. In general, the best times for all the functions were periods of high energy.

Although the results appear quite clear-cut, one criticism that must be dealt with in this kind of research is that subject expectation effects could have produced these results. Such an argument would hold that the participants somehow gleaned the purpose of the research and cooperated in producing expected results. These possibilities always exist in research such as this, but there are several reasons why expectation effects are not likely to be the basis of these results.

First, the subjects would not have known what the expected effects should have been at different times of day. Second, if participants had guessed the experimental hypotheses over the various days of their participation, one would assume that the effects would be stronger at the end of the experiment than at the beginning. But statistical analyses of the trends over the course of the experiment indicated that this was not the case. Third, all participants were explicitly warned to be scrupulously honest in making their self-ratings at each time according to how they felt at that moment. Moreover, these participants were highly motivated to follow instructions. They were volunteers, and their main purpose in participating in these experiments was to learn more about themselves.

Last, and perhaps most important, the results of the third experiment were consistent with those of the first two, even though an entirely different procedure was employed. Moreover, if expectation effects had produced the results obtained in the third experiment, it would be necessary to assume that participants knew the relevant characteristics of their diurnal rhythms when they were first interviewed and that they provided interview information consistent with that knowledge. Or they would have had to rate themselves in the subsequent diurnal rhythm study to be consistent with the interview data. Neither possibility seems likely.

In sum, each of the three experiments described above used a different methodology, particularly the last one as compared to the first two. Nevertheless, the results of all three were consistent. This is a good example of convergent validity, and it provides considerable support for the conclusion that naturally occurring rhythms of energy together with interacting tension states predict quite well various secondary moods and changes in cognitive perspective.

The results of this research raise fundamental issues about the nature of each person's sense of reality. For example, the common perception about personal problems is that outside circumstances, such as events or other individuals, are what influence the seriousness of one's problems (cf., McArthur, 1972), not internal personal changes. However, this research clearly indicates that the seriousness of one's problems is at least in part an internally determined matter. It appears that in some respects reality changes with circadian arousal rhythms!

So far, we have only begun to understand these phenomena, and there are many more questions yet to be answered. One important issue concerns the degree to which the relationship between circadian rhythms and changes in psychological perspective involves cognitive intermediaries. For instance, does awareness of one's own energy level determine other psychological effects, or is this some kind of noncognitive causal process?

I believe a cognitive intermediary does exist, and it may work the following way. When an individual thinks about problems that are likely to require strong personal resources, it is natural for that person to evaluate the resources available to meet those demands. Information of that sort is obtainable if the person simply surveys his or her feelings at that moment. As I have previously discussed, the moods of energy, tiredness, tension, and calmness are excellent indicators of personal resources. Therefore, when a person thinks about a personal problem, he or she also considers *present* personal resources. This process probably occurs so rapidly that one is scarcely aware of it (cf. Carver & Scheier, 1982).

This feedback loop is very adaptive. If a problem had to be met immediately, the ability to assess personal resources quickly for a decision would ensure greater likelihood of success. But there is a subtle error with this logic. Often the problem faced is something that will occur in the future, and the present personal resources may not be the same as will be available later. For example, if one is without energy, and a problem is considered, awareness of this low energy may activate the feedback process to make the problem appear unsolvable. The error occurs because in the future, when the problem must be met, there may be adequate resources to deal with it.

Of course, this feedback process can work both ways. If one thinks about an ongoing problem during high-energy times, it might seem of little or no significance. But in the future, when the problem must be met, the individual may not have the energy to deal with it. Therefore, unrealistically optimistic judgments may be made when one is very energetic, just as unrealistically pessimistic judgments are made during periods of fatigue.

These phenomena can be understood in relation to other related theoretical concepts, for example, the theory of state dependency that was discussed in Chapter 2 (e.g., Overton, 1978, 1984). To recapitulate, this theory holds that perceptions and memories are partially associated with moodlike states (cf. Bower, 1981), and as these states shift, cognitive elements associated with them become more or less available to conscious awareness. In this context, therefore, certain self-descriptive memories, abilities, or lack of ability, may be associated with states of energy and tension, and in the presense of these states, the relevant memories would be activated.

This state dependency theory, together with the concept of arousal rhythms, can be applied to the interactive model of tension and energy. Consider the example of the young man described above whose problems appeared insoluble late at night, but easy to deal with the next morning. Energetic arousal varies in a predictable circadian rhythm that is low at various times of day, including late at night. Furthermore, low energetic arousal predisposes an individual to increased tension or anxiety. Therefore, late in the evening as this young man experienced tense-tiredness, he became increasingly agitated, and he may have had memories of experiences from past tense-tired states. As he focused upon his life, these memories could have made his present circumstances appear hopeless. The next morning, however, the natural state of higher energy and lower tension probably would have been associated with past experiences of success. These memories of past successes could easily have led to a view that his current problems were quite solvable.

Other kinds of questions regarding cognitive intermediaries also bear further investigation. For example, does it matter if one is moving up or down on the energy cycle, or is it the absolute level of energy (and the interacting tension state) that influences personal problem perception? To illustrate, one usually feels energy increasing during the morning hours, and decreasing during portions of the afternoon and evening. Do these differences influence perspective? I think they might (see Chapter 5).

Individual Differences in Daily Rhythms

Rhythms of energetic arousal, and the related subtle changes in psychological perspective, do not have the same cycle shape for every person. Over a number of years, I have observed many different patterns of arousal in individuals.[6] The various cycles differed considerably from each other, and yet each might have represented an endogenous circadian rhythm. Some persons showed steep rises in energy and a peak early in the morning. Others reached their peak much later in the day. Some people had cycles that rose rapidly to a maximum, which remained more or less constant throughout the day until it finally dropped just before sleep. And still others showed several alternating peaks and troughs of about the same amplitude occurring throughout the day.

Although these observations do not qualify procedurally as scientific data, they have prompted me to believe that there are quite a number of variations from the most common rhythm, where the peak is reached in the late morning or early afternoon, drops in the late afternoon, and reaches a subpeak early in the evening. The amount of research regarding these differences is relatively small and by no means has sampled the full extent of possible variations. Therefore, this remains a rich area for future studies. Published research has generally focused on arousal differences between morning and evening personality types, or this research investigated the daily arousal differences associated with extraversion, and components of extraversion such as impulsivity.

Many lay people believe in the concept of morning and evening types, that is, individuals who feel best, work most efficiently, and are happiest at one or the other time. In fact, it is such a well-established concept that most college students with no particular training in this area readily identify themselves as either a morning or evening type. Interestingly enough, the evening type appears to be the most desirable category. In public discussions, most will describe themselves as liking to stay up late at night and as doing good work at that time. This is particularly true of younger students. Few like to admit they are morning types. When it is admitted, it is often by an older, returning student who indicates that he or she used to be an evening type, but now has become a morning type.

Although there were some early theoretical and empirical analyses of morningness and eveningness (e.g., Freeman & Hovland, 1934; Kleitman, 1963), a considerable amount of new research on this topic was stimulated by the publication in 1976 of an English-language questionnaire regarding a morningness-eveningness trait (Horne & Östberg, 1976). In this questionnaire, Horne and Östberg provided standardized responses for people to indicate their sleeping and waking times, their best periods for performance, and the times they preferred various activities. Using scores on the questionnaires, the investigators divide people on a continuum. According to Horne, about 7.5 percent of the population are definite evening types, and another 7.5 percent are definite morning types. Thirty percent are thought to be moderate morning or evening types, and 50 percent are in the middle category. However, probably cultural differences affect this distribution (J. Horne, personal communication, August 22, 1985). Whether one is a morning or evening type seems to be a stable characteristic over time, and a wide variety of behaviors have been found to be associated with these types (see recent review by Kerkhof, 1985).

The general concept of "larks" and "owls," as they are sometimes popularly described, may be related to differing levels of energetic arousal. This idea is supported by studies indicating that people divided into morning or evening types on the basis of Horne and Östberg's questionnaire had different patterns of energetic arousal at morning and evening periods.

Kerkhof and his associates (Kerkhof et al., 1980) selected extreme morning and evening types and gave them AD ACLs, together with various other performance and physiological tests, at two daily sessions. The investigators found that morning types, as indicated by the questionnaire, had greater subjective energy in the morning session, and evening types experienced relatively greater energy in the evening session. Consistent differences were also obtained for body temperature and performance measures.

My colleagues and I recently completed a larger study regarding energetic arousal and morningness-eveningness scores (Thayer, Takahashi, & Pauli, 1988). This study, referred to above, involved self-ratings with AD ACLs every hour of the day for six days. Dividing participants on the basis of their questionnaire scores, morning types reported relatively more energy in the first part of each day over the six-day period, and evening types generally reported more energy in the last part of the day. But because of the variability across experimental participants, the statistical effect only approached significance.

A second analysis of peak hour for energetic arousal in relation to morningness did show the expected effect, however. Those with the highest morningness scores reached a peak of energetic arousal at the third measurement period (8–9:00 A.M.), the middle group reached a peak in the seventh hour, and the lowest scoring group (evening types) peaked during the eighth hour of the day. (Since these participants were not selected in such a way as to statistically represent different levels of morningness, the actual peak hours are much less important than the fact that there were wide differences between the hours.) Other research involving various self-ratings that assess probable elements of energetic arousal, particularly self-ratings of alertness, have also shown reliable differences between morning and evening types (Breithaupt, Hildebrandt, & Werner, 1981; Folkard, Monk, & Lobban, 1979; Froberg, 1977; Watts, Cox, & Robson, 1983).

It should be noted that the common perception that people become more of a morning type as they grow older may be valid. Research by Åkerstedt and Torsvall (Åkerstedt & Torsvall, 1981; Torsvall & Åkerstedt, 1980; see also Tune, 1969) does suggest that morningness increases with age. In one study, these investigators obtained reliable data indicating greater numbers of problems in connection with night shift work as a function of age. But this relationship was reversed with morning shift work.

The reason for this shift to morningness with age, if it does occur, is not clear, particularly because morningness appears to be a characteristic of temperament with possible genetic determination, and thus it may be relatively fixed (cf. Eaves et al., 1988). Of course, this would not preclude a phase shift with age. Declining efficiency of bodily energy systems with age could move people's peak of energetic arousal closer to the restorative elements of night sleep. Still another explanation is that as people get older they are less influenced by what is most socially desirable, and they begin to recognize more clearly their own characteristics of temperament. Therefore, self-descriptions of morningness may become more accurate with increasing age.

In addition, age is probably associated with cycles of energetic arousal in other ways. The life cycle of an individual can be viewed as representing abundant energy resources in youth and gradually decreasing resources with age. As energy availability changes throughout the life cycle, many other aspects of personality could be affected. In particular, there may be subtle psychological perspective changes regarding problem perception and optimism. This is not to say that older persons view their particular problems as more serious and are less optimistic about them. That is probably not the case. But there may be subtle perspective changes with regard to issues and actions that are at least in part determined by available energy resources.

An anecdote related to me by a colleague illustrates the possible interpretations in this regard. On entering a shopping center where some construction work was occurring, he noticed several senior citizens—probably in their eighties—seated on a bench and watching. When he left two hours later, the seniors were still seated in the same place, seemingly absorbed in watching the work. My colleague, who was at retirement age himself, indicated that this might be seen as lamentable by some, who would view it as an example of old people being shunted aside into dull uninteresting lifestyles. But he viewed this activity as probably quite satisfying for those individuals. As age reduces available energy resources, it is possible that preferences and interests change accordingly.

Although the so-called excesses of youth are often attributed to complex social and educational factors, a plausible alternative explanation may involve biological resources of energy reserves. Differing levels of energy resources may underlie older people's judgments that young people enjoy cars that are too fast, music too loud, and parties that go on too long (cf. Farley, 1986; Zuckerman, 1979). What is attractive to one with abundant energy resources may be repugnant to another who fatigues more easily.

We may even speculate about the influence of changing energy resources in relation to crime statistics that show much higher crime rates for adolescents and young adults than for older people. For example, in 1982 the U.S. arrest rate was highest for teens and the twenty-to-twenty-four-year-old group in virtually all categories of crime. To cite one example, the disorderly conduct arrest rates per 10,000 were: those thirteen to nineteen had an arrest rate of 65.7/10,000; twenty to twenty-four, 97.3; twenty-five to thirty-four, 52.6; thirty-five to forty-nine, 25.5; fifty to sixty-four, 11.8; and sixty-five and older, 2.4 (Uniform Crime Report, 1982. Washington, D.C., U.S. Department of Justice, 1983, Table 31, pp. 176–77). Although clearly the changing socioeconomic factors that accompany age changes affect these differences in crime rates, the fact that old people commit relatively few crimes may be due as much to changing energy levels as it is to these other social determinants.

Although these differences in social behaviors for different age groups may be quite documentable, the validity of the basic idea that energy resources decline with age is open to question. Although this decline seems obvious, the available scientific evidence is quite limited, probably because this is a difficult question to investigate. There are no agreed upon physiological measures of absolute energy levels, and comparisons of self-reports of energetic arousal as a function of age have not been made, to my knowledge.

However, there are indications that circadian rhythms for various physiological functions decrease in amplitude as people grow older (Descovich et al., 1974; Iguchi, Kato, & Ibayashi, 1982; Scheving et al., 1974; Touitou et al., 1983;

Weitzman et al., 1982). These functions include body temperature and production of testosterone, melatonin, norepinephrine, and epinephrine. Although these physiological functions are probably related to energetic arousal, the exact relationship is not clear.

One potentially relevant psychological study conducted by Douglas and Arenberg (1978) was carried out over a sixteen-year period as part of the Baltimore Longitudinal Study. These investigators obtained data from a large sampling of males, using the Guilford-Zimmerman Temperament Survey. Among other things, this test measures general activity and the tendency toward an energetic, rapidly moving and working lifestyle. It is a measure of the usual pace of activity. Both cross-sectional and longitudinal components of the study indicated that general activity declined somewhat after age fifty, and it declined quite substantially after seventy years of age. If general activity is closely related to energetic arousal, this study would appear to provide good evidence of declining energy resources with age.

Variations between arousal cycles of extraverts and introverts have been the subject of a number of studies. In one of the first systematic observations, Blake (1967a; see also Colquhoun, 1960) found that introverts have a higher body temperature than extraverts in the first part of the day, and extraverts have higher temperature in the last part. Over the years, a number of studies attempted to replicate the Blake study, using a wide variety of measures of arousal and performance. Early research did appear to support the concept of an interaction between extraversion and time of day, with arousal as the underlying basis (Blake & Corcoran, 1972). However, later research provided mixed results (Kerkhof, 1985).

One possible explanation for the mixed results is that measures of extraversion are complex, combining components of impulsivity and sociability (Schalling, 1978). There is evidence that the impulsivity component may produce the interaction (Revelle et al., 1980). However, this matter is not clear (Eysenck & Folkard, 1980), and there is evidence against this contention (Larsen, 1985).

In these extraversion-introversion studies, several investigators have argued that inconsistencies regarding the interaction of time of day and extraversion may be due to the fact that arousal is multidimensional (Eysenck & Folkard, 1980; Larsen, 1985). This idea was supported in a study previously referred to (Thayer, Takahashi, & Pauli, 1988) in which AD ACL measurements were taken every hour over six days. In this study, participants were also tested for extraversion. Initially, we expected the time of day and extraversion interaction originally obtained by Blake to be replicated with energetic arousal because it is the most general arousal measure. However, no such interaction was obtained. Instead, introverted participants were more *tense* than extraverts for the first two-thirds of the day, and extraverts were more tense in the last portion of the day. This interaction reached a high level of statistical significance.

Firm conclusions cannot be drawn from a single study of this sort, particularly when the results are unexpected. However, it is possible that some of the mixed results (Kerkhof, 1985) occurred because the arousal state assumed to underlie the interaction between extraversion and time of day is more related to tension than to energy, and the two arousal dimensions are sometimes negatively correlated (see Chapter 6). This possibility is supported by a subsequent reanalysis of Blake's original temperature data (Colquhoun & Folkard, 1978), which showed that the extraversion and time of day interaction was most pronounced in those subjects who scored high on neuroticism. Thus, the anxiety or tension component of neuroticism may have strongly contributed to the interaction.

There are many other individual differences in cycles that bear further exploration. For example, a number of personality questionnaires include subtests relating to characteristic levels of energy (e.g., Jackson, 1976). Each of these should be systematically researched in relation to the various rhythms discussed in this chapter.[7] Another important individual difference relates to the ability to modulate arousal cycles, which could be associated with differences in self-awareness, although more basic differences in temperament could be involved. It appears that this ability to modulate arousal is associated with maturity, because children are often poor at this, as can be seen when they become "wound up" at evening playtime and then are unable to sleep. A more basic inability common to some children could be represented by the syndrome of hyperactivity (cf. MacDonald, 1988; Rosenthal & Allen, 1978; Zentall & Zentall, 1983).

Another important, and relatively unexplored, individual difference concerns the psychological perspective changes associated with energetic and tense arousal. During low-energy and high-tension periods, some people seem more able than others to understand that their pessimistic evaluations of personal problems are temporary and mood-related. It is almost as though some are better than others at recognizing their cycles and at recalling perceptions during states quite different from the present one. In particular, there may be individual differences in state dependency.

Other Rhythms of Energetic and Tense Arousal

It is increasingly clear that mood states associated with energy and tension vary in circadian rhythms, or at least in diurnal rhythms. Many believe, however, that other kinds of variations in mood occur. For example, many of my students describe variations on different days. A common report is that a good-mood day is often followed by a bad-mood day, or vice versa.[8] Some indicate multiday mood swings, and others even speak of seasonal mood shifts. Related topics were discussed in Chapter 2 (cf. Caspi, Bolger, & Eckenrode, 1987; Rossi & Rossi, 1977; Stone et al., 1985; Stone & Neale, 1984). Here I shall deal specifically with energetic and tense arousal forming infradian (greater than twenty-four hours) and ultradian (less than twenty-four hours) cycles.

Infradian rhythms of tense arousal have been mainly reported in relation to the female menstrual cycle. In particular, the increased tension in the days just prior to menses and the more general Premenstrual Tension Syndrome (PMS) are topics that have received considerable popular, medical, and scientific attention. These topics are quite sensitive politically, because many people are justifiably concerned that evidence of periodic tension states in females may be used by prejudiced individuals to discriminate against women in the workplace and elsewhere. Therefore, investigators working in this area often exercise a reasonable caution in interpreting the available data.

Patkai recently reviewed a large number of studies about the menstrual cycle and concluded "that the occurrence of some negative moods and somatic complaints in a majority of women before and during menstruation is relatively well established" (Patkai, 1985, p. 95). She goes on to point out: "However, the adverse influence of premenstrual and menstrual periods upon performance is not well supported." Similarly, Asso, in her review of premenstrual effects, indicated that "a possible relationship between the menstrual cycle and cognitive performance is largely negative" (Asso, 1985/86).

In addition to her analyses of the literature on performance and menstrual cycles, Asso and her associates completed a series of well-done studies in which tense arousal was shown to increase during the premenstrual period. In one study (Asso & Braier, 1982), thirty-six women between seventeen and thirty-seven years of age were randomly assigned to be tested during a time either premenstrual (within five days of menstruation) or intermenstrual (middle third of cycle). Most were tested with AD ACLs and a series of objective and physiological tests in the afternoon on the appointed day of their cycle. The results indicated significantly higher levels of tension in the premenstrual period. Other tests used by Asso, particularly skin conductance and other self-report tests, also changed in the expected direction, although not to a statistically significant degree.

In another experiment, Asso (1986) used a "repeated-measures" design to test thirty women between eighteen and thirty-seven years of age with AD ACLs and a series of other physiological and self-report tests. Once again, a highly significant increase in tense arousal was observed in the premenstrual period compared to mid-cycle. In addition, there were statistically significant increases in various other responses taken from a menstrual distress questionnaire (e.g., pain, impaired concentration, behavior change, water retention) as well as in electrodermal levels. Respondents also showed significantly higher levels of depression and hostility in that part of the cycle. These research findings of higher tension in the premenstrual period are consistent with research by Bell (1976), which also employed the AD ACL.

The two studies by Asso are quite interesting in another respect. In both studies, Asso and her associate found not only that tense arousal was higher in the premenstrual period, but they also found that energetic arousal was higher at mid-cycle. In consistency with concepts derived by Eysenck (1967), Asso interprets these differences as indicating greater cortical arousal at mid-cycle and greater autonomic arousal in the premenstrual period. However, as will be discussed further in Chapter 6, a more appropriate interpretation may utilize the concepts of energetic and tense arousal.

The Asso results indicating greater energetic arousal at mid-cycle are consistent with other research findings based on self-report measurements related to

energetic arousal (Moos et al., 1969). However, studies by Parlee (1982) and Bell (1976) indicated that energetic arousal was highest in the premenstrual period. One possible explanation for these conflicting results could be that the tension present in Asso's research participants was higher than for those in Parlee and Bell's participants. Moderate levels of tension increase energetic arousal, but higher levels decrease energetic arousal.

If females do in fact experience greater levels of energetic arousal at mid-cycle, these differences are readily interpretable within a general biological model. In evolutionary development, there would clearly have been a greater reproductive advantage for species members who experience more energy during the mid-cycle phase, the time of their highest fertility. The elevated energy noticed at high fertility periods provides an additional argument for the biological underpinnings of the energetic arousal concept.

The evolutionary utility of higher tension during the premenstrual period is much less clear. Speculating broadly, one possible explanation is that the biologically adaptive heightened energetic arousal at mid-cycle results in decreased energetic arousal premenstrually as a balance in the cyclical process. In turn, reduced energetic arousal might predispose women toward increased tense arousal (see Chapter 6).

The rhythmicities of energetic and tense arousal described as diurnal, circadian, and infradian may not be the only cycles of significance. There is some evidence that energetic arousal varies in ultradian rhythms of about ninety minutes in duration. Thus, there may be periods of energy and tiredness about an hour and a half in length throughout the day, and it is possible that these in turn are modulated by the longer diurnal-circadian rhythms.

This idea of ninety-minute cycles can be traced in part to the early 1960s, when Kleitman (1961, 1963) described a basic rest activity cycle (BRAC) of 80 to 120 minutes. He viewed the cycle as part of the ontogenetic development of sleep-wakefulness rhythms from infancy—when the newborn sleeps most of the time, but awakens periodically for feeding—to adulthood, when sleep occurs only one-third of the time. In adulthood, the ninety-minute REM/non-REM cycles (REM, or rapid eye movement sleep, is usually associated with dreaming) that occur during sleep presumably are related to the early cycles of wakefulness that were necessary at one time due to feeding requirements. Thus, the periodic sleeping and waking of the neonate develops into adult wakefulness and to the continuing waking cycles of alertness and tiredness. Although this idea has been challenged in recent times on a number of grounds (see reviews by Kripke, 1982; Lavie, 1985), still, the logic of his arguments as viewed in a broad perspective is quite compelling.

Whether or not the BRAC cycles do represent the waking counterparts of the REM/non-REM sleep cycle, however, and whether both are remnants of feeding requirements, there have been many indications that wakefulness does vary roughly in ninety-minute arousal rhythms. Such rhythms have been observed in a variety of other bodily and psychological activities, including EEG cycles (Kripke, 1972), daydreaming (Kripke & Sonnenschein, 1978), tendencies to sleep (Lavie & Scherson, 1981), vigilance (Globus et al., 1971; Orr, Hoffman, &

Hegge, 1974), and even hypnotizability (E. L. Rossi, 1985). Moreover, there are indications of similar ultradian rhythms occurring with self-rated mood states of alertness-tiredness (Gertz & Lavie, 1983). This area is a rich one for further investigation, particularly in relation to the various mood phenomena thought to be related to energetic arousal.

Speculations and Applications

Several areas relating to biological rhythms have been quite popular among students in my classes, for which longitudinal mood analyses were optional class projects. For example, there is a good deal of student interest in establishing morningness-eveningness typologies using measurements of arousal as well as a retrospective questionnaire. In addition to morningness and eveningness typologies, the particular peaks and troughs of cycles are usually determinable by identifying high-energy/low-tension periods of the day (optimal times) in comparison with low-energy/high-tension periods (low times). In this latter situation, self-ratings of problem seriousness, optimism, and related states usually show substantial differences between the optimal and less optimal times of day, and generally the overall results are consistent with the research described previously.

One of the most popular areas of study concerns compatibility between persons with differing arousal cycles. For example, to what extent do personal problems result when an extreme morning type lives with an extreme evening type? Can divergent arousal variations between partners account for social conflict?

To find this out, one of my students carried out a study in an attempt to answer some of these questions. He determined that his wife's daily peak of energetic arousal occurred soon after awakening, and that she was very fatigued after 7:00 P.M. in the evening. Apparently, she was an extreme morning type. In contrast, his measured energy level was relatively low throughout the morning, and higher than usual in the late evening hours. He was an extreme evening type.

He described some of the interactions between his wife and himself when there were problems to be discussed. Not surprisingly, she usually chose to raise issues during the morning, when they were both preparing for work and having breakfast. He indicated that in the morning all he could do was groan and tell her to leave him alone. But he was a reasonable sort, and by the end of the evening, he was ready to talk. However, a discussion at that time of night left *her* very irritable, and his persistence often resulted in a fight.

This degree of cycle incompatibility was more extreme than usual, but even lesser differences in energy patterns are often described by my students as causes of conflicts between themselves and a partner. In my view, however, the matter is not at all straightforward in relating incompatibility with rhythm cycle differences and similarities. At first thought, it seems obvious that morning and evening types would be incompatible, but on the other hand, such differences usually leave one partner with more energy than the other to deal with problematic situations. In contrast, if both partners have periods of low energy in common,

this could exacerbate any conflict or stress that occurs during that time. At least one prediction that seems likely is that *knowledge* about differences in cycles between partners, and subsequent allowances for them, would lead to better social interactions.

A small amount of published research already exists on the topic of arousal levels and social interactions. For example, in the study described above (Thayer, Takahashi, & Pauli, 1988), a significant relationship was observed between interview-determined estimates of best and worst hours for getting along with others, and measures of diurnal rhythms collected over six days. High energetic arousal periods were the best times for social interactions, and low energetic arousal, the worst. In another study, Watts (Watts, 1982) investigated the relationship between morningness personality characteristics and roommate relationships. She found that differences in the tendency to be a morning type predicted roommate incompatibility.

Hoskins and Halberg (Hoskins & Halberg, 1983) investigated compatibility in actual interactions by using the AD ACL to determine arousal cycles and a specially designed conflict questionnaire. These investigators collected data about one couple's arousal levels and their perceptions of conflict for thirty-five days. They found a number of significant relationships between conflict scores and both energetic and tense arousal. However, these correlations varied in direction with the individual and with time of day. Some of these differences might have been due to the differing morningness characteristics of the two individuals, as well as to the degree of conflict. But, in any event, these differing results indicate the potential complexity of the theoretical issues involved.

5

Determinants of Energetic and Tense Arousal, Including Cognitive–Mood Interactions

The common perception that exercise results in fatigue is frequently wrong. One of the most interesting things about subjective energy is that often this feeling is immediately *enhanced* by moderate exercise. I am not speaking here of the enhancement that comes over time with physical conditioning. Instead, my point is that on any single occasion energy is often increased by moderate exercise, and the effect can continue for minutes if not hours. At first thought, this doesn't seem logical. After all, exercise involves energy expenditure, and therefore, it should result in tiredness. Nevertheless, on the basis of experimental data, plus some speculative biological theory, it appears that much of the time the immediate effect of moderate exercise is increased energy.

Feelings of fatigue do result from exercise, of course, under certain conditions. For example, if one is already exhausted from physical labor, additional exercise is unlikely to increase energy; instead, the opposite will occur.[1] Similarly, if a person in poor physical condition attempts to run a mile, the immediate effect will be tiredness, if not exhaustion. On the other hand, finger movements or rolling the eyes, which might conceivably be called muscular exercise, will probably not increase energy either. Nevertheless, within these high and low limiting conditions, there exists a level of moderate exercise that has the reliable and immediate effect of increasing energetic arousal.

Exercise and Energetic Arousal: Experimental Demonstrations

A series of experiments that I conducted illustrate well the energizing effects of moderate exercise. Each of these experiments involved young or middle-aged participants whose lifestyles included at least occasional exercise and who were in fairly good physical condition. As an experimental manipulation, these volunteers took brisk ten-minute walks after a period of sedentary activity so that the contrasting effects on mood could be most easily detected. This last point is particularly important because the mood effects from moderate exercise are quite subtle. And, although in the long run these mood changes may have substantial effects on behavior, most common scientific research designs are not well-suited to measure effects so subtle.

The first experiment in this series involved fifty male and female college students divided equally into two groups (Thayer, 1978b). With the first group, participants arrived at a room where they were acquainted with the project and given a short filler task. After about fifteen minutes, they were invited to join the experimenter for a moderately fast ten-minute walk around the campus. Within five minutes of returning from the walk and being seated, the participants completed an AD ACL, rating their immediate feelings of energy and tension. Next, they sat quietly for fifteen more minutes, after which they completed a second AD ACL. With the second group, the participants sat for thirty minutes before completing their first AD ACL; then they walked, and finally they made a second set of ratings.

Statistical analyses of the results indicated a highly significant increase in subjective energy following the walk. Instead of becoming more tired, people had a significant *decrease* in tiredness. Thus, the immediate effect of this simple walk was a significant mood shift and an immediate increase in energetic arousal.

Although the participants were told nothing about the purpose of the experiment, it might be argued that they guessed the purpose and cooperated by giving the preferred results. Or, skeptics might suggest that mere expectations about the exercise produced the rating change, even without any conscious awareness on the part of the walkers. However, evidence indicating the unlikelihood of these explanations was available because of the design employed in this research.

Half the participants completed the first AD ACL after sitting and before they knew there would be a walk, while the other half completed the first set of ratings after the walk and before they knew there would be a period of sitting. Therefore, comparisons could be made of the first AD ACL in one condition with the first AD ACL in the second condition. And these differences, in turn, could be compared with the differences obtained from the two testings of each participant.

If expectation effects had caused these results, it is likely that the energy increases would have been greater between the two testings for each participant than the differences between the first tests that were administered in the two counterbalanced groups (one group that took the first AD ACL after walking versus the group that took it after sitting). But, instead, this analysis showed approximately the same outcome in the two kinds of comparisons (i.e., 41% variance accounted for in the within-subjects comparison, versus a 42% variance in the between-subjects comparison). These essentially equivalent results provide an excellent indication that the increased energy was produced by the exercise and not by expectation effects or by simple cooperation on the part of the participants.

A second experiment (Thayer & Cheatle, 1976) also focused on the effects of exercise on subjective energy, but used a different procedure in order to address slightly different questions. Instead of taking walks outside as an exercise manipulation, the fifty-six participants that completed this experiment used a treadmill that was set at either 2½ or 3¼ miles per hour at a 6-degree incline. At both treadmill speeds, ten minutes of walking under these conditions produced a highly significant increase in energy as well as a reliable decrease in tiredness (with a slightly greater arousal at the lesser speed). This experimental manipulation also produced a significant *decrease* in subjective tension for both speeds. These differences in arousal levels were reliable for both before- and after-walk comparisons, and for comparisons between participants who walked and those in a control condition who merely sat for ten minutes.

The results of this treadmill experiment were consistent with those of the first experiment, but the latter findings occurred in a more controlled setting, with pace and degree of effort more standardized. Moreover, the empty-walled room that contained the treadmill created a somewhat sterile atmosphere. All this minimized the possible effects of cognitive change due to the kinds of environmental influences that would inevitably occur with an outside walk. Thus, the energizing effects of moderate exercise could be more confidently attributed to arousal shifts than to simple cognitive changes.

In a third experiment, an assessment was made of the *length* of time that subjective energy is enhanced following moderate exercise (Thayer, 1987a). This experiment employed a short-term longitudinal design in which manipulations occurred on several occasions over a three-week period. On each occasion, participants made self-ratings of energetic and tense arousal, then took a ten-minute brisk walk, and made additional ratings at fixed time intervals for two hours afterwards.

This experiment incorporated ingestion of a sugar snack as an alternative to taking the walk. To summarize the complete procedure, at a fixed time each day, eighteen participants completed an AD ACL, then they rolled a die, and depending on what number occurred they either took a ten-minute rapid walk or they ate a candy bar. AD ACLs were subsequently taken 30, 60, and 120 minutes after the pretest.

Participants in this experiment followed a fixed procedure, but they walked wherever they happened to be at the scheduled time (e.g., around a block in the neighborhood). Their walk was rapid, and they maintained a relaxed but erect posture. They breathed deeply, and they swung their arms freely in a natural walking motion. Besides time of day and type of walk, other conditions were also held constant, including previous physical activity and food ingestion.

The arousal levels taken at the thirty-minute interval (twenty minutes after the walk) were consistent with the previous research. The first self-rating showed significant increases in energy and decreases in tiredness, and participants also showed significant decreases in tension. But the effects on mood did not end at the thirty-minute interval time. The enhanced energy and decreased tension lasted for at least one hour, and to a lesser degree, there was an enhanced energy effect for two hours. These results are especially impressive if considered in relation to the trade-off in time it took to get them: ten minutes of rapid walking produced at least one hour of enhanced energy and reduced tension. Two other experiments in this series addressed the influence of moderate exercise on arousal (see Chapter 4), and from these studies, it appears that moderate exercise produces an effect similar to that produced by peaks in circadian arousal cycles.

The experiments testing exercise and circadian rhythm on arousal utilized a short-term longitudinal design, and this point is particularly important. It is only through aggregation of ratings over time that the subtle effects of such variables as moderate exercise and circadian rhythms become fully apparent (cf. Epstein, 1980; Rushton, Brainerd, & Pressley, 1983). However, the subtlety of these effects should not be taken as an indication that they have little influence.

Two experiments showing the influence of exercise and circadian rhythm on mood were completed over three-week periods. Participants took AD ACLs at fixed times of day, which represented high and low circadian arousal levels (Thayer, 1987b). In the first experiment, the participants also rated the perceived seriousness of a long-term personal problem at four times of day representing different levels of diurnal arousal. The other experiment used the same basic methodology, but here participants made ratings of their general level of optimism, happiness, and sense of physical well-being twice a day. Participants in both experiments took a rapid ten-minute walk once each day, using the same walking method described in the previous experiment. They took the walk at various times, but never within 1.5 hours of a completed measurement. Immediately after the walk, the participants filled out an AD ACL and rated the seriousness of their problem once again.

The immediate effect of exercise on energetic arousal was evident in both these studies by the differences between post-walk measurements compared to arousal levels at various times of day. In the first experiment, energetic arousal was significantly higher after the walk than at late afternoon, and the differences between the arousal self-ratings were even greater when the post-walk measurement was compared with the waking and before-sleep periods. In this experiment, energetic arousal levels after walking were comparable to those at late morning, the highest measured arousal level of the diurnal cycle. Similar effects were obtained in the second experiment, although waking and before-sleep periods were not included in this study. This similarity of findings considerably increases the reliability of the results.

The indirect effects observed in this study were also important. In both experiments, the rapid walk resulted in significant cognitive-perceptual shifts. After the walk, chronic personal problems appeared significantly less serious. Additionally, the walk increased general optimism to a significant degree. Although statistically significant, these were small effects, and on any one day they were not necessarily present, but when viewed over all the days of the experiment, the effects were quite apparent. Once again, this is an example of small but persistent differences that, in the long run, could be quite influential.

The exact causes of these cognitive-perceptual shifts are difficult to prove in an experiment such as this. Walking appeared to produce the effect, but whether energetic arousal had any influence on these shifts is less demonstrable. However, a careful analysis of the indirect evidence suggests that the changes in perception were due primarily to variations in energetic arousal. This is particularly true if one assumes that tension is reduced by sudden increments of energetic arousal (see Chapter 6).

This analysis is based on comparing relative strengths of effects for energetic arousal, tense arousal, and the other cognitive-perceptual measures. It is also based on analyses of increasing cognitive-perceptual effects for different interactions of energetic and tense arousal. Further theoretical analyses were made possible on the basis of known circadian rhythms and the effects of exercise (see Thayer 1987a, 1987b, for additional consideration of these points).

In these three experiments and others like them, the possibility always exists that some expectation effects of the participants influenced the obtained results, but this is unlikely for a number of reasons. First of all, any influence due to expectation would result in greater effects at the end of a multiple-occasion experiment than at the beginning. But the statistical analyses showed this did not happen. Furthermore, all experimental participants were explicitly warned to be scrupulously honest with all their ratings. And I have found in studies such as these in which multiple ratings are made that the rating task usually becomes quite automatic, and little consideration is given to anything except the immediate ratings.

These studies strongly suggest that increased energetic arousal occurs as a result of moderate exercise, but many questions remain unanswered. For example, it is not clear what amount of exercise is sufficient to produce the effect, nor is it clear what level of exercise results in fatigue instead of increased energy (cf. Hollandsworth & Jones, 1979). Moreover, these processes are likely to be cyclical and time-related. For example, a given amount of exercise may result in an initial period of fatigue followed by increased energy feelings a short while later. Furthermore, these relationships are probably related in a complex way to the overall physical condition of an individual as well as his or her state at the time of the exercise. And, to make matters even more complicated, these relationships are probably in continuous change, as repeated exercise results in bodily development from physical conditioning.

All of these complexities notwithstanding, the effect of moderate exercise on energetic arousal is one of the most reliable effects on mood that I have observed. Within a broad set of limits, moderate exercise usually results in an immediate increase in energetic arousal, and with reliable measurement (e.g., observations over multiple occasions) it is often possible to observe this effect lasting minutes, if not hours, after the exercise. The relationship is so consistent that it probably should be viewed in elemental biological terms (see next section).

The effects of more intense exercise, and particularly systematic training to achieve physical fitness, have recently been the subject of increasing research attention. Folkins and Sime (1981) reviewed the existing literature up to 1980 and observed that there were numerous demonstrations of positive benefits resulting from intense exercise in relation to personality, cognitive functioning, and affect. Of particular interest for this analysis, affective changes generally have involved reductions of stress emotions such as anxiety. However, there was also evidence of improvement in general of mood and states of well-being. Another recent review of the literature by Morgan (1982) also concluded that exercise is associated with improved affect, particularly for people in anxious and depressed states.

It is possible, and I believe probable, that the demonstrated positive benefits of extended exercise and physical fitness training are all mediated by changing levels of energetic arousal. Thus, the recent popular interest in physical fitness may be ascribed in part to the enhanced energy effects obtained from it. Although it is difficult to assess, more intense physical conditioning probably results in overall heightened levels of energetic arousal. If this does occur, the negative relationship between energetic and tense arousal (see Chapter 6) could easily account for the reported anxiety-reducing effects of extended exercise programs.

The effects of energetic arousal on mood and cognition may be the basis for the positive benefits attributed to exercise that are widely reported in the popular media. There is now a large body of books and articles that describe a panoply of psychological changes that presumably occur from running, aerobics, swimming, walking, and other kinds of exercise. Generally, these books do not contain references to scientific research concerning the effects of exercise on mood, but they usually reflect informal reports of experiences by the writers and exercise enthusiasts involved. These positive claims are not surprising; one can hardly speak to a person involved in regular exercise without hearing accounts of beneficial mood changes believed to derive from that exercise. Serious scientists may tend to dismiss these accounts because they are not based on controlled studies, but the consistency of the reports of positive benefits at least suggests that exercise has a powerful influence on mood. In any event, reports by lay people and enthusiasts that mood is strongly affected by exercise are entirely consistent with my research findings.

Biological Considerations

The relationship of energetic arousal to exercise may represent an elemental biological linkage reflecting the importance of the motor system in evolutionary development. I will not attempt a thorough presentation of the pro and con evidence for this idea, but instead, let me refer to several lines of argument that might be brought to bear in support of the linkage. Consider, for example, the often cited views of Nobelist Roger Sperry regarding the central function of the motor system:

> [T]he vertebrate brain was designed primitively for the regulation of overt behavior rather than for mental performance. As one descends the vertebrate scale, purely mental activity becomes increasingly insignificant compared with overt response. Among the salamanders and lower fishes, where thought processes are presumably negligible, the bulk of the nervous appa-

ratus is clearly concerned with the management of motor activity. To the extent that sensation and perception are evident, these would appear to serve directly for the guidance of response. From the fishes to man there is apparent only a gradual refinement and elaboration of brain mechanisms with nowhere any radical alteration of the fundamental operating principles. In man as in salamanders the primary business of the brain continues to be the governing directly or indirectly, of overt behavior. (Sperry, 1952, p. 297)

Sperry goes on to emphasize that this point may seem strange to lay people who are mainly familiar with the cognitive functions of the brain: "Instead of regarding motor activity as being subsidiary, that is, something to carry out, serve, and satisfy the demands of the higher centers, we reverse the tendency and look upon the mental activity as only a means to an end, where the end is better regulation of overt response" (Sperry, 1952, p. 290). And he emphasizes that "the entire output of our thinking machine consists of nothing but patterns of motor coordination" (Sperry, 1952, p. 297).

Although this famous paper was written some years ago, the viewpoint of many brain scientists has not changed dramatically since Sperry wrote those words. The motor system is extraordinarily important in evolutionary development, undoubtedly because it enables the animal to function in all domains of survival. And even though this system is still relatively poorly understood, it is usually accorded respect for its fundamental importance.

When Sperry put forth these ideas, he was not speaking about the motor theory of thought, the popular view held in the early part of the century that all thought required accompanied motor responses. Although that overly simplistic view has been largely disregarded in recent times, there is still a considerable amount of evidence concerning the relationship of the skeletal-muscular system to attention, decision-making, and various kinds of goal-directed behaviors. Malmo's summary analysis of electromyographic (EMG) studies exemplifies this point: "Evidence from the EMG research reviewed . . . provides strong support for the proposition that the motor system is an indispensable part of all activities of the mind" (Malmo, 1975, p. 67).

In the view of both Sperry and Malmo, the motor system is accorded a central significance in the psychic life of the individual.[2] Thus, the ideas that I expressed about the centrality of exercise to energetic arousal do have plausible support in respected psychobiological thought. These ideas are speculative, of course, but they are consistent with other kinds of evidence as well. For example, motor activity is integrally associated with traditional notions of arousal. Sleep deprivation research has shown this clearly. In reviewing a variety of studies, Kleitman wrote:

Cortical activity is thus sustained by, and sustains, the wakefulness system and the skeletal musculature. In the operation of the multiple feedback circuits, wakefulness capacity is limited by muscular endurance. As was shown by the course of events in sleep-deprivation experiments . . . the subjects could maintain wakefulness as long as they were able and willing to maintain muscular activity. Even a well-rested person may have difficulty in remaining awake, if, in addition to the removal of, or decrease in, stimulation through other sense organs, he allows his skeletal musculature to relax. Conversely, tense muscles may be responsible for "insomnia." (Kleitman, 1963, p. 369)

There is other experimental evidence of the relationship between gross voluntary motor activity and sleep-wake divisions. I have summarized this matter by pointing out:

Of course, in a general sort of way, animal researchers have always relied on the absence of motor activity as an indication of sleep. Moreover, Russian researchers working on sleep therapies found decreases in gross motor activity to be an excellent index of the passage between wakefulness and sleep, particularly when adjusted to the idiosyncratic differences among patients (Andreev, 1960). Decreasing motor activity is even an indication of the depth of sleep (Cathala & Guillard, 1961; Rohmer, Schaff, Collard, & Kurtz, 1965). Motor activity is somehow integrally related to sleep and wakefulness. (Thayer, 1985, p. 119)

Other Determinants of Energetic Arousal

In the most general analysis, the basic biopsychological system of energetic arousal is undoubtedly associated with physical health. Healthy persons are more likely than unhealthy ones to experience energy, vigor, and vitality as opposed to unusual levels of fatigue and tiredness. There are many indications of this, but comparing illness with the state of peak physical conditioning makes this relationship obvious.

A good example can be found in the energy decreases commonly associated with illness. Physicians and nurses who are training and studying physical diagnosis learn early that the chief complaint of a wide variety of patients is loss of energy and general fatigue (cf. Lundberg, 1984). In one study recently conducted in the Boston area involving 500 medical patients who were representative of the 30,000 visits/year in this primary care general medical facility, 37 percent of the patients indicated that they had been experiencing severe fatigue (Buchwald, Sullivan, & Komaroff, 1987; also see Kroenke et al., 1988). Sometimes this fatigue is referred to as general malaise. A characteristic of this state is that the individual does not feel strong enough for the usual life pursuits, activity patterns are decreased, and there is a greater tendency to seek rest and sleep.

This relationship between illness and energy has been so frequently observed that the relative balance of fatigue compared to energy and vigor may often be an early indication of sickness (note research on mood and illness reviewed in Chapter 2, particularly Blanchet & Frommer, 1986; Harrigan et al., 1984; King, 1981). From this perspective, it is clear that a general discussion of the determinants of energetic arousal should include such well-known health detractors as cigarette smoking, consuming excessive alcohol, physical inactivity, obesity, and too little or too much sleep (Berkman & Breslow, 1983).

Nutrition is likely to be another important determinant of energetic arousal, although the exact nature of this relationship is not yet understood. It is highly probable that food substances of various sorts influence moods associated with energetic arousal, but this influence has received relatively little scientific attention. The small number of studies done on this topic is curious considering the wide interest in it of the general public. To some extent, the relative lack of research may have to do with the reluctance of the somewhat conservative scientific establishment to become involved in an area that has become so popularized. But in my view, this is not the major reason for the low number of published studies; instead, this paucity of publications is probably related to the difficulties in studying the subtle mood changes that occur from nutritional variations.

A change in diet probably affects people over time, but on any one occasion the effects of a particular food are likely to be masked by other, more powerful elements of an experiment. For example, the experimental participant who ingests a particular food and then rates his or her mood is likely to be more affected by the fact of being in an experiment than by the effects of the food. As I shall argue in Chapter 7, the usual experimental designs make it difficult to research this area, and alternative approaches are necessary.

It is possible to study the short-term effects on mood of various food substances, but because of the subtlety of these reactions, such studies must involve highly reliable measurements, and it may be necessary to use naturalistic settings. One such study was conducted in relation to sugar ingestion (Thayer, 1987a). This experiment, discussed earlier in the context of exercise, involved having subjects take an AD ACL, and then follow a randomly determined selection of one of two experimental conditions: either ingesting a standard-sized candy bar or taking a rapid ten-minute walk. AD ACLs were taken 30, 60, and 120 minutes afterwards. Because it involved multiple repetitions of the experimental conditions over a three-week period, this experiment produced quite reliable measurements of changes in energetic and tense arousal.

In this study it was observed that following the sugar snack, most participants felt more energy initially, but after an hour a majority felt less energy. On the other hand, tension was significantly increased one hour after ingestion of the candy bar. By two hours, this tension effect had dissipated. The changes were subtle and might well be unnoticed on any single occasion. But over time, the small changes were statistically reliable.

A few other studies of the relationship between food and mood have been published, but usually they entailed measurements on a single occasion following ingestion of a particular food, and thus the subtle effects were more difficult to detect. Recently, Wurtman and Wurtman (1986) reviewed a number of experiments involving the ingestion of various substances such as carbohydrate, fat, and protein, as well as neurotransmitter precursors such as tryptophan. The results indicated that these food substances probably affect energetic arousal, but these changes may be moderated by such variables as sex and age. Similar conclusions were drawn by Spring, Chiodo, and Bowen (1987) in a recent review of the effects of carbohydrates and tryptophan on behavior.

It would be quite advantageous to have more research in this area, as it involves a number of important practical applications. For example, various investigators have argued that the major effect of sugar ingestion is increased tiredness (Spinweber, 1981; Wurtman, Hefti, & Malemed, 1981; Wurtman & Wurtman, 1986). This appears to be contrary to popular beliefs that sugar ingestion results in increased tension or anxiety (Dufty, 1975; Fredericks & Goodman, 1969). In the sugar ingestion experiment just described (Thayer, 1987a), one hour after eating a candy bar there was a significant increase in tension, which would seem to contradict the viewpoint that tiredness is the major effect of sugar ingestion. However, it is possible that the natural biological reaction to sugar ingestion in fact may be increased tiredness, but that required activity in this state could be the basis of the observed tension increase. That is, a tired person who is required to continue daily activities may become tense as a reaction to the demand for activity rather than sleep.

Although the immediate effects of various nutritional substances on energetic and tense arousal have not been clearly demonstrated, the mood effects of extremes in diet have been rather convincingly documented. The starvation studies (see Chapter 3 for a fuller discussion) systematically conducted by the Selective Service and the University of Minnesota in the 1940s (Keys et al., 1950) made clear that one of the major mood effects of restricted food intake is reduced energetic arousal. Participants in the study, which was carried out over many months, showed distinct reductions in energy and significantly increased tiredness.

Sleep is another primary influence on energetic arousal. Numerous sleep deprivation studies have demonstrated that as sleep is reduced below normal amounts, energy is reduced and tiredness increases (e.g., Johnson, 1982; Kleitman, 1963). However, there are still many questions about the relationship between sleep and mood that remain unanswered. In my view, the situation is roughly comparable to that of nutrition and mood. Just as nutritional extremes yield predictable mood changes, so sleep extremes clearly affect mood. Nevertheless, attempts to demonstrate correlates of this likely relationship have yielded conflicting results.

For example, if sleep is integrally tied to energetic arousal, it would seem likely that persons who regularly sleep only a few hours per night (short sleepers) would differ from those who characteristically sleep many hours (long sleepers). In fact, some research showed a difference between the two types, albeit one contrary to expectations. Hartmann and his associates (Hartmann, Baekeland, & Zwilling, 1972; Spinweber & Hartmann, 1976) obtained evidence that, among other characteristics, short sleepers were more energetic and less anxious than long sleepers. On the other hand, Webb and Friel (1970, 1971) found no differences between short and long sleepers. And, in what would seem to be the more logical finding, Hicks and Pellegrini (Hicks & Pellegrini, 1977) obtained results indicating that short sleepers have higher anxiety levels than long sleepers.

These conflicting findings can be explained by the many sources of potential error in studies of this sort. Webb (1979) pointed out that error may be present due to inappropriate trait and state characterizations, insufficient measurement technology, and statistical issues concerning confidence levels. Considering these potential sources of error, and consistent with earlier findings that there were no differences between short and long sleepers, Berry and Webb concluded that there is "a general insulation of sleep from day-to-day mood variations" (Berry & Webb, 1985).

Notwithstanding the failure of Webb and his associates to find relationships between sleep and mood, my own view is that this area has been insufficiently investigated. As with nutrition research, mood changes that occur due to variations in sleep require a special kind of methodology in order to be detected. These subtle mood changes require the most reliable measurement and somewhat naturalistic settings for the test.

Because people have the capacity to overcome temporary states of low energy and tension when they are motivated by the requirements of an experiment, the influence of sleep on these states may not be detectable unless numerous measurements are taken over time in naturalistic settings. One methodology that might capture the effects of sleep would be a series of single-person studies conducted over multiple days (see Appendixes). However, such studies are costly and difficult to manage, and they provide less control of certain important variables, particularly expectation effects.

Even with the various problems that exist in studying the effects of sleep on mood, there is a sizable amount of research literature concerning naps and mood changes. For example, Taub and his associates (Taub, 1977, 1982; Taub, Tanguay, & Clarkson, 1976; Taub, Tanguay, & Rosa, 1977) found that naps generally increase energetic arousal, particularly in the case of people who nap regularly. The effects of naps appear to be complex, however, and are influenced by such factors as how many hours one was awake before taking a nap, the time of day the nap is taken, and the duration of the nap (Naitoh, 1981). Measurements taken at various times after a nap showed different nap effects, both because of immediate post-nap inertia (Lubin et al., 1976) and because the effects may not be apparent until a later point in the circadian arousal rhythm (Gillberg, 1985). Finally, it may be true that mere rest has the same effect on mood as sleeping (Daiss, Bertelson, & Benjamin, 1986).

Interactions of Cognition and Energetic Arousal

Although the evidence is limited, there is little doubt that cognitive stimuli affect energetic arousal (cf. Berlyne, 1971; Steele, 1977; Weinberger, 1984; Wright & Brehm, 1984). News that one has just won a lottery prize, for example, would likely result in strong feelings of energy and vigor, and these feelings would probably last for a lengthy period if the prize were sizable enough. Moreover, continued thoughts about the benefits from the prize would maintain the energy over time. Besides good fortune or positive thoughts, energetic arousal would probably be enhanced by a large variety of more mundane factors, such as an unexpected compliment, an interesting conversation, or even a pleasant picture.[3] Cognitively mediated changes in tension are also likely to affect energetic arousal (see Chapter 6).

I believe, however, that there is a much more basic way in which energetic arousal and cognitive factors interact. This has to do with ongoing judgments about one's immediate capability to accomplish various tasks. Thousands of times a day we are confronted with tasks that require resources to accomplish them, and in each case there is a momentary evaluation of the requirements of the task in relation to one's resources to meet it. This rapid evaluation involves an instantaneous assessment of current mood states. Although the assessment occurs so quickly the person scarcely realizes it is occurring, nevertheless, an individual generally obtains information about the basic question, "Do I have the energy to accomplish that task?"

Consider a simple matter such as going to the store to pick up some food for the next morning's breakfast. Let us assume that it is late at night after a hard day's work. When considering whether to go shopping, an individual would rapidly assess his level of tiredness in relation to his knowledge about the resources required to walk to the car, drive to the store, buy the food, drive home, and put the food away. This would not be preceded by well-formed questions about resources and step-by-step task requirements, but in some form those kinds of questions and answers would be part of a decision concerning the action.

This analysis can be extended even further if each step in the sequence were mediated by a process of matching one's resources with the requirements of the task at hand, "Can I get out of this chair?" "Do I have the energy to walk to the car?" and so on. As energy requirements become relevant, an individual continually senses his or her level of energetic arousal.

This process probably would remain at a low level of awareness unless the personal resources do not match or exceed the requirements. Cases in which there is a sense of too little energy to accomplish the task may bring into salient consciousness the thought, "I am too tired for that." Even this microanalysis of daily events may be too gross, however, because in the actual ongoing sequence, a person probably would quickly consider a *range* of options such as walking to the store, driving the car, walking fast to the car, walking slowly to the car, etc. Just as rapidly, there would be choices of the options that match the resources available.

From this analysis, it is clear that there is a constant interaction of cognition and mood. Moreover, this process must be quite complex, because it is likely that, in the process of continually measuring resources against requirements, allotments and rationing of reasonable amounts of energy must be made to accomplish the whole of the tasks required. This explains why a long distance runner is able to marshal his or her resources and not expend all the energy in the first part of a race. That this is a learned behavior can be demonstrated by comparing children with adults. Children may bound over fire hydrants and skip on steps, only to be worn out before the necessary trip is completed, but adults, after much experience, have learned that skipping over steps has its cost at a later time, when that energy may be needed.

This ongoing sensing of energy, coupled with a prudent allotment in relation to daily requirements, is likely to produce adjustments throughout the day as unexpected events occur through the interaction of cognition with arousal. For example, a brief period of exercise may enhance energetic arousal (see first section of chapter) and later result in choosing activities that otherwise would have been avoided. Or, an individual who suddenly realizes that there are more tasks to complete than were previously realized may subtly shift other activities to accommodate the additional energy expenditure. A complete understanding of the determinants of energetic arousal requires an appreciation of cognitive interactions.

Analyses of relationships between self-awareness and behavior are gaining much more currency in the psychological literature in recent years. For example, an analysis of decisions and actions has been provided by Bandura in relation to his theory of self-efficacy (Bandura, 1977, 1986), which he postulates acts as an intermediary between external events and an individual's decisions about action. As Bandura said, "Perceived self-efficacy is defined as people's judgments of operative capabilities—what people think they can do under given circumstances" (Bandura, 1986, p. 391). Beliefs about one's efficacy are assumed to derive from four sources of information—performance accomplishments, vicarious experience, verbal persuasion, and emotional arousal—but it is mainly the last information source that is relevant in this discussion.

In Bandura's system, emotional arousal as a source of feelings of self-efficacy has generally been used to explain fear-related perceptions about success or failure. For example, an individual who is fearful of public speaking will form efficacy beliefs about his capabilities to speak in public partly on the basis of his self-perceived arousal when speaking. However, self-efficacy beliefs are not limited to tense arousal. In some analyses of health practices, Bandura and his colleagues (Ewart et al., 1983; Taylor et al., 1985) theorized that feelings of self-efficacy mediate a variety of behaviors related to decisions about whether a person has the ability or strength to accomplish various tasks. In that research, patients recuperating from heart attacks made decisions about the level of activity to engage in on the basis of self-judgments of efficacy, and these judgments were related to somatic feedback.

Although the earlier analysis of interactions between arousal and cognition is close to Bandura's microanalyses of self-efficacy, there are certain differences. Bandura's view of self-efficacy is related to perceptions about the skills necessary to perform a particular task or family of tasks. He discusses the matter in the following way:

> Self-precepts of efficacy are usually measured in terms of variable use of the subskills one possesses under different situational demands. For example, in measuring driving self-efficacy, people are not asked to judge whether they can turn the ignition key, shift the automatic transmission, steer, accelerate and stop an automobile, blow the horn, monitor signs, read the flow

of traffic, and change traffic lanes. Rather, they judge, whatever their sub-skills may be, the strength of their perceived self-efficacy to navigate through busy arterial roads, congested city traffic, onrushing freeway traffic, and twisting mountain roads. The motor components of driving are trivial, but the generative capability of maneuvering an automobile through congested city traffic and speedy freeways is not. (Bandura, 1986, p. 397)

My description of the interaction between energetic arousal and cognition, in comparison, would be very much related to the actual motor components of driving as it is occurring. This analysis would involve the immediate future capabilities to steer, accelerate and stop the automobile, change traffic lanes, and so on. Energetic arousal is probably *also* involved in each judgment of skill to perform a particular task, as the skill judgment varies with a person's mood (cf. Bandura, 1986, p. 408). But my analysis focuses mainly on the momentary ongoing projections of capability to perform this or that activity. Skills are related to this, but considering all cognition-arousal interactions, a process even more basic than skill judgment, probably occurs.

Requirements Versus Resources Imbalances: Basic Antecedents of Tense Arousal

I indicated previously that cases in which personal resources do not match or exceed the requirements of a task may bring into consciousness the thought, "I am too tired." Subsequently the individual simply avoids or modifies the task at hand. There are other situations in which requirements exceed resources, however, and yet no choice is available to avoid the requirements. Let me provide a potentially useful, but still speculative, theoretical analysis that fixes this imbalance as a basic antecedent of tense arousal. With this analysis, the real or imagined danger that was described in previous chapters as the primary antecedent of tense arousal would be further defined in relation to unavoidable requirements that exceed resources.

Because resources would be assessed through feelings of energy and tiredness, interpretations of danger generally would be relative to the energy one is experiencing. Moreover, in this way of thinking the subjective experience of tension (and related moods)—the main marker of tense arousal—would be integrally associated with energy (in the sense that the balance of tension and energy is the best indication of the effects of threatening circumstances). From this, one can appreciate the relevancy of my description of central mood states in compound terms such as tense-energy, tense-tiredness, calm-energy, and calm-tiredness.

Let us consider several examples of this new analysis of danger. First I offer a rather extreme example that graphically presents the parameters, and then several more likely examples that would not be obvious without this interpretation. If one encounters a large, snarling dog approaching rapidly on a deserted street, there could be little doubt that the situation would be interpreted as dangerous. In this case it is clear that the unavoidable requirements would exceed most people's resources to deal with them. However, in this way of thinking it is not the dog per se that represents danger, but rather the danger exists because of the possibility that one may not be able to react in such a way as to avoid harm. If the dog is securely chained, or if it is behind an impenetrable fence, the danger is lessened or eliminated since no personal reaction is required. Considering this example in relation to mood, tension (and the related feeling of fear) would occur in the presence of a snarling dog that is loose, but it would be greatly reduced if the dog were chained or behind an impenetrable fence.

The danger in this situation is certainly subject to cognitive interpretation, but this interpretation occurs at an elemental level. As one observes the dog approaching, not only is a decision made about its potential to produce bodily injury, but also there is an instantaneous sensing of one's resources (available energy) for reacting to the animal. Tense arousal occurs only if there is a mismatch at this point. A large, snarling dog would generate more tense arousal than a tiny, snarling dog. Thus, the subjective experience of tension would be an indication that at some level of interpretation a judgment was made that unavoidable requirements exceed resources.

This analysis of danger and tense arousal allows extensions to many other more likely situations than the example with the dog. For instance, because resources vary throughout the day, it follows that a given set of requirements may sometimes produce tense arousal, and at other times the same requirements would produce no tension. In Chapter 3 I indicated that for many people the circadian rhythm of energetic arousal reaches its peak at late morning or early afternoon, and it drops in late afternoon. Therefore, an activity such as driving a car might cause no tension at late morning, but the same task, in the same traffic conditions, could be quite tension-inducing at late afternoon.

A couple discussing a problem could remain calm when they are dealing with the problem in the early afternoon, but the same discussion could be very tension-inducing if the individuals are tired late at night. In a similar way, office workers may experience little tension from requirements of typing in the morning, but late in the afternoon they could become quite tense from the same work. Individuals whose resources are depleted because they are hungry and tired may be extremely irritable (an indication of tension), but the same people may be calm and energetic when they are rested and have eaten.

In another way of looking at this, consider the distress that many people experience when they perceive themselves as losing control (Brunson & Matthews, 1981; Fodor, 1984; Glass, 1977). It may be a situation in which so many demands are being placed on them that they no longer are able to manage events. Here, as well as in the above examples, it is possible that the resources-requirements imbalance is at the core of the problem.

Although there has been little systematic investigation of these phenomena from this theoretical perspective, there is some relevant research evidence. For instance, in sleep deprivation research (Kleitman, 1963; Murray, 1965), a common pattern has occurred in which participants were quite cooperative early in the study; then, as deprivation continued and resources dropped, they became tense and irritable. Research described in Chapter 4 concerning perception of personal problems and time of day indicated the same phenomenon (Thayer, 1987b; Thayer, Takahashi, & Pauli, 1988). In those studies, individuals evaluated their problems as more or less serious, and their optimism varied on the basis of the time of day and their natural rhythms of energy.

There are a number of issues yet to be resolved within this theoretical perspective. For example, is this imbalance always a cognitive interpretational process? And if so, to what degree is there conscious awareness of the process? Unfortunately, the parameters of cognition and awareness are quite unclear in relation to these points (cf. Lazarus, 1982; Zajonc, 1980).

It seems to me that there is a continual sensing of resources in the form of energy levels, and as described above, these self-assessments provide information that is useful about decisions concerning daily activities. However, in a situation that is dangerous, and in which one must act quickly, the mismatch between requirements and resources may not be sensed in those terms. Although it is logical that in the course of daily activities the sensing of feelings would come before action, and enter into the decision-making about that action, emergencies may require immediate reflex action (cf. Zajonc, 1984). Here there could be no time to judge one's resources; instead, it may be necessary to act as fully as one's body allows.

Even in emergencies, however, the sense of fear occurs rapidly, although probably not as rapidly as the defensive reflexive activity. For example, if someone jumps out at a person and frightens them, there is little time for interpretation before the defensive action and the fear occur. Yet, if a person reacts with some defensive maneuver, this must indicate that there has been some interpretation made, even if it is only a decision that it is necessary to protect oneself in case this situation is dangerous. Anything that breaks the usual pattern leads to attention, and this is followed by an initial interpretation that may result in a defensive motor act (e.g., crouching and shielding one's vital parts). The subjective experience of fear either occurs simultaneously or shortly thereafter.

If the fear-inducing situation develops more slowly, and there is time for interpretation, then it may be more obvious that the awareness of a resources-requirements imbalance is the basis of the subjective experience of tension. Since few comparative studies have been done of the interactions among a frightening stimulus, cognitive processing, feelings of fear, and skeletal-muscular defensive reactions, it is difficult to know the exact relationships involved. However, based on a logical analysis of functional utility, it would seem more important in an immediate emergency for the skeletal-muscular reaction to occur than for the feeling of fear to be registered in consciousness. In the case of a gradually developing emergency, either the feeling could occur simultaneously with the skeletal-muscular reaction, or the feeling could precede it.

The issue of awareness enters in once again for situations in which there is anxiety, tension, or nervousness, but no apparent awareness of danger. The low-level tension that many people experience under moderate stress is an example of this. Or, in clinical cases, the anxiety that is present is a signal of some sort of threat or danger, and yet the individuals experiencing these feelings may report no problem within awareness. In the present theoretical perspective, I would assume that at some level of functioning the individual's resources do not match the unavoidable requirements, and tension is the inevitable result.

The role of cognition and conscious awareness is also unclear in relation to internally generated pain. Anyone who has awakened from sleep with a tooth-ache or some other internally generated pain can testify that muscles are often tense, and immediately upon awakening there is a subjective experience of ten-sion. In addition, there may be a somewhat similar tension response some time after sugar ingestion (Thayer, 1987a). Various other kinds of systemic disrup-tions, such as food allergies (King, 1981), may also produce tension. These would seem to be noncognitive reactions in which the imbalance between resources and requirements appears to be totally outside of conscious awareness.

Even in these cases, however, cognition may play a significant part. For example, chronic pain has been found to be greater late in the day (Rogers & Vilkin, 1978) when energetic arousal is known to drop (see Chapter 4). It may not be too great a theoretical extension to suggest that the internal sensation is interpreted as pain only when one senses that because of lowered resources there is an inability to deal with the continued strong sensations. This might even account for the success of pain-reducing techniques such as hypnosis if one assumes that the hypnotic state can modify the interpretational process. In the case of the tension that occurs some time after sugar ingestion, another kind of cognitive intercession may occur (Thayer, 1987a). If the natural biological reac-tion to sugar ingestion is tiredness, as some scientists argue (e.g., Wurtman & Wurtman, 1981), then an individual not allowed to sleep and forced to continue daily activities may become tense because the low resources (indicated by tired-ness) do not match the requirements present in the individual's ongoing daily activities.

Cognitive-Affective Interactions Involving Subtle but Persistent Negative Mood States

Moods often motivate an individual to action. Strong negative moods may be more unpleasant than physical pain,[4] and avoiding them can be quite important to the person experiencing these unpleasant states. The extremes to which this can lead are readily apparent in suicide statistics.

Subtle negative moods can also motivate avoidance if they are sufficiently persistent. These motivational effects sometimes appear disproportionate to the strength of the moods involved. Subtle but persistent moods can impel one to strong action even though they are only mildly apparent in consciousness. Although there is not yet much research data to support these assertions, indirect evidence does support them.

An example of the disproportionate influence might be found in the case of a mildly anxious person who is dieting and trying not to eat tasty and longed-for foods. The person avoids these foods for a lengthy period even though a mild uneasiness is continuously present, and even though he or she knows that the anxiety could be temporarily eliminated by eating. If this low level of anxiety persists, it may at last overcome personal resolve. At a point of breakdown, the individual might gorge on otherwise unacceptable foods and give up the diet entirely. Here the mild anxiety has had a strong effect even though it would appear to be only weakly motivating.

Or consider the mildly depressed person who has been on an exercise program, thus successfully overcoming the depression. Each time that the exercise is to be carried out, however, the individual must overcome fatigue and low-level tension in order to begin. But the mild depression is chronic, and eventually it has an effect. The individual finally breaks the schedule and gives up the exercise program completely.

Still another example may be cited in the case of Premenstrual Tension Syndrome, or PMS. As indicated in the previous chapter, the evidence about moods associated with this condition is mixed, perhaps because the mood effects are very subtle. It may be true that PMS begins with a slight increase in tension that many are able to disregard, at least for a time. But the fact that this mildly uncomfortable condition is present all the time during the premenstrual period, and the fact that the individual knows it recurs month after month may eventually lead to extreme reactions of irritability, anger, or depression during this time that may appear disproportionate to the discomfort of the condition at any one moment.

The influence of subtle moods such as these is not well understood because the moods can be so easily overcome. A slightly depressed person can perform some action in any single situation, even though he or she feels little energy. Or a mildly anxious individual can withstand the anxiety with just a small amount of self-discipline. Thus, on any one occasion, a subtle negative mood can easily be overridden. In fact, the ease with which these moods can be overcome suggests that their motivational effects are trivial.

Yet these persistent moods sometimes become disproportionately influential. This probably occurs because the moods interact with cognitive influences. As these mood effects seem to be cumulative, they cannot be adequately gauged unless measurements are taken over a long period of time.

There appears to be at least three kinds of cognitive reactions that together or separately may account for the motivational process. The first possibility is one in which the mood acts as a signal or cue for stronger moods to come. In this case, at some low level of awareness the individual may notice the mood, realize that it is mild, but also seek to avoid it before it becomes stronger. In other words, action is taken to reduce the mood before it reaches unpleasant proportions. A kind of anticipatory avoidance process is the core of this behavior.

A second possibility is that at some point the individual not only recognizes the subtle mood, but also recognizes that it has been present for a long time. This case would lead to an irrational view that the unpleasant affective state can never be escaped and a kind of panic reaction may occur. The cognitive script might go something like this: "There is that feeling again. It is the same one that I have been feeling for a long time. I can't escape it. I will always have this unpleasant feeling!"

A third possibility arises from the fact that a dysphoric mood may precipitate an unwanted behavior, and awareness that this behavior has occurred results in discouragement, which subsequently leads to an even more negative mood. Breaking a diet is a good example. Once the discipline is lost that enabled the individual to avoid food, a perception of personal failure occurs (see discussions of related cognitive influences in Ruderman, 1986; Ruderman, Belzer, & Halperin, 1985; Ruderman & Wilson, 1979). The failure may be seen as one of many, and this becomes the stimulus for a much more negative mood state.

In each of the above cognitive reactions, the individual may react more extremely than is warranted by the initial mood. Possibly these reactions are due to a loss of self-efficacy (Bandura, 1986), but in any event, all these processes appear to involve beliefs that are irrational. In the first case, the beliefs are irrational because the mood probably would not become strong enough to require anticipatory avoidance. In the second case, it is unlikely that the mood would continue in its present form for the indefinite future, although a kind of state dependency makes it appear as though it would. The third process in which failure is perceived, and which in turn leads to a strong negative mood, is also likely to be unreasonable, since the transgression is often only slight and might not indicate a substantial personal failure.

An individual is probably not fully aware of these processes, as the cognitive sequence is likely to be so rapid that the individual has little sense of the dynamics involved. Moreover, tiredness, reduced energy, or heightened anxiety may be important antecedents of the shift from a subtle mood to an extreme reaction. Thus, normal inhibitory mechanisms would be reduced.

Bioevolutionary Analyses of Tense Arousal

In Chapter 3 I described tense arousal as a reaction to real or imagined danger that involves bodily preparation for physical activity, and later I theorized that it may serve as a response to unavoidable requirements that exceed bodily resources. Humans as well as most animals exhibit certain characteristic patterns of behavior when danger is imminent. One of the first reactions is attention to the danger stimulus so that its extent can be assessed. When a person is anxious or nervous—tense arousal states that denote danger of some sort—the associated response of focusing attention on the danger has often been misunderstood, because it appears that the individual is easily distracted and has a very short attention span. However, a much better interpretation is that this focused attention is an adaptive response that allows a person to continuously scan the surroundings in order to locate the problem. The purpose of these rapid fluctuations in attention would be clear if the danger were obvious, but in the case of anxiety or simple nervousness, the stimulus is often unknown. Moreover, the individual may not even be aware that any problem exists.

Another elemental response to danger is motor inhibition (cf. Gray, 1982). Such a response may well be adaptive because it enables the individual to ready him or herself for action and to minimize detection by a predator until an action decision can be made. Consider a Cro-Magnon ancestor making his way through the forest at night and back to the safety of his abode. He hears a sound that might indicate danger, but its direction and proximity is unclear. He would stop and crouch—frozen—while directing maximal attention to locating and judging the danger.

This defensive freeze response is extremely interesting, because it provides a possible understanding of the characteristic bodily reactions associated with tense arousal, even in mild form. In addition to stopping all movement in order to avoid detection, assuming this posture in the presence of imminent danger ensures maximal protection in case the danger is quite close. The characteristic crouch protects vital bodily areas; the head is slightly forward, the chin down, the neck tight, the shoulders hunched, and the arms, abdominal area, buttocks, and legs are tight as well.

Not only is this response used when a predator is nearby, but the same pattern, to a lesser extent, is characteristic of a nervous or slightly tense person. The neck, shoulders, and back are tight, and the muscles are knotted. The individual is slightly hunched forward, and facial muscles are also taut, enabling maximal attention to danger. In effect, it is a protective posture associated with the inhibitory muscular pattern that provides maximal avoidance of detection. These bodily responses may be more or less evident depending on the extent and nearness of the danger. Intense fear is associated with a clearly defined bodily response; mild nervousness or anxiety is associated with a lesser, but nonetheless characteristic, bodily response.

Viewing the danger response as an inhibitory muscular pattern provides an explanation for otherwise poorly understood aspects of mild tension, anxiety, and nervousness. For example, the tapping fingers and wiggling foot of a nervous person are slight releases of the muscular inhibition. These muscular actions occur particularly in the peripheral musculature, probably because tension there cannot be completely maintained. Nervous pacing may also represent a primitive attempt to release muscular inhibition.

Even the breathing pattern of an anxious person bespeaks inhibition. Instead of the full breathing of an athlete engaged in unrestrained physical activity, the fearful person breathes in a shallow, rapid pattern. The necessary gas exchange is accomplished with short panting breaths, indicating that the muscles surrounding the thoracic cavity are in an inhibitory pattern, as well as the rest of the musculature.[5]

The behavior that occurs together with this focused attention and skeletal-muscular inhibition is characterized by caution. The cautious individual may continue with the tasks at hand, but these tasks are accomplished more slowly and deliberately, and with a certain discontinuity of action. By observing an anxious person, one can see the residual defensive freeze pattern represented. This bodily pattern has evolved over millions of years, and although its evolutionary underpinning may not be understood, its usefulness is still evident.

These bodily patterns are not independent of subjective states. There is a continuum of moods or emotions of danger—at one extreme feelings of terror and great fearfulness, and at the other, uneasiness or slight nervousness. Anxiety, whether intense or mild, is another feeling of danger, but this emotion indicates that the object of danger is outside of awareness. Tension, the marker term that describes all of these variations of arousal, usually represents a middle state of danger. It implies not only the muscular inhibitory involvement, but also the correlated subjective state. However, all the states of tense arousal involve a characteristic skeletal-muscular and subjective interaction.

The concept of inhibition as a central characteristic of fear, anxiety, and tension appears to conflict with the long-standing biological concept of the "fight or flight" response under emergency conditions. This idea, which to some extent was suggested by McDougall (1908), was developed much more fully by Cannon (1929/1963), who argued that the various bodily changes associated with reactions to emergencies had great use. The fight or flight concept became widely accepted in popular, and to some extent in scientific, thinking. Despite its wide acceptance, certain aspects of the fight or flight response were never well supported by scientific evidence (e.g., Martin & Lacey, 1914). Cannon (1929/1963) himself recognized that fear may be "paralyzing until there is a *definite deed to perform*" (p. 198). Thus, in his view, action would be inhibited until either fighting or fleeing becomes appropriate, which would make Cannon's view of the initial response to danger, and my own view, identical.

Although Cannon's emergency theory has become widely accepted, there always were well thought out criticisms (e.g., Rogoff, 1945). After a thorough analysis of a wide variety of physiological and behavioral evidence concerning Cannon's theory, Arnold (1945) stated flatly that "fear must be enervating rather than energizing" (p. 40). Arnold's point is that fear produces caution (and inhibition) instead of unrestrained action.

In addition to the central role played by epinephrine (adrenaline) and other agents of bodily activation in emergency responses, a large part of the logic behind Cannon's fight or flight concept is that both fighting and fleeing require massive muscular exertion, all of which means there is a comparable physical response to various emergency emotions. This viewpoint is quite similar to the one outlined in this book, that both energetic and tense arousal utilize skeletal-muscular activity, one to mediate ongoing behavior, and the other to prepare the individual for whatever action may be necessary for survival (e.g., fight or flight). Furthermore, the systems of the body that participate in vigorous activation, including the general metabolic, cardiovascular, respiratory, and endocrine systems, do not show clear differentiations between energetic and tense arousal. Both kinds of arousal involve these same systems because skeletal-muscular activity is involved in either case.

But what of the acts of fight or flight? When either fighting or fleeing occurs, muscular inhibition is released. The rabbit that has crouched frozen while the fox approached suddenly darts for whatever safety can be found when the predator passes the outer perimeter of the rabbit's flight distance. Although inhibition was functional up to a point, there comes a time when any inhibition becomes dysfunctional. When fight or flight are the only means for survival, animals that persist in exhibiting inhibition would have very poor survival potential.

Although the moods that would accompany the shift from a pattern of inhibition to one of action have not been studied in the theoretical context of arousal, it seems logical that efficient emergency action in the form of fleeing or fighting would *not* be associated with fear. Since fear and other aspects of tense arousal are the feelings of caution and inhibition, another type of feeling would be associated with efficient action. When an individual is frozen, fear is consciously felt, but when action occurs, the conscious mood is subjective energy.

In the next chapter, I shall examine the relationship of the two relevant mood systems—the moods of inhibition and the moods of action. They represent quite different states of being, and they are not independent. Instead, they form a complex relationship that has a functional basis.

6

The Natural Interaction
of Energetic and Tense Moods:
A Multidimensional Arousal Model

Moods of energy and tension interact in a complex manner. Under certain conditions, increases in subjective tension are associated with increased subjective energy, but under other conditions, reduced energy occurs with heightened tension. In psychometric terms, the two mood dimensions appear to be orthogonal, but this apparent independence actually masks differing relationships between these moods at different levels of arousal. These relationships are very important, because different patterns of energy and tension are basic elements of a variety of other common mood states.

In this chapter a model is described that I believe accounts for the interactions between subjective energy and tension better than any other (Thayer, 1978b, 1985, 1986). There are several other multidimensional models of arousal, and some of these will be discussed. However, point by point comparisons are not possible, because there has been little focus on these mood interactions outside of the arousal concepts presented here.

Several parts of this model still require further experimental verification, and there are important unknowns in a number of parameters. Nevertheless, the broad theoretical outlines appear to match observations of energy and tension interactions. Furthermore, additional tests may be readily derived to evaluate its assumptions.

Because few controlled experimental studies exist that are applicable to this model, I have attempted to argue its validity from diverse kinds of formal and informal evidence. This is not fully satisfactory, but in any event, the moods under discussion are well-known and are experienced by most people on a daily basis. In the final analysis, an important test of a model such as this is its consistency with these experiences, a consistency that I hope will be apparent in the pages that follow.

Summary of Mood Interactions

A basic overview of the elements of this model may be helpful in understanding the various interactions to be discussed. The interactions of energy- and tension-related moods may be conceptualized in three patterns, which are represented in Figure 6–1. In the first of these patterns, determinants of arousal, such as perceived danger and stress, produce increased subjective tension together with a changing pattern of subjective energy. As tension increases, energy at first increases as well. But at some level of arousal, the direction of this relationship changes, and thereafter, further increases in tension are associated with decreases in energy (see Figure 6–1a). In psychometric terms, this interaction

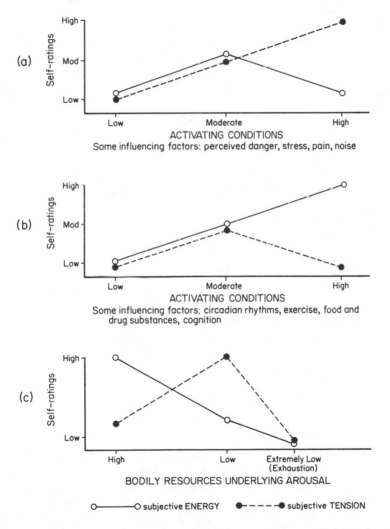

FIGURE 6–1. The complex interaction of mood states under conditions of real or imagined danger.

pattern involves a positive correlation between energetic and tense arousal from low to moderate levels, and a negative correlation from moderate to high levels.

The second pattern holds only in the case of threatening or ongoing danger conditions that directly or indirectly affect the individual. In this case, other determinants of arousal, such as circadian rhythms and exercise, first produce increased subjective energy together with increased subjective tension, but as energy increases further there is decreased tension (Figure 6–1b). In psychometric terms, the same pattern of positive correlation between energetic and tense arousal from low to moderate levels, and negative correlation from moderate to high levels, is represented here. Thus, at low levels of arousal the two moods increase and decrease together, but at higher arousal levels, an increase in one mood is associated with a decrease in the other.

Finally, the relationship between subjective energy and tension must be understood in relation to the changing bodily resources that underlie arousal. Under conditions of danger, lowered resources first result in increased tension as well as decreased energy. After a state of exhaustion occurs, however, tension decreases as well (see Figure 6–1c).

Early Experimental Evidence

The beginnings of this multidimensional model can be traced to an experiment conducted in my laboratory a number of years ago (Thayer & Moore, 1972). The findings of this research were quite serendipitous, but in retrospect they appear to have indicated remarkably well the way that moods of energy and tension interact with different levels of activating conditions.

This research involved three levels of stress, studied in an experimental design involving different groups of subjects. Stress was manipulated by instructions and setting, and feelings of energy and tension were measured by self-ratings (AD ACL scores). One hundred and sixteen male college students, randomly divided among the three stress conditions, rated their arousal before and after a verbal-learning task. The stress manipulation included variations in instructions about the importance of the experiment, and in the higher stress conditions there were admonitions to do as well as possible, with a characterization of the task as related to intelligence.[1]

As expected, experimental participants reported increasing amounts of tension at each of the three levels of manipulated stress. Because tension or anxiety are usually thought to be a reaction to stress, it would seem that the manipulations were appropriate. Since one theoretical basis for this research was the then current view of arousal as unidimensional, we expected that as the stress manipulation caused tension to increase, tiredness would decrease (and subjective energy increase) or at least remain unchanged. Such an expectation was consistent with a view of arousal as forming a single continuum that varies from low to high levels (Duffy, 1962). However, this did not occur.

As expected in the moderate stress condition, the participants rated their tiredness as less and energy greater than in the low stress condition. They were apparently energized by the moderate amount of stress. But entirely unexpected was the finding that at high levels of stress, the experimental participants reported *more* tiredness and *less* energy than was present at moderate levels (see Figure 6–2). The picture that emerged from these results was that measures of energy and tension are positively correlated from low to moderate levels, but negatively correlated from moderate to high levels.

The Covariation of Energy and Tension

The covariation of energy and tension from low to moderate stress that occurred in the experiment described above is consistent with traditional activation models. In her pioneering work on the topic, Duffy documented the wide variety of bodily systems that show a parallel response of increasing activation from diverse kinds of stimulation (Duffy, 1962, 1972). She did not view this activation as localized in the brain, but as manifested throughout the body. From Sternbach's description of the matter in his textbook on psychophysiology, it is evident that this covariation of activated systems is well-known.

> Many different situations produce rather similar activating effects. Increased muscle tension, apparent SNS activity, and EEG-desynchronization can be produced by most emotions [perhaps not depression], by mental activity, physical exercise, changes in sensations—in short by almost any *change* in conditions. In this sense activation seems to be a set of responses in the individual alerting him for whatever may come next, in the nature of a generalized preparatory act. (Sternbach, 1966, pp. 72–73)

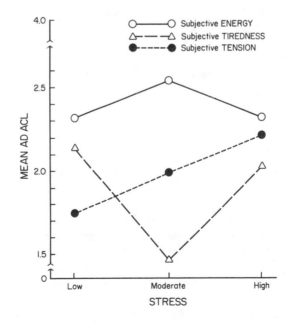

FIGURE 6–2. Mood changes as a function of three levels of stress.

Historically, general activation theories maintained that all bodily systems vary on a continuum from low to high intensity, varying with increasing personal demand (Malmo, 1959). Although there are well-conceived arguments that there are exceptions to this principle (Lacey, 1967; Neiss, 1988; Vanderwolf & Robinson, 1981), little question exists of this kind of generalized bodily response in the broader perspective of a resting individual who suddenly engages in physical activity, or who merely prepares for it. The general metabolic demands associated with gross motor activity require such a relationship. In this broader perspective of many bodily systems responding to personal demand with increasing activation, we might expect moods—subjective manifestations of bodily arousal changes—to exhibit covariation also. In other words, moods might be expected to covary in the same way that the cardiovascular and respiratory systems covary with increasing demand.

In fact, the common perception regarding moods of tension and energy probably is that these two subjective states are correlated. In my experience, people make little distinction between them. Feelings of energy are often associated with at least a slight degree of tension. Moreover, if the positive elements of anxiety are analyzed, this emotion is often regarded as a motivator (e.g., V. L. Allen, 1985; Sugarman & Freeman, 1970; Zuckerman, 1979), or at least as not debilitating. To quote one of my students writing about anxiety, "It gets one going."

Examples of this relationship are common. Consider, for instance, the following scenario representing the covariation of energy and tension. A person is relaxing and feeling mildly tired, thinking about little in the way of activity. Suddenly he recalls a previously forgotten but important deadline that is two days hence. Anxiety immediately arises, but if the deadline is two days away, the perceived danger is only moderate. The anxiety energizes the person and causes him to work steadily and productively.

Many people live their lives at these levels of tension and associated energy. In any university one can find a large percentage of students who procrastinate, who never start studying for an exam or preparing a paper until threatened failure is almost upon them. They do not seem depressed or chronically tired by their practices. Instead, the potential danger seems mildly pleasant, or at least not sufficiently unpleasant to be avoided. One might even assume that they enjoy the mood of "tense-energy" that predominates with these practices.

The concept of the Type A personality, originally conceived by Friedman and Rosenman (1974), strongly suggests this kind of tension-energy relationship. For such persons, there is never sufficient time; there is too much to do, so it is necessary to rush continually to complete well the tasks at hand. The tension within these individuals is evident in Rosenman's description of a number of characteristics of the extreme Type A individual: "He may employ a tense, teeth-clenching jaw-grinding posture. . . . He frequently sits poised on edge of chair. . . . He may squirm or move about if you talk too slowly for him or tap fingers on legs or desk with impatience." And yet, the energetic arousal of these persons is also evident in Rosenman's description of this personality type as having "a general expression of vigor and energy, alertness and confidence"

(Rosenman, 1978, pp. 55–69). Such individuals appear to exhibit simultaneously both energy and tension.

But in these various examples, only a moderate amount of tension would exist in relation to energy, and a positive correlation between measures of these moods thus could be expected. Tense-energy is the mood state that is characteristic of this interaction. The change from a positive correlation to negative occurs only when moderate levels of intensity are exceeded.

The assumption that a positive correlation exists between tense and energetic arousal implies that tension increases as conditions generating greater degrees of energetic arousal are present, just as energy increases with conditions generating tense arousal. But as I conceive of these relations, the former association does not necessarily occur. That is, subjective tension increases following an increment in subjective energy *only* in the presence of ongoing danger conditions, and this represents a limiting condition for this model.

Threat or danger can have an effect, of course, even if it is not obviously present. That is, troubling circumstances in a person's life may create chronic tension or anxiety even though there is little awareness of the dynamics.[2] In this case, increases in energetic arousal up to a moderate point might be expected to bring increases in tense arousal.

One example of this correlation often occurs in the case of diurnal rhythms of energetic arousal. In Chapter 4, such a relationship was described. Energy typically rises sharply in the first several hours after awakening, with tension also rising, but in an apparently delayed response and to a lesser degree. Thus, the positive correlation occurs between energetic and tense arousal, but tense arousal could be seen as a delayed response to energetic arousal rather than the reverse.

High Tension and Low Energy

Although there are many examples in which subjective energy and tension seem directly related, there are also examples in which a mixed pattern of low energy and high tension clearly occurs, and the negative correlation part of this model may be observed (see Figure 6–1a). Perhaps the best documented instances of these mixed arousal occurrences are with conditions of chronically high anxiety or with depression. A continuing state of high anxiety would certainly characterize high arousal, and yet the fatigue and tiredness that usually reflect low arousal states is also found in these cases. For example, in two large-scale studies of anxiety neurotics, some of the most commonly observed symptoms other than anxiety were: "tires easily," "feelings of tiredness not related to physical exertion," and "fatigued all of the time" (Miles, Barrabee, & Finesinger, 1951; Wheeler et al., 1950). These symptoms reflect both high and low arousal acting simultaneously.

Another example of this mixed arousal pattern occurs with many kinds of depression, particularly those in which motor agitation is a component part. The following is a partial listing of diagnostic characteristics for major depressive episodes as taken from DSM III, the system developed by the American Psychiatric Association (1980) and widely used to identify this malady: "insomnia or hypersomnia," "psychomotor agitation or retardation," "loss of interest or pleasure in usual activities," "loss of energy, fatigue." Once again, the high arousal condition, as evidenced by psychomotor agitation and insomnia, occurs together with low arousal, as indicated by fatigue and loss of energy.

A similar mood pattern was reflected in my own research on less severe types of depression. Two studies focused on energy and tension ratings over a number of days whenever participants felt depressed, and on control days that were as similar to the depression days as possible, but without the depression (Bassin & Thayer, 1986; Thayer & Wettler, 1975). In both of these studies, the periods of depression were associated with statistically reliable patterns of low energy and tiredness together with high tension.

Chronic anxiety states and depressive episodes are not the only conditions in which this mixed pattern occurs. Indeed, many people experience tense-tiredness daily, reflecting the associated arousal pattern. For example, in my research on diurnal cycles of university students, this pattern occurred regularly at certain times of day, especially when those students were under stress (see Chapter 4). A period of particular susceptibility was mid to late afternoon, when energetic arousal dropped but stress remained high. A similar period occurred late at night when tiredness was present, but ruminations about personal problems maintained a state of tension.

Some might argue that the tiredness present with anxiety and depression is of little significance because it is a simple matter of energy depletion that occurs with chronic anxiety. This is possible, of course, and I shall discuss the matter further when considering physiological mechanisms and biological issues. However, the theoretically important point that tension and tiredness seemingly can characterize both high and low arousal at the same time should not be overlooked. Moreover, a reasonable argument can be made that the feelings of tiredness and fatigue present with anxiety may not result from natural energy depletion, but instead may come about quite rapidly, even instantaneously, under certain circumstances.

Take, for example, a case in which a problem has been bothering a person for some time. The awareness of anxiety is present whenever the problem-related thoughts occur, but during periods when the thoughts are not present, there is an apparent absence of anxiety. When those thoughts do occur, however, not only is there a sharp increase in anxiety but also a distinct feeling of fatigue. Each time that the person thinks of the problem, the sinking feeling recurs immediately, or, put another way, a feeling of profound tiredness. These feelings may also be associated with feelings of resignation.

Another less clear, but perhaps quite relevant, example of this rapidly occurring mixture of anxiety and fatigue was recently suggested by a colleague. It concerns the dynamics of procrastination. She related to me the common experience of putting off tasks that were somewhat unpleasant while she worked quite energetically on other, secondary activities. When she finally sat down to deal with the aversive tasks, she would suddenly feel too tired to complete them. But putting them aside again, her energy for other activities would return. In this example and the previous one, the existence of low energy seems somewhat paradoxical because it often occurs without significant energy expenditure. Thus, mere thoughts about conflictual areas or unpleasant circumstances result in sudden increments of anxiety and decreased energy.

In all the examples discussed in this section, the pattern of high tension and tiredness together with low energy is a variation of the assumed negative correlation between dimensions of tense and energetic arousal. It is similar to the high stress condition in the experiment described at the beginning of this chapter (see Figure 6–2). In contrast, the examples of the previous section indicated a positive relationship between tension and energy, a relationship similar to the effects observed between low and moderate stress conditions in the first experiment.

Within the theoretical model presented here, the positive correlation between tense and energetic arousal is assumed to begin shifting to a negative correlation at moderate levels of intensity. One problem with this assumption, however, is that there is no independent measure of the "moderate" point, and so predicting exactly where the shift will occur is not easy. To make matters more complicated, the moderate point, or the place at which the positive correlation changes to negative, probably varies with the physical resources of the individual. When resources are low, the moderate point is relatively low, but as resources increase, that moderate point also increases.

It follows then that the tiredness or fatigue associated with high tension would not be present if an individual is fully rested and healthy, which would mean greater personal resources at hand. But one who is depleted of resources due to demanding activities or due to a naturally low time of day would shift from tense-energy to tense-tiredness under lesser degrees of stress. Another way of looking at this is that a young person in good physical condition who is faced with a future emergency might be energized by the requirements (tense-energy), but an older person in poor physical condition might experience tense-tiredness under those same requirements. Or, in relation to natural diurnal rhythms, the same moderate stressor might result in tense-energy in the morning and tense-tiredness in the late evening.

The point of moderate intensity is sufficiently related to individual resources that, conceivably, it might be higher or lower in relation to the perceived importance of the arousal-producing conditions (there may be stable individual differences as well, cf. Eysenck, 1967; Larsen & Diener, 1987; Strelau, 1983; Zuckerman, 1979). It is possible, for example, that a perceived emergency could result in tense-energy for a lengthy period as usually untapped resources are mobilized. The concept of "general adaptation syndrome" described by Selye (1978) in relation to chronic stress is perhaps relevant in this case.

Low Energy and Vulnerability to Tension

The assumption of a negative correlation between dimensions of energetic and tense arousal carries another important implication. Low levels of energy appear to increase vulnerability to tension, anxiety, and fearfulness. This vulnerability is readily apparent from research on sleep deprivation. Although anxiety was not the primary focus in most deprivation research, there have been a number of observations that sleep-deprived subjects grow irritable and tense, particularly in the early stages. After reviewing more than a dozen studies, Murray (1965) stated, "Sleep deprivation traditionally produces an increase in irritability; it is a classic symptom" (p. 245). And he goes on to conclude, "Anxiety occurs mostly at the beginning and is related to subject and staff concern of physical health, as well as to the existing personality of the subject."

It appears that the vulnerability to increased tension under conditions of increasing fatigue is a general biological phenomenon. In addition to sleep deprivation, the large-scale Selective Service starvation experiment conducted in 1944 (see Chapter 3) offers another example of this association of low energy to increased tension. Healthy young men deprived of normal food intake for twenty-four weeks not only reported substantially increased tiredness, but they also became increasingly anxious (Keys et al., 1950). Their tension-associated reactions were clearly apparent: "Irritability increased to the point that it became an individual and group problem. Although the men were well aware of their hyperirritability, they were not altogether able to control their emotionally charged responses; outbursts of temper and periods of sulking and pique were not uncommon" (p. 836).

The increased vulnerability to tension under conditions of tiredness is recognized in general medical practice as well. In his clinical textbook, *The Management of the Anxious Patient,* Meares (1963) makes the point that fatigue may be an early symptom of anxiety, and he also indicates that "the individual's susceptibility to anxiety is increased by fatigue" (p. 55). Meares draws an interesting distinction between fatigue caused by "nervous factors" and that brought on by purely physical expenditure. In his view, the former type of fatigue brings particular susceptibility to anxiety. This distinction could be valid, but in the present theoretical model I have adopted the more general biological conception of any energy expenditure as leading to fatigue, and therefore, to greater susceptibility to tension.

Meares also speaks of a state of apathy that develops from exhaustion. This condition of apathy was also noted by Murray (1965) in the later stages of sleep deprivation, and by Keys et al. (1950) in their descriptions of extended periods of food deprivation.

The phenomenon of low energetic arousal producing a predisposition for increased tense arousal is well known in everyday life experiences. For example, many parents of small children are aware that these young people are least patient and most irritable when tired. Increased fearfulness, one aspect of tense arousal, is also greatest when children are tired. A good illustration of this occurred once when I took my then five-year-old to Disneyland. Upon arriving in the early afternoon, she chose to go on a very fast ride, and she loved it. She took the ride several more times that day, but the last time in the evening—past her usual bedtime—the ride proved frightening. She refused to take it again until another daytime visit.

Adults also frequently experience this increased susceptibility to tension when tired. Consider the times when minor arguments and confrontations with loved ones have their greatest effect—periods of tiredness and general fatigue. Minor problems in the late afternoon, or in the evening after a hard day's work can be very tension-inducing.

High Energy and Low Tension

Under conditions of threat or potential danger it appears that there is a kind of dynamic balance between energetic and tense arousal. A change in one is associated with a similar change in the other at lower levels, and a reciprocal change at higher levels. One implication of this is that moderate to high levels of tension *decrease* as energy *increases* (see Figure 6–1b). Thus, the negative correlation between dimensions is once again represented, but in the opposite way to the cases described in the previous section.

In my view, this dynamic balance between energy and tension is most observable in relation to physical exercise. Because it is now clear that one of the major effects of exercise under many circumstances is the immediate increase in energetic arousal (see Chapter 5), this prediction about decreases in tension can be tested through observations of the effects of exercise. The current widespread interest in vigorous physical activity as a therapeutic adjunct to programs aimed at reducing anxiety and depression may be understood in the context of this relationship.

Psychotherapists who treat anxious and depressed clients put these individuals on regular exercise schedules. There is now more scientific literature supporting these prescriptions (e.g., McCann & Holmes, 1984), but a surprisingly small amount of formal research has been done on the relationships involved. This provides another example of practitioners going beyond the fully accepted scientific research and using whatever treatments appear to work.

Although systematic scientific investigations do support the idea that exercise reduces tension and anxiety, the causal association is not easy to demonstrate conclusively. The problem is that experiments concerning anxiety reduction through exercise may be criticized because of expectations held about exercise by experimental participants. Thus, it is difficult to conduct "blind" studies. Nevertheless, many experiments have been done, and thoughtful scientific reviews argue that the weight of the evidence supports the idea that exercise reduces anxiety (e.g., Folkins & Sime, 1981; deVries, 1981).

One of the most convincing series of experiments was carried out by H. A. deVries, who worked with electromyographic recordings of muscle tension as a function of exercise. In one experiment, deVries and Adams (1972) demonstrated that moderate amounts of exercise are better tension reducers than meprobamate, a tranquilizer commonly used to reduce anxiety. Subjects were given either the tranquilizer, a lactose placebo, or told to exercise by walking a treadmill, and the effect on tension of all these conditions was measured immediately after, thirty minutes after, and one hour after the substance ingestion or exercise took place. The exercise was the only treatment that showed a significant effect.

The research findings of deVries are entirely consistent with my own experiments (see Chapter 4) that, over three-week periods, employed a number of ten-minute rapid walks in relation to self-ratings of energy and tension (Thayer, 1987a, 1987b). This relatively small amount of moderate exercise resulted in statistically significant increases in energy ratings and decreases in tension ratings. As energy increased following the walks, tension immediately decreased.

Certain experiences of athletes further illustrate this relationship. One of my former students, who was a track-and-field competitor, described a highly relevant instance in this regard. He spoke of track meets where he would often observe well-conditioned athletes yawning and evidencing other signs of fatigue while they waited for their event to begin. He interpreted this behavior as anxiety-related, and thus illustrative of the inverse relation of the two kinds of arousal as described above. But once the event began, the athletes moved around vigorously, the anxiety apparently gone. Surges of energy were then the dominant subjective state.

Although the present model appears to predict accurately the anxiety-reducing effects of exercise, some important uncertainties still remain. Because low to moderate increases in energetic arousal would be associated with increases in tense arousal, it might be expected that some forms of exercise would increase rather than decrease anxiety. This may have been the case in an experiment on psychiatric hospital patients carried out by Dodson and Mullens (1969). Their experiment included jogging, light exercise, and no-exercise control conditions. As expected, jogging resulted in less tension and more alertness. But the light exercise unexpectedly resulted in more anxiety among the patients. Unfortunately, the absence of an independent measure of the moderate point, at which the relationship between energetic and tense arousal changes direction, represents a distinct uncertainty about the theoretical model. And in the case of data such as those gathered by Dodson and Mullens, it is necessary to resort to an argument that appears somewhat circular.

The apparent dynamic balance between energetic and tense arousal also seems to describe a number of effects produced by fairly well-known psychoactive drugs. I should point out that evidence for this is complex, and for the most part it was gathered from animal research. Therefore, there are obvious limitations for understanding these drug effects on moods in humans. Nevertheless, a number of psychological reactions to sedative-hypnotic drugs strongly suggests a kind of dynamic balance between two arousal systems.

For example, in their excellent review of the behavioral effects of barbiturates, Susan and Leslie Iversen (1975) describe a paradoxical activating effect of these agents, nominally classed as depressants. They stated, "In large doses barbiturates suppress ongoing behavior and induce sleep. But in small doses they increase rather than decrease behavioral output, and this facilitory effect may well be related to their value as anxiety-reducing drugs" (p. 180). They based this conclusion on a survey of the literature on animal experiments in which behaviors such as delayed response, reactions to punishment, and various kinds of discrimination tasks were studied under different dosages of barbiturates.

The Iversens also describe the potentiation effects between amphetamines (nominal stimulants) and barbiturates under certain circumstances, a finding that supports my theoretical model. In particular, the two classes of drugs potentiate each other on unconditioned and reinforced behaviors, but they have very different effects on punishment-related behaviors. For these behaviors, amphetamines intensify the effects of punishment, but barbiturates reduce these effects.

Although this apparently paradoxical facilitating effect is most pronounced with barbiturates, it has also been observed with the class of drugs often described as minor tranquilizers (Iversen & Iversen, 1975). The effects of the benzodiazepines, of which the best-known prescription drug is Valium, at least superficially resemble the effects of stimulants at certain dosage levels. Because this drug is so widely used in the United States and worldwide, its mood-altering properties are well known. This shift in the dynamic balance is probably the basis of Valium users reporting "high" feelings as the tension remits.

The apparently paradoxical activating effects of many depressant drugs has been widely observed with alcohol (cf. Hull & Bond, 1986). While this drug is usually classed as a CNS depressant, it is clear that many people are activated by it, particularly in small amounts and in the preliminary stages of intoxication. At the beginning of a party, one can often observe animated and energetic behavior following the initial imbibing of alcoholic drinks. Although this is not necessarily the case (Goodwin, 1977), these activating effects are often attributed to the depression of "higher centers" of the brain, thus releasing inhibitions. This popular explanation is entirely consistent with the concept of a dynamic balance between energetic and tense arousal. The "inhibitions" in this case would be mediated by tense arousal, and their elimination represents a reduction of this kind of arousal.

Still another seemingly paradoxical effect concerning an arousal-related drug and behavior may be cited as possible evidence for the model. It concerns effective treatment of hyperactivity in children, or, as it is now often labeled, Attention Deficit Disorder. Hyperactive children appear to exhibit high levels of tension. They are often overly active, restless, and fidgety. But frequently, these young people can be helped with amphetamines and other stimulants, a perplexing phenomenon (Rosenthal & Allen, 1978). How is it possible to calm down a seemingly overaroused young person with a drug that increases arousal? But if one assumes a dynamic balance between tense and energetic arousal, a plausible explanation might be that aphetamines increase energetic arousal, and thus the tension of the hyperactivity is reduced.

As I shall argue in Chapter 8, this apparent dynamic balance between energy and tension may well account for some of the druglike effects of sugar ingestion (Thayer, 1987a). That is, sugar may often be sought as a tension-reducer as well as a temporary stimulant. This is in addition to, and perhaps as underlying, the effects of taste. Other common drugs of choice, such as caffeine and tobacco, may also temporarily affect this dynamic balance.

One last example occurs in the case of stress management. Selye, the progenitor of many leading ideas in this area, originally employed forced exercise as a stressor in his studies of resulting physiological effects (Selye, 1956). But today we find that exercise programs are almost always employed, not as stressors, but as useful aspects of stress management. Of course, the key here is the amount of exercise. Many kinds of exercise regimes lead to enhanced energy, subsequently reducing tension-associated stress. This effect of exercise to increase one kind of arousal at the same time it reduces another kind of arousal is an example of the dynamic balance between energy and tension.

Exhaustion

The theoretical model that includes direct and inverse relations of energy and tension also accounts for one other significant mood variation. It appears that fatigue and declining energy predispose an individual to increased tension only up to a point. When physical resources decline sufficiently, a state of exhaustion occurs, and the otherwise high degree of subjective tension sharply declines (see Figure 6–1c).

The mood state that develops from this decline has been described variously as apathy, depression (but not in the psychomedical sense), or reduced affective response. This state appears to be a predictable biological reaction to diminished physical resources. The feelings associated with exhaustion are quite important theoretically because they strongly suggest the relationship between elemental moods and metabolic state.

The mood of exhaustion is clearly evident from reading accounts of starvation (nonexperimentally induced) in the Russian famine of 1918–22, the World War II civilian and prisoner experiences, and accounts of severe privation by isolated individuals (see literature review in Keys et al., 1950). Before becoming exhausted, these persons often went through an interim phase characterized by irritability and increased anxiety, perhaps associated with actions to relieve the problem. This, in turn, was followed by a pervasive apathy. In this state there was reduced responsiveness to stimulation, even painful stimulation. Behavior appeared listless, and there was little affective variation.

Conditions leading to this state appear to create a decline in energetic arousal. In my view, the interim phase of irritability and increased anxiety represents the negative correlation described between tension and energy. And when the last phase of apathy occurs, energetic arousal is at an extremely low point and a distinct depression of subjective tension occurs. In this last condition, the individual attempts to conserve resources (probably nonconsciously), and thus limit the energy expenditure that may occur with emotional expression or active resistance to environmental stressors.

There are many recorded examples of this decline in energy and the subsequent state of apathy. Consider, for instance, an incident related by Bettelheim (1943) that occurred during his internment in Buchenwald, a German concentration camp. He writes that prisoners were already severely stressed by malnutrition, hard labor, and freezing temperatures. On one occasion, a group of prisoners who had worked more than twelve hours with little food were forced to stand exposed to freezing temperatures all night. Many of them collapsed and died. Toward the end of this incident, an "utter indifference swept the prisoners. . . . They did not care whether the guards shot them; they were indifferent to acts of torture committed by the guards" (p. 434). This state is described often in the accounts of horrific experiences in concentration camps. And we see it once again in the psychiatric interviews of U.S. prisoners of war repatriated in 1953 (Strassman, Thaler, & Schein, 1956). The investigators of these prisoners describe the major condition as apathy.

Although these prolonged and extreme environmental stressors produce chronic states of apathy, a similar state can be observed in the exhaustion produced under less lethal circumstances. For instance, apathy developed in subjects in the controlled semistarvation studies carried out in Minnesota (Keys et al., 1950), and it was also observed in a variety of sleep-deprivation experiments. Kleitman (1963) writes, for example, of the tendency of sleep-deprived subjects to have decreased responsiveness to pain or other types of stimulation. Murray's (1965) summary of sleep-deprivation studies emphasizes the "decline of activity, talkativeness, and sociability," and a "narrowing of interests." He writes, "Energy is conserved, fatigue reduced, and hostile conflict is avoided by a modulation of affect" (p. 216).

A similar mood state appears to occur occasionally in everyday life circumstances. This state is not only produced by the types of severe stress described above, but it may be observed on those occasions when there has been sleep loss over an extended period, or when high psychological stress has occurred, usually for a lengthy time. It is also likely that this exhaustion-related mood follows lengthy and extended physical expenditures such as sometimes occur for mountain climbers and backpackers.[3] This exhaustion may appear episodically at certain times in the diurnal cycle (see Chapter 4), such as late in the waking day.

In my view, three kinds of anecdotal examples illustrate this mood particularly well. In the first one, a friend was experiencing a serious internal infection that dragged on for days, with alternate periods of near death followed by temporary remission. In the times of near death she was conscious, but her mood was one of apparent equanimity. She seemed to care little about her fate, a state faintly reminiscent of the prisoner example related by Bettelheim. Notably, however, on the occasions when she slightly recovered her strength, she felt anxious about her condition and about the possibility that she might not survive. Thus, with partial recovery, she experienced tense-tiredness, but as the condition periodically worsened, she experienced the calmness associated with exhaustion.

The second example occurred with a faculty member at my university. He was preparing a report for a meeting in which he expected a considerable amount of acrimony and even personal attack. Because of this project and his other work, he got very little sleep for over two weeks. As the day of the most important public presentation approached, he found himself increasingly tense, and the night before the event he got very little sleep. When he arose on the final day he was exhausted, but a strange mixture of calmness and imperturbability was present. In the meeting there were emotional outbursts by some and many hostile questions, but he handled them without affective response. His mood, which might have appeared apathetic, could be described as quite pleasant in the sense that the previous concerns were absent. One distinct subjective characteristic was the seemingly total absence of anxiety and tension.

Similar kinds of reduced responsiveness, together with an absence of tension, seem to be present after lengthy and physically demanding backpacking trips. At the end of a long and taxing hike, the usual concerns about snakes, bugs, and fastidious eating conditions seem to be totally absent. If there are unpleasant insects on food, they are casually brushed aside, and people with mild snake phobias react nonchalantly to a nearby reptile. It appears that the energy expended on the hike reduces the amount of energy available to expend on minor fears and anxieties. Once again, there is an apparent depression of subjective tension at very low levels of energetic arousal.

Selected Physiological Mechanisms

The literature reviewed in Chapter 2 makes clear that there is a physiological underpinning to mood—particularly psychopathological mood states. Exactly what constitutes this substrate and how it functions is still unclear, however. Although a detailed analysis of the anatomy and physiology that could underlie the arousal interactions is outside the scope of this book, several relevant lines of thought will be briefly mentioned.

The evidence for the covariation of multiple psychophysiological systems from low to moderate levels is fairly well established, at least for limited degrees of arousal. There is no clear indication, however, of what physiological mechanisms underlie the relationship in which moderate to high levels of tense arousal are associated with reduced energetic arousal, or in which increased energetic arousal is associated with reduced tense arousal. In this section, therefore, I will discuss several possible physiological bases for this inverse relationship.

In general, at least two kinds of processes should be considered. The inverse relationship may be mediated by the central nervous system, or it may be determined by more peripheral metabolic mechanisms. And of course, some combination of the two is possible. If a sharp rise in tension results in an immediate drop in energy, or if energy increments are immediately followed by tension reduction, the rapidity of the response suggests some sort of brain reaction is involved in the process. On the other hand, if the effects of arousal occur within minutes or more after the stimulus, then general metabolic processes might be implicated.

First, let us briefly consider central mediation. The brain processes that might mediate mood are quite complex and largely unknown. However, one relevant and widely cited dual arousal model was presented some years ago by Routtenberg (1968), who reviewed the substantial body of evidence for the reciprocal interaction of functions associated with the reticular activating system and those associated with the limbic system. Although the brain functions that

Routtenberg focused on were not completely identical with the assumed functions of energetic and tense arousal, there is overlap, and in any event the demonstration of reciprocal interactions between the brain systems is of interest for this discussion.

There is some difference of opinion on the matter (cf. Carlson, 1986), but the reticular activating system is widely assumed to mediate general bodily arousal (Moruzzi & Magoun, 1949; Mountcastle, 1980), particularly psychomotor activity and sleep-wake patterns (Kalat, 1984). Because energetic arousal is thought to mediate these same functions, the reticular activating system must be seriously considered as the neural underpinning of these moods, or at least as playing a central role in the mediation.

The most obvious mediator of tense arousal, on the other hand, would probably be the limbic system (MacLean, 1949, 1970; Papez, 1937), based on the substantial amount of evidence identifying this general system with emotion and emotional expression (see also Buck, 1984; Carpenter & Gruen, 1978; Plutchik, 1980). Tension, anxiety, and fear—the main characteristics of tense arousal—are widely assumed to be mediated by structures in the limbic system.

Although Routtenberg's theory of the reticular and limbic systems interacting dynamically offers a strong theoretical basis for what constitutes the neural substrate of energetic and tense arousal, several other dynamic oppositional systems have been suggested, each with a slightly different neural underpinning. For different reasons, each set of brain systems could mediate energetic and tense arousal. It may be possible, for example, that the primary mediators lie mainly within the limbic system (cf. Gray, 1975; McGuinness & Pribram, 1980; Pribram & McGuinness, 1975), or the opposing feelings could be related to lateralized cerebral cortical functions. In the latter regard, two interesting theories were recently proposed by Fox and Davidson (1984), and by Tucker and Williamson (1984). These theories offer plausible evidence that opposing negative and positive, or depression and elation, moods are lateralized by the two hemispheres of the cerebral cortex.

The increasing evidence linking brain chemistry and mood provides further support for the role of central mediation in the two systems of arousal. Unfortunately, the more that is known, the more complex this science becomes (Panksepp, 1986). It is evident that certain neurotransmitter systems, in particular those involving norepinephrine, dopamine, and serotonin, are related to arousal and sleep (Carlson, 1986; Kalat, 1984; Panksepp, 1986). Moreover, noradrenergic agonists such as amphetamine clearly produce arousal, and the catecholamine and indolamine systems have been hypothesized as playing a central part in affective disorders (Bunney & Davis, 1965; Schildkraut, 1965; van Praag, 1978). These psychopathologies probably involve some sort of imbalance of energetic and tense arousal (Bassin & Thayer, 1986; Thayer & Wettler, 1975). Finally, studies of the pharmacologic actions of various anti-anxiety agents have implicated these neurotransmitters (Sepinwall & Cook, 1978).

There is intriguing evidence of an oppositional relationship between norepinephrine and dopamine that bears further examination in relation to energetic and tense arousal interactions. Antelman and his associates (Antelman & Caggiula, 1977; Antelman & Chiodo, 1984) have presented a good deal of support for the theory that norepinephrine exerts a modulatory effect on dopamine, especially during stressful situations. If one takes gross motor activity as the marker of energetic arousal, there is a strong possibility that the energetic arousal system has an important dopaminergic underpinning (Mason, 1984). There is also some evidence that the noradrenergic system may mediate anxiety (Redmond & Huang, 1979) and thus may be a major neurochemical substrate of tense arousal. This possible interaction bears further investigation.

Neuropeptides, in particular the enkephalins and endorphins, may very well be associated with the exhaustion stage described in the present model of tense and energetic arousal.[4] The analgesic effects of these endogenous opioids have been well established by research in the past decade (Carlson, 1986; Iversen, Iversen, & Snyder, 1983). These effects may be the bases of the high thresholds to pain that are apparent in the apathy associated with sleep and other kinds of severe deprivation.

The reciprocal relationship between energetic and tense arousal may be explained in another way. First, it should be noted that an obvious explanation for the fact that high tension produces low energy is that the substantial energy expenditure associated with tension would naturally result in fatigue. But this does not adequately explain other elements of the model, such as the fact that the tension and tiredness generated by danger are often relieved by moderate exercise. It follows that exercise, which clearly involves an energy expenditure, could not reduce tension and fatigue if these states were only produced by an excessive amount of energy expenditure. There is, however, a mechanism associated with skeletal-muscular tension, a central component of tense arousal, that could possibly account for the observed relationship. I stated previously that fear, anxiety, and tension are characterized by muscle tension with an absence of directed motor activity. In addition, respiration is shallow and uneven. This picture of muscle strain and inadequate oxygen consumption is suggestive of a process that physiologists call anaerobic energy metabolism.

This metabolic process occurs when an individual engages in rapid, emergencylike actions, such as running up two flights of stairs as fast as possible or making a fifty-yard dash at top speed (de Vries, 1986; Lamb, 1984; Shephard, 1982). It is also involved in isometric tension exercises, as when muscles are held as tightly as possible for a minute or so. The latter example suggests a kind of muscle tension, particularly for certain muscle groups in the shoulders, neck, and back, that may be similar to what occurs at high levels of tense arousal.

At the physiological level, anaerobic metabolism, which breaks down energy stored in tissue as quickly as possible to supply the muscles, results in rapid increases in lactic acid and some reduction in basic energy supplies (e.g., creatine phosphate and glycogen). At the psychological level, it results in subjective fatigue fairly quickly, but not immediately. The exact physiological basis for this fatigue is not clear, but it probably occurs because this type of metabolism operates without oxygen and is a very inefficient energy supply system. The increases in lactic acid are particularly noteworthy due to the association of blood lactate with symptoms of anxiety (Pitts & Allen, 1982; Pitts & McClure, 1967).

Thus, the anaerobic processes that may be associated with skeletal-muscular tension—characterized by an uneven breathing pattern producing an oxygen deficiency, rapidly occurring fatigue, and increased lactic acid formation—suggest tense arousal. Using this metabolic process to explain the fatigue associated with tension is particularly attractive because it also possibly accounts for the effect of exercise in reducing tension. The mechanism for this is a second kind of energy metabolism—aerobic metabolism.

As opposed to the anaerobic energy supply system, the aerobic metabolism is much more efficient (deVries, 1986; Lamb, 1984; Shephard, 1982). It utilizes oxygen and can draw upon a wide base of carbohydrate, fat, and protein sources. Although anaerobic metabolism can produce a large amount of energy rapidly, as might be necessary in an emergency, the energy supply cannot be sustained, possibly due to excess lactic acid accumulation in the muscles. Aerobic metabolism, on the other hand, is a slower supply system, but it can efficiently break down the acidic by-products of the anaerobic activities as well as utilize wider sources of energy, which may account for the increased feelings of energy that result from moderate exercise.

Using these two metabolic processes to explain the reciprocal relationship between energetic and tense arousal seems valid intuitively, but there are problems with this explanation as well. First, anaerobic metabolism is usually associated with short-term maximal exercise. There has been little investigation of this metabolic process in relation to low-level tension of the sort associated with anxiety. Moreover, it may be possible to account for a number of the phenomena discussed above by increased epinephrine and not necessarily by increased skeletal-muscular isometric tension. Nevertheless, the metabolic process explanation remains promising.

Even if anaerobic versus aerobic metabolic processes cannot account for the critical interactions under discussion, focusing on skeletal-muscular tension as a key physiological element of tense arousal may still be quite valid. It is possible that at the peripheral level the bodily state associated with tense arousal differs from energetic arousal primarily because of skeletal-muscular tension. Thus, the distinctive subjective components of tense arousal (e.g., feelings of fear, anxiety, and tension) may in part be conditioned reactions to physiological arousal states associated with danger in which skeletal-muscular tension acts as the signal system. Of course, even though skeletal-muscular tension may be a key component, a variety of evidence from brain research (see above) suggests that the differences between energetic and tense arousal do not occur only at the peripheral level. But there could be limbic system processes that produce skeletal-muscular inhibition as well as other general arousal reactions in times of danger, and that reduce inhibition as the danger passes.

This is quite speculative, but there is a pharmacological model that accounts for the dissociation of different peripheral physiological systems and their possible effects on feelings of energy and tension. This model is based on the effects of the well-known drug nicotine (Domino, 1973; Gilbert, 1979). Nicotine causes bodily arousal, including a generalized cardiovascular effect. For example, smoking one cigarette raises a resting heart rate from five to forty beats per minute. However, nicotine also results in reduced skeletal-muscular tension. Thus, a tense person smoking a cigarette experiences both activation and deactivation in different bodily systems. The effects on mood of this drug will be discussed more fully in Chapter 8, but suffice it to say here that smoking may temporarily energize a person and at the same time reduce tension, an effect quite similar to the assumed reciprocal relationship between energetic and tense arousal.

Mood and Biology

Most of the ideas in this section were presented in the first several chapters, but let me summarize them here in relation to the multidimensional model under discussion. The position taken in this book is that moods are naturally occurring signal systems of underlying bodily processes; they are not disembodied subjective states with no biological function. In a general sense, the moods of energy and tension provide useful information about the most elemental states of being. They indicate readiness for activity, or the need for rest and recuperation; they warn of danger, or they provide indications of safety. The model under discussion involves a kind of multilevel systems approach in which there exists something like a monitoring and decision-making level. Furthermore, I assume that the information provided by the sensing of arousal levels may be useful for long-term planning or at least for social communication.

Adaptive needs would probably be served by an elemental arousal system that mediates appetitive behaviors of all sorts, particularly those involving gross voluntary motor activity and affected by sleep-wake diurnal cycles. In fact, this arousal system may be so integrally tied to gross voluntary motor activity that it should be viewed as more than just an appetitive system. It may be viewed as an action system.

But threats to survival also require attention, and in many cases a different kind of physical reaction. Therefore, it may have been evolutionarily useful for a second type of arousal to be activated during these emergency situations. This system may be regarded as mediating arousal plus inhibition. In a certain respect, the two systems interacting represent stop-and-go, or excitation and inhibition, functions.

This complex interaction could be explained in the following way. A distal threat requires attention and caution, but ongoing appetitive behaviors are still appropriate, including gross motor activity. In fact, these behaviors may be hastened so as to be completed more quickly in the presence of potential danger. A proximal threat, on the other hand, requires temporary suspension of all appetitive behaviors so the danger can be dealt with, and it often necessitates that the individual stop and evaluate the danger and bodily resources. However, at some point it may be necessary to overcome inhibition so that unrestrained action can occur. Finally, in the event of severe long-lasting threat, it may be necessary to overcome inhibitions associated with threat and anxiety and to re-engage appetitive behaviors sufficiently for basic survival.

These ideas could be the bases of the interactions between mood systems described in the multidimensional model. In the presence of danger, a mood prevails that can be variously described as anxiety, tension, or fearfulness. An individual experiencing this mood is alerted that something is wrong, and the mood predisposes vigilance, caution, and physiological preparation for action should it be necessary. The mood that predisposes ongoing or appetitive activities is also affected in a complex way.

Thus, low to moderate degrees of threat not only raise tension as an indication of danger, but they also raise energy so as to complete necessary tasks with facility. For this distal threat, ongoing and appetitive behaviors continue as before, but they are hastened. This represents the assumed positive correlation between energetic and tense arousal from low to moderate levels of intensity.

But it is clear that at some point, increases in tension are no longer associated with increasing energy. Instead, the opposite relationship occurs. This may be understood in relation to increasing danger requiring suspension of ongoing appetitive behaviors to deal with the threat. In these cases, it is best for the individual to wait until the threat can be evaluated. At this point, the dominant mood is anxiety or tension combined with reduced subjective energy; tension is the signal to prepare for action, but reduced energy is a signal to stop ongoing motor activity.

The above relationship between moods shows a negative correlation from moderate to high levels of intensity. The opposite configuration of heightened energy and lowered tension would occur in the event of a requirement for fight or flight. In this case, survival would be enhanced by uninhibited action.

Within the model under consideration, the last set of relations between moods occurs following exhaustion. This extreme state of depleted resources threatens survival itself, and so the arousal systems must predispose self-preservative behaviors. Thus, the tension that occurs with less severe tiredness would be absent following extreme exhaustion, because tension predisposes physiological preparation to action, and this is antithetical to needed rest and recuperation. Such a set of relations is necessary because sleep, reduced or prevented by tension, must occur when exhaustion is present or the individual will perish. With exhaustion, therefore, we find reduced responsiveness to stimulation, heightened pain thresholds, and restricted affective response. Not only is energetic arousal extremely low, but subjective tension is absent so that the necessary rest or sleep can occur.[5]

Other Arousal Models in Comparison

To fully understand the present model, it is useful to consider it in relation to the arousal concepts included in other models. A number of different conceptualizations might be chosen for this discussion, but the four below include assumptions that provide significant comparisons with the central concepts described in this chapter. My emphasis here is not on complete summaries and evaluations of these alternative models, but instead on the significant points of comparison.

H. J. Eysenck

Eysenck's arousal model is the most widely researched of any of the multidimensional conceptualizations (Eysenck, 1967; Eysenck & Eysenck, 1985). The three dimensions of this model were primarily determined by questionnaire data, but subsequently they have been the subject of extensive experimental research. Only two of these dimensions, extraversion and neuroticism, are discussed here because they bear the greatest relevance to concepts of arousal. The two dimensions, or types, as Eysenck calls them, are really psychophysiological systems, with assumed neural underpinnings and psychological manifestations.

Compared to extraverts, introverts are thought to have chronically high levels of cortical arousal, a condition affected primarily by the reticular activating system. This, in turn, results in tendencies for the two kinds of personality to seek out or avoid stimulation in order to maintain optimal levels. The second personality dimension includes neurotics or highly emotional types as compared to low emotionality counterparts. Neuroticism is associated with reactivity of the limbic system, and its related physiological reactions can often be seen in higher levels of autonomic activation.

Although the two arousal systems (named arousal and activation) are clearly interrelated, Eysenck has focused little on their interaction. He regards them as partially independent except under conditions of extreme emotion (e.g., war, severe stress, etc.) or in the case of highly emotional people. In the latter circumstances, arousal and activation are equivalent (Eysenck, 1967, p. 233). Although Eysenck's types appear similar to the two arousal dimensions discussed extensively in this book, his proposed pattern of interaction is different from the complex pattern described in my model.

This difference in interaction patterns may be due to what psychologists have called a trait versus state orientation. Although Eysenck utilizes such variables characterizing state as arousal and activation, his main concepts center around the types or traits of extraversion and neuroticism, and the arousal interactions within each type. As part of the Eysenck model, the assumed differences in cortical arousal and in autonomic activation exist as semipermanent personality dispositions that are probably determined by hereditary factors (Eaves et al., 1988). In comparison, energetic and tense arousal are clearly state variables, and the theoretical analyses of these systems involve quite transitory processes and reactions. Even the less transitory biological cycles associated with energy and tension change fairly frequently with natural bodily variations.

The fact that Eysenck's dimensions of activation and arousal are thought to be mediated by the limbic and reticular activating systems suggests a parallel with the systems of energetic and tense arousal because of my supposition of a similar anatomical mediation. This similarity could arise because the interactions of energetic and tense arousal are affected to some extent by the more general personality dispositions of neuroticism and extraversion. For example, there is evidence that neurotics, as defined by Eysenck, have a greater tendency toward tense arousal than low neurotic counterparts. An examination of questionnaire items (e.g., self-identification as a nervous or irritable type) readily demonstrates this point, and in addition, studies have shown a substantial correlation between well-known anxiety measures and neuroticism (Eysenck & Eysenck, 1985, p. 210). A study from my laboratory verifies this point. In that study, neuroticism correlated significantly with tense arousal as rated at hourly periods over six days (Thayer, Takahashi & Pauli, 1988).

Although this evidence of reactivity to tense arousal among neurotics is somewhat persuasive, there is mixed evidence about the relationship between energetic arousal and extraversion, as might occur if the two models were symmetrical. As evidence in support of symmetry, Eysenck assumes that introverts have chronically higher levels of cortical arousal than extraverts, and in the study from my laboratory mentioned above, introverts in fact reported more energetic arousal over six-day periods than extraverts (Thayer et al., 1988). But these differences were small and not statistically significant.

But there is also conflicting evidence about symmetry between the two models. In another study from my laboratory, extraverts experienced greater amounts of energetic arousal following moderate exercise than introverts (Thayer et al., 1987). Moreover, it is known that extraverts prefer physical activity more than introverts (Eysenck & Eysenck, 1965; Furnham, 1981), and as we have seen in Chapter 5, gross voluntary motor activity is one of the major determinants of energetic arousal. Introverts could have greater reactivity to energetic arousal, of course, because it is possible that extraverts have learned to utilize physical activity as a means of most efficiently raising arousal to preferred levels.

J. A. Gray

Although Gray's (1975, 1982) multidimensional model has points of great similarity to Eysenck's model, there are differences in Gray's conception of arousal, and these yield interesting comparisons with energetic and tense arousal. Gray has argued for the existence of two semipermanent personality dimensions, impulsivity and anxiety, that rotate 45 degrees in psychometric space from Eysenck's comparable dimensions. In my view, the latter differences favor Eysenck's interpretation (cf. Zuckerman, Kuhlman, & Camac, 1988), although there is evidence to contradict this opinion (see, for example, Gray, 1982; Revelle et al., 1980). However, it appears that Gray's model differs significantly from Eysenck's on another basis, and it is here that important comparisons can be made with the model under discussion in this chapter.

Although Gray often argues that his model is based on traits, as is Eysenck's, a careful analysis leads to the conclusion that Gray's model is most powerful as an indication of state functions. Gray proposes two oppositional brain systems that are associated with reward and punishment, and a third arousal system that interacts with the two. In an excellent review, Fowles (1980) points out that Gray's system actually involves elements of three kinds of arousal. In particular, Gray has made an extensive analysis of ongoing reward-seeking behaviors in relation to behaviors associated with anxiety and inhibition, which appear to have the greatest similarity with the energetic and tense arousal systems. Gray's reward-seeking, or appetitive, system mediates ongoing behavior, just as energetic arousal is assumed to do. And his behavioral inhibition system can produce increases in arousal together with reduced motor behavior, just as tense arousal is assumed to do (see Chapter 5).

With the exception of Gray's analyses of anxiety as a basis of personality types, very little of his work concerns human feelings and moods. Instead, most of his research has involved animals. Thus, the effects of anti-anxiety drugs on animal reward-seeking and response inhibition—a major basis of his theoretical analyses—has limited usefulness for interpreting mood, and thus it is difficult to make good comparisons.

Notwithstanding these limitations, it is apparent that Gray's behavioral inhibition system has substantial parallels with tense arousal. In addition, his appetitive system has some parallels with energetic arousal. Finally, Gray's two systems in interaction bear a strong resemblance to the dynamic balance assumed between energetic and tense arousal from moderate to high levels. It is unclear, however, if Gray's model has any parallels with the direct relationship between energetic and tense arousal from low to moderate levels, or with the mood phenomena of the exhaustion stage, as postulated in the model presented in this book.

G. Mandler

The theory of emotion proposed by Mandler includes a combination of traditional activation or arousal theory and a sophisticated version of cognitive psychology (Mandler, 1975, 1984). His ideas appear to derive in part from the pioneering concepts of Miller, Galanter, and Pribram (1960) concerning hierarchically organized plans and feedback loops, and from the theory of Schachter (1964) about nonspecific arousal interacting with cognitive interpretation. For Mandler, emotions and moods are combinations of "arousal and meaning analysis." Consistent with this idea, he dissects the conscious awareness of emotion, which he sees as the joint product of arousal and evaluative cognitions.

Arousal varies on a single dimension, in Mandler's view, and it is defined entirely in terms of autonomic nervous system functioning. It serves as both an activator of certain action patterns and as a kind of signal system for evaluating situations requiring choices and actions. The way that Mandler (1984) perceives the subtle interplay of autonomic arousal and cognition is apparent in the following: "One particular set of cognitive and environmental conditions that turns arousal into anxiety is a general state of helplessness, or the unavailability of task- or situation-relevant plans or actions" (p. 244).

Mandler's theory is similar to the model presented in this book in a number of ways. There is obvious overlap between his concept of autonomic arousal as a signal system and the ideas presented in this chapter and previous ones about arousal-related moods as indicators of important bodily states. However, the specific signals that autonomic arousal conveys, in his view, are not necessarily the same as the information about personal resources and danger provided by energy- and tension-related moods. For example, the way that feelings of energy convey subtle indications of self-efficacy or that tiredness indicates the need for rest and recuperation have no obvious parallel in Mandler's work. However, the idea that danger often represents a cognitive interpretation that precedes arousal is similar to Mandler's theory (cf. Lazarus, 1966).

Mandler's conception of nonspecific arousal as an activator of certain action tendencies is similar to the model presented in this book. But an important difference is that energetic and tense arousal represent two dimensions, while Mandler assumes only one. His assumption that arousal is a function only of autonomic nervous system reaction provides no parallel to the danger-related arousal plus inhibition that integrally involves skeletal-muscular reactions. Finally, there is no equivalent in Mandler's model to the complex interaction pattern assumed herein regarding energetic and tense arousal.

D. Watson and A. Tellegen

Recently, Watson and Tellegen (1985) reanalyzed a number of different psychometric studies of mood. They then presented an excellent analysis of a number of different mood studies resulting in what they called the consensual structure. Since mood is a central topic of this book, it is perhaps appropriate to consider their analysis of this structure at this point, even if it does not represent an original arousal model per se.

These two investigators correlated six extensive self-report studies of mood. They then factor analyzed each and found substantial overlap. Finally, they compared factors based on corresponding verbal descriptors from the various studies, and again there was a great deal of similarity across studies. Since the six analyses employed a wide variety of mood descriptors, this reanalysis represented a consensus across studies of the psychometric dimensionality of mood.

The result of this research was a two-dimensional model that included in the first dimension such descriptors as: active, elated, enthusiastic, excited, peppy, strong; and on the opposite pole, drowsy, dull, sleepy, and sluggish. The second dimension included: distressed, fearful, hostile, jittery, nervous, scornful; and on the opposite pole, at rest, calm, placid, and relaxed (Watson & Tellegen, 1985, p. 221). Because of the hedonic colorings of the words included in the two dimensions, Watson and Tellegen chose to call the two dimensions positive and negative affect.

It is not surprising that Watson and Tellegen's two dimensions largely overlap with the model of energetic and tense arousal presented in this book, because these investigators used early research on the AD ACL (see Chapter 3) as a major part of their analysis. At the same time, it is useful to note that the two-dimensional analysis presented here, and based to a large extent on AD ACL research, is consistent with other independent investigations of mood (see Borgatta, 1961; Hendrick & Lilly, 1970; Lebo & Nesselroade, 1978; McNair, Lorr, & Droppleman, 1971; Russell & Ridgeway, 1983).

A difference between Watson and Tellegen's conclusions and those of the present model concerns the labels given to these dimensions. Inevitably, this is a somewhat arbitrary process based on the apparent meaning of the various descriptors included in the emerging factors. Should these dimensions be called positive and negative affect or energetic and tense arousal? Clearly the two dimensions do possess positive and negative affective tone (see additional discussion in Thayer, 1986), and at least to some extent, both sets of labels are correct. But are positive and negative affective tone the central defining characteristics of these dimensions rather than energetic and tense arousal? Or is it possible that both sets of labels apply equally well, but that they concern different aspects of biopsychological functioning? These are questions for which answers are not available at the present time. For now, however, I believe in the suitability of energetic and tense arousal as labels.

Perhaps a more important difference between Watson and Tellegen's analysis and the analysis leading to the present model is the assumed relationship between the two dimensions. For these two investigators, the dimensions labeled positive and negative affect are thought to be orthogonal. In comparison, I have hypothesized a relationship between energetic and tense arousal that *appears* to be orthogonal, but actually is a complex mixture of positive and negative correlations at different levels of intensity.

Summary of a Multidimensional Arousal Model

The multidimensional arousal model featured in this book includes two biopsychological systems that interact in a complex manner. These systems are assumed to have biological underpinnings and to be mediated by neurophysiological and neurochemical substrates. However, the greatest amount of evidence is psychological, and indeed the systems are named for their subjective manifestations. Thus, energetic and tense arousal are descriptive terms that denote feelings and mood states. The best evidence for this model comes from observing these subjective states in naturally occurring variations.

Energetic arousal appears to be a general appetitive or action system that also has an important signal function for self-monitoring and decision-making. It is most readily identifiable through feelings that range from energy, vigor, and liveliness to states of fatigue and tiredness. Variations in this system are readily observable in relation to diurnal (circadian) cycles, gross voluntary motor activity (e.g., exercise), ingestion of basic food substances (also psychoactive drugs), and sleep. Physical conditioning and health obviously affect energy and tiredness. Also, there are powerful cognitive influences on energetic arousal. Finally, tension affects energetic arousal in a complex way.

The second hypothesized system, tense arousal, appears to be activated by danger, real or imagined. Generally, this system depends on a strong cognitive link between the danger stimulus and the biopsychological reaction. Its immediate manifestations are feelings of tension, anxiety, or fearfulness on one extreme, and calmness or quietness on the other. Tense arousal is a kind of preparatory-emergency system that facilitates the most efficient way to evaluate the danger and the preferred methods for meeting it. Behaviorally, tense arousal is associated with danger-responsive attention patterns and skeletal-muscular tension. This muscular tension appears to produce a kind of inhibitory behavior pattern that optimizes avoidance of the potential danger in conjunction with preparation for emergency action. But the emergency action itself (e.g., fight or flight) may be affected by energetic arousal.

The mood of energetic arousal has a positive affective tone, and in its higher levels it is closely associated with optimism and increased self-esteem. In states of low energy and tiredness, the mood is one of reduced optimism and a more conservative self-evaluation and regard of personal problems. Tense arousal, on the other hand, has a negative affective tone and can, in conjunction with energetic arousal, accentuate negative evaluations of self and personal problems. States of low energy and tension, for example, are associated with strong concerns about personal problems and low self-esteem, but high energy and calmness appear to facilitate positive or benign evaluations.

The interaction of energy and tension is complex (see Figure 6–3). Measures of these feelings are positively correlated from low to moderate levels and negatively correlated from moderate to high levels. The point at which a change in

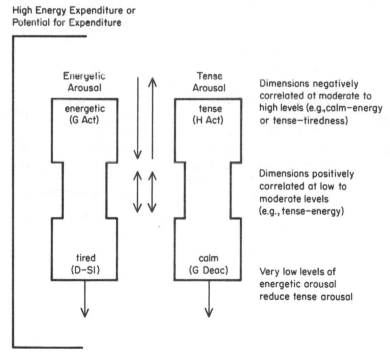

FIGURE 6–3. A two-dimensional arousal model applicable under conditions of real or imagined danger.

correlated function occurs is not well defined, but in general it is related to the resources of the individual.

A kind of dynamic balance exists between energy and tension under conditions of danger. This balance is also evident in the tension-reducing effects of exercise. Changes in feelings of energy with time of day also appear to affect tension. During the first third of the day, when most people experience the highest energy, tension is relatively low. On the other hand, an individual is predisposed to increased tension during naturally occurring low points in the diurnal energy cycle, such as mid to late afternoon and late in the evening.

This dynamic balance can also be observed when subjective energy decreases as tension or anxiety rises. For instance, reminders of personal problems or encounters with danger that generate high anxiety or fear have the effect of lowering subjective energy. The complex nature of this interaction is apparent, however, in the fact that moderate anxiety or fear may increase subjective energy.

An additional element of this model is represented in states of very low energetic arousal. Exhaustion significantly reduces subjective tension. This tension reduction apparently follows a stage of increasing vulnerability to tension as energy drops. But when energy has dropped sufficiently so that exhaustion occurs, tension is apparently eliminated. Thus, a tired person may be irritable and anxious, but an exhausted person experiences little anxiety.

The subjective manifestations of energetic and tense arousal in interaction are descriptively labeled "tense-energy" and "tense-tiredness" or "calm-energy" and "calm-tiredness." Chapter 8 describes the common mood associations of these subjective states. Generally, calm-energy and calm-tiredness represent optimal mood states, while tense-energy and tense-tiredness are less optimal. However, these latter states are typical in modern-day society.

This model includes speculations about the possible evolutionary bases of these mood systems and their interaction pattern. To briefly summarize, these arousal systems efficiently mediate a variety of ongoing and emergency-related behaviors appropriate to the demands of safety and maintenance of life functions. In consciousness, the moods provide signals indicating bodily resources and requirements for recuperation, danger, or safety. The mood of exhaustion facilitates conservation of resources and rest, even in the presence of danger. Thus, in the context of danger these mood systems may be viewed as having stop-and-go functions. A predominance of energy in relation to tension facilitates ongoing behavior, but greater tension than energy is a signal to stop or to be cautious.

7

Issues Relating to Formal and Informal
Research on Mood

Much of the traditional experimental research on mood involves nomothetic designs that are usually carried out in a laboratory setting. Typically, behavior is assessed on only a single occasion, or at most, two occasions (e.g., pre and post experimental conditions). Probability models that are used to evaluate research results often depend on multiple replications across subjects. Discussions of the limitations arising from these traditional procedures in relation to general psychological research have become increasingly prominent in the recent scientific literature. Particularly noteworthy in this context are the ideas of Epstein (1980, 1983) and Rushton, Brainerd, and Pressley (1983). Recently Larsen (1988) has provided an excellent organizational framework for considering these issues. In this chapter, I shall address some of these issues as well as ones that have not been widely considered, and in particular, I shall apply these ideas to mood.

Reliability of Mood Measurements Through Data Aggregation

Prevailing daily moods generally are very subtle. They exercise a small but continuing influence on behavior. Such moods can be overridden on any single occasion by a variety of immediate situational influences that can have powerful psychological effects. These situational influences may exercise their control through emotional activation that is more subjectively salient than the prevailing mood, or the effects may occur through activation of strong cognitive predispositions.

In order to adequately study the effects of long-term or prevailing mood states, it is necessary to obtain extremely reliable measurements that do not inordinately reflect the impact of incidental situations on the moods that are of interest.[1] We know that the reliability of a measurement derives from the ratio of the "real" measurement variance and the "error" variance. If one's interest is in the prevailing background mood state, therefore, incidental situational influences increase the error variance in any one measurement, thereby decreasing the reliability of that measurement.

As a general rule, one of the best ways to approach this problem is through observations of subtle moods on multiple occasions and with aggregation of mood measurements across those occasions. This experimental procedure enhances the reliability of the mood measurement as an indicator of long-term mood. If a subtle but persistent mood state can be assessed on a number of occasions, the immediate situational influences are averaged out, since they tend to occur and to be distributed in a random fashion. This is one basis of the well-known Spearman-Brown formula that is widely used in psychometrics. For example, this formula shows that a single test item measures an underlying phenomenon less reliably than multiple items.

These arguments may be made more clear by using examples. It should be apparent from the discussion of rhythmic mood variations in Chapter 4 that energetic arousal rises and falls according to circadian rhythms, forming a background pattern in the lives of most people. These moods tend to influence behavior in a number of small but important respects. Studying the diurnal portions of these rhythms requires sampling mood states at various times of the day. For example, a person could make a self-rating with the AD ACL at the beginning of each hour from awakening to sleep. This method would probably show that self-ratings of energy are higher in the first third of the day than at other times. However, if one's interest is in the endogenous biological mood rhythm, the reliability of any single self-rating of energy might be poor. For example, even though energy tends to be highest in the morning, at 11:00 A.M. the person may be having an unusually stressful experience and tension could reduce the natural energy feelings during that period (see Chapter 6). At 4:00 P.M., the person may not be experiencing a natural afternoon drop in energy because they have recently engaged in some energizing exercise that is not part of their typical behavior pattern (see Chapters 4 and 5). At 11:00 P.M., when the endogenous energy rhythm normally would be low, the person may be attending a lively party, and subjective energy could be unusually high (see Chapter 5). In each of these cases, the self-ratings would be unreliable measures of the endogenous mood rhythm because incidental influences (random error sources) would be influencing the ratings to a greater degree than the endogenous rhythm.

The solution to this problem would be to take energy ratings over a number of days and to aggregate them into means for each hour (cf. Thayer, Takahashi, & Pauli, 1988). Since immediate situational influences sometimes result in higher energy ratings than usual and sometimes in lower than usual ratings, measures that are aggregated over a number of days would cancel out these one-time-only effects. Thus, the cumulative self-ratings would more reliably measure the endogenous rhythm than a measurement taken on only one occasion.

Although reliable measurement is essential for all good scientific research, it is especially important in research with subtle mood states because, by their nature, these affective conditions are quite difficult to assess. If research designs employed in mood study do not adequately measure these states due to their subtlety, then the results may be interpreted as indicating that certain moods do not exist or that they are of little significance. I believe that circumstances such as this could have occurred with regard to measuring the effects of food on mood. In Chapters 2 and 5, the existing scientific research on this topic was described, and one of the most striking aspects about this literature is its paucity. Even though there is vast public interest in this topic and widely held beliefs about the effects of nutrition on mood, only a small number of published scientific studies document any relationship.

The lack of data about the food-mood relationship could be explainable by the fact that food variations within normal limits, have only a minimal effect on mood on any single occasion. As was indicated in Chapter 5, small but persistent mood effects can become influential in the behavior of a person over time. Often a kind of cumulative effect occurs. Therefore, long-term variations in eating habits could significantly influence prevailing moods. That is, on any one occasion, and within normal variations of eating habits, a particular food constituent could have almost undetectable effects on the mood of the person ingesting the food. And yet, a subtle but continuing food-mood association could eventually have dramatic effects. If this were the case, research that does not adequately deal with these matters would be likely to show no mood effects. Thus, simply because few documented studies indicating a food-mood association have been published, it might be erroneously concluded that no relationship exists.

The Value of Naturalistic Versus Laboratory Test Conditions in the Study of Mood

The reliability issue is also related to a second experimental design consideration in relation to food and mood research as well as other kinds of long-term mood studies. This issue concerns naturalistic versus laboratory experimental procedures. From a careful examination of this issue, one may easily draw the conclusion that laboratory conditions often impede rather than facilitate understanding of mood. This is because these conditions may produce situational effects that are unintended, but nonetheless powerful (Thayer, 1987a, 1987b).

As an indication of how this occurs, consider that if food-mood associations are very subtle, and if experimental designs rely on mood measurements taken once only and under artificial laboratory conditions, the mood effects of a food substance might be particularly difficult to detect because the incidental psychological effects of the experimental procedures themselves may be much more potent than the effects of the food. Thus, under typical laboratory conditions, the ingestion of a food substance could result in little or no experimental mood variation. Therefore, although the inability of researchers to demonstrate a relationship under fully controlled laboratory conditions may appear to indicate that no relationship exists, this conclusion could be quite misleading.

Let us consider the matter further with a specific example relating to the effects of sugar ingestion on mood. Suppose it is hypothesized that regular candy consumption affects long-term mood levels. Carried out in the laboratory and involving the most strict controls, the experiment would probably utilize a substance primarily composed of simple carbohydrates carefully proportioned for nutrient quality and quantity. The substance tested would not likely be a familiar candy bar, but instead something that could be better controlled.

If the usual experimental procedures are employed, subjects would arrive at the laboratory at the appointed time, or perhaps two hours earlier so that the lack of ingestion of other substances could be assured. At the time the sugar snack is supposed to be taken, the critical substance or some similar-tasting placebo would be administered, and subjects would be carefully instructed on how to complete the necessary pre- and post-ingestion self-ratings. Again, going by common practice, the subjects ingest the substance only on a single occasion, or at the most, a couple of occasions. In order to obtain enough data to evaluate the critical and placebo conditions necessary for an inferential statistical model, multiple subjects would be employed, each taking part only once or twice.

In this example, the context of the strictly controlled experiment could well influence the subject so much that whatever subtle mood effects might derive from the candy could easily go undetected. For the experimental participant, the experience of coming to a laboratory, being in an experiment, having investigators carefully observe one's behavior, and being under an unusual one-time-only routine, could have a powerful psychological effect. Thus, in this case strict laboratory procedures could provide a poor indication of the way that regular sugar ingestion affects prevailing moods. This is not to say that strict laboratory procedures are useless in other kinds of psychological research. On the contrary, these procedures have served behavioral science extremely well, and psychology in general has advanced greatly with the aid of these powerful scientific control conditions. But in the study of subtle, long-term mood states, the value of these procedures may be limited. In experimental psychological terms, procedures that incorporate control of all possible confounding variables are so effective in reducing Type I errors (improper acceptance of experimental hypotheses) that the reciprocal Type II errors (rejection of correct hypotheses) become much more likely to occur.

There is an alternative procedure involving naturalistic conditions and cumulative data collecting that may provide better answers to the critical questions. But this procedure is not widely used in scientific research for reasons that will be discussed more fully below. Suppose that a group of highly dependable volunteer participants (or a single individual) who, on typical days over a multiweek period and in the natural setting of their daily lives, do not eat or drink anything from 1:30 until 3:30 in the afternoon. At 3:30, a self-rating of mood is taken, which, although it involves systematized ratings, can be completed in only a few seconds and is done with materials that can be carried around on the person. These pre-ingestion ratings could be followed by eating the same amount each day of the person's usual choice of candy. Post-ingestion ratings would be taken immediately after eating the candy, and then thirty minutes, one hour, and two hours later.

This procedure could involve candy ingestion on some days and no ingestion on others, with the two levels acting as a control. (Other comparison conditions could be easily added, and random procedures could be used to determine whether the ingestion or no-ingestion condition is to occur following the initial self-rating.) All of this could be accomplished without a great deal of disruption in the lives of the experimental participants. If such a study were repeated on many occasions so that the procedure were no longer unusual (the greater the number, the higher the reliability of the obtained measurements), and if the results were analyzed for stability, the information obtained would be extremely useful (see Thayer, 1987a, for a study using some of these procedures).

It is worthwhile to examine the question of what kind of information is sacrificed and gained from these naturalistic procedures. First of all, the mood effect of candy in general would be better understood by using less precisely determined quantities and types, particularly if several kinds of candy were chosen for the experimental variable. In addition to determining the physiological effects of the sugar content of the candy, taste and other sensory cues would be involved; therefore, using familiar candy bars as opposed to a carefully controlled laboratory substance would enhance external generalization.

Less certain, however, would be exactly what constituents of the candy may be producing the effect. For instance, an effect from candy in general may be occurring because the carbohydrates increase concentrations of tryptophan and serotonin, or the mood effect may be due to a sudden increase in blood glucose and the subsequent insulin infusions that stabilize and reduce the glucose levels. Using the procedures outlined above makes these physiological influences more difficult to evaluate. Even though the question of the influential constituent is important scientifically, it is not essential to the more general question of how regularly eaten candy bars affect daily mood states. That kind of information is better obtained by the naturalistic observational procedure described.

With this naturalistic procedure, there is also some uncertainty regarding the possible influence of expectation effects on any obtained relationship between mood and candy ingestion. It is, of course, possible that the candy has little significant physiological effect. Although current research and opinion (e.g., Christensen, White, & Krietsch, 1985; see also Spring, Chiodo, & Bowen, 1987) suggests that expectation effects are not highly likely in regard to many food-mood relationships, nevertheless, there could be some kind of firmly held (or even unconscious) belief by the individual about the effects of candy that is producing the effect rather than the effect occurring because of the physiological influences of candy ingestion itself.

Thus, one of the drawbacks of naturalistic experimental procedures is that there is a greater possibility that subject expectations could account for any observed mood change than there would be with traditional laboratory procedures. This is because using procedures carried out over multiple occasions and with undisguised experimental treatments, makes it impossible to fully control subject awareness and any existing expectations.

Nevertheless, these expectation effects are not as likely to be influential if certain precautions are observed. For example, when using such naturalistic methods, it is essential that subjects attempt to be scrupulously honest in each rating. Second, a similar procedure must be followed on each testing occasion.

Third, if naïve subjects are deemed necessary, the obviousness of the experimental hypothesis should be evaluated and minimized, if possible. Finally, any observed effects should be analyzed by occasions because if the mood effects occur in about the same intensity across occasions, expectations are less likely to be confounded variables in the obtained relationship. With all this, it has been my experience that if expectations are considered at all by the participants, these thoughts are limited to only the first couple of measurement occasions. Experimental participants often report that when self-ratings are made repeatedly, the process soon becomes somewhat automatic, and little thought is given to the significance of each rating (cf. Thayer, 1987a, 1987b).

Even with these various precautions, however, expectation effects still are not fully controlled under naturalistic multiple-occasion designs. But in a certain sense, this makes little difference, as expectations are part of the overall relationship between sugar-snacking and mood change. Naturally, it would be important to know if expectation effects are implicated, but this can be determined once a sugar-mood relationship has been observed. Then, more precisely controlled experiments could be conducted to determine exactly what processes are at the base of this relationship, and it is here that controlled laboratory research may be particularly valuable.

Historically, expectation effects have not been fully documented, but the mere possibility of these distorting influences has been quite influential. Every formal introduction to experimental psychology cautions naïve researchers to control these "demand characteristics" lest subjects try to learn the purpose of the experiment and to respond so as to validate the expected hypotheses. However, as Berkowitz and Donnerstein (1982) point out when referring to this possible motivation on the part of experimental subjects, this "motivational conception . . . has been more widely accepted and exposed to less critical scrutiny than probably any other motivational analysis in contemporary psychology." Moreover, in discussing various aspects of this point, they go on to indicate that "Future historians of social science surely will marvel at how this reasoning has been accepted in the absence of clear evidence supporting it" (p. 250; see also Berkowitz & Troccoli, 1986).

Certainly, this is a complicated issue with room for differences of opinion. But in any event, even though there may be a possibility of expectation effects confounding results in many kinds of research, this is not an all-or-none matter. The mere possibility of demand characteristics or other kinds of subject expectation effects should not automatically invalidate otherwise well-controlled research. A more balanced approach would be to consider the findings in relation to the *possibility* of confounding expectation effects and in relation to other kinds of available research evidence. Conclusions could be drawn on the basis of the overall research evidence instead of on the basis of a single piece of research.

Another reason that longitudinal naturalistic designs are often not used in scientific research relates to sometimes excessive concerns involving subject compliance with the requirements of the experiment. If participants are to complete ratings on a number of occasions within their natural life settings, the experimenter cannot be entirely certain that the procedures will be followed. This problem requires consideration about how participants are recruited for research and about what their motivation for participating is.

Clearly, students completing unsupervised self-ratings as part of a course requirement might not be careful in following required procedures, and they might even be tempted to falsify results just to complete the requirement. It is essential in such designs, if they are conducted for scientific purposes, that participants be highly motivated to be honest and scrupulous in maintaining planned procedures and that conditions are arranged to minimize noncompliance. For example, experimental participants should be given every opportunity to stop participating, with no consequences involved, if for any reason they choose to do so. In the case of volunteers, who are more highly motivated, compliance with planned procedures is much less of a problem. A volunteer participant can usually be trusted to carry out even complex procedures with care, or if they can't carry out the procedures, they can be trusted to inform the experimenter.

In addition to concerns about expectation effects and subject compliance, there are other problems involving the difficulty of collecting data with naturalistic and multiple-occasion procedures (cf. Epstein, 1980). Typically, these procedures involve a great deal of data, and the mere logistics of data collection become quite substantial. In addition, there is the problem of the time required of experimental participants, as well as of their motivation to participate. Needless to say, in planning a research project it is much easier just to schedule one-hour sessions for each participant and to obtain the services of these individuals on the basis of a university subject pool. It is difficult to evaluate the importance of these problems, but I suspect they are quite significant in maintaining traditional practices.

Some moderately successful techniques might be mentioned that have been used to get around some of these problems. For example, in a number of studies Diener, Emmons, and Larsen (e.g., Larsen et al., 1986) collected data from students enrolled in semester-long independent research courses. In addition to the credit, the students participated to learn something about themselves, and about personality testing and research methods. In some of my research, I have found that if the task is not onerous, volunteers participate largely to gain self-information, especially if they are promised extensive debriefing, and their personal test results, which may be potentially useful in their own lives. Whichever procedure for using participants is followed, an experimenter is still confronted with the problem of generalization. Are the results obtained from these kinds of volunteers representative of results that might be obtained from the general population? To some extent, this is an empirical question that can be experimentally investigated. But it is difficult to evaluate these effects definitively.

Considering all these matters, it is clear that naturalistic research designs have a number of advantages, but there are potential error sources as well. However, there may be no alternative to using naturalistic designs if one is to gain a general understanding of long-term mood dynamics. Even with the various limitations, naturalistic research designs may be so essential in gaining meaningful information on critical questions that avoiding them could significantly impede understanding of daily mood dynamics.

The attempt to reduce or eliminate all expectation effects, as well as concerns about subject compliance, may have influenced a whole generation of researchers, particularly researchers on mood. Thus, procedures in which all possible sources of error could not be completely controlled were often eschewed in favor of controlled laboratory experiments. Investigators were probably discouraged from conducting many studies involving longitudinal designs in naturalistic settings, and from including self-reports as dependent variables. Moreover, implicit attitudes about the necessity of laboratory conditions may have cast doubt on the systematic self-study of mood, with the unfortunate result that a valuable tool for the observation and control of dysphoric mood states was underutilized.

Self-Study for the Understanding of Mood Dynamics

When considering the procedures involved with naturalistic research designs in the study of mood, the usually assumed distinctions between controlled scientific research and systematic self-study begin to break down. An individual may conduct a reasonably good scientific experiment on him or herself if a number of simple principles are borne in mind. Furthermore, due to the wide individual differences that exist with regard to mood dynamics, these quite feasible self-studies may be more valuable for the person conducting the experiment than some sort of generalized information gained from more traditional experiments conducted under controlled laboratory conditions.

In my advanced experimental psychology classes (university, senior level), usually I have tried to include at least one short-term longitudinal design involving naturalistic observations. In this design, each student does an experiment on him or herself with occasions being the source of replications rather than different persons. Students in these classes are quite sophisticated, and therefore, more elaborate controls and statistical procedures can be introduced. In experiments of this sort, the relative effects of several levels of an experimental variable can be examined, and these different levels can be randomly introduced following pretesting on each occasion (experiments are usually conducted over many occasions through a multiweek period).

In addition, designs can be used that are factorial (two or more crossed variables), and mixed (manipulated and correlational variables). All of the obtained results can be statistically analyzed with sophisticated techniques. Repeated-measures analyses of variance can be employed to analyze the multiple observations taken by a single person on him or herself (see Appendix IV for examples of these designs). Finally, if students in a class are conducting the same self-experiment, it is possible to evaluate the group effects using traditional statistical analyses.

Although these advanced design experiments with their sophisticated techniques for data analysis are extremely popular among senior experimental psychology students, simpler versions can be easily conducted by laypeople. For example, an individual who frequently finds him or herself depressed may profitably make self-ratings of depression, energy, and tension, as well as simple situational designations, at various critical times of the day over a number of days. From these, a determination can be made if there are any recurring patterns that relate to underlying circadian rhythms or to specific situations and conditions. Methods of analyzing the results obtained from these self-studies need not involve complicated descriptive or inferential statistics. Simple averages taken over a number of occasions will provide good information about a number of basic mood dynamics.

Once an individual becomes somewhat skilled at the simplest methods, procedures can be incorporated that allow joint self-study of two or more variables. For example, in addition to this self-monitoring over time, a person may also incorporate studies of such potentially important mood influences as moderate exercise, sugar ingestion, or even amount of sleep. The self-experimenter will most likely find that the various mood influences have different effects at different times of day, or under different conditions of stress and physical health. The benefit gained by a person from these procedures will be the development of a personalized psychology of mood.

These techniques are so valuable that one may ask why systematized self-study is not practiced more often. Certainly there is a natural tendency for an individual to observe him or herself when dysphoric moods occur. But often the self-observation may be only minimal. Usually the individual just tries to remember what external event happened to cause the mood instead of systematically observing behavior to determine if a relationship does exist between mood and these other factors. There is not sufficient appreciation of the power of self-observational techniques. Moreover, many may feel that systematic self-observational procedures are beyond their ability.

It is hard to judge the real influence on self-study that concerns about expectation effects may have, but this influence could be quite substantial. The same kinds of hesitancy that scientists have regarding the use of longitudinal designs, naturalistic settings, and self-reports may exist with average laypeople concerning systematic self-observation. In any event, for whatever reason, the attitude seems to exist among the general public that planned self-observations have only limited value.

Although some experts may react defensively to the idea of laypeople taking diagnosis and mood change evaluation into their own hands through systematic self-observation, such an attitude would be quite short-sighted. Experts have genuine value in setting up self-observation programs and in helping clients to interpret results. If stable rhythms and influences relating to mood do occur, self-observational procedures are particularly valuable because the individual making the observations is likely to derive much more actual personal benefit and be more impressed with the results than they would be through mere authoritative directions from an expert. This occurs both because the results include the individual differences that characterize that person, and also because information gained by systematic self-observation is likely to be more immediately meaningful to the individual. I have found that people who have conducted these kinds of self-analyses often trust the results as especially good predictors of future mood dynamics, a point discussed more fully in the next chapter.

8

Toward an Understanding of Nonpathological Mood States: Evidence, Speculations, and Applications

There are a number of features that any comprehensive understanding of mood must incorporate. After first indicating what these essential features are, some observations and speculations will be provided about the ways in which energy and tension moods meet these criteria. Parts of this understanding were more fully developed elsewhere in this book, but ideas specific to mood will be added in the present discussion. This chapter also includes hypothetical scenarios of mood relations that might occur in life circumstances characterized by varying degrees of stress, and some theory is provided about the ways in which food and drugs are often used as mood modulators. Last, practical applications will be offered concerning maintenance of optimal moods based on this understanding.

Essential Features of Mood

Current evidence suggests at least eight essential features ought to be incorporated in any comprehensive understanding of mood. The first feature is that mood involves conscious awareness. Moods may be judged by behaviors, or they may even be inferred by bodily postures, but first and foremost, mood is part of consciousness. Certainly no conclusions concerning mood could be drawn without some sort of description or self-rating by an individual of how he or she feels. Although some moods such as low-level depression may be unrecognized by a person suffering from the malady, nevertheless, that individual would be aware of such telltale feelings as tiredness or an absence of energy.

A second essential feature is that mood is an enduring reaction not usually identified with a particular stimulus. A temporary affective reaction that is brought about by a particular stimulus is probably best described as an emotion, although certainly emotions and moods are closely related. But generally speaking, moods have temporal continuity, and they often appear to the individual experiencing them to be relatively independent of any particular cause.

A third feature is that mood is often assigned a positive or negative hedonic value. In scientific usage, writers are undoubtedly aware that this hedonic continuum may be conceptualized in various ways, but a common approach is to designate a mood or multiple moods simply as "positive" or "negative" (see Chapter 2). In the popular culture, there is less concern with the specificity of a term, and people speak simply about a "good mood" or a "bad mood." In recent times, people sometimes use terms such as "up" or "down" to describe moods. Putting moods in positive or negative categories may inappropriately eliminate finer distinctions, such as sexual, angry, or contemplative moods. Nonetheless, a positive-negative assessment is in such wide usage that any credible analysis ought to account for this hedonic valence.

A fourth essential feature in understanding mood is its relationship with the depression-elation continuum. A large proportion of the scientific literature on mood deals with depression and its opposite state. Much of this research and theory comes from medical treatment of severe depression, but any general psychotherapeutic practice includes extensive involvement with low-level depressive conditions as well. Moreover, the literature on nonpathological moods often incorporates depression. And finally, in the popular culture, depression is probably the most commonly identified mood outside of simple positive and negative designations.

A fifth essential feature for understanding mood is the inclusion of a physiological base. As used here, the term "physiological" incorporates psychophysiological, neurophysiological, neurochemical, and general anatomical (usually the brain) substrates of mood. Within this general categorization, it seems to me there is indisputable evidence for a physiological basis or component element of mood. Although one sometimes finds authors describing a mood-related topic such as affect as though it were somehow disembodied and not tied to a physiological base, this is not a defensible position, either logically or on the basis of existing scientific evidence.

A sixth feature necessary for understanding mood is that this affective state is related to central biological principles and functions, including the likelihood of an evolutionary basis. The overwhelming evidence from over a hundred years of biological science is that important elements of our being have developed through natural selection and through adaptation to the requirements of the environment. Mood is unlikely to be an exception.

The cyclicity of moods provides fundamental evidence of their biological underpinnings. This cyclicity is most strong for certain types of mood—for example, energy, tiredness, or related states of alertness—but it is highly likely that all sorts of moods have cyclical characteristics. Sleep is one of the most important cyclical functions, and although the effects of sleep have not been demonstrated with regard to a wide variety of moods, nevertheless, at least in extreme conditions a relationship between sleep and mood is highly probable.

Other biological functions associated with eating and nutrition probably influence mood as well. These mood effects are most apparent in extreme states of food deprivation, but it is likely that certain types of food subtly modify moods even in nonextreme circumstances. The small amount of formal evidence that exists concerns mainly carbohydrate ingestion, but future research will yield further relationships.

Exercise is linked with still other biological functions that undoubtedly influence mood. Although there is relatively more scientific evidence about the relationship between exercise and mood than there is about the relations between sleep or nutrition and mood, a paucity of hard data still exists. Quite possibly, this is due to the subtlety of mood reactions arising from associated biological functions. In addition to research on mood and exercise, there is wide experience with exercise as a mood modulator in general psychological and psychiatric clinical practice, particularly in regard to depression. But it is frustrating to document this usage because the clinicians who regularly prescribe exercise seldom publish their results.

The seventh essential feature in understanding mood is the close relationship between this affective state and cognitive processes. Here there is quite a lot of published evidence, especially regarding broad categories. In Chapter 2, for example, the literature was reviewed on the cognitive antecedents of mood and mood-memory associations, and it is impressive in its demonstration that mood and cognition are closely related.

The eighth and final essential feature that I would include for a comprehensive understanding of mood is the mood-behavior association. The formal literature is only beginning to document the interactions between mood and behavior, and yet the evidence is already strong that mood influences memory, perception, and probably a wide variety of other functions (see Chapter 2). As in the case of cognition, these associations are likely to be highly complex, involving feedback loops and ongoing mood-behavior interactions. The effects of mood on behavior may not be dramatic except in extreme conditions (e.g., depression and suicide), and yet it seems likely that subtle but persistent moods can have a substantial effect on behavior over time.

An Understanding of Mood Based on Energy and Tension[1]

The eight essential features described above are clearly associated with moods of energy and tension. For example, energetic and tense moods are elementary states of consciousness. Although they are probably based on general psychophysiological arousal processes as well as a variety of biochemical substrates, feelings of energy and tension are close correlates of many other commonly identified moods, and they appear to be essential elements of these moods. Energy and tiredness occur cyclically during regularly occurring biological processes. These affective states[2] last for minutes or hours in circadian or other rhythms, or they exhibit gradual change with such influences as physical exertion. Biologically meaningful variables such as sleep, nutrition, exercise, and general health are likely antecedents of these states.

There is a clear mood-behavior relationship involving energy and tension. Subjective energy predisposes activity, while tiredness prompts rest. Tension is associated with caution and vigilance while attempting to locate the source of danger, and calmness reflects the absence of danger, thus enabling more carefree behavior. Various cognitive factors interact with energy and tension both directly and indirectly. For example, tension probably depends in large part on cognitive interpretations of danger, and events that are construed in a positive light may increase subjective energy. Moreover, cognitive processes associated with everything from simple decisions to self-efficacy estimations are likely to be influenced by the immediate levels of energy and tension.

In order to understand the overall mood life of an individual with respect to the hedonic tone of energy and tension moods, it is necessary to consider two types of context: a nonstressful environmental setting in which no important problems exist, and a context characterized by significant personal problems and by environmental stress. These two contexts might be viewed as differing on a dimension of real or imagined personal danger. The trouble-free nonstressful situation might occur, for example, on an extended vacation at a pleasant beach resort. In this sort of existence, natural cycles of energy and tiredness would be the dominant mood pattern. For most persons, higher energy would occur in the first third of the day, after significant sleep from the night before, but the cycle would probably conform to the overall physical activity pattern of the person. General health and nutrition would play a part, and regular patterns of cognitive activity might also influence the cycle.

In this nonstressful state, the moods of calm-energy and calm-tiredness might be expected to predominate. Their hedonic valence would range from highly positive for calm-energy (Thayer, 1978a) to more neutral but still positive feelings associated with calm-tiredness. States of calm-energy would be associated with optimism, happiness, and physical well-being (Thayer, 1987b).

These cycles of calm-energy and calm-tiredness produce what are probably optimal moods. They are not only pleasurable, but energetic periods are associated with enhanced learning, thinking, and general intellectual activity (Thayer, Takahashi, & Pauli, 1988). A possible challenge to this idea about optimal moods comes from anecdotal reports[3] suggesting that large amounts of work are not necessarily accomplished in these mood states. Instead, behavior without tension is characterized by relaxation and little pressure to perform any particular task. But this does not mean that the overall mood implies indolence, because activity occurs periodically in this mood state as energy increases and decreases in a rhythmic pattern.

Characteristic moods differ for an individual with a lifestyle full of personal problems and environmental stress. Low-level anxiety, fearfulness, or nervousness would most likely be the prevailing moods of this individual. Unlike the positive moods, these negative (tension-related) moods do not arise naturally from cyclical biological processes, but they are quite understandable in biological terms. They represent a reaction to danger in the most general sense, at least cognitive interpretations of danger.

These tension-related moods do not occur independently of energy and tiredness, but are combined with them. Depending on the degree of energy that is present, tense-energy may have a quite positive hedonic valence (Thayer, 1978a). Certain personality types are particularly likely to perceive this mood as positive. Type A personalities, for example, seem to enjoy the driving experience of mild tension and its associated energy (Friedman & Rosenman, 1974; Matthews, 1982). Judging by anecdotal reports, this tense-energy state results in high productivity for many people. It predisposes speed and reduces the desire for relaxation. There is a certain pressure to perform associated with tense-energy, so work production may be increased. However, the quality of production may not be as great as that associated with calm-energy. But so far, there is little empirical evidence of the relative influence on productivity of the two kinds of moods, and so this conclusion remains speculative.

Tense-energy is a state valued by many, but fatigue inevitably occurs and the somewhat pleasurable state changes to tense-tiredness. This mood is distinctly negative in affective tone (Thayer, 1978a). While experiencing tense-tiredness, people view their problems as more serious (Thayer, 1987b, experiment 1), and they are considerably less optimistic and happy, with lower levels of physical well-being, than they are while experiencing calm-energy (Thayer, 1987b, experiment 2).

Although major depression is not likely to be fully understood on the basis of these moods alone, tense-tiredness is characteristic of the depressed individual. A loss of energy is one of the central phenomena of depression. And at least certain types of agitated depression, if not all forms of this dysphoria, are associated with underlying anxiety (American Psychiatric Association, 1980).

Other well-known characteristics of depression include a negative appraisal of personal circumstances, a distinct lack of optimism, and general unhappiness. Low self-esteem is also often present in depression. Empirical studies from my laboratory have shown that all of these characteristics are associated with tense-tiredness. In one longitudinal study (Thayer, 1987b, experiment 1), the most negative appraisals of personal problems occurred during the most tense-tired states that were experienced over a three-week period. And in another study, optimism and happiness were lowest in this tense-tired mood state as recorded over an extended period (Thayer, 1987b, experiment 2).

In other research (Rubadeau, 1976; Rubadeau & Thayer, 1976), self-esteem, energy, and tension were rated on multiple occasions over a seven-week period by twenty-three male and female students at fixed times of day. In order to reduce any effects of reaction to measurement, we used the Adjective Generation Technique (Allen & Potkay, 1973), as well as more common self-esteem rating scales. The expected negative correlations between tension and self-esteem were obtained for most participants, but we did not expect the positive correlations between energetic arousal and self-esteem.[4] Thus, self-esteem was lowest during the lowest energy periods, while heightened energy favored increased self-esteem.

Other studies directly aimed at examining moderate depressive states have also been conducted. In one such study (Thayer & Wettler, 1975), eight women volunteers were recruited who had been experiencing periodic states of depression, but who had not sought professional help and were not on medication. Over multiple occasions, these women rated their depression as well as their energy and tension states. Additional ratings of depression, energy, and tension were made on days when depression was felt as well as on nondepressed days that were matched as closely as possible in every factor to the depression days. Characteristic patterns of tiredness, low energy, and tension were found at the times of highest depression. Recently, this study was repeated (Bassin & Thayer, 1986), and the same pattern of tense-tiredness was again associated with depression.

Tense-tired mood states may not account for major depression, but this mood configuration could provide a considerable understanding of low-level depressive states. The absence of energy is often a primary sign of this debilitating condition, a point Gaylin (1979) makes very well:

> To feel tired, independent of a source, is as close (excepting grief) as most of us come to the feelings of that clinical state called "depression." Feelings of depression are, I suspect, more often than not misread. Customarily, individuals who are depressed will not even be aware of being in the grip of an emotional state. They are more likely to complain of exhaustion, fatigue, boredom, weariness. When a patient states that he is chronically tired, and then describes the fact that he has had a precipitous weight loss and insomnia, the psychiatrist knows that—barring physical illness—he is getting a classical description of depression. (p. 102)

Low-level depression can affect behavior considerably. Individuals experiencing chronic states of tense-tiredness may appear normal in other respects, but their lives pass with few accomplishments. They may spend a great deal of time watching television or simply doing nothing even though there are tasks to be accomplished and activities to be pursued. In my experience, this condition is particularly apparent in those times when an individual is not forced by schedule or work requirements to accomplish various activities, but when activity depends entirely on self-initiation. Further evidence that this type of depression is related to energy cycles is that the depressed behavior is heightened when subjective energy is naturally low, as in late afternoon or in the last half of the day, when circadian rhythms of energetic arousal are often decreased.

If depression were composed of no other element than tense-tiredness, then one would expect it to recede periodically as energy is enhanced, but depressions do not necessarily show these cycles.[5] However, tense-tiredness may interact with cognitive variables to predispose the individual to give up and adopt a kind of learned helplessness (Metalsky et al., 1987; Seligman, 1976). If the naturally occurring mood of tense-tiredness is an important element of depression, then it would be essential in the study of depressive conditions to note factors likely to contribute to tense-tiredness, such as chronic insomnia, nutritional deficiencies, and generally poor health, as well as the more commonly assumed antecedents of depression such as stress and personal problems.

Hypothetical Scenario Regarding the Mood States of a Person Under Stress

These theoretical concepts may be made more understandable with a practical example. Let us consider the changing mood state of a person experiencing heavy stress. Suppose that a fifty-year-old man is unexpectedly informed at 10 A.M. one morning that he is going to lose a seemingly secure job which he has held for twenty-five years. Suppose further that this individual has been healthy, and that in the recent past there were few significant problems in his life. He has been eating a balanced diet, sleeping well, and the night before he had a good night's sleep.

Initially, the news of the job loss would be extremely tension-provoking. On hearing about it, he might feel a mixture of high anxiety with a sharp drop in energy and a profound feeling of fatigue (see Chapter 6). This feeling could last for quite some time, and indeed, his mood during that morning might be described as one of tense-tiredness. However, because his physical resources are high, and because the information comes in the morning, as his endogenous energy cycle is increasing (see Chapter 4), the energy drop might not last longer than a few minutes. After that, the high tension that he feels might be mixed with moderately high energy, at least sufficiently for him to begin rationally evaluating the situation, gather more information, and consider alternative actions for himself. Thus, his predominant mood during this morning might be characterized by tension and a moderate degree of subjective energy (tense-energy).

In the afternoon and that night, however, his mood could change dramatically. As his endogenous energy rhythm begins to decrease, he would become more and more vulnerable to increasing anxiety (see Chapters 5 and 6). The mood of tense-energy that he felt during the morning would likely change to one of tense-tiredness. This reaction could be expected to occur in the mid to late afternoon, a period when many people experience a sharp energy decline. But in any event, it is very likely that during the evening, tense-tiredness would be present.

This increasingly tired state would predispose him not only to increasing tension, but also to a variety of correlated cognitive changes. For example, the problem which was serious but manageable might now appear hopeless (Thayer, 1987b, experiment 1). The prospects for finding another job and salvaging himself economically might seem very slight. His general optimism probably would decrease significantly, and he would become extremely unhappy (Thayer, 1987b, experiment 2). His immediate feelings of self-esteem might decrease considerably during this period (Rubadeau, 1976; Rubadeau & Thayer, 1976).

In the afternoon and the evening not only would his mood be characterized as tense-tiredness, but depression could very well occur. While experiencing this mood, his memories as well as his general perceptions probably would be quite negative. His thinking would be dominated not only with the problem, but also with other negative aspects of his life. He would be experiencing a kind of state dependency, or mood congruence, in which the tone of his thoughts would match the negative hedonic tone of his mood (see Chapter 2).

That night, the continuing tension would probably cause him to toss and turn for hours before dozing off for short periods of fitful sleep. Thoughts about his problems would probably fill his mind. Try as he might not to think about them, he would be unable to stop these negative ruminations. As he awakens periodically from the fitful sleep, he might reach the maximum pessimism level somewhere in the middle of the night, when his endogenous energy rhythm reaches its lowest point.

As morning comes, he would begin to feel better, reflecting the gradually increasing cycle of energetic arousal. And by 8 or 9 A.M., his mood may be considerably more positive than the night before. The tense-tiredness would give way once again to tense-energy, although the energy experienced would probably be lower than the day before. As his energy increases, his mood would improve. The problem of a job loss might seem less serious, and he would become slightly more optimistic about the future. He might also begin to feel better about himself.

With the re-emergence of tense-energy, his depression might lift, and the feeling of paralysis that he experienced the night before might give way to more energetic feelings, and therefore, to action that would remedy the problem. This lessening of tense-tiredness would be more likely if his physical routines were not entirely disrupted. For example, if he continued to eat and to exercise, energy would be enhanced (see Chapter 6).

As the second day wears on, however, his energy again would decline in the late afternoon, or perhaps even earlier, because at this point his physical resources would be lessened by the continuous tension and lack of sleep. By the evening of the second day, the depression might be even greater than the day before, and he could be more disabled than he was. During this day, his mood might be described as a mixture of tense-energy and increasing tense-tiredness. Depression could increase as energy declines.

The second night, sleep might be even more difficult to obtain than it was the first night due to the unremitting tension. Depending on his physical resources, exhaustion might be very near. Late this night, he might become so exhausted that his mood would shift from tense-tiredness to a kind of apathy-related calmness in which all feelings would be reduced (see Chapter 6). Bothersome thoughts or even disruptive events would have little or no effect. For a while at least, the anxiety that he had been experiencing continuously would seem to disappear. Finally, he might sink into a deep sleep. But even this sleep would not last the whole night; probably he would awaken in the early morning hours, again feeling depressed.

This same pattern could continue for days, with slightly more positive moods in the naturally occurring high-energy hours, and negative moods as energy declines. Unless events changed and the source of the stress was reduced, the individual would gradually become more and more debilitated through sleep deprivation and the probable disruption of other biological processes. He would appear to be normal at some times, only to become increasingly more depressed at other times.

The gradually increasing negative mood would be reflected in his physical state. The individual might experience the characteristic skeletal-muscular tension as he first learns about his job loss, and to varying degrees as tense-tiredness continues. There would be tight muscles in the shoulders, neck, face, and elsewhere that would be consistent with tense-tiredness. This skeletal-muscular pattern is a kind of residual of the preparatory-emergency state that accompanies danger, in which the bodily reaction includes arousal plus skeletal-muscular inhibition (see Chapters 3 and 5). This tension would be accompanied by tapping fingers, a rapidly shaking foot, or pacing as the impact of the problem becomes greater.

There would be other indications of tension in the individual's inability to concentrate. As he tries to work, for example, he might find his attention wandering. Once again, this is a residual biological pattern that emanates from functional reactions to danger that emerged in the evolutionary past (see Chapter 3).

Figure 8–1 summarizes the continuing debilitation, the changing levels of energy across days, and the points of relatively better mood (tense-energy) and less optimal mood (tense-tiredness). The first portion of that figure (Figure 8–1a) indicates the naturally occurring diurnal rhythm of energetic arousal that

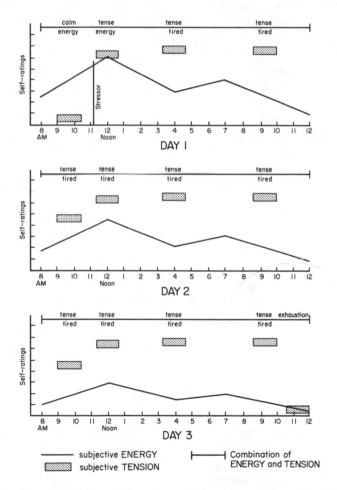

FIGURE 8–1. Theoretical description of mood changes over three days following sudden severe shock.

might be expected on the first day. Prior to the news of job loss, we might assume calm-energy would be experienced by this healthy individual who had previously lived under conditions of minimal stress. However, immediately following the stress, tension would rise sharply and remain high thereafter. Thus, there would be periods of relatively more energy (tense-energy) and relatively less (tense-tiredness).

On the second day (Figure 8–1b), energy would still be elevated in the first third of the day following whatever sleep was obtained the night before, although some debilitation would have occurred. And by the third day (Figure 8–1c), the amplitude of the energetic arousal cycle would be greatly reduced from the debilitating effects of two nights of poor sleep and high tension during the day. Therefore, brief periods of tense-energy might be experienced in the mornings of the second and third days, but subjective energy would be relatively low compared to the tension. Most of these days would be characterized by tense-tiredness. Other related moods could be expected, such as pessimism, unhappiness, and perhaps depression. Finally, near the end of the third day and possibly as early as the end of the first day, exhaustion could be expected to occur. Here the mood would be one of calm-tiredness.

Most people experience these reactions to stress. However, there are likely to be many individual differences in this pattern. For example, the age of the person probably would affect his reactions, not only because the stressor is likely to have a different meaning for individuals at different life cycle stages, but more important for this example, because the available energy resources probably vary with age (see Chapter 4). Thus, in this respect, a stressor such as the one described could affect a twenty-year-old man much less severely than a fifty-year-old man, who may have poorer health and a less good physical condition. Other individual differences relating to physical health, bodily condition, and long-term sleep and nutritional deficiencies could also result in varying the effects on mood of the stressor.

Some of these individual differences in reaction to a stressor might be due to characteristic personality traits. For example, an individual high on Eysenck's (1967) neuroticism dimension would probably react with a much greater degree of tension to a stressful situation (Thayer, Takahashi, & Pauli, 1988). Also, some individuals might show a greater degree of tense arousal to stimulation in general (Diener et al., 1985; Farley, 1986; Strelau, 1983). Furthermore, the diurnal cycles that affect mood may be affected by the degree of morningness of the individual.

The mood patterns that I described might be expected to differ as the degree of stress differs. An individual under moderate degrees of stress might experience relatively greater amounts of tense-energy compared to tense-tiredness. The pessimism or increased personal problem perception might be considerably lower for this individual as compared to the person experiencing heavy stress. The predominant mood for this individual would be much more positive on the whole, depression would seldom occur, and if it did, it would occur only occasionally, as personal resources diminish from time to time.

Self-Determined Mood Modulation: Use of Sugar Snacks, Caffeine, Tobacco, and Other Drugs

People use various strategies to modulate their mood from one day to the next, if not from moment to moment. In a number of ways, people attempt to perpetuate their good moods and even to enhance them. And perhaps to an even greater degree, various strategies are regularly employed to eliminate bad moods.

In Chapter 5, a theoretical mircoanalysis was provided of the way that energy-tiredness moods and cognition may interact to influence momentary decisions about behavior. Here I wish to go further, suggesting that people regularly sense their levels of arousal, and that they employ techniques that were successful in the past to enhance their mood. This is done by modulating energy and reducing tension. Some of these self-management techniques are consciously employed, but probably there is only low awareness about the process much of the time.

The idea that people regulate their moods is not new. For example, Cialdini, Darby, and Vincent (1973) proposed the "negative state relief" model, in which they suggested that negative moods result in various mood-elevating behaviors, including helping others in social situations. This concept has been supported by various research (e.g., Baumann, Cialdini, & Kendrick, 1981; Cialdini, Baumann, & Kendrick, 1981; Manucia, Baumann, & Cialdini, 1984; see also Carlson & Miller, 1987). More recently, Morris and Reilly (1987) presented an excellent review of the wide variety of strategies people use to modify mood, including self reward, alcohol consumption, distraction, expressive behavior, cognitive transformations (e.g., altering interpretations), problem-directed action, and affiliation (e.g., seeking associations with others). Of the various mood-management techniques reviewed, they concluded that the use of alcohol for tension reduction provides the most convincing case for the existence of mood-elevating behaviors (see also Clark and Isen's [1982] discussion of self-regulation of moods).[6]

Most of the empirical evidence of attempts to regulate arousal with drugs and other food substances is indirect or based on retrospective report. Yet, it is quite persuasive when taken as a whole. Let us consider some of this evidence before the particular role of energetic and tense arousal is analyzed.

A number of studies indicate that at least certain types of people appear to reduce anxiety by eating, usually carbohydrates. Ruderman (1986) recently reviewed the research and concluded that restrained eaters (e.g., dieters) significantly increase their consumption when in a dysphoric mood (especially anxiety and depression). However, this tendency may not be universal as Ruderman noted because several studies have shown that unrestrained eaters (e.g., nondieters) tend to decrease consumption in dysphoric moods.

Small increases in arousal occur after eating carbohydrates as well as some other foods. It is well-known, for example, that blood glucose is raised following carbohydrate ingestion, and there is a small increment in metabolic rate. But the evidence that subjective arousal states are affected is limited. In one experiment that was described earlier (Thayer, 1987a), participants ate a sugar snack on multiple occasions and at fixed times of the day over a three-week period. They then rated their mood soon after ingestion, an hour later, and two hours later. Significant mood patterns were obtained, with energy first increasing twenty minutes after ingestion and then decreasing after one and two hours. Similarly, subjective tiredness first decreased and then increased at one and two hours. Subjective tension was significantly higher one hour after ingestion, but not immediately following the sugar snack. The observed tiredness effects have been repeated in other studies, but the tension effects have received less support (Spring, Chiodo, & Bowen, 1987). Although these mood changes were reliable, they were quite subtle, and they may have been obtained only because of the sensitivity of measurement that was made possible by the longitudinal design of the experiment (see Chapter 7).

In other studies, Rosenthal et al. (1986) found that a carbohydrate lunch significantly reduced depression. Lieberman, Wurtman, and Chew (1986) found that carbohydrate snackers experienced reduced depression following a lunch with high proportions of carbohydrates. As depression typically involves reduced energy and increased tension, changes in these states could have been the basis of the depression reduction. In the latter two studies, participants who did not crave carbohydrates showed no reduced depression after eating them.

Tobacco use probably is employed quite often to affect arousal. In one survey of over 2,000 smokers, Ikard, Green, and Hŏrn (1969) found that pleasurable relaxation was the reason given for tobacco use by most smokers. Russell, Peto, and Patel (1974) found that anxiety often proved to be a stimulus to smoke, in both the general and a smoking clinic population. Warburton and Wesnes (1978) obtained similar results with university students. Frith (1971) asked subjects to imagine themselves in both high and low arousal settings, and individual differences were obtained that indicated some people (e.g., males) were more likely to smoke in a low arousal setting, and others (e.g., females) were more likely to smoke in high arousal settings. This apparently paradoxical high and low arousal effect is quite interesting, and it will be discussed later.

A number of studies have shown that the effects of smoking on arousal and mood are consistent with assumed energy and tension changes. For example, much research indicates that nicotine results in autonomic arousal (e.g., heart rate increments from five to forty beats per minute), but that skeletal-muscular tension is reduced by this substance (Domino, 1973; Gilbert, 1979; Mangan & Golding, 1984). These differing physiological effects may indicate a process is occurring in which energetic arousal increases while tense arousal decreases (see Chapter 6).

Studies focusing specifically on mood have shown that smoking results in tension-reduction effects. Heimstra (1973) found that smoking reduced self-reported anxiety and aggression in conjunction with various taxing activities and a stressful movie. Ague (1973) deprived smokers of cigarettes for a period of time and then allowed them to smoke cigarettes that had varying nicotine content. Smoking high-nicotine cigarettes resulted in reports of feeling greater pleasantness and relaxation.

Alcohol is another substance that may be widely used to modify arousal. This drug is generally regarded as a CNS depressant, although the exact mechanisms of its action are not fully understood (Wesnes & Warburton, 1983). However, these depressant effects often have the net result of enhancing positive moods, especially in low doses. Hull and Bond (1986) reviewed fourteen studies, which were rather homogeneous in their findings that alcohol increased positive mood and reduced negative mood states.

Experimental studies have shown that under unpleasant conditions, alcohol consumption is often increased, probably as a means of affecting mood. Marlatt, Kosturn, and Lang (1975) found that insults delivered by an experimental confederate increased alcohol consumption among those who were objects of the remarks in a staged wine-tasting experiment, particularly if there were no opportunity to retaliate against the insulter. Hull and Young (1983) found that people who were told they had failed on an intellectual task increased their alcohol consumption, again in a staged wine-tasting experiment. This was especially true for persons scoring high on the Self-Consciousness Inventory (Fenigstein, Scheier, & Buss, 1975). In both of these experiments, the manipulations probably were tension-inducing, and quite possibly the alcohol was used by the subjects to reduce their tension.

Caffeine is a common drug that people often use to affect arousal. It is common knowledge that many "get themselves going" in the mornings and at other times with coffee, or drink it when they are tired and need an uplift (Gilliland & Bullock, 1983–84). And in fact, there is a considerable amount of research demonstrating that caffeine does result in physiological arousal (see reviews by Gilliland & Bullock, 1983–84; Sawyer, Julia, & Turin, 1982).

Nevertheless, one may question if caffeine results solely in the desired energy increases, or if tension increases are the primary effect. Small studies on regular coffee drinkers that my students have conducted as part of Psychology of Mood classes have frequently shown slight but significant increases in subjective tension after ingesting approximately 100 mg of caffeine (one cup of strong coffee). However, energy increases sometimes occurred instead (similar mixed effects were obtained by Anderson, 1987). Although small quantities *may* enhance energy, larger amounts seem to result in tension increases. For example, Gilliland and Andress (1981) found that moderate coffee drinkers (M = 2.5 cups/day) as well as high consumers (M = 8.1 cups/day) had increased trait anxiety and self-rated depression as compared to low drinkers (M = .6 cup/day) and those who usually abstained. There were a series of other undesirable effects as well with coffee drinking.

In addition to commonly employed prescription or over-the-counter drugs, various illicit drugs (or illicitly obtained prescription drugs) are used by many to affect arousal. Perhaps the best known of these drugs in use today are amphetamines, methamphetamines, and cocaine. These substances are CNS stimulants that appear to produce arousal mainly through action on norepinephrine (Angrist & Sudilovsky, 1978; Grinspoon & Bakalar, 1985). They cause a number of peripheral arousal effects, including increases in heart rate, blood pressure, and respiration.

In lower doses, and prior to physiological adaptation, these drugs cause feelings of relaxed alertness, energy, vitality, and assertiveness. At this level of use, the mood state that occurs is clearly one of calm-energy, or tense-energy with relatively more energy than tension. However, in larger doses, the relaxed alertness gives way to a kind of driven feeling and to behaviors, such as extreme talkativeness and heightened motor activity, that indicate high arousal states (Angrist & Sudilovsky, 1978; Post, 1976). Here the mood reflects continued high energy, but greater degrees of tension as well.

Cocaine in particular has become a popular illicit drug at the present time. Numerous reports indicate that it is taken extensively by some elements of the entertainment industry and business, where sustained high-energy activity in a limited time period is greatly valued. Apparently it is also used in the general population to conteract depression and to maintain a state of euphoria and sociability in social settings (Grinspoon & Bakalar, 1985).

All of the drugs and food substances described appear to affect arousal levels. And although the evidence is not conclusive on this point, it is likely that people regularly use these substances to modulate mood. In other words, people sense their arousal levels and attempt to "self-medicate" if those levels are undesirable in some way. Is it possible to formulate general principles that apply to all usages of these various substances? I believe it is, although certain qualifications must be recognized before any general principles can be assumed.

First of all, there are likely to be individual differences that affect personal orientations toward these substances. For example, use of carbohydrates during times of tension may be restricted to certain types of persons (e.g., dieters). Furthermore, it may be inappropriate to assume that all explanations of usage can be based on direct physiological shifts in arousal, since the motivation may be indirect, as in smoking to satisfy oral needs or to give oneself something to do with one's hands (Gilbert, 1979).

Even with these qualifications, it is probably true that the substances described are still often used to regulate moods. For some people, all of these substances appear to enhance positive mood, at least over a short time period and when they are ingested in small amounts. This overall mood enhancement seems to work with some of these drugs through a reduction of negative moods, and with others, through an increase in positive moods.

An analysis of the arousal changes resulting from these substances and based on a single arousal continuum cannot account for this mood enhancement. For example, alcohol is a CNS depressant. Yet, in low doses this substance produces euphoria, and generally it enhances positive mood. On the other hand, cocaine and amphetamines are CNS stimulants that increase general physiological arousal. However, these drugs also enhance euphoria, and in low doses they appear to reduce tension as well.

Further evidence that mood enhancement is not based on a single arousal continuum can be found in the effects of carbohydrate ingestion. At least initially, ingestion of simple carbohydrates increases blood glucose and results in small increases in metabolic rate. Sugar snacks also appear to increase subjective energy and decrease tiredness, at least for a short time. However, some people eat more carbohydrates when they are anxious, and thus the immediate motivation appears to be tension reduction.

Tobacco smoking is apparently used by some people to reduce tension, but nicotine causes autonomic arousal. Furthermore, reports by people of the circumstances under which they smoke indicate that some smoke primarily in high arousal situations, and seemingly as a means of reducing that arousal. Others, however, smoke in low arousal situations, apparently to increase arousal.

Caffeine is used by many to wake themselves up or to increase arousal generally. This effect is not aversive, and indeed there is at least indirect evidence that low doses of caffeine enhance subjective energy. However, there is also evidence that regular use of even small amounts of caffeine may increase tension and cause a variety of other negative effects.

Although a single arousal continuum cannot mediate the complex mood enhancement that some people derive from these substances, the positive mood effects can be understood with reference to the two-dimensional arousal model proposed in this book. Energy, with its positive hedonic tone, and tension, with its negative hedonic tone, are directly correlated from low to moderate levels, and inversely correlated from moderate to high levels (see Chapter 6).

Keeping these relationships in mind, it is likely that substances that reduce relatively high levels of tension (e.g., alcohol) would also enhance energy, with a net effect of mild euphoria and a generally positive mood shift. Similarly, substances that enhance energy directly (e.g., cocaine) would also reduce tension. And substances that have *mild* tension-inducing effects (possibly caffeine) would also increase subjective energy.

As indicated in Chapter 6, studying the effects of nicotine may offer particular insight into the physiological bases of these arousal systems. The increased autonomic arousal that nicotine produces is often accompanied by decreased skeletal-muscular arousal (Domino, 1973; Gilbert, 1979; Mangan & Golding, 1984). Given the assumption in the present two-dimensional model that both energy and tension are associated with physiological arousal, but that tense arousal involves skeletal-muscular inhibition, it is quite possible that smoking results in small increases in energy together with decreases in tension. Thus, observations that cigarettes offer satisfaction in both low and high arousal situations become understandable in relation to attempts to raise energy and/or to reduce tension.

Given the possibility that various substances affect mood through changes in both energetic and tense arousal, let us further consider certain daily mood variations in relation to carbohydrate-snacking, which might provide a behavior pattern that holds for all of the substances discussed. Elsewhere (Thayer, 1987a) I have argued that sugar-snacking may be based on an attempt to raise energy. That is, a craving for simple carbohydrates may develop in low energy times or during periods of slight tension when personal demands are high.

Often people are only vaguely aware of this motivation. Instead of thinking, "I need energy to deal with this situation," the individual may think, "This snack will make me feel better," or "It will help me to get through this activity." The small energy surge that a sugar snack produces may not be labeled as such; instead, any introspections that occur might identify only a global sense of feeling better.

A simple conditioning effect would be fundamental in understanding the motivation to snack. Thousands of times in the past when a vague feeling of discomfort (tense-tiredness) was followed by a sugar snack, the uncomfortable feeling disappeared. With these multiple conditioning trials, it is not surprising that tense-tiredness would elicit thoughts and desires for something sweet. The sweet thing may be whatever is available or within recent consciousness (ice cream in the refrigerator or a box of candy nearby). With this pattern, one can see the basis for sugar craving—tense-tiredness coupled with thoughts about the desirable food.

This reasoning is complicated somewhat by the possible effects of taste. Is it possible that the craving has nothing to do with energy, but instead is related only to a desire for a sweet and good-tasting substance? Of course, taste may be an important aspect of the motive, but a biological need for energy could still underlie the general process. Aside from the special case of substances like saccharin, good-tasting foods usually produce relatively rapid increases in blood glucose. Therefore, people may associate these foods with energy increases (cf. Mook, 1974). Also, a distinction might be made between a mild urge brought about by a localized taste sensitivity that can be satisfied with a small sweet, and a stronger, more persistent urge that is related to the basic motive of raising energy.

In any event, if the energy-raising motive is a valid concept, a similar conditioning effect could easily hold for the other substances described. For example, if a cigarette both raises energy and reduces tension, then the craving for this substance is likely to be strong in low-energy or slightly tense conditions. And the relief from these feelings that occurs by smoking could produce a potential conditioning effect that would involve over 7,000 trials a year for a pack-a-day smoker! Such a conditioned effect is likely to be extremely powerful.

Coffee, alcohol, or other drugs may work in much the same way. The uncomfortable feeling that initiates the use of the substance—most likely tense-tiredness—is repeatedly paired with at least temporary cessation following the substance use. In each case, the uncomfortable feeling and the thoughts about the substance would represent the vague craving that motivates the use.

This conditioned effect could be extremely insidious, because awareness of the dynamics might not be present, and therefore counteractive behaviors would not be initiated. Thus, the individual may be unable to anticipate the times that the desire will occur (e.g., low energy times of day, or with disturbing thoughts or unpleasant events). Also, alternative means of dealing with the tense-tiredness (see below) may not be wisely employed without awareness of these dynamics.

Furthermore, the negative effects that can derive at a later period from the use of the substance probably would have little influence on the user's viewpoint because they occur too long after the initial conditioning. For example, even though tension and tiredness apparently develop an hour after eating a sugar snack (Thayer, 1987a), these changes have little conditioning effect because of the temporal separation of the unpleasantness from the initial stimulus conditions and the immediate behavioral response. What is likely to be more important for the conditioned effect is the energy surge that immediately follows sugar ingestion.

With this understanding of self-regulation of mood based on a conditioned behavior to enhance energy, recent observations about cross-substance associations become much more understandable. For example, most people who have attempted to stop smoking are aware that their weight often increases, suggesting increased eating occurs. Consistent with that idea, Grunberg (1986) has documented the existence of a craving for simple carbohydrates among former smokers who are trying to avoid cigarettes. Similarly, cocaine users who are attempting to avoid the substance often seek sugar in unusually large amounts. Quite possibly, this low awareness conditioned motive to enhance energy can explain other times when there are cravings for sweets. For example, Rosenthal and his associates (Rosenthal et al., 1986; Rosenthal & Heffernan, 1986) have observed that people with seasonal depressive disorder often crave simple carbohydrates in the winter months when their depression is greatest. As indicated earlier, depression is often characterized by tense-tiredness.

Tense-tiredness may not be the only eliciting condition of the various kinds of substance use discussed. It is quite possible that people have learned to repeat those behaviors that maintain good moods. Therefore, even when individuals are experiencing a good mood, they might sense slight diminutions in that mood and attempt to allay them. What better way of maintaining the good mood than to use some substance that enhances subjective energy?

Unanswered Questions About Mood

There are a number of questions about mood that remain unanswered. These are matters for which evidence may suggest one theoretical solution, but the issues are complex, and upon further research, another solution could prove to be more correct. Let me briefly describe a few of the more important unanswered questions, and also indicate my views on these matters.

Is There a Separate Hedonic Continuum?

Previously, I indicated that energetic arousal was found to have a positive hedonic tone, and tense arousal a negative tone (Thayer, 1978a). Moods associated with these kinds of arousal are pleasant or unpleasant. Thus, calm-energy is a positive mood and tense-tiredness is negative. Furthermore, if energy is fairly high in relation to tension, tense-energy may also be pleasurable. But there is a possibility of a separate, different pleasure dimension of mood. Do variations of energetic and tense arousal fully account for the positive and negative hedonic tone of moods? Or are there other mood characteristics that have to do specifically with pleasure and its opposite state, and that are not the same as energetic and tense arousal?

There is a rich early history of theory concerning a pleasure dimension of emotion, affect, or mood (e.g., Nowlis & Nowlis, 1956; Schlosberg, 1954; Young, 1967). Physiological research on the so-called pleasure or reward centers of the brain in animals (Olds, 1962; Olds & Milner, 1954) also suggests this dimension, and findings concerning opioid receptors in the brain and the isolation of endogenous opiatelike substances (Akil & Watson, 1983; Miller, 1983; Post et al., 1984) suggest a possible biochemical substrate of subjective pleasure.

More recently, Watson and Tellegen (1985) sought to arrive at a consensual structure of mood by reanalyzing and combining a variety of self-rating studies of affect. The two dimensions they obtained were labeled positive and negative affect, and they were found to be orthogonal, or independent.

Although Watson and Tellegen concluded that positive and negative affect are sufficient to account for the important variations in mood, in their reanalysis they obtained what may be a separate pleasantness dimension that loaded in psychometric space at a 45-degree angle to positive and negative affect (moderate correlation with each). This possible pleasantness-unpleasantness dimension included such self-descriptive adjectives as content, happy, kindly, pleased, satisfied, and warmhearted versus blue, grouchy, lonely, sad, sorry, and unhappy (cf. Russell, 1978, 1980). At one pole, the pleasantness dimension would be correlated with two dimensions that they labeled High Positive Affect (active, elated, enthusiastic, excited, peppy, strong) and Low Negative Affect (at rest, calm, placid, relaxed). The bipolar opposite, or unpleasantness pole, would be correlated with Low Positive Affect (drowsy, dull, sleepy, sluggish) and High Negative Affect (distressed, fearful, hostile, jittery, nervous, scornful).

The dimensions that Watson and Tellegen labeled as Positive and Negative Affect substantially overlap energetic and tense arousal as I have been discussing these mood dimensions. Therefore, if one takes Watson and Tellegen's interpretations as valid, it would appear that pleasantness-unpleasantness is correlated but not identical, with energetic and tense arousal. But this conclusion is tentative, however, because dimension labels (e.g., Pleasantness) are somewhat arbitrary. For example, the adjective grouping that Watson and Tellegen labeled Positive Affect and that I have called energetic arousal might also be labeled "pleasantness," based on the positive hedonic tone of several of the self-descriptive adjectives included in that dimension.

That this matter remains unsettled is illustrated by other research as well. Isen, Daubman, and Nowicki (1987) used another research approach, and they concluded that pleasant feelings have effects different from the effects produced by arousal. As part of their studies of creative problem-solving, these researchers manipulated pleasant affect with a short comedy film. They also manipulated arousal by requiring research participants to step up and down from a cement block for two minutes. Expected performance differences on various cognitive tasks (e.g., problem-solving) were obtained with the film manipulation but not with the exercise condition.

These results would seem to suggest that at least for certain cognitive processes, pleasant feelings are not identical to arousal feelings. However, there are other interpretations to these results than made by Isen and her colleagues. First, a comedy film that makes people laugh probably would be tension-reducing, as humor often is (Burger, 1986; Shurcliff, 1968). Further, the physical activity of laughing is likely to be physiologically arousing. Another point is that the stepping task may have been perceived as aversive by participants, therefore becoming tension-inducing. Thus, it is conceivable that the film temporarily produced calm-energy, and the stepping task, tense-energy. Or, if the exercise task was physically draining, it may have produced tense-tiredness. Still, these alternative interpretations are not based on any hard data, and the original conclusions of Isen, Daubman, and Nowicki may be correct. If that is the case, their research provides further evidence that pleasant affect is slightly different from the positive affective tone of certain arousal states.

After surveying all this evidence, one is still left with the question as to whether pure pleasantness is separate from arousal-produced positive affect. At the present time, I am uncertain. Variations in energetic and tense arousal account for many aspects of mood, and on the basis of parsimony I must tentatively conclude that there is not a separate pleasure dimension. However, the physiological and biochemical evidence about particular processes and anatomical loci of the brain that may mediate pleasure suggests that a separate pleasure dimension of mood may exist. Also, there are factor analytically defined dimensions that may be pure reflections of pleasure, further adding to the uncertainty. Finally, the research of Isen suggests that arousal elements of mood may not be identical with the pleasure elements of mood. But none of this evidence is conclusive. The findings using animals as subjects do not address the question directly, and alternative explanations exist for the findings of Isen as well as for the factor analytic data.

It is conceivable that the brain and other relevant systems of the body are organized in such a way that arousing conditions influence neural centers or biochemical processes that specifically result in feelings of pleasure. However, important anatomical-biochemical divisions might still exist between the major substrates of arousal and those of pleasure and its opposite condition. Further research may indicate that under natural conditions these various processes usually operate together, but sometimes they could be fractionated.

For example, there may be certain drugs that directly affect brain functions related to subjective pleasure, but which have little or no effect on energetic and tense arousal. Two drugs that might be cited in this regard are heroin and cocaine (Ray, 1972). Heroin produces a distinctly pleasurable affective rush, but at the same time it enervates the body and leaves the user in a dreamy, semi-somnolent state. Thus, it would appear in this case that subjective pleasure is not related to heightened energetic arousal.[7] On the other hand, cocaine also produces pleasurable affect, but the pleasure is associated with subjective energy, increased self-esteem, and the perception of enhanced abilities.

Are Depression, Anger, and Sexual Arousal Pure States?

Other questions about mood remain unanswered. For instance, many forms of depression have as their primary symptoms tense-tiredness, pessimism about the future, low self-esteem, and general unhappiness. This combination of subjective effects apparently is related to lowered energetic and heightened tense arousal (Bassin & Thayer, 1986; Thayer & Wettler, 1975). However, can depression be fully understood on the basis of these arousal patterns, or is there some additional bodily condition that is unique to depressive conditions?

It would appear that something else is involved, because people who are tense and tired and who also feel pessimistic and unhappy may not feel depressed. On the other hand, low-level depression could go unrecognized except for these symptoms. It is possible that lengthy periods of tense-tiredness, in combination with cognitive variables, could form such unpleasant subjective conditions that the individual eventually becomes depressed (e.g., learned helplessness [Metalsky et al., 1982; Seligman, 1975] or some such phenomenon develops).

I have been describing low-level depression, but even major depressions have no clear physiological marker that is unique to the disorder, and which could not be attributed to protracted states of tension and low energy. As indicated in Chapter 2, there has been a great deal of research on the neurochemical bases of depression (e.g., neurotransmitter imbalances in the monoaminergic system), but at this time the physiological mechanisms of action in these disorders remain unclear (Mason, 1984; McNeal & Cimbolic, 1986). Certainly, extreme behavioral correlates of depression, such as suicide, seem to differentiate this malady from simple states of tense-tiredness and its associated cognitive reactions. Moreover, the long-term nature of major depression seems to set this disorder apart. But as yet, the underlying physiological dynamics have not been unambiguously clarified. Therefore, the extent to which depression is a unique or pure mood condition remains unanswered.

Other questions concern states such as anger and sexual arousal. So far, I have avoided discussing moods associated with these biological states. However, it is quite possible that anger and sexual antecedents influence mood in a unique way, and that a complete theory would account for moods that are affected by these states. It is also possible, however, that moods associated with anger and sexual arousal are variations of interactions among energetic arousal, tense arousal, and cognitive factors.

Events Versus Natural Processes as Mood Antecedents

A personal incident will introduce the last unanswered question about mood that I wish to deal with here. One morning my twelve-year-old daughter told me that she was in a good mood. When I asked her what causes good moods, she said, "A lot of times, good moods happen when people have something good to look forward to." I mention this incident only because it probably represents a common viewpoint about mood. Many believe that moods are primarily created and maintained by events in one's life (cf. McArthur, 1972). Naturally occurring internal processes are either overlooked or undervalued as mood determinants.

Contrary to this point of view, my main discussions of mood antecedents focused on naturally occurring processes such as circadian rhythms, exercise, sleep, and nutrition. These, together with cognitive interpretations, were assumed to exercise the major influences on mood. It seems clear, however, that events are important mood antecedents as well. But what is not clear is the *relative* importance of external events versus natural internal processes and cognitive constructions in determining and maintaining mood. In experimental-statistical terms, what proportions of mood variance are accounted for by the two classes of influence?

Several points might be considered in addressing this question. First of all, negative moods are probably more influenced by life events than positive ones. As the standard mood state may well be positive or at least neutral, shifts to negative moods probably occur with threatening environmental circumstances. Thus, given good health, physical fitness, adequate sleep, and satisfactory nutrition, positive or neutral moods would be the norm. However, stressors such as time pressures, evaluation anxiety, personal misfortune, and so on produce negative moods. These external events create tense arousal, and moods associated with this condition are subjectively experienced as negative. Therefore, the question of the relative importance of events versus natural processes would be answered partly on the basis of the type of mood (positive or negative).

But a second point to consider is that moods often override external events. Even the most negative events may have little affective impact when the individual is in a good mood, and very positive events may not change a bad mood. Every person has had the experience of feeling so good that an event, which otherwise would be quite negative, has little or no effect. The opposite experience is also common, particularly with depressed people. Of course, a sufficient number of positive events probably would eliminate the negative mood (e.g., Lewinsohn & Amenson, 1978), but at least within a short time period negative moods often appear to be unaffected by a positive event. Therefore, there are occasions in which mood is relatively unaffected by events.

A third point is that events, personal processes, and cognitive constructions strongly interact. Thus, a problem is viewed as more serious when the individual is tired and tense than when she or he is feeling energetic and calm (Thayer, 1987b). Time of day, nutritional condition, and amount of sleep appear to be quite important when interpreting the personal significance of events. Therefore, it is probably the interaction of events and natural processes that accounts for the major proportion of mood variance.

A final point that should be discussed concerning the significance of events to mood relates to the fact that people are often unable to identify the determinants of their own moods. If events do influence moods, this inability to identify the causes of mood change indicates some failing in awareness of the relevant dynamics.[8] It is unclear whether this lack of awareness is due to some sort of unconscious mechanism such as that posited by Psychoanalytic theory (e.g., Brenner, 1955; Gaylin, 1979) or to some other basis of limited awareness (e.g.,

Hilgard, 1977; see also recent reviews in special issue of *Personality & social psychology bulletin, 13,* 1987).

Within this book, the implications of limited awareness of negative mood antecedents were not systematically discussed. However, this matter may be quite important, because this limitation would reduce the utility of the signal function of mood states. One particular outcome of this limitation would be a reduced ability to self-modify negative moods. For example, an individual with a continuing personal problem may give little conscious consideration to the matter, and yet it could result in chronic tension. Over time this tension would reduce energy and contribute to various negative mood states. With no or little awareness of the problem's existence or effect, changing the negative mood caused by it is quite problematic.

A likely reason for the inability of people to identify the causes of mood is that they generally are not aware of slowly changing natural processes, and therefore, they do not see their significance in mood formation. Shifts in circadian energy rhythms, for example, are so gradual that often they go undetected. And mood effects from nutritional influences are so subtle as to defy analysis with any but the most reliable assessments. Moreover, these mood shifts are so weak on any one occasion that well-known expectation effects can probably devalue their significance or overcome them. Nevertheless, as I have tried to show, these subtle internally generated moods are present and influential when considered over time.

In any event, it appears that as people become more aware of these natural states, the reasons for mood shifts become much more clear. The very process of self-observation sharpens awareness.

Applications: Systematic Self-Observation

Many people have asked me, "How can I control my moods?" This book is not about the control of mood states in this sense, nor has my research dealt in large measure with the issue, but in the course of many years of research and teaching, I have often thought about it.

In my view, the most important key to mood control is systematic self-observation. This enables individuals to be aware of their own idiosyncratic mood reactions so that appropriate modifications can be made. Intelligent adults usually are able to reduce negative moods and enhance positive ones when adequate feedback is available about basic mood reactions. Often when dysphoric mood reactions are present, one finds an individual who is not clearly perceiving basic interactions among events, natural processes, and mood effects.

This inability to observe mood dynamics accurately is understandable. Moods are difficult to observe reliably, but accurate observations are not impossible. The greatest problem occurs with subtle background moods that may be overridden on any single occasion, but that influence behavior over time. Strong moods such as intense anxiety are obvious even to the casual and poorly trained observer. But subtle moods offer problems, first in discrimination, and second in accurate rating.

Systematic self-observation of moods is especially important due to the wide differences that exist among individuals, even with the basic processes that were described in previous chapters. Variance between subjects accounts for one of the most sizable portions of variability in research on mood. One person reacts strongly to exercise, and another does not. One individual experiences increased depression at night, and another feels most depressed in the morning.

Although there are substantial individual differences, stable relationships exist for each person between energy and tension states on one hand, and various other moods and perceptions on the other. Moreover, it is possible to detect these individual differences through careful assessments of changing mood states in daily life processes. A longitudinal approach is essential, however (see Chapter 7). Observations on one occasion only or merely for two or three times are too unreliable. In observing diurnal energy cycles, for example, one should collect observations on several days that are not markedly unusual in relation to events and personal physical condition.

One of the changes that begins to occur after an individual systematically observes him or herself for a period of time is that an awareness develops. Subjective feelings become much more salient than they were in the past. And with this enhanced awareness, the person often notices relationships that were unnoticed before. It is at this stage of self-understanding that changes can be made that have real effects on mood.

In previous chapters, it was postulated that moods of energy and tension could have evolved through bioevolutionary development. They serve as indicators of readiness for action, the need for rest, and the nearness of danger or safety. However, without awareness of these subjective signal systems, the individual is at a disadvantage.

The reasons for this variability in awareness probably have to do in part with the learning history of the individual. Most adults have had lots of practice identifying energy and tiredness, but less experience with tension and calmness. This learning history probably begins with parents noting how their child is feeling and supplying words to describe those feelings. For example, a parent sees a child yawning and says, "You are tired".

Indications of tiredness or energy are much more salient and well-known than those of tension and calmness. For many people, little practice with identifying tension in their early years is likely to have occurred. Moreover, even in adulthood there may be serious impediments to awareness of these subjective feelings. For example, fear, anxiety, and tension are socially undesirable states, especially for men. Undoubtedly this reduces self-awareness of these states. Another problem regarding identification is that chronic states of low-level tension may eventually become the norm, so that the individual no longer recognizes the condition.[9]

Many people first identify their low-level tension states by noting things that they are doing or thoughts that they are having, and only then do they realize that they are tense. For example, an individual will note that he is tapping his fingers or wiggling his foot. Another person notices tight muscles in her neck or back, or she notices that the muscles of the jaw are taut. Uncomfortable stomach sensations are also common indicators of tension. Other relevant signs are feelings of impatience and irritability. One good self-observer described to me recurrent thoughts that she recognizes as accompanying tension, and I suspect that this phenomenon is not uncommon. She said that when she is tense, she always thinks about ice cream. In other words, tension-related thoughts (in this example, thoughts related to tension reduction) may serve as indicators of tension.

These signs may be the initial indication of tension, but on further introspection, a subtle but distinctive feeling is found to be present. Moreover, as self-ratings lead to ever more refined discriminations among moods, this subjective state becomes much more apparent. A similar process occurs with the absence of tension.

Distinguishing the feeling of calmness may be even more difficult than it is for tension because the bodily signs and behavioral reactions are not as apparent. Persons who regularly practice relaxation or tension-reduction exercises (e.g., meditation, visualization, natural breathing) seem able to identify this state very well. Those who exercise regularly also seem to be good at this discrimination. Perhaps repeatedly experiencing periods of calmness in immediate conjunction with tension states allows internal cues to become more apparent.

It appears that most adults are best at identifying and making self-ratings of tiredness and energy. They are next best at identifying tension, and poorest at identifying calmness. However, appropriately identifying all these states seems to improve with multiple observations and self-ratings.

Applications: Projects, Measurement Materials, and Designs for Systematic Self-Observation

Intelligent adults can usually modify moods to a more positive level if accurate feedback is available. To do this, one needs measurement materials to assess core elements of mood. Moreover, using procedures to control some of the more important confounding variables is quite useful in this process. With the right materials and procedures, even an untrained observer can obtain self-understanding much more quickly.

Several kinds of basic self-observational projects yield excellent feedback, which in turn can enable people to deal more effectively with dysphoric mood states. One of these projects is a systematic assessment of diurnal energy cycles, with a noting of tension variations at different points in the cycle (see Chapter 4). This project is fairly easily accomplished by using self-ratings with the AD ACL taken at the top of each hour over several typical days. It does require, however, that a number of days be assessed, because moods are subtle and unusual events on any one day can raise or lower both tension and energy scores. However, once the background endogenous rhythm is established, it is possible to predict very accurately the times of day that positive and negative moods (e.g., optimism, depression) will naturally occur.

A second basic self-observational project involves assessing mood before and after brief periods of moderate exercise, such as brisk walks (see Chapter 5). Once again, this project requires that these assessments be made on a number of occasions so as to reduce random or extraneous error sources that otherwise would influence energy and tension scores. It is useful, in this regard, to schedule these exercise periods at different times of the day so as to determine when the exercise is most effective. Once this information is obtained, the individual usually becomes aware of the integral relationship between exercise and mood.

This same experimental design can be effectively employed with various other possible mood influences. For example, a particular kind of food (e.g., sugar) or drug (e.g., caffeine) can be studied in relation to energy and tension changes. The effects on mood of different durations of sleep can also be studied this way, although here it is useful to take measurements at several times in the day following a particular sleep variation so as to observe its full effects, as well as take measurements on multiple occasions when this particular sleep variation was employed.

These various self-observational projects are not always definitive because expectation effects that may confound the results could occur. Also, in general, the fewer times the self-observational sequence is repeated, the lower the reliability of the results. But intelligent adults can usually overcome expectation effects when they are aware of their possible existence and especially when self-observations occur on multiple occasions.

Some of the best systematic self-observational procedures are described in the Appendixes, which include complete measurement materials for longitudinal studies. The materials include various forms of the AD ACL, other mood markers, and designs that I have used successfully and for which self-study was a primary part.[10]

Applications: Moderate Exercise for Short-Term Mood Modulation

Once self-observation confirms relationships among energy, tension, and other mood states, it is likely that enhanced energetic arousal and reduced tense arousal will be sought. In Chapter 5, some of the growing evidence that exercise is effective in overall mood enhancement was reviewed. I would say that assuming typical health, exercise, sleep, and nutritional conditions, the single most important natural mood modulator is exercise, and the most effective way of enhancing mood is through increased exercise.

In the usual research design that employs exercise, it is assumed that physical conditioning is the object of this activity. With improved physical condition, overall energetic arousal is probably increased, if not in amplitude, then in the amount of time in which subjective energy is sustained. Clearly, this is beneficial for optimal mood states. However, moderate exercise can be very effective as a short-term mood modulator, even though a person's physical condition is not substantially improved. Brisk walks of five to ten minutes enhance mood for up to one or two hours (Thayer, 1987a). These brisk walks, or comparable forms of moderate exercise, can be extremely useful during those periods when a temporary relief of dysphoric moods is desirable. Thus, short periods of moderate exercise may serve as excellent therapeutic interventions.

One experiment that demonstrated these potentially beneficial effects involved randomly alternating brisk ten-minute walks with the ingestion of a candy bar at fixed times of day over a three-week period (Thayer, 1987a). This experiment was described previously, but let us here consider the potential short-term therapeutic effects suggested by the experimental results. Although the mood effects from these manipulations were quite subtle, reliable differences in mood ratings for two hours were obtained. Both the sugar snack and the brisk walk resulted in increased energy and decreased tiredness, but the effects were greater for the walk than for the candy ingestion. Moreover, ratings of energy showed reliable increases for at least one hour after the walk. In comparison, the majority of participants felt more tired one hour after eating the candy bar, and by two hours there was no longer any effect.

The comparative value of the walk versus the candy was even more apparent for ratings of tension. Although the candy may have had a temporary tension-reducing effect, by one hour after ingestion, tension increased. In comparison, tension was significantly reduced by the ten-minute walk; ratings reached the lowest degree ten minutes after the walk, but even 110 minutes after the walk there were small but reliable decreases in tension.

The walk was clearly superior to the candy in the overall effects on energetic and tense arousal. These results strongly suggest that brief moderate exercise may be substituted for a sugar snack with excellent mood effects. Considering that sugar cravings probably develop in conjunction with a conditioned desire for mood enhancement, using moderate exercise may be an excellent method of alleviating these urges.

This mood effect from exercise may also be used by dieters. Diets are often rigorously maintained, only to be broken periodically when resolve is weak or when tense-tiredness temporarily overcomes inhibitions. It is difficult for the dieter to avoid those periods of weakness through pure cognitive resolve, particularly at certain times. One significant problem is that even though the diet may only have been broken a single time, this suspension has continuing effects. Once the diet is broken, the individual is often so dispirited that he or she gives up the diet altogether.

But suppose that a person were to substitute a five- or ten-minute walk on those occasions of periodic weakness. Since the immediate mood change that follows a brisk walk is superior to the satisfaction gained from food, the walk would appear to be an excellent alternative. If the tense-tiredness were relieved by the walk even for only one hour, the worst of the weak period might be over, and the individual might be able to avoid the temptation to break the diet altogether.

Temporary alleviation of the urge to smoke may also be possible through using brief periods of exercise. Recently, my students and I have been conducting research on this (e.g., Thayer & Peters, 1987). Volunteers who smoke one to two packs of cigarettes a day follow a randomized schedule in which five-minute brisk walks are sometimes completed before smoking, with the aim of determining the effect of this brief exercise. On twelve separate occasions in their natural life settings, these participants use a procedure in which a forty-five-minute period of nonsmoking inactivity (e.g., reading or working at a desk) is followed by making self-ratings of their urge to smoke and of their current states of energy and tension (using AD ACLs). They then open an envelope to determine whether they are to walk briskly for five minutes or continue their previous activity. Following that five minutes of walking or other activity, they complete a second set of self-ratings, after which they are free to smoke whenever they wish. However, they are asked to record the time that the next cigarette is taken.

At this time, ten participants have completed the experimental procedure, and the results are quite positive. The time before smoking the next cigarette has been increased following the five-minute walk by a statistically significant 50 percent (13.1 minutes in the walk condition versus 8.8 minutes in the control condition). Consistent with this, the rated urge to smoke was decreased in the walk condition, although this effect was weaker than the time effect. An analysis of the self-ratings suggests that a mood change is the basis of this reduced urge. The walk produced significantly increased subjective energy compared to the control condition, and those individuals with the greatest increases in subjective energy chose to wait the longest before smoking the next cigarette.

The practical implications of this research are great for those individuals who use cigarettes to temporarily raise energy or reduce tension. For the smoker attempting to stop, the urge to smoke becomes greater and greater until eventually the individual succumbs and lights a cigarette. However, this urge is probably stronger at certain times (perhaps acute tense-tiredness periods that follow cyclical patterns) and under certain conditions (Gilbert, 1979; Leventhal & Cleary, 1980). If an individual were able to substitute a short walk, and gain a comparable or superior mood effect, the number of cigarettes that are smoked might be substantially reduced.

Another recent study by Bassin and myself (1986) suggests that short brisk walks may also be employed to allay moderate depression. This experiment involved seven women who were feeling depressed several times a week, but who were not being treated for the condition. The design of the experiment required participants to complete depression checklists and AD ACLs when the depression occurred, and then either to walk briskly for fifteen minutes or to continue the activity in which they had been engaged. A second set of self-ratings were completed after the walk. This whole sequence was done twice. The same procedure was repeated on control days that were as similar in important respects to the depression days as possible, except that the depression was absent.

The results indicated that in the depressed state the walk reliably reduced subjective depression. Furthermore, a relationship with arousal states was suggested, because the walk also increased energy and decreased tension. Thus, it appears from this research that if an individual is depressed, a short brisk walk will lessen the feeling. As with snacking and smoking, short periods of moderate exercise seem to be excellent therapeutic interventions.

Although the value of moderate exercise as a therapeutic intervention may be quite high theoretically, it is not clear that people left on their own will use this method. In the depression experiment just described, sixteen enthusiastic volunteers began the research, but only seven completed all phases. This substantial dropout rate occurred even though the walk appeared to have the same positive mood effect for the dropouts as it did for those who completed the experiment. In discussing these results, one of my students offered a possible explanation for this high dropout rate. She said that when she is depressed, she doesn't have the energy to walk. This is ironic, because the very activity (exercise) that might be most beneficial in times of depression is the activity that may be least desired.

A similar analysis might be valid in the case of sugar-snacking and smoking. If these substances are employed as self-medications that enhance mood, and if periods of tense-tiredness are often the precipitating conditions for substance use, then the individual may feel too tired to walk or engage in similar exercise at the very time when the walk would be of most benefit. Use of the undesirable substances, however, is very easy, and tense-tiredness offers no impediment to this behavior.

Even with this limitation, these physical activities may still be self-initiated if the individual is able to overcome cognitively the effects of tense-tiredness. That is, individuals who are aware of the comparative effects of exercise may be able to force themselves to take the walks. And once engaged in this physical activity, the immediately enhanced energy feelings would probably sustain a short brisk walk. In advising people on this, I have suggested that they not think in terms of a ten-minute brisk walk, but that they merely begin to walk slowly and for a short distance, after which they can increase their pace and walking time if they feel up to it. Usually, by the time they have walked even a short distance, they feel like continuing the walk or speeding it up.

Applications: Recognition and Accommodation to Time of Day Mood Effects

Systematic self-observation will probably verify the effects of time of day on energy, tension, and a variety of other mood variables. However, individual differences make self-observation over several days particularly important. Although many individuals experience peak energy in the late morning, decreases in late afternoon, and sharp declines in the late evenings (see Chapter 4), others may have patterns that differ from this typical cycle. But the relationship between peaks and troughs of energy and other mood states is likely to be consistent across persons, at least over time. And this consistency can be used in personal planning to optimize mood.

Three studies that were described briefly earlier will illustrate this. In one study, participants rated the apparent seriousness of an ongoing personal problem at various times of day and over a three-week period (Thayer, 1987b, experiment 1). Very subtle changes in problem perception were observed, with the problem appearing more serious in the late afternoon and evening than in the late morning. In general, the perceived seriousness of the problem varied with the energy and tension levels of the individual. Measures of calm-energy predicted that the problem would be rated as less serious, while tense-tiredness measures predicted ratings of greater seriousness. A second study (Thayer, 1987b, experiment 2) employed a similar procedure, but in this experiment, optimism was measured, and its ratings varied with time of day. Again, the effects were subtle, but consistent.

A third study (Thayer, Takahashi, & Pauli, 1988) focused on such moods and related behaviors as depression, self-esteem, and positive interactions with others. This study employed a retrospective rating procedure in which participants first indicated the times of day at which various moods and other psychological functions typically are best and worst for them. Later, the same individuals rated energy and tension every hour over six typical days, from waking to sleep. Comparative analyses of the retrospective reports, together with the measurements of actual cycles, indicated that the periods previously designated by participants to be best inevitably were times when measured energy was highest. The reports of when functioning was at its worst were found to be those times of day when measured energy was lowest. These relationships held even though individuals indicated different optimal times of day for the various functions, and diurnal rhythms were different for each person.

These three studies suggest that if naturally occurring low points of energetic arousal were recognized and compensated for, moods might be optimized. As an example, if one knew the periods of the day when energy is low and tension high, the individual might avoid thinking about personal problems at those times. Simply knowing that there are periods when depressing thoughts are more likely to occur might mitigate their effects.

Another way of accomplishing this might be by reminding oneself that this is the time of day when energy usually is low and tension high. If an individual recognizes that these cyclical processes occur naturally, and that mood can be expected to be negative at these times, the dysphoric moods need not be attributed to negative life circumstances. It is probably more comforting and less likely to result in increasing depression if one attributes negative moods to natural bodily processes than to external events, which are difficult to change.

Other personal strategies could be employed, such as avoiding discussions and arguments with others at times of tense-tiredness. Also, it is sometimes possible to plan stressful activities for times of day when energy is naturally high, and therefore, the effects of stress-produced tension are reduced. In each of these cases, knowledge of naturally occurring energy cycles and subsequent vulnerability to increased tension might enable an individual to control his or her mood.

Applications: Enhancing Mood Through Increasing Long-Term Energetic Arousal and Decreasing Tense Arousal

As a general rule, any long-term routines that increase energetic arousal are likely to enhance mood. Therefore, mood is probably improved through such well-known practices for maintaining good health as obtaining sufficient sleep, regular exercise, balanced nutrition, and avoiding toxic substances (cf. Berkman & Breslow, 1983). The likely effect of following a healthy regimen is heightened and more sustained subjective energy.

Although the evidence about mood enhancement is strong regarding exercise, less empirical proof can be marshalled in relation to other health practices, perhaps because longitudinal research designs necessary for investigating these rather subtle effects are not widely used. For example, some research indicates that variations in amount of sleep have little effect on mood (Berry & Webb, 1985). Yet, in my experience with mood journals kept by students over lengthy time periods, lack of sleep is usually an important predictor variable of subjective tension.

Although there is little formal empirical proof, the relationship between sleep and mood seems quite logical. Insufficient sleep probably reduces overall energetic arousal, leaving the individual susceptible to increased tense arousal. Thus, greater tense-tiredness occurs, and related negative moods develop as a reaction. Moreover, this probably becomes a cycle of increasing tension resulting in decreased sleep, and in turn, further increased tension.

This cycle may lead to gradually developing insomnia. Insomnia can be described as excessive tense-tiredness at times when sleep is appropriate. Within the theoretical model proposed in this book, tension is a reaction to danger that results in arousal and a state of vigilance for the sources of threat in the environment. This heightened arousal is incompatible with the low arousal necessary for sleep.

Heightened energetic arousal indirectly results in reduced tense arousal, or at least in states of tense-energy that are somewhat positive hedonically. However, by directly reducing tense arousal, the optimal mood state of calm-energy may be achieved. Of primary importance in this respect is the development of means of coping with stressful life circumstances and personal problems. Of course, this is much easier said than done. And much of the time it may require psychotherapeutic aid.

But it is also possible to reduce tension through self-directed activity. Regularly practiced relaxation or stress management methods such as meditation, visualization, yoga, natural breathing, and so on may be quite effective in directly reducing tension and, therefore, in enhancing energy. Without daily practice with these techniques, however, they are not likely to be helpful in acute tension-inducing circumstances.

To summarize these methods of application, mood enhancement is probably best accomplished initially through systematic self-observation. This enables an individual to become aware of the relationships among energy, tension, and various dysphoric and optimal mood states, as well as to become aware of individual differences in mood response that may be a part of each of these relationships.

In general, optimal moods are attained by increasing energetic arousal and decreasing tense arousal. Short-term techniques for accomplishing this include utilization of brief periods of moderate exercise, and the monitoring and shifting of schedules in relation to endogenous diurnal energy cycles. Long-term practices likely to be extremely useful in this regard are routines that enhance health, sleep, and diet, all of which probably increase subjective energy, a core component of optimal mood states.

In addition to increasing energetic arousal, directly reducing tense arousal is also likely to optimize mood. Coping with or reducing stressful life circumstances and personal problems is important for this, but regularly practicing relaxation or stress management techniques may reduce chronic tense arousal.[11] And often these techniques can be put to good use during temporary tension-inducing circumstances.

The Activation-Deactivation Adjective Check List (AD ACL)

The AD ACL is a multidimensional test of various transitory arousal states, including energetic and tense arousal (see Chapter 3). It has been used widely in many psychophysiological (e.g., Mackay, 1980) and psychological contexts,* and it has taken a variety of language forms (e.g., Bohlin & Kjellberg, 1973—Swedish version; Grzegolowska-Klarkowska, 1980—Polish version; Mackay et al., 1978—Anglicized version). Within the wider dimensions of energetic and tense arousal are four subscales—Energy (General Activation), Tiredness (Deactivation-Sleep), Tension (High Activation), and Calmness (General Deactivation).

The above parenthetical designations were given in the 1960s (Thayer, 1967), before the multidimensional arousal model was conceptualized in its present form. If these parenthetical names were to be modifed at the present time, they would be somewhat different. For example, the parenthetical name associated with Tiredness would probably now be *General Deactivation,* thus indicating that it is likely to represent the opposite pole from *General Activation.* Other names associated with Tension and Calmness might be High and Low Preparatory-Emergency Activation (or Arousal), thus indicating the likely function of these kinds of arousal.

The self-rating response format used in this test originally followed a format employed by Nowlis (1965) with the Mood Adjective Check List. This four-point self-rating system is slightly unconventional in comparison with the more usual three-, five-, or seven-point formats used in a number of other adjective checklists. Also, the verbal anchors of the AD ACL (as well as of the Mood Adjective Check List), although quite meaningful, are not completely symmetrical.

In order to determine if these somewhat unconventional features result in important differences, a study was recently completed to compare factor structures using different self-rating formats (Thayer, 1986). In this research, little difference was observed between the usual AD ACL format and others. Additional evidence for the validity of the AD ACL format may be found in other studies that employed it, and that obtained findings consistent with both mood and general arousal theories (Purcell, 1982; Watson & Tellegen, 1985). Therefore, the format most often employed with the AD ACL appears to be satisfactory. Alternatively, other more conventional

---

* In addition to studies reviewed in this book, see *Social Science Citation Index* with Thayer (1967, 1978a, 1986) as search references.

formats probably can be employed with little difference in results so long as the factor groupings are maintained.

Following is the AD ACL Short Form with the self-descriptive adjectives of Energy (A1), Tiredness (A2), Tension (B1), and Calmness (B2). Scoring is based on four possible points for each adjective. A common procedure in many studies has been to score only A1 and B1, since they are the best indications of energetic and tense arousal, respectively. A2 and B2 are particularly useful if the primary purpose of a study is to focus on the low arousal states of each dimension (Tiredness and Calmness). However, use of the full range of dimensions tends to reduce somewhat the strength of the relationships observed between arousal and other behaviors. This may be because people often do not make good discriminations of states of calmness, or it may occur because different processes underlie the pole opposites of each dimension (see Chapter 3).

AD ACL Short Form

Each of the words on the back describes feelings or mood. Please use the rating scale next to each word to describe your feelings *at this moment.*

EXAMPLES:

relaxed (vv) v ? no If you circle the double check (vv) it means that you *definitely feel* relaxed *at the moment.*

relaxed vv (v) ? no If you circle the single check (v) it means that you feel slightly relaxed *at the moment.*

relaxed vv v (?) no If you circle the question mark (?) it means that the word does not apply or you cannot decide if you feel relaxed *at the moment.*

relaxed vv v ? (no) If you circle the no it means that you are *definitely not* relaxed *at the moment.*

Work rapidly, but please mark all the words. Your first reaction is best. This should take only a minute or two.

(Back page)

(vv) v ? no : definitely feel
vv (v) ? no : feel slightly
vv v (?) no : cannot decide
vv v ? (no) : definitely do not feel

active vv v ? no	drowsy vv v ? no	
placid vv v ? no	fearful vv v ? no	
sleepy vv v ? no	lively vv v ? no	
jittery vv v ? no	still vv v ? no	
energetic vv v ? no	wide-awake vv v ? no	
intense vv v ? no	clutched-up vv v ? no	
calm vv v ? no	quiet vv v ? no	
tired vv v ? no	full-of-pep vv v ? no	
vigorous vv v ? no	tense vv v ? no	
at-rest vv v ? no	wakeful vv v ? no	

The AD ACL is scored by assigning 4, 3, 2, and 1, respectively to the "vv, v, ?," and "no" scale points, and summing or averaging the five scores for each subscale. (An appropriate cardboard template can be easily constructed.) In order of appearance, the subscale adjectives are as follows: Energetic (active, energetic, vigorous, lively, full-of-pep); Tired (sleepy, tired, drowsy, wide-awake, wakeful); Tension (jittery, intense, fearful, clutched-up, tense); Calmness (placid, calm, at-rest, still, quiet). Scoring for "wakeful" and "wide-awake" must be reversed for the Tiredness subscale. Also, if full bipolar dimensions of energetic and tense arousal are of interest (see above), Tiredness and Calmness scores must be reversed (but not wakeful and wide-awake, in this case) before summing the ten scores.

The AD ACL Long Form (Thayer, 1967, 1978a) includes additional activation adjectives as well as filler adjectives to disguise the purpose of the test. It contains the same instructions except that respondents are told that the test will take only a couple of minutes to complete. Based on previous analyses (Thayer, 1967, 1978a), the following adjectives are included on this form. The designations A1, A2, A3, and A4 after each significantly loaded activation adjective represent the subscales of Energy, Tiredness, Tension, and Calmness, respectively.

In order of appearance, the adjectives are: carefree, serious, peppy (A1), pleased, placid (A4), leisurely (A4), sleepy (A2), jittery (A3), intense (A3), grouchy, energetic (A1), egotistic, calm (A3, A4), suspicious, tired (A2), regretful, stirred-up (A3), warm-hearted, vigorous (A1), engaged-in-thought, at-rest (A4), elated, drowsy (A2), witty, anxious (A3), aroused, fearful (A3), lively (A1), defiant, still (A4), self-centered, wide-awake (A1, A2), skeptical, activated (A1), sad, full-of-pep (A1), affectionate, quiet (A4), concentrating, sluggish (A1, A2), overjoyed, quick (A1), nonchalant, quiescent (A4), clutched-up (A3), wakeful (A1, A2), rebellious, active (A1), blue, alert (A1), tense (A3). Since different numbers of activation adjectives are included in the four factors, these factor scores must be averaged instead of just summed if interfactor comparisons are to be made.

Self-Study Designs to Determine Diurnal Rhythms of Energetic Arousal

This self-study design will enable an investigator to determine natural biological rhythms of energetic arousal. If lifestyles are sufficiently stable, these rhythms may be endogenous, but whether endogenous or not it is useful to know about regularly appearing patterns of these daily rhythms. Other useful information may also be gained from this kind of study. For example, from assessments of tense arousal together with energetic arousal (AD ACL), information can be gained about optimal and low periods within each day. Also, on the basis of the information provided below, individuals may judge their degree of "morningness" or "eveningness" (Horne & Östberg, 1976) relative to normative arousal scores.

Procedure

Self-ratings of energetic arousal should be made at the top of each hour from waking to sleep. (Digital watches that can be set to signal the wearer each hour may be purchased inexpensively, reducing the likelihood that a rating time may be missed.) In addition to the hourly ratings, complete an AD ACL on awakening and just before going to sleep (unless these times occur within fifteen minutes of the hourly measure). For this study, choose days (three or more days would be best) on which waking and retiring times are at the same clock hours, and which represent typical activity patterns and characteristic stress levels. Avoid measurement days when unusual events or activities are anticipated (e.g., anything likely to have an unusual impact on either energetic or tense arousal). If self-ratings have begun and an unusual event occurs that is likely to affect arousal strongly, discontinue the rating process and begin another day.

Since a large number of self-ratings must be made with this design, it may be useful to employ shortened versions of the AD ACL. For example, in university classes in which diurnal rhythms were the subjects of self-study, eight-item versions—including the adjectives energetic, tense, drowsy, still, jittery, tired, vigorous, and quiet—have been successfully employed. In this case, energetic, vigorous, drowsy, and tired represent energetic arousal. Tense, jittery, still, and quiet represent tense arousal; however, still and quiet were often dropped from the scoring because some participants were uncertain about how to make these discriminations.

Results

Simple Analyses. Score energetic and tense arousal based on the descriptions provided in Appendix I. Develop a table in which time of measurement is represented in the first of several rows. In subsequent rows, place energetic arousal scores for those time periods. Thus, a given time period will have as many scores (rows) as days in the study. Finally, a last row will include averages for each of the hours. In another set of rows, the same procedure can be used to calculate averages for tense arousal. Since it may be useful to compare energetic and tense arousal curves for certain interpretations, it is advisable to transform the means to four-point scales (particularly if tense arousal is scored on an abbreviated scale).

It is useful to have the first, second, third, and so forth measures of the day be the same clock hours on every measurement day. That is why the instruction was given that typical days should be employed on which awakening and retiring times are the same. Calculate averages* for each hour, and plot the two curves of energetic and tense arousal on a graph, with hours on the horizontal axis and AD ACL scores on the vertical axis.

More Complex Analyses. Depending on how many days were observed, it may be possible to compute a repeated-measures analysis of variance (days × hours) to determine if the curve represents reliable variations in energetic arousal. Time-series statistics may also be employed to fit various periodic frequency functions to the data (e.g., Gottman, 1981). Thus, a spectral analysis will allow a determination of what sine-cosine functions represent the best fit.

Interpretation

The likelihood that the energetic arousal curve derived from this study represents an endogenous cycle is related to the extent that the days chosen are typical (representative) of one's usual lifestyle. If awakening and retiring times in an individual's life differ widely, this curve may represent only the energy cycle that derives from the amount and quality of sleep, and the activity pattern of the days under study.

Inspection of relative levels of energetic and tense arousal should indicate optimal and poor periods of the day. Periods when energy is high and tension is low (calm-energy) should be better for many behavioral functions than periods when tension is high and energy is low (tense-tiredness). Periods when energy and tension are both high (tense-energy) may be optimal times for some people (e.g., Type A personalities), particularly in relation to amount of work produced.

Morningness versus eveningness characteristics may be estimated by comparing one's first and last scores of the day with the normative scores provided below. It may also be useful to compare these designations of morningness with questionnaire scores derived from the self-scoring Morningness-Eveningness Questionnaire (Horne & Östberg, 1976).

Following are normative energetic arousal scores (four-point scale) for morning and evening periods. These scores were obtained from twenty-one college students who monitored their energetic arousal levels each hour over three days using shortened versions of the AD ACL (see above), with adjectives including energetic, tired, drowsy, and vigorous. (See also Thayer, 1978b, Figure 2 for additional Energy-scale levels obtained with the standard AD ACL Short Form.) By comparing one's own

---

* Various indexes of a central tendency may be employed (e.g., Thayer, Takahashi, & Pauli, 1988).

scores against these normative results, some determination of tendency toward morningness or eveningness may be made. (Note that in the study from which these normative scores were obtained, if an individual's waking hour and first daily measurement, or sleep and last daily measurement, occurred within fifteen minutes of each other, only one measure was taken, and the same score was recorded in the waking [or sleep] and first hour columns.)

	Waking and First Hours				*Sleep and Last Hours*			
	Waking	1st	2nd	3rd	3rd	2nd	1st	Sleep
Mean	1.7	1.9	2.6	3.0	2.4	1.9	1.5	1.4
Standard deviation	.61	.71	.69	.65	.58	.65	.39	.36

Alternative Study

For one reason or another, it may not be feasible to study arousal rhythms throughout the waking hours of several days. An alternative self-study project is to focus on selected segments of several days, gathering self-ratings every half hour during those periods. These may be periods associated with a particular routine such as work, or some other activity that is especially stressful. In this case, it is often useful to anchor the self-monitoring periods with morning awakening, lunch, or dinner as a beginning, and another eating time or sleep at the end. This will not only serve as a reminder about when to begin and end the project, but in addition, these sleep or activity anchors may be studied in relation to the preceding or succeeding mood cycles.

Correlational Analyses of Energy, Tension, and Various Other Mood and Behavioral Processes

This self-study design makes possible analyses of relationships among energy, tension, and a wide variety of other mood and behavioral processes that may be affected by these kinds of arousal.

Procedure

Self-ratings should be completed concurrently on one or more mood and/or behavioral processes. Several rating scales are provided below for possible use. Each set of ratings should be made according to how the individual feels at that moment. Times for completion are optional, but interpretations will be enhanced if these self-ratings are made on at least twenty occasions, and if occasions are chosen so as to maximize the variability of energy and tension scores. For example, self-ratings of other mood states may be completed at the same time as AD ACLs are taken in a biological rhythm study (see Appendix II). Alternatively, ratings may be taken randomly at various times of the day over several days and in various situations that are likely to produce different levels of arousal.

Below are various general-purpose self-rating scales that may be employed. Other rating scales may be readily constructed and substituted if desired. Some of these rating scales are patterned after studies of mood described in previous chapters.

At this moment, how *depressed* do you feel?

1	2	3	4	5	6	7
Not at all	Slightly		Somewhat	Very		Extremely

The same rating scale may be used for moods such as optimistic, happy, physical well-being, and a variety of others. In addition, changing perceptions of a long-term personal problem (see Chapter 4) may be studied with the above rating scale by using the following question: "At this moment, how *serious* does the *problem* appear?" Global mood states may be studied with the following scale.

At this moment, rate your overall *mood.*

1	2	3	4	5	6	7
Very bad	Bad		Neither good nor bad	Good		Very good

The above rating scale may be used to measure self-esteem by substituting the following question: "At this moment, how *good* do you feel about *yourself?*" Finally, various subjective urges (see Chapter 8) may be studied with the following scale.

At this moment, my *urge* to *snack* (or smoke a cigarette) is:

1	2	3	4	5	6	7
Very weak	Weak		Neither strong nor weak	Strong		Very strong

If very small numeric variations occur in self-ratings using this seven-point scale, the scale may be increased to fourteen or twenty-one points, with the verbal anchors spread out equally.

Results

Simple Analyses. Score Energy and Tension as previously indicated (Appendix I), and correlate the results with the scores derived from whatever other self-rating(s) was made. Any standard correlation statistic (e.g., Pearson Product Moment Correlation) is sufficient for this analysis. But if users of this study have no access to this statistical procedure, scores for the different variables may be plotted on a graph, with the sequence of ratings on the horizontal axis (e.g., 1 through 20), and the AD ACL and rating scale scores on the vertical axis. Two or more vertical axes may be employed to represent the different ratings. This will ensure that the subsequently drawn curves overlap one another and that interpretations may be made more easily.

More Complex Analyses. More complex analyses may be made by considering non-AD ACL ratings in four categories: (a) periods when both Energy and Tension are high, (b) Energy is high and Tension is low, (c) Tension is high and Energy is low, and (d) both Energy and Tension are low. For example, depression ratings may be compared in the calm energy period and the tense-tired period. Appropriate statistical analyses of these comparisons would involve repeated-measures analyses of variance, or *t* tests. In addition to these discrete comparisons, somewhat similar results may be obtained with multiple regression analyses.

Interpretation

Interpretation of correlation coefficients depends on the number of observations taken. For example, if observations were taken on twenty occasions, a coefficient of .44 would be necessary to conclude that this relationship is statistically significant (p < .05). In general, if a sizable number of observations are taken, .2–.4 correlations are considered low, but they may involve a definite relationship, .4–.7 correlations are considered moderate, but they may involve a substantial relationship, and .7–.9 correlations are considered high, and they may involve a marked relationship.

If data are analyzed only by graphical representations, qualitative analyses must be made on the basis of converging or diverging high and low points on the various curves. In general, a relationship is represented if energy, tension, and other self-ratings covary with each other.

If the more complex analyses for different arousal configurations, which are described above, yield reliable differences among other mood and behavioral processes, it is possible that arousal states underlie the observed differences. This may lead to better understanding of such known arousal antecedents as circadian rhythms, exercise, nutrition, and sleep.

Experimental Studies of Antecedents
of Energy and Tension

These self-study designs will enable analyses to be made of a wide variety of influences on subjective energy and tension states. With these designs, it is possible to evaluate the effects of antecedents ranging from commonly ingested substances such as sugar and caffeine to lifestyle routines such as those associated with regular exercise, naps, and sleep length. These self-experiments may focus upon immediate effects, or, with relatively little extra effort, mood effects lasting over several hours may be assessed. In addition to studying one kind of mood antecedent, the interaction of two or more antecedents may be studied with factorial designs.

Procedure

Choose days on which events and activities that are likely to influence energetic and tense arousal are quite similar. Whenever possible, attempt to hold constant other influences on arousal when studying a particular antecedent. For example, unless it is varied systematically, time of day that a rating is taken should be the same on each of the days of the experiment. As a procedural example, moderate exercise will be considered next, but the same methodology can be applied to numerous other antecedents.

To best determine the effects of moderate exercise, each session of exercise should occur following a sedentary period (at least thirty to forty-five minutes apart). Take an AD ACL immediately after the sedentary period and just before the exercise. Complete the moderate exercise (e.g., five to fifteen minutes of brisk walking*), wait five or ten minutes for physiological stabilization, and complete a second AD ACL. To recognize the full effects of exercise, it is useful to take additional measurements thirty and sixty minutes after the first post-exercise measurement. (Inexpensive digital watches with stop-watch functions and alarms increase the ease with which these time period increments are remembered.)

Although these pre- and post-measurements are sufficient for interpretable results, the interpretations will be enhanced if a no-exercise control condition is

---

* Note that brisk walking may be harmful to anyone with a history of cardiovascular problems as well as various other medical problems. If there is any question about your ability to complete this walk without medical problems, consult your physician before doing it.

included. (Different intensities or lengths of exercise may also be employed as control conditions.) The control conditions should utilize the same time periods, during which the AD ACLs are taken, as the exercise condition, and the control conditions should incorporate more or less the same extra-experimental conditions as occur in the exercise condition. This is one way of holding constant extraneous variables that otherwise would lead to ambiguous interpretations. Thus, the no-activity or continued-activity control should be preceded by an AD ACL, and post AD ACLs should be taken at the same times as they would occur in the exercise condition.

The exercise and no-exercise control conditions may be alternated, but it is preferable to use a procedure in which the pre AD ACL is taken, and then the exercise or no-exercise condition is randomly chosen. This can be accomplished by choosing from lots designating each condition or by casting a coin or die.

It is advisable to complete this procedure a number of times for each condition. The more it is done, the more reliable the results will be. Completing exercise and no-exercise conditions on only one occasion increases the likelihood that other influences have caused any differences in mood state. But completing each condition on ten separate occasions will substantially increase the likelihood that any observed differences are due to the exercise.

With this kind of basic design, it is quite feasible to cross a second or even a third variable with the exercise (a factorial design). For example, the exercise and no-exercise conditions may be completed in the morning and the afternoons in comparable numbers to determine if the time of day that exercise occurs has any effect on arousal states.

Other antecedents of arousal may also be studied with these procedures. For example, the effects of sugar snacks or caffeine may be studied fairly easily. In testing, however, care should be taken that no food or liquid other than the sugar snack or coffee that is part of the experiment is taken either an hour prior to the substance ingestion or during the post-ingestion self-ratings. It should be noted that a no-caffeine condition may result in its own arousal effects—withdrawal—if coffee is usually ingested during that time. As was true in the exercise example, it is advisable to test for the mood effects of the substance for a period of time after the immediate post-ingestion self-rating, because the immediate effect may be different than one that occurs a half hour or an hour later.

As was true in the exercise example, factorial designs are very useful here. For instance, time of day may be profitably studied, or other alternatives such as the effects on mood of moderate exercise versus a sugar snack may be studied in a single experiment.

The effects of different lengths of night sleep and of naps represent certain time-based experimental problems. The main problem is that mood effects that are assessed immediately after night sleep or after a nap may not be good indications of the overall effects of the sleep. That is, mood effects from different lengths of sleep may not show up until hours after the nap or until late afternoon in the case of different night-sleep lengths. Thus, in these kinds of sleep experiments, care should be taken to make systematic self-ratings some time after one has awakened.

Results

Simple Analyses. Score energetic and tense arousal based on descriptions provided in Appendix I. Compute averages for each condition (pre, post-1, post-2, etc.), and either place them in a table, or graph the results in such a way that the horizontal axis represents the pre- to post-condition(s) and the vertical axis represents the AD ACL scores.

More Complex Analyses. Repeated-measures analyses of variance are the easiest way to evaluate the obtained effects. With this method of analysis, factors correspond to independent variables (e.g., pre, post-1, post-2; A.M., P.M.; exercise, no exercise; etc.), and replications correspond to occasions. Thus, an analysis of variance may be completed on one person's data alone.

Interpretation

Graphical representations of pre- to post-, and experimental versus control, conditions can often indicate important differences. However, without the use of statistical models it is not possible to determine if the observed differences are due merely to chance.

In general, each of the above analyses should be completed twice, once for energetic arousal scores and once for tense arousal scores. However, it is possible to evaluate the effects of arousal antecedents on energetic and tense arousal together. This can be done informally by observing circumstances in which subjective energy and tension levels diverge following a given antecedent. For example, moderate exercise appears to raise energy and decrease tension (see Chapter 5). On the other hand, small increments in tension may raise energy as well (see Chapter 6).

NOTES

CHAPTER 2

1. Recently Skinner (1987) provided an interesting reminder about the radical–behaviorist psychology of the 1960s and early 1970s.

2. Relevant here is a recent survey of my university Senior Level classes. Respondents indicated that good moods last about one day, but even the longest estimate is only one week. Bad moods have shorter durations, a half day on the average, and these moods usually last anywhere from a half hour to two or three days.

3. Another indication that Watson and Tellegen's positive and negative affect are not reciprocal opposites comes from the findings of different behavioral correlates with each (e.g., Clark & Watson, 1988).

4. For an excellent review of both positive and negative findings from over thirty studies that have used the Velten procedure, see D. M. Clark (1983).

5. This is a system of general bodily arousal primarily characterized by subjective states that range from feelings of energy to tiredness.

6. The peak, or acrophase, of the cortisol rhythm is early morning (Minors & Waterhouse, 1981), and with the expected lag time, it could account for the late morning or early afternoon peak of energetic arousal.

7. Post et al. (1984). This research involved many more elements, but only findings relevant to mood in normal participants are presented here.

8. Based on research by Christensen, White, and Krietsch (1985), expectancy effects may not be a substantial problem.

CHAPTER 3

1. Alternative conceptualizations of arousal based on biological meaningfulness can be found in Gray (1982) and Vanderwolf and Robinson (1981).

2. The classic distinction between fear and anxiety was made by Freud (1953–55). With fear, the object (or basis) of the danger is known, but in anxiety it is not.

3. There have been numerous variations on this hypothesis that apparent differences are entirely due to cognitive labeling (cf. Schachter, 1964).

4. Drugs that reduce or increase arousal may act quite differently with respect to overt behavioral processes. For example, barbiturates are often used to induce sleep and sometimes to reduce anxiety. On the other hand, the various kinds of tranquilizers in their optimal effect reduce anxiety, but they do not increase tiredness. Apparently paradoxical effects may also be seen with cocaine, which produces increased energy (arousal), but reduces pain. In its street usage, cocaine seems to have an appeal based on its anti-anxiety effects. Common recreational drugs such as caffeine and nicotine, which also have arousal effects, are used by many as calming agents.

The recreational use of alcohol similarly reduces anxiety, consistent with the property of this drug as a CNS depressant, but in the short term it often provides a euphoric (arousal) effect. And finally, hyperkinetic children are often prescribed drugs such as Ritalin (an amphetamine) and even caffeine to help reduce their hyperactivity by increasing arousal. Further discussion of these apparently paradoxical drug effects and their relationship with the multidimensional arousal model is in Chapters 6 and 8 (see also Goodman & Gilman, 1985; Grinspoon, 1976; Marks, 1985).

CHAPTER 4

1. It is true, however, that the experimental literature has not clearly documented this interaction (e.g., Folkard, 1983).

2. Alertness is an alternative descriptor for General Activation, one of the elements of energetic arousal (Thayer, 1967).

3. In Thayer (1987b), the highest tense arousal ratings were in mid to late afternoon.

4. However, Folkard et al. (1985) have recently shown that alertness and sleep/wake cycles may not be as closely associated as once thought.

5. Wever (1982) has found that vigorous physical activity does not affect circadian temperature rhythms, but the shape and peak of energetic arousal cycles may be affected by such activity.

6. A class I sometimes teach entitled Self-Observation includes projects that involve multiday self-studies of arousal variations.

7. Note the use by Douglas and Arenberg (1978) of the Guilford-Zimmerman Temperament Survey.

8. These reciprocal processes may be a function of various mood perturbations and of the body's tendency to maintain homeostasis (cf. Panksepp, 1986).

CHAPTER 5

1. Some of the earliest research on stress employed forced treadmill activity (Selye, 1956).

2. A somewhat similar position was taken by Lang (1979) in his presidential address to the Society for Psychophysiological Research. He presented persuasive evidence that emotional imagery includes a motor program that is the prototype for overt behavioral expression. Although Lang focused on motor responses as efferent correlates of emotional imagery, the close association between motor responses and cognitive processes is likely to occur in both directions, in my view.

3. Thanks to Nancy Voils for pointing out that there is a growing popular literature and some related scientific literature about the effect of clothing and other changeable personal characteristics on mood. Probably, energetic arousal is enhanced by the perception that one looks good.

4. Osmond, Mullaly, & Bisbee (1985) interviewed thirty depressed psychiatric in-patients who had previously experienced severe physical pain from injury, illness, or surgery. When asked to compare the two conditions, subjects indicated that depression was worse and that they would rather re-experience pain than the depression.

5. Supporting this argument was an interesting doctoral dissertation by J. L. Hager (Cornell Univ., 1976), in which she studied the respiration patterns of individuals who were subjected to either a stress-inducing film or a brief period of vig-

orous exercise. She found arousal in both groups, but the respiratory patterns were quite different. Exercisers breathed more rapidly and deeply, while those that were stressed breathed fast and shallowly.

CHAPTER 6

1. Participants were thoroughly debriefed before leaving the experiment so that there would be no detrimental effects from this manipulation.

2. Some kind of nonconscious mechanism of influence must be assumed. It might be the classic Freudian mechanism, or an alternative such as Hilgard's (1977) neodissociation model.

3. If this is in fact the case, the relationship of this and related moods to simple energy dynamics is more certain.

4. Panksepp (1986) argues persuasively that the opiate system underlies the re-establishment of homeostatic function following all kinds of stressful perturbations.

5. This assumed function could account for the observations of Malmo and Surwillo (1960) of increasing activation as sleep deprivation continues. If sleep deprivation results in a functional dissociation between levels of the nervous system mediating consciousness and peripheral systems registering increasing stress, then the decrease in anxiety experienced during exhaustion may be largely subjective (perhaps a central nervous system phenomenon) and may not represent total physiological deactivation (at least not autonomic deactivation). Therefore, conscious awareness could adequately assess the general physiological condition only under somewhat normal circumstances. However, the increased activation observed by Malmo has been attributed by Murray (1965) to artifactual processes related to subject treatment and measurement procedures.

CHAPTER 7

1. It is clear, of course, that a number of situations, or even a single powerful situation, may strongly affect long-term mood, if not control it entirely (see Chapter 8). My reference is to incidental situations that are infrequent in occurrence and that are not sufficiently potent to significantly shift background mood levels over time.

CHAPTER 8

1. Moods related to anger or sexual arousal may not be interpretable within this theoretical context.

2. Within the traditional division of mind into affect and cognition (e.g., Isen, 1984; Lazarus, 1984; Zajonc, 1980), these states are clearly affective. Moreover, moods of tension (including anxiety, fearfulness, etc.) are certainly emotional in character. Whether moods of energy and tiredness are also emotional is open to interpretation, but I regard them at least as central elements of common emotions.

3. I have systematically gathered university student reports involving retrospective analyses of these states.

4. Eighteen of twenty-three subjects showed positive correlations for Energy versus self-esteem; twenty-one of twenty-three subjects showed negative correlations for Tension vs. self-esteem. Combining individual correlations by summation of standard score transformations with appropriate divisions yielded probabilities that such combined values would occur by chance as less than 1 in 10,000 for both Energy and Tension.

5. Certain forms of depression have been observed to follow circadian rhythms (e.g., Mendels, 1970; Winokur, Clayton, & Reich, 1969), but this is still an area with a great number of unknowns.

6. An interesting new model of mood management was recently presented by Zillman (1988a, 1988b).

7. My thanks to Martin Fiebert for suggesting the example of heroin.

8. This is not to say that people cannot identify the moods themselves; but they cannot identify the causes of their moods just as they often cannot identify the causes for other behaviors (e.g., Nisbett & Wilson, 1977).

9. Experience with biofeedback (e.g., Brown, 1977) has demonstrated this.

10. These materials and procedures may be freely copied and used for research, self-study, or nonprofit educational purposes with citation of appropriate sources.

11. In addition to the well-known effects of such tension-reducing practices as natural-breathing, muscle relaxation, and meditation, Hanley and Chinn (in press) recently demonstrated the effects of guided imagery on both tense and energetic arousal.

REFERENCES

Ague, C. (1973). Nicotine and smoking: Effects upon subjective changes in mood. *Psychopharmacologia, 30,* 323–328.

Åkerstedt, T., Patkai, P., & Dahlgren, K. (1977). Field studies of shiftwork: II. Temporal patterns in psychophysiological activation in workers alternating between night and day work. *Ergonomics, 20,* 621–631.

Åkerstedt, T., & Torsvall, L. (1981). Shift work shift-dependent well-being and individual differences. *Ergonomics, 24,* 265–273.

Akil, A., & Watson, S. J. (1983). Beta-endorphin and biosynthetically related peptides in the central nervous system. In L. L. Iversen, S. D. Iversen, & S. H. Snyder (Eds.), *Handbook of psychopharmacology: Neuropeptides* (Vol. 16). New York: Plenum.

Allen, B. P., & Potkay, C. R. (1973). Variability of self-description on a day-to-day basis: Longitudinal use of the Adjective Generation Technique. *Journal of personality, 41,* 638–652.

Allen, B. P., & Potkay, C. R. (1981). On the arbitrary distinction between states and traits. *Journal of personality and social psychology, 41,* 916–928.

Allen, V. L. (1985). Arousal, affect, and self-perception: The role of the physical environment. In C. D. Spielberger, I. G. Sarason, & P. B. Defares (Eds.), *Stress and anxiety* (Vol. 9), pp. 79–93. Washington, D.C.: Hemisphere.

Alloy, L. B., & Ahrens, A. H. (1987). Depression and pessimism for the future: Biased use of statistically relevant information in predictions for self versus others. *Journal of personality and social psychology, 52,* 366–378.

American Psychiatric Association (1980). Task force on nomenclature and statistics. *Diagnostic and statistical manual of mental disorders* (DSM-III) (3rd ed.). Washington, D.C.: American Psychiatric Association.

Anderson, K (1987). Impulsivity and caffeine: A within and between subjects test of the Yerkes-Dodson Law. Paper presented at the annual meeting of the International Society for the Study of Individual Differences, Toronto, Canada.

Andreassi, J. L. (1980). *Psychophysiology: Human behavior and physiological response.* New York: Oxford University Press.

Andreev, B. V. (1960). *Sleep therapy in the neurosis.* New York: Consultants Bureau.

Andrew, R. J. (1974). Arousal and the causation of behaviour. *Behaviour, 51,* 135–165.

Angrist, B., & Sudilovsky, A. (1978). Central nervous system stimulants: Historical aspects and clinical effects. In L. L. Iversen, S. D. Iversen, & S. H. Snyder (Eds.), *Handbook of psychopharmacology* (Vol. 11). New York: Plenum.

Antelman, S. M., & Caggiula, A. R. (1977). Norepinephrine-dopamine interactions and behavior. *Science, 195,* 646–653.

Antelman, S. M., & Chiodo, L. A. (1984). Stress: Its effect on interactions among biogenic amines and role in the induction and treatment of disease. In L. L.

Iversen, S. D. Iversen, and S. H. Snyder (Eds.), *Handbook of psychopharmacology* (Vol. 18). New York: Plenum.

Arnold, M. B. (1945). Physiological differentiation of emotional states. *Psychological review, 52,* 35–48.

Aschoff, J. (1965). Circadian clocks. Amsterdam: North-Holland.

Asso, D. (1985/86). Psychology degree examinations and premenstrual phase of the menstrual cycle. *Women & health, 10,* 91–104.

Asso, D. (1986). The relationship between menstrual cycle changes in nervous system activity and psychological, behavioral and physical variables. *Biological psychology, 23,* 53–64.

Asso, D., & Braier, J. R. (1982). Changes with the menstrual cycle in psychophysiological and self-report measures of activation. *Biological psychology, 15,* 95–107.

Asterita, M. F. (1985). *The physiology of stress.* New York: Human Sciences Press.

Backstrom, T., Saunders, D., Leask, R., Davidson, D., Warner, P., & Bancroft, J. (1983). Mood, sexuality, hormones, and the menstrual cycle: II. Hormone levels and their relationship to the premenstrual syndrome. *Psychosomatic medicine, 45,* 503–507.

Baker, G.H.B. (1987). Psychological factors and immunity. *Journal of psychosomatic research, 31,* 1–10.

Bandura, A. (1977). Self-efficacy: Toward a unifying theory of behavioral change. *Psychological review, 84,* 191–215.

Bandura, A. (1986). *Social foundations of thought and action: A social cognitive theory.* Englewood Cliffs, N.J.: Prentice-Hall.

Barnett, P. A., & Gotlib, I. H. (1988). Psychosocial functioning and depression: Distinguishing among antecedents, concomitants, and consequences. *Psychological bulletin, 104,* 97–126.

Baron, R. A., Russell, G. W., & Arms, R. L. (1985). Negative ions and behavior: Impact on mood, memory, and aggression among Type A and Type B persons. *Journal of personality and social psychology, 48,* 746–754.

Bassin, R. B., & Thayer, R. E. (1986). Self-reported Depression, Moderate Exercise, and Arousal Level. Paper presented at Western Psychological Association, Seattle, Wash.

Baucom, D. H., & Aiken, P. A. (1981). Effects of depressed mood on eating among obese and nonobese dieting and nondieting persons. *Journal of personality and social psychology, 41,* 577–585.

Baumann, D. J., Cialdini, R. B., & Kendrick, D. T. (1981). Altruism as hedonism: Helping and self-gratification as equivalent responses. *Journal of personality and social psychology, 40,* 1039–1046.

Beck, A. T. (1967). *Depression: Clinical, experimental and theoretical aspects.* New York: Hoeber.

Beck, A. T., Ward, C. H., Mendelsohn, M., Mock, J. E., & Erbaujh, J. K. (1961). An inventory for measuring depression. *Archives of general psychiatry, 4,* 561–571.

Becker, J. (1974). *Depression: Theory and research.* Washington, D.C.: Winston & Sons.

Bell, B. (1976). Self-reported activation during the premenstrual and menstrual phases of the menstrual cycle. *Journal of interdisciplinary cycle research, 7,* 193–201.

Belsher, G., & Costello, C. G. (1988). Relapse after recovery from unipolar depression: A critical review. *Psychological bulletin, 104,* 84–96.

Benassi, V. A., Sweeney, P. D., & Defour, C. L. (1988). Is there a relationship between locus of control orientation and depression? *Journal of abnormal psychology, 97,* 357–367.

Berkman, L. F., & Breslow, L. (1983). *Health and ways of living: The Alameda County study.* New York: Oxford University Press.

Berkowitz, L. (1987). Mood, self-awareness, and willingness to help. *Journal of personality and social psychology, 52,* 721–729.

Berkowitz, L., & Donnerstein, E. (1982). External validity is more than skin deep: Some answers to criticisms of laboratory experiments. *American Psychologist, 37,* 245–257.

Berkowitz, L., & Troccoli, B. T. (1986). An examination of the assumptions in the demand characteristics thesis: With special reference to the Velten mood induction procedure. *Motivation and emotion, 10,* 337–349.

Berlyne, D. E. (1971). *Aesthetics and psychobiology.* New York: Appleton-Century-Crofts.

Berry, D.T.R., & Webb, W. B. (1985). Mood and sleep in aging women. *Journal of personality and social psychology, 49,* 1724–1727.

Bettelheim, B. (1943). Individual and mass behavior in extreme situations. *Journal of abnormal and social psychology, 38,* 417–452.

Biro, V., & Stukovsky, R. (1985). Changed self-ratings of young women during the phases of their cycle. *Studia psychologica, 27,* 239–244.

Blake, M.J.F. (1967a). Relationship between circadian rhythm of body temperature and introversion-extraversion. *Nature, 215,* 896–897.

Blake, M.J.F. (1967b). Time of day effects on performance in a range of tasks. *Psychonomic science, 9,* 349–350.

Blake, M.J.F., & Corcoran, D.W.J. (1972). Introversion, extraversion and circadian rhythms. In W. P. Colquhoun (Ed.), *Aspects of human efficiency: Diurnal rhythm and loss of sleep.* London: English Universities Press.

Blanchet, P., & Frommer, G. P. (1986). Mood change preceeding epileptic seizure. *Journal of nervous and mental disease, 174,* 471–476.

Blaney, P. H. (1986). Affect and memory: A review. *Psychological bulletin, 99,* 229–246.

Bohlin, G., & Kjellberg, A. (1973). Self-reported arousal during sleep deprivation and its relation to performance and physiological variables. *Scandinavian journal of psychology, 14,* 78–86.

Borgatta, E. I. (1961). Mood, personality, and interaction. *Journal of general psychology, 64,* 105–137.

Boring, E. G. (1953). A history of introspection. *Psychological bulletin, 50,* 169–189.

Bower, G. H. (1981). Mood and memory. *American psychologist, 36,* 129–148.

Boyle, G. J. (1985). The paramenstrum and negative moods in normal young women. *Personality and individual differences, 6,* 649–652.

Breithaupt, H., Hildebrandt, G., & Werner, M. (1981). Circadian type questionnaire and objective circadian characteristics. In A. Reinberg, N. Vieus, & P. Andlauer (Eds.), *Night and shift work: Biological and social aspects.* Oxford: Pergamon Press.

Brenner, C. (1955). *An elementary textbook of psychoanalysis.* Garden City, N.Y.: Doubleday.

Brewin, C. R. (1985). Depression and causal attributions: What is their relation? *Psychological bulletin, 98,* 297–309.

Broadbent, D. E. (1971). *Decision and stress.* London: Academic Press.

Brody, N. (1988). *Personality: In search of individuality.* New York: Academic Press.

Brooks, G. A., & Fahey, T. D. (1984). *Exercise physiology: Human bioenergetics and its applications.* New York: Wiley.

Brown, B. B. (1977). *Stress and the art of biofeedback.* New York: Harper & Row.

Brown, F. M. (1982). Rhythmicity as an emerging variable for psychology. In F. M. Brown & R. C. Graeber (Eds.), *Rhythmic aspects of behavior.* Hillsdale, N.J.: Erlbaum.

Brown, J. D. (1984). Effects of induced mood on causal attributions for success and failure. *Motivation and emotion, 8,* 343–353.

Brown, J. D., & Taylor, S. E. (1986). Affect and the processing of personal information: Evidence for mood activated self-schemata. *Journal of experimental social psychology, 22,* 436–452.

Brunson, B. I., and Matthews, K. A. (1981). The Type A coronary-prone behavior patterns and reactions to uncontrollable stress: An analysis of performance strategies, affect, and attributions during failure. *Journal of personality and social psychology, 40,* 906–918.

Buchwald, A. M., Strack, S., & Coyne, J. C. (1981). Demand characteristics and the Velten Mood Induction procedure. *Journal of consulting and clinical psychology, 49,* 478–479.

Buchwald, D., Sullivan, J. L., & Komaroff, A. L. (1987). Frequency of "Chronic Active Epstein-Barr Virus Infection" in a general medical practice. *Journal of the American Medical Association, 257,* 2303–2307.

Buck, R. (1984). *The communication of emotion.* New York: Guilford.

Buckalew, L. W., & Rizzuto, A. (1982). Subjective response to negative air ion exposure. *Aviation, space, and environmental medicine, 53,* 822–823.

Bunney, W. E., & Davis, J. W. (1965). Norepinephrine in depressive reactions: A review. *Archives in general psychiatry, 13,* 483–494.

Bunney, W. E., & Hamburg, D. A. (1963). Methods for reliable longitudinal observation of behavior: Development of a method for systematic observation of emotional behavior on psychiatric wards. *Archives of general psychiatry, 9,* 280–294.

Burger, J. M. (1986). *Personality: Theory and research.* Belmont, Calif.: Wadsworth.

Burghardt, G. M. (1985). Animal awareness: Current perceptions and historical perspective. *American psychologist, 40,* 905–919.

Buss, A. H., & Plomin, R. (1984). *Temperament: Early developing personality traits.* Hillsdale, N.J.: Erlbaum.

Campbell, D. E. (1982). Lunar-lunacy research: When enough is enough. *Environment and behavior, 14,* 418–424.

Cannon, W. B. (1929/1963). *Bodily changes in pain, hunger, fear and rage.* New York: Harper & Row.

Caplan, B. (1983). Staff and patient perception of patient mood. *Rehabilitation psychology, 28,* 67–77.

Carlson, M., & Miller, N. (1987). Explanation of the relation between negative mood and helping. *Psychological bulletin, 102,* 91–108.

Carlson, N. R. (1986). *Physiology and behavior* (3rd ed.). Boston: Allyn and Bacon.

Carpenter, W. T., & Gruen, P. H. (1978). The limbic-hypothalamic-pituitary-adrenal system and human behavior. In L. L. Iversen, S. D. Iversen, & S. H. Snyder (Eds.), *Handbook of psychopharmacology: Biology of mood and antianxiety drugs* (Vol. 13). New York: Plenum.

Carr, D. B., Bollen, B. A., Skriner, G. S., Arnold, M. A., Rosenblatt, M., Beitins, I. Z., Martin, J. B., & McArthur, J. W. (1981). Physical conditioning facilitates the exercise-induced secretion of beta-endorphin and beta-lipotropin in women. *New England journal of medicine, 305,* 560–563.

Carver, C. S., & Scheier, M. F. (1982). Control theory: A useful conceptual framework for personality-social, clinical, and health psychology. *Psychological bulletin, 92,* 111–135.

Cash, T. F., Rimm, D. C., & MacKinnon, R. (1986). Rational-irrational beliefs and the effects of the Velten mood induction procedure. *Cognitive therapy and research, 10,* 461–467.

Caspi, A., Bolger, N., & Eckenrode, J. (1987). Linking person and context in the daily stress process. *Journal of personality and social psychology, 52,* 184–195.

Cathala, H. P., & Guillard, A. (1961). La réactivité au cours du sommeil physiologique de l'homme. *Pathologie et biologie, Paris, 9,* 1357–1375.

Charry, J. M., & Hawkinshire, F. B. W., V. (1981). Effects of atmospheric electricity on some substrates of disordered social behavior. *Journal of personality and social psychology, 41,* 185–197.

Christensen, L., Krietsch, K., White, B., & Stagner, B. (1985). Impact of a dietary change on emotional distress. *Journal of abnormal psychology, 94,* 565–579.

Christensen, L., White, B., & Krietsch, K. (1985). Failure to identify an expectancy effect in nutritional research. *Nutrition and behavior, 2,* 149–159.

Christie, M. J., & McBrearty, E. M. (1979). Psychophysiological investigations of post lunch state in male and female subjects. *Ergonomics, 22,* 307–323.

Cialdini, R. B., Baumann, D. J., & Kendrick, D. T. (1981). Insights from sadness: A three-step model of the development of altruism as hedonism. *Developmental review, 1,* 207–223.

Cialdini, R. B., Darby, B. L., & Vincent, J. E. (1973). Transgression and altruism: A case for hedonism. *Journal of experimental social psychology, 9,* 502–516.

Clark, D. M. (1983). On the induction of depressed mood in the laboratory: Evaluation and comparison of the Velten and musical procedures. *Advances in behavioural research and therapy, 5,* 27–49.

Clark, D. M., & Teasdale, J. D. (1982). Diurnal variations in clinical depression and accessibility of memories of positive and negative experiences. *Journal of abnormal psychology, 91,* 87–95.

Clark, L. A., & Watson, D. (1988). Mood and the mundane: Relations between daily life events and self-reported mood. *Journal of personality and social psychology, 54,* 296–308.

Clark, M. S., & Isen, A. M. (1982). Toward understanding the relationship between feeling states and social behavior. In A. H. Hastorf & A. M. Isen (Eds.), *Cognitive social psychology.* New York: Elsevier/North-Holland.

Clark, M. S., Milberg, S., & Erber, R. (1984). Effects of arousal on judgments of others' emotions. *Journal of personality and social psychology, 46,* 551–560.

Clark, M. S., Milberg, S., & Ross, J. (1983). Arousal cues arousal-related material in memory: Implications for understanding effects of mood on memory. *Journal of verbal learning and verbal behvavior, 22,* 633–649.

Clements, P. R., Hafer, M. D., & Vermillion, M. E. (1976). Psychometric, diurnal, and electrophysiological correlates of activation. *Journal of personality and social psychology, 33,* 387–394.

Cohen, R. M., Weingartner, H., Smallberg, S. A., Pickar, D., & Murphy, D. L. (1982). Effort and cognition in depression. *Archives of general psychiatry, 39,* 593–597.

Coleman, R. E. (1975). Manipulation of self-esteem as a determinant of mood of elevated and depressed women. *Journal of abnormal psychology, 84,* 693–700.

Collins, A., Eneroth, P., & Landgren, B. M. (1985). Psychoneuroendocrine stress responses and mood as related to the menstrual cycle. *Psychosomatic medicine, 47,* 512–527.

Colquhoun, W. P. (1960). Temperament, inspection efficiency, and time of day. *Ergonomics, 3,* 377–378.

Colquhoun, W. P. (1971). *Biological rhythms and human performance.* London: Academic Press.

Colquhoun, W. P. (1982). Biological rhythms and performance. In W. Webb (Ed.), *Biological rhythms, sleep, performance.* Chichester: Wiley.

Colquhoun, W. P., & Folkard, S. (1978). Personality differences in body-temperature rhythm, and their relation to its adjustment to night work. *Ergonomics, 21,* 811–817.

Colt, W. D., Wardlaw, S., & Frantz, A. (1981). The effect of running on plasma beta-endorphin. *Life sciences, 28,* 1637–1640.

Conroy, R.T.W.L., Elliot, A. L., Fort, A., & Mills, J. N. (1969). Circadian rhythms before and after a flight from India. *Journal of physiology, 204,* 85P.

Cooper, P. J., & Bowskill, R. (1986). Dysphoric mood and overeating. *British journal of clinical psychology, 25,* 155–156.

Costa, P. T., & McCrae, R. R. (1980). Influence of extraversion and neuroticism on subjective well-being: Happy and unhappy people. *Journal of personality and social psychology, 38,* 668–678.

Coyne, J. C., & Gotlib, I. H. (1983). The role of cognition in depression: A critical appraisal. *Psychological bulletin, 94,* 472–505.

Cramer, R. E., McMaster, M. R., Lutz, D. J., & Ford, J. G. (1986). Sport fan generosity: A test of mood, similarity, and equity hypotheses. *Journal of sport behavior, 9,* 31–37.

Cruickshank, P. J. (1984). A stress and arousal mood scale for low vocabularly subjects: A reworking of Mackay et al. (1978). *British journal of psychology, 75,* 89–94.

Cunningham, M. R. (1979). Weather, mood, and helping behavior: Quasi experiments with the sunshine samaritan. *Journal of personality and social psychology, 37,* 1947–1956.

Curran, J. P., & Cattell, R. B. (1976). Manual for the Eight State Questionnaire. *Multivariate experimental clinical research, 7,* 113–132.

Daiss, S. R., Bertelson, A. D., & Benjamin, L. T. (1986). Napping versus resting: Effects on performance and mood. *Psychophysiology, 23,* 82–88.

Davidson, R. J. (1984). Affect, cognition, and hemispheric specialization. In C. E. Izard, J. Kagen, & R. B. Zajonc (Eds.), *Emotions, cognition, and behavior.* Cambridge: Cambridge University Press.

Dejonc, R., Rubinow, D. R., Roy-Byrne, P., Hoban, C., Grover, G. N., & Post, R. M. (1985). Premenstrual mood disorder and psychiatric illness. *American journal of psychiatry, 142,* 1359–1361.

Dejours, P. (1964). Control of respiration in muscular exercise. In W. O. Fenn, & H. Rahn (Eds.) *Handbook of physiology: Respiration* (Vol. 1). Washington, D.C.: American Physiological Association.

Deldin, P. J., & Levin, I. P. (1986). The effect of mood induction in a risky decision-making task. *Bulletin of the psychonomic society, 24,* 4–6.

Dermer, M., & Berscheid, E. (1972). Self-report of arousal as an indicant of activation level. *Behavioral science, 17,* 420–429.

Descovich, G. C., Montalbetti, N., Kuhl, J.F.W., Rimondi, S., Halberg, F., & Ceredi, C. (1974). Age and catecholamine rhythms. *Chronobiologia, 1,* 163–171.

deVries, H. A. (1981). Tranquilizer effect of exercise: A critical review. *Physician and sports medicine,* November 1981, 46–55.

deVries, H. A. (1986). *Physiology of exercise for physical education and athletics* (4th ed.). Dubuque, Ia.: Brown.

deVries, H. A., & Adams, G. M. (1972). Electromyographic comparison of single doses of exercise and meprobamate as to effect on muscular relaxation. *American journal of physical medicine, 51,* 130–141.

Diener, E., & Emmons, R. A. (1985). The independence of positive and negative affect. *Journal of personality and social psychology, 47,* 1105–1117.

Diener, E., & Iran-Nejad, A. (1986). The relationship in experience between different types of affect. *Journal of personality and social psychology, 50,* 1131–1138.

Diener, E., Larsen, R. J., Levine, S., & Emmons, R. A. (1985). Intensity and frequency: Dimensions underlying positive and negative affect. *Journal of personality and social psychology, 48,* 1253–1265.

Dillon, K. M., & Baker, K. H. (1985/86). Positive emotional states and enhancement of the immune system. *International journal of psychiatry in medicine, 15,* 13–18.

Dodson, L. C., & Mullens, W. R. (1969). Some effects of jogging on psychiatric hospital patients. *American correctional therapy journal, 23,* 130–134.

Domino, E. F. (1973). Neuropsychopharmacology of nicotine and tobacco smoking. In W. L. Dunn (Ed.), *Smoking behavior: Motives and incentives.* New York: Wiley.

Douglas, K., & Arenberg, D. (1978). Age changes, cohort differences, and cultural change on the Guilford-Zimmerman Temperament Survey. *Journal of gerontology, 33,* 737–747.

Duffy, E. (1962). *Activation and behavior.* New York: Wiley.

Duffy, E. (1972). Activation. In N. S. Greenfield & R. A. Sternbach (Eds.), *Handbook of psychophysiology.* New York: Holt.

Dufty, W. F. (1975). *Sugar blues.* Radnor, Pa.: Chilton.

Eason, R. G., & Dudley, L. M. (1971). Physiological and behavioral indicants of activation. *Psychophysiology, 7,* 223–232.

Eastwood, M. R., Whitton, J. L., & Kramer, P. M. (1984). A brief instrument for longitudinal monitoring of mood states. *Psychiatry research, 11,* 119–125.

Eaves, L. J., Eysenck, H. J., & Martin, N. G. (1988). *Genes, culture and personality: An empirical approach.* New York: Academic Press.

Eckenrode, J. (1984). Impact of chronic and acute stressors on daily reports of mood. *Journal of personality and social psychology, 46,* 907–918.

Edmondson, H. D., Roscoe, B., & Vickers, M. D. (1972). Biochemical evidence of anxiety in dental patients. *British medical journal, 4,* 7–9.

Eliasz, A. (1985). Mechanisms of temperament: Basic functions. In J. Strelau, F. Farley, & A. Gale (Eds.), *Biological foundations of personality and behavior* (Vol. 1), pp. 45–59. New York: Hemisphere.

Emmons, R. A., & Diener, E. (1986). Influence of impulsivity and sociability on subjective well-being. *Journal of personality and social psychology, 50,* 1211–1215.

Epstein, S. (1980). The stability of behavior. II: Implications for psychological research. *American psychologist, 35,* 790–806.

Epstein, S. (1983). A research paradigm for the study of personality and emotions. In M. M. Page (Ed.), *Personality—Current theory and research: 1982 Nebraska symposium on motivation.* Lincoln: University of Nebraska Press.

Ewart, C. K., Taylor, C. B., Reese, L. B., & DeBusk, R. F. (1983). Effects of early postmyocardial infarction exercise testing on self-perception and subsequent physical activity. *American journal of cardiology, 51,* 1076–1080.

Eysenck, H. J. (1967). *The biological basis of personality.* Springfield, Ill.: Thomas.

Eysenck, H. J., & Eysenck, M. W. (1985). *Personality and individual differences: A natural science approach.* New York: Plenum.

Eysenck, H. J., & Eysenck, S.B.G. (1965). *Manual for the Eysenck Personality Inventory.* London: Hodder & Stoughton. (San Diego, Edits.)

Eysenck, M. W. (1982). *Attention and arousal: Cognition and performance.* Berlin: Springer-Verlag.

Eysenck, M. W., & Folkard, S. (1980). Personality, time of day, and caffeine: Some theoretical and conceptual problems in Revelle et al. *Journal of experimental psychology: General, 109,* 32–40.

Eysenck, M. W., & Hepburn, L. (1987). Introversion-extraversion and changeability of mood. Paper presented at the International Society for the Study of Individual Differences, Toronto, Canada.

Farley, F. (1986). The big T in personality. *Psychology today, 20,* 44–52.

Fenigstein, A., Scheier, M. F., & Buss, A. H. (1975). Public and private self-consciousness: Assessment and theory. *Journal of consulting and clinical psychology, 43,* 522–527.

Fibiger, W., Singer, G., Miller, A. J., Armstrong, S., & Datar, M. (1984). Cortisol and catecholamines changes as functions of time-of-day and self-reported mood. *Neuroscience and biobehavioral reviews, 8,* 523–530.

Fodor, E. M. (1984). The power motive and reactivity to power stresses. *Journal of personality and social psychology, 47,* 853–859.

Foley, K. M., Kourides, I. A., Inturrisi, C. E., Kaiko, R. F., Zaroulis, C. G., Posner, J. B., Houde, R. W., & Li, C. H. (1979). Beta-endorphin: Analgesic and hormonal effects in humans. *Proceedings of the national academy of science, USA, 76,* 5377–5381.

Folkard, S. (1982). Circadian rhythms and human memory. In F. M. Brown & R. C. Graeber (Eds.), *Rhythmic aspects of behavior.* Hillsdale, N.J.: Erlbaum.

Folkard, S. (1983). Diurnal variation. In R. Hockey (Ed.), *Stress and fatigue in human performance.* Chichester: Wiley.

Folkard, S., Hume, K. I., Minors, D. S., Waterhouse, J. M., & Watson, F. L. (1985). Independence of the circadian rhythm in alertness from the sleep/wake cycle. *Nature, 313,* 678–679.

Folkard, S., Knauth, P., Monk, T. H., & Rutenfranz, J. (1976). The effect of memory load on the circadian variation in performance efficiency under a rapidly rotating shift system. *Ergonomics, 19,* 479–488.

Folkard, S., Monk, T. H., & Lobban, M. C. (1978). Short and long-term adjustment of circadian rhythms in "permanent" night nurses. *Ergonomics, 21,* 785–799.

Folkard, S., Monk, T. H., & Lobban, M.. C. (1979). Towards a predictive test of adjustment to shift work. *Ergonomics, 22,* 79–91.

Folkins, C. H., & Sime, W. E. (1981). Physical fitness training and mental health. *American psychologist, 36,* 373–389.

Folstein, M. F., & Luria, R. (1973). Reliability, validity, and clinical application of a visual analogue mood scale. *Psychological medicine, 3,* 479–486.

Forgas, J. P., Bower, G. H., & Krantz, S. E. (1984). The influence of mood on perceptions of social interaction. *Journal of experimental social psychology, 20,* 497–513.

Fort, A. (1968). The effects of rapid change in time zone on circadian variation in psychological functions. *Journal of physiology, 200,* 124P.

Fowles, D. C. (1980). The three arousal model: Implications of Gray's two-factor learning theory for heart rate, electrodermal activity and psychopathy. *Psychophysiology, 170,* 87–104.

Fox, N. A., & Davidson, R. J. (1984). Hemispheric substrates of affect: A developmental model. In N. A. Fox & R. J. Davidson (Eds.), *The psychobiology of affective development.* Hillsdale, N.J.: Erlbaum.

Frankenhaeuser, M. (1975). Experimental approaches to the study of catecholamines and emotion. In L. Levi (Ed.), *Emotions: Their parameters and measurement.* New York: Raven Press.

Frankenhaeuser, M. (1978). Psychoneuroendocrine approaches to the study of emotion as related to stress and coping. In H. E. Howe & R. E. Dienstbier (Eds.), *1978 Nebraska symposium on motivation.* Lincoln: University of Nebraska Press.

Fredericks, C., & Goodman, H. (1969). *Low blood sugar and you.* New York: Constellation International.

Freeman, G. L., & Hovland, C. I. (1934). Diurnal variations in performance and related physiological processes. *Psychological bulletin, 31,* 777–799.

Freud, S. (1953–55). *The standard edition of the complete psychological works,* trans. James Strachey. 24 vols. London: Hogarth.

Friedman, M., & Rosenman, R. H. (1974). *Type A behavior and your heart.* New York: Knopf.

Frith, C. D. (1971) Smoking behavior and its relation to the smoker's immediate experience. *British journal of social and clinical psychology, 10,* 73–78.

Froberg, J. E. (1977). Twenty-four patterns in human performance, subjective and physiological variables and differences between morning and evening active subjects. *Biological psychology, 5,* 119–134.

Frost, R. O., Graf, M., & Becker, J. (1979). Self-devaluation and depressed mood. *Journal of consulting and clinical psychology, 47,* 958–962.

Frost, R. O., & Green, M. L. (1982). Duration and post-experimental removal of Velten Mood Induction procedure effect. *Personality and social psychology bulletin, 8,* 341–342.

Furnham, A. (1981). Personality and activity preference. *British journal of social psychology, 20,* 57–68.

Gage, D. F., & Safer, M. A. (1985). Hemisphere differences in the mood state-dependent effect for recognition of emotional faces. *Journal of experimental psychology: Learning, memory, and cognition, 11,* 752–763.

Galbo, H. (1983). *Hormonal and metabolic adaptation to exercise.* New York: Verlag.

Garzino, S. (1982). Lunar effects on behavior: A defense of the empirical research. *Environment and behavior, 14,* 395–417.

Gaylin, W. (1979). *Feelings: Our vital signs.* New York: Harper & Row.

Gershon, S., & Shaw, F. H. (1961). Psychiatric sequelae of chronic exposure to organophosphorus insecticides. *Lancet, 1,* 1371–1374.

Gertz, J., & Lavie, P. (1983). Biological rhythms in arousal indices: A potential confounding effect in EEG feedback. *Psychophysiology, 20,* 690–695.

Gilbert, D. G. (1979). Paradoxical tranquilizing and emotion-reducing effects of nicotine. *Psychological bulletin, 86,* 643–661.

Gillberg, M. (1985). Effects of naps on performance. In S. Folkard & T. H. Monk (Eds.), *Hours of work: Temporal factors in work scheduling.* Chichester: Wiley.

Gilligan, S. G., & Bower, G. H. (1984). Cognitive consequences of emotional arousal. In C. E. Izard, J. Kagan, & R. Zajonc (Eds.), *Emotion, cognition and behavior,* pp. 547–588. New York: Cambridge University Press.

Gilliland, K. (1980). The interactive effect of introversion-extraversion with caffeine induced arousal on verbal performance. *Journal of research in personality, 14,* 482–492.

Gilliland, K., & Andress, D. (1981). Ad lib caffeine consumption, symptoms of caffeinism and academic performance. *American journal of psychiatry, 138,* 512–514.

Gilliland, K., & Bullock, W. (1983–84). Caffeine: A potential drug of abuse. *Advances in alcohol and substance abuse, 3,* 53–73.

Glass, D. C. (1977). *Behavior patterns, stress, and coronary disease.* Hillsdale, N.J.: Erlbaum.

Glassman, A. (1969). Indolamines and affective disorder. *Psychosomatic medicine, 31,* 107–114.

Globus, G. G., Drury, R. L., Phoebus, E. C., & Boyd, R. (1971). Ultradian rhythms in human performance. *Perceptual and motor skills, 33,* 1171–1174.

Golub, S. (1981). Premenstrual and menstrual mood changes in adolescent women. *Journal of personality and social psychology, 41,* 961–965.

Goodman, L. S., & Gilman, A. (Eds.). (1985). *The pharmacological basis of therapeutics* (7th ed.). New York: Macmillan.

Goodwin, D. W. (1977). Alcohol. In M. E. Jarvik (Ed.), *Psychopharmacology in the practice of medicine,* pp. 407–416. New York: Appleton-Century-Crofts.

Gotlib, I. H., & Meyer, J. P. (1986). Factor analysis of the Multiple Affect Adjective Check List: A separation of positive and negative affect. *Journal of personality and social psychology, 50,* 1161–1165.

Gottman, J. M. (1981). *Time series analysis: A comprehensive introduction for social scientists.* Cambridge: Cambridge University Press.

Graeber, R. C. (1982). Alterations in performance following rapid transmeridian flight. In F. M. Brown & R. C. Graeber (Eds.), *Rhythmic aspects of behavior.* Hillsdale, N.J.: Erlbaum.

Gray, J. A. (1975). *Elements of a two-process theory of learning.* London: Academic Press.

Gray, J. A. (1982). *The neuropsychology of anxiety: An inquiry into the functions of the septo-hippocampal system.* Oxford: Oxford University Press.

Green, A. R., & Nutt, D. J. (1983). Antidepressants. In D. G. Grahame-Smith & P. J. Cowan (Eds.), *Psychopharmacology 1: Part I Preclinical psychopharmacology,* pp. 1–37. Amsterdam: Excerpta Medica.

Grinspoon, L. (1976). *Cocaine: A drug and its social evolution.* New York: Basic Books.

Grinspoon, L., & Bakalar, J. B. (1985). *Cocaine: A drug and its social evolution* (rev. ed.). New York: Basic Books.

Grunberg, N. E. (1986). Nicotine as a psychoactive drug: Appetite regulation. *Psychopharmacology bulletin, 22,* 875–881.

Grzegolowska-Klarkowska, H. J. (1980). Use of defense mechanisms as determined by reactivity and situational level of activation. *Polish psychological bulletin, 11,* 155–168.

Hager, J. L. (1976). The human respiratory response in state anxiety. (Doctoral dissertation, Cornell University.) *Dissertation Abstracts International, 37,* 5423B.

Halberg, F. (1969). Chronobiology. *Annual review of physiology, 31,* 675–725.

Hanley, G. L., & Chinn, D. (in press). Stress management: An integration of multidimensional arousal and imagery theories with case study. *Journal of mental imagery.*

Harrigan, J. A., Kues, J. R., Ricks, D. F. & Smith, R. (1984). Moods that predict coming migraine headaches. *Pain, 20,* 385–396.

Hartmann, E. (1982–83). Effects of L-tryptophan on sleepiness and on sleep. *Journal of psychiatric research, 17,* 107–113.

Hartmann, E., Baekeland, F., & Zwilling, G. (1972). Psychological differences between long and short sleepers. *Archives of general psychiatry, 26,* 463–468.

Healy, D., & Williams, J.M.G. (1988). Dysrhythmia, dysphoria, and depression: The interaction of learned helplessness and circadian dysrhythmia in the pathogenesis of depression. *Psychological bulletin, 103,* 163–178.

Heimstra, N. W. (1973). The effects of smoking on mood change. In W. L. Dunn (Ed.), *Smoking behavior: Motives and incentives.* Washington, D.C.: Winston.

Heine, D., & Steiner, M. (1986). Standardized paintings as a proposed adjunct instrument for longitudinal monitoring of mood states: A preliminary note. *Occupational therapy in mental health, 6,* 31–37.

Hendrick, C., & Lilly, R. S. (1970). The structure of mood: A comparison between sleep deprivation and normal wakefulness conditions. *Journal of personality, 38,* 453–465.

Hicks, R. A., & Pellegrini, R. J. (1977). Anxiety levels of short and long sleepers. *Psychological reports, 41,* 569–570.

Hilgard, E. R. (1977). *Divided consciousness: Multiple controls in human thought and action.* New York: Wiley.

Hinz, L. D., & Williamson, D. A. (1987). Bulimia and depression: A review of the affective variant hypothesis. *Psychological bulletin, 102,* 150–158.

Hockey, R. (1983). *Stress and fatigue in human performance.* Chichester: Wiley.

Hollandsworth, Jr., J. G., & Jones, G. E. (1979). Perceptions of arousal and awareness of physiological responding prior to and after running 20 kilometers. *Journal of sports psychology, 1,* 291–300.

Hollon, S. D., DeRubeis, R. J., & Evans, M. D. (1987). Causal mediation of change in treatment of depression: Discriminating between nonspecificity and noncausality. *Psychological bulletin, 102,* 139–149.

Horne, J. A. (1983). Mammalian sleep function with particular reference to man. In M. Andrew (Ed.), *Sleep mechanisms and functions.* Wokingham, U.K.: Van Nostrand.

Horne, J. A., & Östberg, O. (1976). A self-assessment questionnaire to determine morningness-eveningness in human circadian rhythms. *International journal of chronobiology, 4,* 97–110.

Horton, J. R., & Yates, A. J. (1987). The effects of long-term high and low refined-sugar intake on blood glucose regulation, mood, bodily symptoms and cognitive functioning. *Behaviour research and therapy, 25,* 57–66.

Hoskins, C., & Halberg, F. (1983). Circadian relations among level of activation, conflict, and body temperature assessed by chronobiologic serial section. *Psychological reports, 52,* 867–876.

Howarth, E., & Hoffman, M. S. (1984). A multidimensional approach to the relationship between mood and weather. *British journal of psychology, 75*, 15–23.

Hull, J. G., & Bond, C. F. (1986). Social and behavioral consequences of alcohol consumption and expectancy: A meta-analysis. *Psychological bulletin, 99*, 347–360.

Hull, J. G., & Young, R. D. (1983). Self-consciousness, self-esteem, and success-failure as determinants of alcohol consumption in male social drinkers. *Journal of personality and social psychology, 44*, 1097–1109.

Humphreys, M. S., & Revelle, W. (1984). Personality, motivation, and performance: A theory of the relationship between individual differences and information processing. *Psychological review, 91*, 153–184.

Hyland, M. E. (1987). Control theory interpretation of psychological mechanisms of depression: Comparison and integration of several theories. *Psychological bulletin, 102*, 109–121.

Iguchi, H., Kato, K. I., & Ibayashi, H. (1982). Age-dependent reduction in serum melatonin concentrations in healthy human subjects. *Journal of clinical endocrinology and metabolism, 55*, 27–29.

Ikard, F. F., Green, D. E., & Horn, D. (1969). A scale to differentiate between types of smoking as related to the management of affect. *International journal of addictions, 4*, 649–659.

Ingram, R. E. (1984). Toward an information-processing analysis of depression. *Cognitive therapy and research, 8*, 443–478.

Isen, A. M., (1984). Toward understanding the role of affect in cognition. In R. S. Wyer & T. K. Srull (Eds.), *Handbook of social cognition* (Vol. 3), pp. 179–236. Hillsdale, N.J.: Erlbaum.

Isen, A. M., Clark, M., & Schwartz, M. F. (1976). Duration of the effect of good mood on helping: "Footprints on the sands of time." *Journal of personality and social psychology, 34*, 385–393.

Isen, A. M., Daubman, K. A., & Nowicki, G. P. (1987). Positive affect facilitates creative problem solving. *Journal of personality and social psychology, 52*, 1122–1131.

Isen, A. M., & Gorgoglione, J. M. (1983). Some specific effects of four affect-induction procedures. *Personality and social psychology bulletin, 9*, 136–143.

Isen, A. M., & Levin, P. F. (1972). The effect of feeling good on helping: Cookies and kindness. *Journal of personality and social psychology, 21*, 384–388.

Isen, A. M., & Nehemia, G. (1987). The influence of positive affect on acceptable level of risk: The person with a large canoe has a large worry. *Organizational behavior and human decision processes, 39*, 145–154.

Iversen, L. L., Iversen, S. D., & Snyder, S. H. (Eds.). (multiyear). *Handbook of psychopharmacology.* New York: Plenum.

Iversen, L. L., Iversen, S. D., & Snyder, S. H. (1983). *Handbook of psychopharmacology: Neuropeptides* (Vol. 16). New York: Plenum.

Iversen, S. D., & Iversen, L. L. (1975). *Behavioral pharmacology.* New York: Oxford University Press.

Jackson, D. N. (1976). *Jackson Personality Inventory manual.* Port Huron, Mich.: Research Psychologists Press.

Janal, M. N., Colt, E.W.D., Clark, W. C., & Glusman, M. (1984). Pain sensitivity, mood and plasma endocrine levels in man following long-distance running: Effects of naloxone. *Pain, 19*, 13–25.

Janowsky, D. S. (1980). The cholinergic nervous system in depression. In J. Mendels & J. D. Amsterdam (Eds.), *The psychobiology of affective disorders*, pp. 83–89. New York: Karger.

Johnson, E., & Tversky, A. (1983). Affect, generalization, and the perception of risk. *Journal of personality and social psychology, 45*, 20–31.

Johnson, L. C. (1982). Sleep deprivation and performance. In W. B. Webb (Ed.), *Biological rhythms, sleep, and performance.* Chichester: Wiley.

Johnson, L. C., Tepas, D. I., Colquhoun, W. P., & Colligan, M. J. (1981). *Biological rhythms, sleep, and shift work: Advances in sleep research* (Vol. 7). New York: Spectrum Publications.

Johnson, M. H., & Magaro, P. A. (1987). Effects of mood and severity on memory processes in depression and mania. *Psychological bulletin, 101*, 28–40.

Jones, M. T., Bridges, P. K., & Leak, D. (1968). Relationship between cardiovascular and sympathetic responses to the psychological stress of an examination. *Clinical science, 35*, 73–79.

Kalat, J. W. (1984). *Biological psychology* (2nd ed.). Belmont, Calif.: Wadsworth.

Kales, A., & Kales, J. D. (1984). *Evaluation and treatment of insomnia.* New York: Oxford University Press.

Karpman, V. L. (1987). *Cardiovascular system and physical exercise.* Boca Raton, FL: CRC Press.

Kavanagh, D. J., & Bower, G. H. (1985). Mood and self-efficacy: Impact of joy and sadness on perceived capabilities. *Cognitive therapy and research, 9*, 507–525.

Kendell, R. E., Mackenzie, W. E., West, C., McGuire, R. J., & Cox, J. L. (1984). Day-to-day mood changes after childbirth: Further data. *British journal of psychiatry, 145*, 620–625.

Kerkhof, G. A. (1985). Inter-individual differences in the human circadian system: A review. *Biological psychology, 20*, 83–112.

Kerkhof, G. A., Korving, H. J., Willemse-Geest, H.M.M., & Rietveld, W. J. (1980). Diurnal differences between morning type and evening type subjects in self-rated alertness, body temperature and the visual and auditory evoked potential. *Neuroscience letters, 16*, 11–15.

Ketai, R. (1975). Affect, mood, emotion, and feeling: Semantic considerations. *American journal of psychiatry, 132*, 1215–1217.

Keys, A., Brozek, J., Henschel, A., Mickelsen, O., & Taylor, H. L. (1950). *The Biology of human starvation.* Minneapolis: University of Minnesota Press.

King, D. S. (1981). Can allergic exposure provoke psychological symptoms? A double-blind test. *Biological psychiatry, 16*, 3–19.

Kirchenbaum, D. S., Tomarken, A. J., & Humphrey, L. L. (1985). Affect and adult self-regulation. *Journal of personality and social psychology, 48*, 509–523.

Kirchler, E. (1985). Job loss and mood. Special issue: Unemployment. *Journal of economic psychology, 6*, 9–25.

Kirkcaldy, B. D. (1984). The interrelationship between trait and state variables. *Personality and individual differences, 5*, 141–149.

Kleitman, N. (1961). The nature of dreaming. In G.E.W. Wolstenholme & M. O'Connor (Eds.), *The nature of sleep.* London: Churchill.

Kleitman, N. (1963). *Sleep and wakefulness* (rev. and enlarged ed.). Chicago: University of Chicago Press.

Klonowicz, T., Ignatowska-Switalska, H., & Wocial, B. (1986). Hypertension and response to stress: Need for stimulation. In J. Strelau, F. Farley, & A. Gale

(Eds.), *Biological foundations of personality and behavior* (Vol. 2), pp. 45–59. New York: Hemisphere.

Kripke, D. F. (1972). An ultradian biological rhythm associated with perceptual deprivation and REM sleep. *Psychosomatic medicine, 34,* 221–234.

Kripke, D. F. (1982). Ultradian rhythms in behavior and physiology. In F. M. Brown & R. C. Graeber (Eds.), *Rhythmic aspects of behavior.* Hillsdale, N.J.: Erlbaum.

Kripke, D. F., & Sonnenschein, D. (1978). A biologic rhythm in waking fantasy. In D. Pope & J. L. Singer (Eds.), *The stream of consciousness.* New York: Plenum.

Kroenke, K., Wood, D. R., Mangelsdorff, A. D., Meier, N. J., & Powell, J. B. (1988). Chronic fatigue in primary care. *Journal of the American Medical Association, 260,* 929–934.

Lacey, J. I. (1967). Somatic response patterning and stress: Some revisions of activation theory. In M. Appley & R. Trumbull (Eds.), *Psychological stress.* New York: Appleton-Century-Crofts.

Laird, J. D., Wagener, J. J., Halal, M., & Szegda, M. (1982). Remembering what you feel: Effects of emotion on memory. *Journal of personality and social psychology, 42,* 646–657.

Lamb, D. R. (1984). *Physiology of exercise: Responses and adaptations* (2nd ed.). New York: Macmillan.

Lang, P. J. (1979). A bio-informational theory of emotional imagery. *Psychophysiology, 16,* 495–512.

Larsen, R. J. (1985). Individual differences in circadian activity rhythm and personality. *Personality and individual differences, 6,* 305–311.

Larsen, R. J. (1988). A process approach to personality research: Using time as a facet of data. Symposium on emerging issues in personality theory. University of Michigan, Ann Arbor.

Larsen, R. J. & Diener, E. (1985). A multitrait-multimethod examination of affect structure: Hedonic level and emotional intensity. *Personality and individual differences, 6,* 631–636.

Larsen, R. J., & Diener, E. (1987). Affect intensity as an individual difference characteristic: A review. *Journal of research in personality, 21,* 1–39.

Larsen, R. J., Diener, E., & Emmons, R. A. (1986). Affect intensity and reactions to daily life events. *Journal of personality and social psychology, 51,* 803–814.

Larson, R., Csikszentmihalyi, M., & Graef, R. (1980). Mood variability and the psychosocial adjustment of adolescents. *Journal of youth and adolescence, 9,* 469–490.

Lavie, P. (1985). Ultradian cycles in wakefulness—Possible implications for work-rest schedules. In S. Folkard & T. H. Monk (Eds.), *Hours of work.* Chichester: Wiley.

Lavie, P., & Scherson, A. (1981). Ultrashort sleep-wake schedule 1: Evidence of ultradian rhythmicity in "sleep-ability." *Electroencephalography and clinical neurophysiology, 52,* 163–174.

Lazarus, R. S. (1966). *Psychological stress and the coping process.* New York: McGraw-Hill.

Lazarus, R. S. (1982). Thoughts on the relations between emotion and cognition. *American psychologist, 37,* 1019–1024.

Lazarus, R. S. (1984). On the primacy of cognition. *American psychologist, 39,* 124–129.

Lazarus, R. S., & Folkman, S. (1984). *Stress, appraisal, and coping.* New York: Springer.

Lebo, M. A., & Nesselroade, J. R. (1978). Intraindividual differences and dimensions of mood change during pregnancy identified in five P-technique factor analyses. *Journal of research in personality, 12,* 205–224.

Lefcourt, H. M., Miller, R. S., Ware, E. E., & Sherk, D. (1981). Locus of control as a modifier of the relationship between stressors and moods. *Journal of personality and social psychology, 41,* 357–369.

Levenson, R. W. (1983). Personality research and psychophysiology: General considerations. *Journal of research in personality, 17,* 1–21.

Levenson, R. W., & Gottman, J. M. (1983). Marital interaction: Physiological linkage and affective exchange. *Journal of personality and social psychology, 45,* 587–597.

Levenson, R. W., & Gottman, J. M. (1985). Physiological and affective predictors of change in relationship satisfaction. *Journal of personality and social psychology, 49,* 85–94.

Leventhal, H., & Cleary, P. D. (1980). The smoking problem: A review of the research and theory in behavioral risk modification. *Psychological bulletin, 88,* 370–405.

Leventhal, H., & Tomarken, A. J. (1986). Emotion: Today's problems. *Annual review of psychology, 37,* 356–610.

Lewinsohn, P. M., & Amenson, C. S. (1978). Some relations between pleasant and unpleasant mood-related events and depression. *Journal of abnormal psychology, 87,* 644–654.

Lewy, A. J. (1984). Human melatonin secretion (II): A marker of the circadian system and the effects of light. In R. M. Post & J. C. Ballenger (Eds.), *Neurobiology of mood disorders.* Baltimore: Williams & Wilkins.

Lieberman, H. R., Wurtman, J. J., & Chew, B. (1986). Changes in mood after carbohydrate consumption among obese individuals. *American journal of clinical nutrition, 44,* 772–778.

Lindsley, D. B. (1951). Emotion. In S. S. Stevens (Ed.), *Handbook of experimental psychology.* New York: Wiley.

Linn, M. W., Linn, B. S., & Jensen, J. (1984). Stressful events, dysphoric mood, and immune responsiveness. *Psychological reports, 54,* 219–222.

Lubin, A., Hord, D. J., Tracy, M. L., & Johnson, L. C. (1976). Effects of exercise, bedrest, and napping on performance decrement during 40 hours. *Psychophysiology, 13,* 334–339.

Lundberg, G. G. (1984). Lassitude: A primary care evaluation. *Journal of the American Medical Association, 251,* 3272–3276.

Luttinger, D., Hernandez, D. E., Nemeroff, C. B., & Prange, A. J. (1984). Peptides and nociception. *International review of neurobiology, 25,* 185–242.

Lyons, W. E. (1986). *The disappearance of introspection.* Cambridge, MA: MIT Press.

MacDonald, K. B. (1988). *Social and personality development: An evolutionary synthesis.* New York: Plenum.

Mackay, C. J. (1980). The measurement of mood and psychophysiological activity using self-report techniques. In I. Martin & P. H. Venebles (Eds.), *Techniques of psychophysiology,* New York: Wiley.

Mackay, C. J., Cox, T., Burrows, G. C., & Lazzarini, A. J. (1978). An inventory for the measurement of self-reported stress and arousal. *British journal of social and clinical psychology, 17,* 283–284.

MacLean, P. D. (1949). Psychosomatic disease and the "visceral brain." Recent developments bearing on the Papez theory of emotion. *Psychosomatic medicine, 11*, 338–353.

MacLean, P. D. (1970). The limbic brain in relation to the psychoses. In P. Black (Ed.), *Physiological correlates of emotion*. New York: Academic Press.

Madigan, R. J., & Bollenbach, A. K. (1986). The effects of induced mood on irrational thoughts and views of the world. *Cognitive therapy and research, 10*, 547–562.

Malmo, R. B. (1959). Activation: A neurophysiological dimension. *Psychological review, 66*, 367–386.

Malmo, R. B. (1975). *On emotions, needs, and our archaic brain*. New York: Holt.

Malmo, R. B., & Surwillo, W. W. (1960). Sleep deprivation: Changes in performance and physiological indicants of activation. *Psychological monographs, 74*, 1–24.

Mandler, G. (1975). *Mind and emotion*. New York: Wiley.

Mandler, G. (1984). *Mind and body: Psychology of emotion and stress*. New York: Norton.

Mangan, G. L., & Golding, J. F. (1984). *The psychopharmacology of smoking*. Cambridge: Cambridge University Press.

Manucia, G. K., Baumann, D. J., & Cialdini, R. B. (1984). Mood influences on helping: Direct effects or side effects? *Journal of personality and social psychology, 46*, 357–364.

Markoff, R. A., Ryan, P., & Young, T. (1982). Endorphins and mood changes in long-distance running. *Medicine and science in sports and exercise, 14*, 11–15.

Marks, J. (1985). *The benzodiazepines*. Lancaster, Pa.: MTP Press.

Marlatt, G. A., Kosturn, C. F., & Lang, A. R. (1975). Provocation to anger and opportunity for retaliation as determinants of alcohol consumption in social drinkers. *Journal of abnormal psychology, 84*, 652–659.

Martin, E. G., & Lacey, W. H. (1914). Vasomotor reflexes from threshold stimulation. *American journal of physiology, 33*, 212–228.

Mason, S. T. (1984). *Catecholamines and behaviour*. Cambridge: Cambridge University Press.

Matheny, K. B., & Blue, F. R. (1977). The effects of self-induced mood states on behavior and physiological arousal. *Journal of clinical psychology, 33*, 936–940.

Matthews, G., Jones, D. M., & Chamberlain, A. G. (in preparation). *Refining the measurement of mood: The Unwist Mood Adjective Checklist*.

Matthews, K. A. (1982). Psychological perspectives on the Type A behavior pattern. *Psychological bulletin, 91*, 293–323.

McArthur, L. A. (1972). The how and the why: Some determinants and consequences of causal attribution. *Journal of personality and social psychology, 22*, 171–193.

McBride, G. (1971). Theories of animal spacing: The role of flight, fight, and social distance. In A. H. Esser (Ed.), *Behavior and environment*. New York: Plenum.

McCann, L. I., & Holmes, D. S. (1984). Influence of aerobic exercise on depression. *Journal of personality and social psychology, 46*, 1142–1147.

McClelland, D. C., Floor, E., Davidson, R. J., & Saron, C. (1980). Stressed power motivation, sympathetic activation, immune function and illness. *Journal of human stress, 6*, 11–19.

McClelland, D. C., Ross, G., & Patel, V. (1985). The effect of an academic examination on salivary norepinephrine and immunoglobulin levels. *Journal of human stress, 11*, 52–59.

McDougall, W. (1908). *Introduction to social psychology.* London: Methuen.

McGuinness, D., & Pribram, K. H. (1980). The neuropsychology of attention: Emotional and motivational controls. In M. C. Wittrock (Ed.), *The brain and psychology.* New York: Academic Press.

McNair, D. M., Lorr, M., & Droppleman, L. F. (1971). *Manual: Profile of Mood States.* San Diego: Educational and Industrial Testing Service.

McNeal, E. T., & Cimbolic, P. (1986). Antidepressants and biochemical theories of depression. *Psychological bulletin, 99,* 361–374.

Meares, A. (1963). *The management of the anxious patient.* Philadelphia: Saunders.

Mehrabian, A. (1987). *Eating characteristics and temperament: General measures and interrelationships.* New York: Springer Verlag.

Mendels, J. (1970). *Concepts of depression.* New York: Wiley.

Mendels, J., & Amsterdam, J. D. (Eds.). (1981). *The psychobiology of affective disorders.* New York: Karger.

Mendels, J., Stinnett, J. L., Burns, D., & Frazer, A. (1975). Amine precursors and depression. *Archives of general psychiatry, 32,* 22–30.

Metalsky, G. I., Abramson, L. Y., Seligman, M.E.P., Semmel, A., & Peterson, C. (1982). Attributional styles and life events in the classroom: Vulnerability and invulnerability to depressive mood reactions. *Journal of personality and social psychology, 43,* 612–617.

Metalsky, G. I., Halberstadt, L. J., & Abramson, L. Y. (1987). Vulnerability to depressive mood reactions: Toward a more powerful test of the diathesis-stress and causal mediation components of the reformulated theory of depression. *Journal of personality and social psychology, 52,* 386–393.

Metcalf, M. G., & Hudson, S. M. (1985). The premenstrual syndrome: Selection of women for treatment trials. *Journal of psychosomatic research, 29,* 631–638.

Miles, H.H.W., Barrabee, E. L., & Finesinger, J. E. (1951). Evaluation of psychotherapy, with a follow-up study of 62 cases of anxiety neurosis. *Psychosomatic medicine, 13,* 83–105.

Miller, G. A., Galanter, E., & Pribram, K. H. (1960). *Plans and the structure of behavior.* New York: Holt.

Miller, R. J. (1983). The Enkephalins. In L. L. Iversen, S. D. Iversen, & S. H. Snyder (Eds.), *Handbook of psychopharmacology: Neuropeptides* (Vol. 16). New York: Plenum.

Minors, D. S., & Waterhouse, J. M. (1981). Circadian rhythms and the human. In A. H. Esser (Ed.), *Behavior and environment,* pp. 53–68. New York: Plenum.

Monjan, A. A. (1984). Effects of acute and chronic stress upon lymphocyte blastogenesis in mice and humans. In E. L. Cooper (Ed.), *Stress, immunity, and aging,* pp. 81–108. New York: Marcel Dekker.

Monk, T. H., & Folkard, S. (1983). Circadian rhythms and shift work. In R. Hockey (Ed.), *Stress and fatigue in human performance.* Chichester: Wiley.

Monk, T. H., Leng, V. C., Folkard, S., & Weitzman, E. D. (1983). Circadian rhythms in subjective alertness and core body temperature. *Chronobiologia, 10,* 49–55.

Mook, D. G. (1974). Saccharin preference in the rat: Some unpalatable findings. *Psychological review, 81,* 475–490.

Moos, R. H., Kopell, B. S., Melges, F. T., Yalom, I. D., Lunde, D. T., Clayton, R. B., & Hamburg, D. A. (1969). Fluctuations in symptoms and moods during the menstrual cycle. *Journal of psychosomatic research, 13,* 37–44.

Morgan, W. P. (1982). Psychological effects of exercise. *Behavioral medicine update, 4,* 25–30.

Morley, J. E., & Levine, A. S. (1980). Stress-induced eating is mediated through endogenous opiates. *Science, 209,* 1259–1261.

Morris, W. N., & Reilly, N. P. (1987). Toward the self-regulation of mood: Theory and research. *Motivation and emotion, 11,* 215–249.

Moruzzi, G., & Magoun, E. W. (1949). Brain-stem reticular formation and activation of the EEG. *Electroencephalography and clinical neurophysiology, 1,* 455–473.

Mountcastle, V. B. (1980). Medical physiology (14th ed.). St. Louis: Mosby.

Munte, T. F., Heinze, H. J., Kunkel, H., & Scholz, M. (1984). Personality traits influence the effects of diazepam and caffeine on CNV magnitude. *Neuropsychobiology, 12,* 60–67.

Murray, E. J. (1965). *Sleep, dreams, and arousal.* New York: Appleton-Century-Crofts.

Naitoh, P. (1981). Circadian cycles and restorative power of naps. In L. C. Johnson, D. I. Tepas, W. P. Colquhoun, & M. J. Colligan (Eds.), *Biological rhythms, sleep and shift work: Advances in sleep research* (Vol. 7), pp. 553–580. New York: Spectrum Publications.

Natale, M., & Bolan, R. (1980). The effect of Velten's mood-induction procedure for depression on hand movement and head-down posture. *Motivation and emotion, 4,* 323–333.

Natsoulas, T. (1970). Concerning introspective "knowledge." *Psychological bulletin, 73,* 89–111.

Neiss, R. (1988). Reconceptualizing arousal: Psychobiological states in motor performance. *Psychological bulletin, 103,* 345–366.

Nisbett, R. E., & Wilson, T. D. (1977). Telling more than we can know: Verbal reports on mental processes. *Psychological review, 84,* 231–259.

Nowlis, V. (1965). Research with the Mood Adjective Check List. In S. S. Tomkins, & C. E. Izard (Eds.), *Affect, cognition, and personality,* pp. 352–389. New York: Springer.

Nowlis, V., & Nowlis, H. H. (1956). The description and analysis of moods. *Annals New York Academy of Science, 65,* 345–355.

Olds, J. (1962). Hypothalamic substrates of reward. *Physiological reviews, 42,* 554–604.

Olds, J., & Milner, P. (1954). Positive reinforcement produced by electrical stimulation of the septal area and other regions of the rat brain. *Journal of comparative and physiological psychology, 47,* 419–427.

Orr, W., Hoffman, H., & Hegge, F. (1974). Ultradian rhythms in extended performance. *Aerospace medicine, 45,* 995–1000.

Osmond, H., Mullaly, R., & Bisbee, C. (1985). Mood pain: A comparative study of clinical pain and depression. *Journal of orthomolecular psychiatry, 14,* 5–12.

Overton, D. A. (1978). Major theories of state dependent learning. In B. T. Ho, D. W. Richards, & D. L. Chute (Eds.), *Drug discrimination and state dependent learning.* New York: Academic Press.

Overton, D. A. (1984). State dependent learning and drug discriminations. In L. L. Iversen, S. D. Iversen, & S. H. Snyder (Eds.), *Handbook of psychopharmacology: Drugs, neurotransmitters, and behavior* (Vol. 18). New York: Plenum.

Owens, H., & Maxmen, J. S. (1979). Mood and affect: A semantic confusion. *American journal of psychiatry, 136,* 97–99.

Panksepp, J. (1986). The neurochemistry of behavior. *Annual review of psychology, 37,* 77–107.

Panksepp, J., Siviy, S. M., & Normansell, L. A. (1985). Brain opioids and social emotions. In M. Reite & T. Field (Eds.), *The psychobiology of attachment and separation.* New York: Academic Press.

Papez, J. W. (1937). A proposed mechanism of emotion. *Archives of neurology and psychiatry, 38,* 725–743.

Parlee, M. B. (1982). Changes in moods and activation levels during the menstrual cycle in experimentally naïve subjects. *Psychology of women quarterly, 7,* 119–131.

Patkai, P. (1985). The menstrual cycle. In S. Folkard & T. H. Monk (Eds.), *Hours of work.* Chichester: Wiley.

Patkai, P., Åkerstedt, T., & Pettersson, K. (1977). Field studies of shiftwork: I. Temporal patterns in psychophysical activation in permanent night workers. *Ergonomics, 20,* 611–619.

Pedersen, N. L., Plomin, R., McClearn, G. E., & Friberg, L. (1988). Neuroticism, extraversion, and related traits in adult twins reared apart and reared together. *Journal of personality and social psychology, 55,* 950–957.

Peele, S. (1983). *The science of experience.* Lexington, MA: Lexington Books.

Pepper, G. M., & Krieger, D. T. (1984). Hypothalamic-pituitary-adrenal abnormalities in depression: Their possible relation to central mechanisms regulating ACTH release. In R. M. Post & J. C. Ballenger (Eds.), *Neurobiology of mood disorders.* Baltimore: Williams & Wilkins.

Persinger, M. A. (1983). Winter blahs and spring irritability: The chronic but subtle behavioral operations. *Perceptual and motor skills, 57,* 496–498.

Peters, R., & McGee, R. (1982). Cigarette smoking and state-dependent memory. *Psychopharmacology, 76,* 232–235.

Peterson, C., & Seligman, M.E.P. (1984). Causal explanations as a risk factor for depression: Theory and evidence. *Psychological review, 91,* 347–374.

Pignatiello, M. F., Camp, C. J., & Rasar, L. A. (1986). Musical mood induction: An alternative to the Velten technique. *Journal of abnormal psychology, 95,* 295–297.

Pittman, T. S., & Heller, J. F. (1987). Social motivation. *Annual review of psychology, 38,* 461–489.

Pitts, F. N., & Allen, R. E. (1982). Beta-adrenergic blockade in the treatment of anxiety. In R. J. Mathew (Ed.), *The biology of anxiety.* New York: Brunner/Mazel.

Pitts, F. N., & McClure, J. N. (1967). Lactate metabolism in anxiety neurosis. *New England journal of medicine, 227,* 1329–1336.

Plutchik, R. (1980). *Emotion: A psychoevolutionary synthesis.* New York: Harper.

Polivy, J. (1981). On the induction of emotion in the laboratory: Discrete moods or multiple affect states? *Journal of personality and social psychology, 41,* 803–817.

Polivy, J., & Doyle, C. (1980). Laboratory induction of mood states through the reading of self-referent mood statements: Affective changes or demand characteristics? *Journal of abnormal psychology, 89,* 286–290.

Post, R. M. (1976). Clinical aspects of cocaine: Assessment of acute and chronic effects in animals and man. In S. J. Mule (Ed.), *Cocaine: Chemical, biological, clinical, social, and treatment aspects.* Cleveland: CRC Press.

Post, R. M., & Ballenger, J. C. (Eds.). (1984). *Neurobiology of mood disorders* (Vol. 1). Baltimore: Williams & Wilkins.

Post, R. M., Pickar, D., Ballenger, J. C., Naber, D., & Rubinow, D. R. (1984). Endogenous opiates in cerebrospinal fluid: Relationship to mood and anxiety. In R.

M. Post & J. C. Ballenger (Eds.), *Neurobiology of mood disorders*. Baltimore: Williams & Wilkins.

Pribram, K. H., & McGuinness, D. (1975). Arousal, activation and effort in the control of attention. *Psychological review, 82,* 116–149.

Purcell, A. T. (1982). The structure of activation and emotion. *Multivariate behavioral research, 17, 221–251.*

Pyszczynski, T., & Greenberg, J. (1987). Self-regulatory perseveration and the depressive self-focusing style: A self-awareness theory of reactive depression. *Psychological bulletin, 102,* 122–138.

Quattrone, G. A. (1985). On the congruity between internal states and action. *Psychological bulletin, 98,* 3–40.

Ransford, C. P. (1982). A role for amines in the antidepressant effect of exercise: A review. *Medicine and science in sports and exercise, 14,* 1–10.

Ray, O. S. (1972). *Drugs, society, and human behavior.* St. Louis: Mosby.

Redmond, D. E., & Huang, Y. H. (1979). Current concepts. 2. New evidence for a locus coeruleus-norepinephrine connection with anxiety. *Life sciences, 25,* 2149–2162.

Revelle, W., Humphreys, M. S., Simon, L., & Gilliland, K. (1980). The interactive effect of personality, time of day, and caffeine: A test of the arousal model. *Journal of experimental psychology: General, 109,* 1–31.

Rholes, W. S., Riskind, J. H., & Lane, J. W. (1987). Emotional states and memory biases: Effects of cognitive priming and mood. *Journal of personality and social psychology, 52,* 91–99.

Riskind, J. H. (1983). Nonverbal expressions and the accessibility of life experience memories: A congruence hypothesis. *Social cognition, 2,* 62–86.

Riskind, J. H., & Rholes, W. S. (1983). Somatic versus self-devaluative statements in the Velten Mood Induction procedure: Effects on negativistic interpretations and on depressed mood. *Journal of social and clinical psychology, 1,* 300–311.

Riskind, J. H., Rholes, W. S., & Eggers, J. (1982). The Velten Mood Induction procedure: Effects on mood and memory. *Journal of consulting and clinical psychology, 50,* 146–147.

Robinson, R. G. (1983). Investigating mood disorders following brain injury: An integrative approach using clinical and laboratory studies, *Integrative psychiatry, 1,* 35–39.

Robinson, R. G., Lipsey, J. R., Bolla-Wilson, K., Bolduc, P. L., Pearlson, G. D., Rao, K., & Price, T. R. (1985). Mood disorders in left-handed stroke patients. *American journal of psychiatry, 142,* 1424–1429.

Robinson, R. G., Lipsey, J. R., Rao, K., & Price, T. R. (1986). Two-year longitudinal study of poststroke mood disorders: Comparison of acute-onset with delayed-onset depression. *American journal of psychiatry, 143,* 1238–1244.

Rogers, E. J., & Vilkin, B. (1978). Diurnal variations in sensory and pain thresholds correlated with mood states. *Journal of clinical psychiatry, 39,* 431–438.

Rogoff, J. M. (1945). A critique on the theory of emergency function of the adrenal glands: Implications for psychology. *Journal of general psychology, 32,* 249–268.

Rohmer, F., Schaff, G., Collard, M., & Kurtz, D. (1965). La motilité spontanée, la fréquence cardiaque et la fréquence respiratoire au cours du sommeil chez l'homme normal. *Electroencephalographie et neurophysiologie clinique, 2,* 192–207.

Romano, J. M., & Turner, J. A. (1985). Chronic pain and depression: Does the evidence support a relationship? *Psychological bulletin, 97,* 18–34.

Rooijen, L. V., & Vlaander, G.P.J. (1984). Dramatic induction of depressive mood. *Journal of clinical psychology, 40,* 1318–1322.

Rosenhan, D. L., Salovey, P., & Hargis, K. (1981). The joys of helping: Focus of attention mediates the impact of positive affect on altruism. *Journal of personality and social psychology, 40,* 899–905.

Rosenman, R. H. (1978). The interview method of assessment of the coronary-prone behavior pattern. In T. M. Dembroski, S. M. Weiss, J. L. Shields, S. G. Haynes, & M. Feinleib (Eds.), *Coronary-prone behavior,* pp. 55–69. New York: Springer-Verlag.

Rosenthal, N. E., Genhart, M. J., Cabellero, B., Jacobsen, F. M., Skwerer, R. O., Wurtman, J. J., & Spring, B. J. (1986). Carbohydrate craving in seasonal affective disorder. Paper presented at the annual meeting of the American Psychological Association, Washington, D.C.

Rosenthal, N. E., & Heffernan, M. M. (1986). Bulimia, carbohydrate craving, and depression: A central connection? In R. J. Wurtman & J. J. Wurtman (Eds.), *Nutrition and behavior* (Vol. 7). New York: Raven Press.

Rosenthal, N. E., Sack, D. A., Carpenter, C. J., Parry, B. L., Mendelson, W. B., & Wehr, T. A. (1985). Antidepressant effects of light in seasonal affective disorder. *American journal of psychiatry, 142,* 163–170.

Rosenthal, R. H., & Allen, T. W. (1978). An examination of attention, arousal, and learning dysfunctions of hyperkinetic children. *Psychological bulletin, 85,* 689–715.

Rossi, A. S., & Rossi, P. E. (1977). Body time and social time: Mood patterns by menstrual cycle phase and day of the week. *Social science research, 6,* 273–308.

Rossi, E. L. (1985). *Dreams and the growth of personality: Expanding awareness in psychotherapy* (2nd ed.). New York: Brunner/Mazel.

Roth, D., & Rehm, L. P. (1980). Relationships among self-monitoring processes, memory, and depression. *Cognitive therapy and research, 2,* 149–157.

Rotton, J., & Kelly, I. W. (1985). Much ado about the full moon: A meta-analysis of lunar-lunacy research. *Psychological bulletin, 97,* 286–306.

Routtenberg, A. (1968). The two-arousal hypothesis: Reticular formation and limbic system. *Psychological review, 75,* 51–80.

Rowell, L. B. (1974). Human cardiovascular adjustments to exercise and thermal stress. *Physiological review, 54,* 71–159.

Rubadeau, J. (1976). The relationship between self-esteem, activation levels, and other situational determinants. Unpublished master's thesis, California State University, Long Beach.

Rubadeau, J., & Thayer, R. E. (1976). The relationship of self-esteem and self-reported activation level over a seven-week period. Paper presented at Western Psychological Association.

Rubin, R. T., Miller, R. G., Clark, B. R., Poland, R. E., & Arthus, R. J. (1970). The stress of aircraft carrier landings. II. 3-methoxy-4-hydroxyphenylglycol excretion in naval aviators. *Psychosomatic medicine, 32,* 589–597.

Ruderman, A. J. (1985). Dysphoric mood and overeating: A test of restraint theory's disinhibition hypothesis. *Journal of abnormal psychology, 94,* 78–85.

Ruderman, A. J. (1986). Dietary restraint: A theoretical and empirical review. *Psychological bulletin, 99,* 247–262.

Ruderman, A. J., Belzer, L. J., & Halperin, A. (1985). Restraint, anticipated consumption, and overeating. *Journal of abnormal psychology, 94,* 547–555.

Ruderman, A. J., & Wilson, G. T. (1979). Weight, restraint, cognitions, and coun-terregulation. *Behaviour research and therapy, 17,* 581–590.

Rushton, J. P., Brainerd, C. J., & Pressley, M. (1983). Behavioral development and construct validity: The principle of aggregation. *Psychological bulletin, 94,* 18–38.

Russell, J. A. (1978). Evidence of convergent validity on the dimensions of affect. *Journal of personality and social psychology, 36,* 1152–1168.

Russell, J. A. (1980). A circumplex model of affect. *Journal of personality and social psychology, 39,* 1161–1178.

Russell, J. A., & Mehrabian, A. (1977). Evidence for a three-factor theory of emotions. *Journal of research in personality, 11,* 273–294.

Russell, J. A., & Ridgeway, D. (1983). Dimensions underlying children's emotion concepts. *Developmental psychology, 19,* 795–804.

Russell, M.A.H., Peto, J., & Patel, U. A. (1974). A classification of smoking by factorial structure of motives. *Journal of the Royal Statistical Society, 137,* 313–333.

Ryle, G. (1949). *The concept of mind.* New York: Barnes & Noble.

Saltin, B. (1973). Metabolic fundamentals in exercise. *Medicine and science in sports and exercise, 5,* 137.

Sanders, D., Warner, P., Backstrom, T., & Bancroft, J. (1983). Mood, sexuality, hormones and the menstrual cycle: I. Changes in mood and physical state: Description of subjects and method. *Psychosomatic method, 45,* 487–501.

Sanders, J. L., & Brizzolara, M. S. (1982). Relationships between weather and mood. *The journal of general psychology, 107,* 155–156.

Sawyer, D. A., Julia, H. L., & Turin, A. C. (1982). Caffeine and human behavior: Arousal, anxiety, and performance effects. *Journal of behavioral medicine, 5,* 415–439.

Schachter, S. (1964). The interaction of cognitive and physiological determinants of emotional state. In L. Berkowitz (Ed.), *Advances in experimental social psychology* (Vol. 1), pp. 49–80. New York: Academic Press.

Schalling, D. (1978). Psychopathy-related personality variables and the psychophysiology of socialization. In R. D. Hare & D. Schalling (Eds.), *Psychopathic behavior: Approaches to research* (pp. 85–106). Chichester: Wiley.

Scherer, K. R. (1986). Vocal affect expression: A review and a model for future research. *Psychological bulletin, 99,* 143–165.

Scheving, L. E., Roig, C., Halberg, F., Pauly, J. E., & Hand, E. A. (1974). Circadian variations in residents of a "senior citizens" home. In L. E. Scheving, F. Halberg, & J. E. Pauly (Eds.), *Chronobiology.* Tokyo: Igaku Shoin.

Schildkraut, J. J. (1965). The catecholamine hypothesis of affective disorders: A review of the supporting evidence. *American journal of psychiatry, 122,* 509–522.

Schildkraut, J. J., Orsulak, P. J., Schatzberg, A. F., & Rosenbaum, A. H. (1984). Urinary MHPG in affective disorders. In R. M. Post & J. C. Ballenger (Eds.), *Neurobiology of mood disorders.* Baltimore: Williams & Wilkins.

Schlosberg, H. (1954). Three dimensions of emotion. *Psychological review, 61,* 81–88.

Schnore, M. M. (1959). Individual patterns of physiological activity as a function of task differences and degree of arousal. *Journal of experimental psychology, 58,* 117–128.

Schwarz, N., & Clore, G. L. (1983). Mood, misattribution, and judgments of well-being: Informative and directive functions of affective states. *Journal of personality and social psychology, 45,* 513–523.

Seligman, M.E.P. (1975). *Helplessness: On depression, development, and death.* San Francisco: Freeman.

Seligman, M.E.P. (1976). *Learned helplessness and depression in animals and men.* Morristown, N.J.: General Learning Press.

Selye, H. (1956). *The stress of life.* New York: McGraw-Hill.

Selye, H. (1978). *The stress of life: Revised edition.* New York: McGraw-Hill.

Sepinwall, J., & Cook, L. (1978). Behavioral pharmacology of antianxiety drugs. In L. L. Iversen, S. D. Iversen, & S. H. Snyder (Eds.), *Handbook of psychopharmacology: Biology of mood and antianxiety drugs* (Vol. 13). New York: Plenum.

Shacham, S. (1983). A shortened version of the Profile of Mood States. *Journal of personality assessment, 47,* 305–306.

Shephard, R. J. (1982). *Physiology and biochemistry of exercise.* New York: Praeger.

Sherrington, C. (1947). *The integrative action of the nervous system* (2nd ed.). New Haven: Yale University Press.

Shurcliff, A. (1968). Judged humor, arousal, and the relief theory. *Journal of personality and social psychology, 4,* 360–363.

Singer, J. A., & Salovey, P. (1988). Mood and memory: Evaluating the network theory of affect. *Clinical psychology review, 8,* 211–251.

Skinner, B. F. (1987). Whatever happened to psychology as the science of behavior? *American psychologist, 42,* 780–786.

Slade, P. (1984). Premenstrual emotional changes in normal women: Fact or fiction? *Journal of psychosomatic research, 28,* 1–7.

Slavney, P. R., & Pauker, S. (1981). The reliability of clinical mood assessment: Patients' self-reports vs. observer ratings. *Comprehensive psychiatry, 22,* 162–166.

Smoller, J. W., Wadden, T. A., & Stunkard, A. J. (1987). Dieting and depression: A critical review. *Journal of psychosomatic medicine, 31,* 429–440.

Soyka, F., & Edwards, A. (1976). *The ion effect.* New York: Bantam.

Sperry, R. W. (1952). Neurology and the mind-brain problem. *American scientist, 40,* 291–312.

Spielberger, C. D., Gorsuch, R., & Lushene, R. (1970). *The State-Trait Anxiety Inventory (STAI) test manual form X.* Palo Alto, Calif.: Consulting Psychologists Press.

Spinweber, C. L. (1981). L-tryptophan in psychiatry and neurology. *Psychopharmacology bulletin, 17,* 81–82.

Spinweber, C. L., & Hartmann, E. (1976). Long and short sleepers: Male and female subjects. *Sleep research, 5,* 112.

Spring, B., Chiodo, J., & Bowen, D. J. (1987). Carbohydrates, tryptophan, and behavior: A methodological review. *Psychological bulletin, 102,* 234–256.

Steele, R. S. (1977). Power motivation, activation, and inspirational speeches. *Journal of personality, 45,* 53–64.

Sternbach, R. A. (1966). *Principles of psychophysiology: An introductory text and readings.* New York: Academic Press.

Stone, A. A. (1987). Event content in a daily survey is differentially associated with concurrent mood. *Journal of personality and social psychology, 52,* 56–58.

Stone, A. A., Cox, D. S., Valdimarsdottir, H., Jandorf, L., & Neale, J. M. (1987). Evidence that secretory IgA antibody is associated with daily mood. *Journal of personality and social psychology, 52,* 988–993.

Stone, A. A., Hedges, S. M., Neale, J. M., & Satin, M. S. (1985). Prospective and cross-sectional mood reports offer no evidence of a "Blue-Monday" phenomenon. *Journal of personality and social psychology, 49,* 129–134.

Stone, A. A., & Neale, J. M. (1984). Effects of severe daily events on mood. *Journal of personality and social psychology, 46,* 137–144.

Strassman, H. D., Thaler, M. B., & Schein, E. H. (1956). A prisoner of war syndrome: Apathy as a reaction to severe stress. *American journal of psychiatry, 112,* 998–1003.

Strelau, J. (1983). *Temperament, personality, activity.* New York: Academic Press.

Strube, M. J., Turner, C. W., Patrick, S., & Perrillo, R. (1983). Type A and Type B attentional responses to aesthetic stimuli: Effects on mood and performance. *Journal of personality and social psychology, 45,* 1369–1379.

Sugarman, D. A., & Freeman, L. (1970). *The search for serenity: Understanding and overcoming anxiety.* New York: Macmillan.

Sutker, P. B., Libet, J. M., Allain, A. N., & Randall, C. L. (1983). Alcohol use, negative mood states, and menstrual cycle phases. *Alcoholism: Clinical and experimental research, 7,* 327–331.

Taub, J. M. (1977). Napping behavior, activation, and sleep function. *Waking and sleeping, 1,* 281–290.

Taub, J. M. (1982). Effects of scheduled afternoon naps and bedrest on daytime alertness. *International journal of neuroscience, 16,* 107–127.

Taub, J. M., & Berger, R. J. (1974). Diurnal variations in mood as asserted by self-report and verbal content analysis. *Journal of psychiatric research, 10,* 83–88.

Taub, J. M., Tanguay, P. E., & Clarkson, D. (1976). Effects of daytime naps on performance and mood in a college student population. *Journal of abnormal psychology, 85,* 210–217.

Taub, J. M., Tanguay, P. E., & Rosa, R. R. (1977). Effects of afternoon naps on physiological variables, performance and self-reported activation. *Biological psychology, 5,* 191–210.

Taylor, C. B., Bandura, A., Ewart, C. K., Miller, N. H., & DeBusk, R. F. (1985). Exercise testing to enhance wives' confidence in their husbands' cardiac capability soon after clinically uncomplicated acute myocardial infarction. *American journal of cardiology, 55,* 635–638.

Taylor, M. J., & Cooper, P. J. (1986). Body size overestimation and depressed mood. *British journal of clinical psychology, 25,* 153–154.

Teasdale, J. D. (1983). Negative thinking in depression: Cause, effect, or reciprocal relationship? *Advances in behavioral research and therapy, 5,* 3–25.

Teasdale, J. D., & Fogarty, S. J. (1979). Differential effects of induced mood on retrieval of pleasant and unpleasant events from episodic memory. *Journal of abnormal psychology, 88,* 248–257.

Teasdale, J. D., & Taylor, R. (1981). Induced mood and accessibility of memories: An effect of mood state or mood induction procedure? *British journal of social and clinical psychology, 20,* 39–48.

Teasdale, J. D., Taylor, R., & Fogarty, S. J. (1980). Effects of induced elation-depression on the accessibility of happy and unhappy experiences. *Behaviour research and therapy, 18,* 339–346.

Tellegen, A. (1985). Structures of mood and personality and their relevance to assessing anxiety, with an emphasis on self-report. In A. H. Tuma & J. D. Maser (Eds.), *Anxiety and the anxiety disorders.* Hillsdale, N.J.: Erlbaum.

Tellegen, A., Lykken, D. T., Bouchard, T. J., Wilcox, K. J., & Rich, S. (1988). Personality similarity in twins raised apart and together. *Journal of personality and social psychology, 54,* 1031–1039.

Teplov, B. M. (1972). The problem of types of human nervous activity and methods of determining them. In V. D. Nebylitsyn & J. A. Gray (Eds.), *Biological bases of individual behavior,* pp. 1–10. New York: Academic Press.

Thayer, R. E. (1967). Measurement of activation through self-report. *Psychological reports, 20,* 663–678.

Thayer, R. E. (1970). Activation states as assessed by verbal report and four psychophysiological variables. *Psychophysiology, 7,* 86–94.

Thayer, R. E. (1971). Personality and discrepancies between verbal reports and physiological measures of private emotional experiences. *Journal of personality, 39,* 57–69.

Thayer, R. E. (1978a). Factor analytic and reliability studies on the Activation-Deactivation Adjective Check List. *Psychological reports, 42,* 747–756.

Thayer, R. E. (1978b). Toward a psychological theory of multidimensional activation (arousal). *Motivation and emotion, 2,* 1–34.

Thayer, R. E. (1985). Activation (arousal): The shift from a single to a multidimensional perspective. In J. Strelau, A. Gale, & F. H. Farley (Eds.), *The biological bases of personality and behavior* (Vol. 1), pp. 115–127. Washington, D.C.: Hemisphere.

Thayer, R. E. (1986). Activation-Deactivation Adjective Check List: Current overview and structural analysis. *Psychological reports, 58,* 607–614.

Thayer, R. E. (1987a). Energy, tiredness, and tension effects of a sugar snack versus moderate exercise. *Journal of personality and social psychology, 52,* 119–125.

Thayer, R. E. (1987b). Problem perception, optimism, and related states as a function of time of day (diurnal rhythm) and moderate exercise: Two arousal systems in interaction. *Motivation and emotion, 11,* 19–36.

Thayer, R. E. (1987c). *Walking as a mood modulator.* Paper presented at the Sanka symposium on fitness walking, National Press Club, Washington, D.C.

Thayer, R. E., & Cheatle, M. (1976). *The effect of treadmill walking on energy and tension.* California State University, Long Beach, unpublished manuscript.

Thayer, R. E., Cook, M. W., Hooe, E. S., & Lotts, D. J. (1987). *Exercise-induced arousal change as a function of extraversion, neuroticism, and psychoticism.* Paper presented at International Conference on Personality and Individual Differences, Toronto, Canada.

Thayer, R. E., & Moore, L. E. (1972). Reported activation and verbal learning as a function of group size (social facilitation) and anxiety-inducing instructions. *The journal of social psychology, 88,* 277–287.

Thayer, R. E., & Peters, D. P. (1987). *Smoking reduction, mood, and short brisk walks.* California State University, Long Beach, unpublished manuscript.

Thayer, R. E., Takahashi, P. J., & Pauli, J. A. (1988). Multidimensional arousal states, diurnal rhythms, cognitive and social processes, and extraversion. *Personality and individual differences, 9,* 15–24.

Thayer, R. E., & Wettler, A. (1975). *Activation patterns in self-reported depression states.* California State University, Long Beach, unpublished manuscript.

Tiggemann, M., & Winefield, A. H. (1984). The effects of unemployment on the mood, self-esteem, locus of control, and depressive affect of school-leavers. *Journal of occupational psychology, 57,* 33–42.

Tom, G., Poole, M. F., Galla, J., & Berrier, J. (1981). The influence of negative air ions on human performance and mood. *Human factors, 23,* 633–636.

Tomkins, S. S. (1981). The quest for primary motives: Biography and autobiography of an idea. *Journal of personality and social psychology, 41,* 306–329.

Torsvall, L., & Åkerstedt, T. (1980). A diurnal type scale: Construction, consistency, and validation in shift work. *Scandinavian journal of work, environment, and health, 6,* 283–290.

Touitou, Y., Bogdan, A., Reinberg, A., Beck, H., & Touitou, C. (1983). Small amplitude circadian and circannual rhythms of temperature in elderly human subjects. *Chronobiologia, 10,* 165.

Tucker, D. M. (1981). Lateral brain function and the conceptualization of emotion. *Psychological bulletin, 89,* 19–46.

Tucker, D. M., & Williamson, P. A. (1984). Asymmetric neural control in human self-regulation, *Psychological review, 91,* 185–215.

Tulving, E., & Thompson, D. M. (1973). Encoding specificity and retrieval processes in episodic memory. *Psychological review, 80,* 352–373.

Tune, G. S. (1969). The influence of age and temperament on the adult human sleep-wakefulness pattern. *British journal of psychology, 60,* 431–442.

Underwood, B., & Froming, W. J. (1980). The mood survey: A personality measure of happy and sad moods. *Journal of personality assessment, 44,* 404–414.

Underwood, G. (1982). *Awareness and self-awareness: Aspects of consciousness* (Vol. 3). London: Academic Press.

Ursin, H., Baade, E., & Levine, S. (1978). *Psychobiology of stress: A study of coping men.* New York: Academic Press.

Vanderwolf, C. H., & Robinson, T. E. (1981). Reticulo-cortical activity and behavior: A critique of the arousal theory and a new synthesis. *The behavioral and brain sciences, 4,* 459–514.

van Praag, H. M. (1978). Amine hypotheses of affective disorders. In L. L. Iversen, S. D. Iversen, & S. H. Snyder (Eds.), *Handbook of psychopharmacology: Biology of mood and antianxiety disorders* (Vol. 13). New York: Plenum.

Velten, E. C. (1967). The induction of elation and depression through the reading of structured sets of mood-statements. (Doctoral dissertation, University of Southern California). *Dissertation Abstracts International, 28,* 1700B.

Velten, E. C. (1968). A laboratory task for induction of mood states. *Behaviour research and therapy, 6,* 473–482.

Vestre, N. D. (1984). Irrational beliefs and self-reported depressed mood. *Journal of abnormal psychology, 93,* 239–241.

Viney, L. L. (1986). Expression of positive emotion by people who are physically ill: Is it evidence of defending or coping? *Journal of psychosomatic research, 30,* 27–34.

Wadden, T. A. (1984). Mood changes in behavioral weight loss programs. *Journal of psychosomatic research, 28,* 345–346.

Wadden, T. A., Stunkard, A. J., & Smoller, J. W. (1986). Dieting and depression: A methodological study. *Journal of consulting and clinical psychology, 54,* 869–871.

Warburton, D. M., & Wesnes, K. A. (1978). Individual differences in smoking and attentional performance. In R. E. Thornton (Ed.), *Smoking behavior: Physiological and psychological influences,* pp. 19–43. Edinburgh: Churchill Livingston.

Watson, D. (1988a). Intraindividual and interindividual analyses of positive and negative affect: Their relation to health complaints, perceived stress, and daily activities. *Journal of personality and social psychology, 54,* 1020–1030.

Watson, D. (1988b). The vicissitudes of mood measurement: Effects of varying descriptors, time frames, and response formats on measures of positive and negative affect. *Journal of personality and social psychology, 55,* 128–141.

Watson, D., & Tellegen, A. (1985). Toward a consensual structure of mood. *Psychological bulletin, 98,* 219–235.

Watts, B. L. (1982). Individual differences in circadian activity rhythms and their effects on roommate relationships. *Journal of personality, 50,* 374–383.

Watts, C., Cox, T., & Robson, J. (1983). Morningness-eveningness and diurnal variations in self-reported mood. *The journal of psychology, 113,* 251–256.

Webb, W. B. (1979). Are short and long sleepers different? *Psychological reports, 44,* 259–264.

Webb, W. B. (1982). *Biological rhythms, sleep, and performance.* Chichester: Wiley.

Webb, W. B., & Friel, J. (1970). Characteristics of "natural" long and short sleepers: A preliminary report. *Psychological reports, 27,* 63–66.

Webb, W. B., & Friel, J. (1971). Sleep stage and personality characteristics of "natural" long and short sleepers. *Science, 171,* 587–588.

Weinberger, J. (1984). Reactions to uncertainty: A comparison of three motivational theories. *Motivation and emotion, 8,* 109–140.

Weiner, B. (1985). An attributional theory of achievement motivation and emotion. *Psychological review, 92,* 548–573.

Weingartner, H., Miller, H., & Murphy, D. L. (1977). Mood-state-dependent retrieval of verbal associations. *Journal of abnormal psychology, 86,* 276–284.

Weitzman, E. D., Moline, M. L., Czeisler, C. A., & Zimmerman, J. C. (1982). Chronobiology of aging: Temperature, sleep-wake rhythms and entrainment. *Neurobiology of aging, 3,* 299–309.

Wesnes, K., & Warburton, D. M. (1983). Stress and drugs. In R. Hockey (Ed.), *Stress and human performance.* Chichester: Wiley.

West, J. B. (1974). *Respiratory physiology—The essentials.* Baltimore: Williams and Wilkins.

Wever, R. A. (1982). Behavioral aspects of circadian rhythmicity. In F. M. Brown & R. C. Graeber (Eds.), *Rhythmic aspects of behavior.* Hillsdale, N.J.: Erlbaum.

Wheeler, E. O., White, P. D., Reed, E. W., & Cohen, M. E. (1950). Neurocirculatory asthenia (anxiety neurosis, effort syndrome, neurasthenia). *Journal of the American Medical Association, 142,* 878–889.

Whybrow, P. C., Akiskal, H. S., & McKinney, W. T. (1984). *Mood disorders: Toward a new psychobiology.* New York: Plenum.

Williams, D. G. (1981). Personality and mood: State-trait relationships. *Personality and individual differences, 2,* 303–309.

Wilson, T. D., Hull, J. G., & Johnson, J. (1981). Awareness and self-perception: Verbal reports on internal states. *Journal of personality and social psychology, 40,* 53–71.

Wilson, T. D., Laser, P. S., & Stone, J. I. (1982). Judging the predictors of one's own mood: Accuracy and use of shared theories. *Journal of experimental social psychology, 18,* 537–556.

Winokur, G., Clayton, P. J., & Reich, T. (1969). *Manic depressive illness.* Saint Louis: Mosby.

Wispe, L. (1980). The role of moods in helping behavior. *Representative research in social psychology, 11,* 2–15.

Wright, R. A., & Brehm, J. W. (1984). The impact of task-difficulty upon perceptions of arousal and goal attractiveness in an avoidance paradigm. *Motivation and emotion, 8,* 171–181.

Wright, W. F., & Bower, G. H. (1981). Mood effects on subjective probability assessments. Stanford University, unpublished manuscript (as described in Gilligan & Bower, 1984).

Wundt, W. (1896). *Grundriss der psychologie.* Leipzig: Engelmann.

Wurtman, R. J., Hefti, F., & Malemed, E. (1981). Precursor control of neurotransmitter synthesis. *Pharmacological review, 32,* 315–335.

Wurtman, R. J., & Wurtman, J. J. (1986). *Nutrition and the brain: Food constituents affecting normal and abnormal behaviors* (Vol. 7). New York: Raven Press.

Wyer, R. S., & Carlston, D. E. (1979). *Social cognition, inference, and attribution.* Hillsdale, N.J.: Erlbaum.

Young, P. T. (1967). Affective arousal: Some implications. *American psychologist, 22,* 32–40.

Zajonc, R. B. (1980). Feeling and thinking: Preferences need no inferences. *American psychologist, 35,* 151–175.

Zajonc, R. B. (1984). On the primacy of affect. *American psychologist, 39,* 117–123.

Zentall, S. S., & Zentall, T. R. (1983). Optimal stimulation: A model of disordered activity and performance in normal and deviant children. *Psychological bulletin, 94,* 446–471.

Zevon, M. A., & Tellegen, A. (1982). The structure of mood change: An idiographic/nomothetic analysis. *Journal of personality and social psychology, 43,* 111–122.

Zillman, D. (1988a). Mood management: Using entertainment to full advantage. In L. Donohew, H. E. Sypher, & E. T. Higgins (Eds.), *Communication, social cognition, and affect,* pp. 147–171. Hillsdale, N.J.: Erlbaum.

Zillman, D. (1988b). Mood management through communication choices. *American behavioral scientist, 31,* 327–340.

Zuckerman, M. (1979). *Sensation seeking: Beyond the optimal level of arousal.* Hillsdale, N.J.: Erlbaum.

Zuckerman, M., Kuhlman, D. M., Camac, C. (1988). What lies beyond E and N? Factor analyses of scales believed to measure basic dimensions of personality. *Journal of personality and social psychology, 54,* 96–107.

Zuckerman, M., & Lubin, B. (1965). *The Multiple Affect Adjective Check List.* San Diego: Educational and Industrial Testing Service.

Zuckerman, M., & Lubin, B. (1985). *Manual for the MAACL-R: The Multiple Affect Adjective Check List.* San Diego: Educational and Industrial Testing Service.

Author Index

Abramson, L. Y., 41, 42, 152, 166, 211
Adams, G. M., 119–120, 201
Ague, C., 158, 195
Ahrens, A. H., 36, 195
Aiken, P. A., 39, 196
Åkerstedt, T., 72, 80, 195, 213, 220
Akil, A., 27, 164, 195
Akiskal, H. S., 43, 221
Allain, A. N., 30, 218
Allen, B. P., 19, 151, 195
Allen, R. E., 126, 213
Allen, T. W., 83, 121, 215
Allen, V. L., 114, 195
Alloy, L. B., 36, 195
Amenson, C. S., 41, 167, 209
American Psychiatric Association, 7, 54, 116, 151, 195
Amsterdam, J. D., 25, 211
Anderson, K., 24, 159, 195
Andreassi, J. L., 48, 195
Andreev, B. V., 95, 195
Andress, D., 24, 159, 204
Andrew, R. J., 46, 48, 195
Angrist, B., 159, 160, 195
Antelman, S. M., 125–126, 195
Arenberg, D., 82, 192, 201
Arms, R. L., 40, 196
Armstrong, S., 27, 202
Arnold, M. A., 28, 199
Arnold, M. B., 7, 108, 196
Arthus, R. J., 26, 215
Aschoff, J., 67, 196
Asso, D., 84, 85, 196
Asterita, M. F., 51, 196

Baade, E., 51, 220
Backstrom, T., 30, 196, 216
Baekeland, F., 97, 205
Bakalar, J. B., 8, 159, 160, 204
Baker, G.H.B., 37, 196
Baker, K. H., 37, 201
Ballenger, J. C., 3, 28, 43, 164, 191, 213–214
Bancroft, J., 30, 196, 216
Bandura, A., 100–101, 106, 196, 218
Barnett, P. A., 43, 196
Baron, R. A., 40, 196

Barrabee, E. L., 115, 211
Bassin, R. B., 54, 116, 125, 152, 166, 173, 196
Baucom, D. H., 39, 196
Baumann, D. J., 43, 157, 196, 199, 210
Beck, A. T., 18, 33, 196
Beck, H., 81, 220
Becker, J., 21, 53, 54, 196, 203
Beitins, I. Z., 28, 199
Bell, B., 85, 196
Belsher, G., 43, 196
Belzer, L. J., 106, 215
Benassi, V. A., 19, 197
Benjamin, L. T., 98, 200
Berger, R. J., 18, 218
Berkman, L. F., 96, 176, 197
Berkowitz, L., 43, 142, 197
Berlyne, D. E., 98, 197
Berrier, J., 40, 219
Berry, D.T.R., 98, 176, 197
Berscheid, E., 70, 201
Bertelson, A. D., 98, 200
Bettelheim, B., 122–123, 197
Biro, V., 30, 197
Bisbee, C., 192, 212
Blake, M.J.F., 71, 82, 197
Blanchet, P., 37, 95, 197
Blaney, P. H., 4, 9, 22, 33, 34, 35, 197
Bluc, F. R., 20, 22, 210
Bogdan, A., 81, 220
Bohlin, G., 18, 72, 178, 197
Bolan, R., 20, 22, 212
Bolduc, P. L., 29, 214
Bolger, N., 42, 83, 199
Bolla-Wilson, K., 29, 214
Bollen, B. A., 28, 199
Bollenbach, A. K., 36, 210
Bond, C. F., 121, 159, 206
Borgatta, E. I., 133, 197
Boring, E. G., 10, 197
Bouchard, T. J., 45, 219
Bowen, D. J., 4, 38, 97, 141, 158, 217
Bower, G. H., 8, 9, 22, 33–34, 35, 36, 78, 197, 203, 204, 207, 222
Bowskill, R., 39, 200
Boyd, R., 85, 204

223

Boyle, G. J., 30, 197
Braier, J. R., 84, 196
Brainerd, C. J., 74, 91, 137, 216
Brehm, J. W., 98, 222
Breithaupt, H., 80, 197
Brenner, C., 167, 197
Breslow, L., 96, 176, 197
Brewin, C. R., 43, 197
Bridges, P. K., 26, 207
Brizzolara, M. S., 40, 216
Broadbent, D. E., 32, 197
Brody, N., 45, 198
Brooks, G. A., 48, 49, 198
Brown, B. B., 194, 198
Brown, F. M., 67, 198
Brown, J. D., 34, 36, 198
Brozek, J., 55, 97, 118, 122, 123, 207
Brunson, B. I., 102, 198
Buchwald, A. M., 21, 198
Buchwald, D., 37, 95, 198
Buck, R., 125, 198
Buckalew, L. W., 40, 198
Bullock, W., 24, 159, 204
Bunney, W. E., 18, 25, 125, 198
Burger, J. M., 165, 198
Burghardt, G. M., 10, 64, 198
Burns, D., 26, 211
Burrows, G. C., 18, 61, 178, 209
Buss, A. H., 47, 159, 198, 202

Cabellero, B., 158, 163, 215
Caggiula, A. R., 125–126, 195
Camac, C., 131, 222
Camp, C. J., 23, 213
Campbell, D. E., 41, 198
Cannon, W. B., 7, 51, 108, 198
Caplan, B., 19, 198
Carlson, M., 43, 157, 198
Carlson, N. R., 125, 126, 198
Carlston, D. E., 64, 222
Carpenter, C. J., 40, 215
Carpenter, W. T., 125, 198
Carr, D. B., 28, 199
Carver, C. S., 77, 199
Cash, T. F., 19, 199
Caspi, A., 42, 83, 199
Cathala, H. P., 95, 199
Cattell, R. B., 16, 200
Ceredi, C., 81, 201
Chamberlain, A. G., 18, 210
Charry, J. M., 40, 199
Cheatle, M., 90, 219
Chew, B., 158, 209
Chinn, D., 194, 205
Chiodo, J., 4, 38, 97, 141, 158, 217
Chiodo, L. A., 126, 195
Christensen, L., 38–39, 141, 191, 199
Christie, M. J., 38, 199
Cialdini, R. B., 43, 157, 196, 199, 210
Cimbolic, P., 3, 4, 25, 26, 166, 211
Clark, B. R., 26, 215

Clark, D. M., 20, 23, 33, 191, 199
Clark, L. A., 42, 191, 199
Clark, M. S., 23, 24, 32, 33, 43, 157, 199, 206
Clark, W. C., 28, 206
Clarkson, D., 98, 218
Clayton, P. J., 194, 221
Clayton, R. B., 84–85, 211
Cleary, P. D., 173, 209
Clements, P. R., 68, 199
Clore, G. L., 10, 64, 217
Cohen, M. E., 53, 115, 221
Cohen, R. M., 36, 199
Coleman, R. E., 21, 200
Collard, M., 95, 214
Collins, A., 30, 200
Colquhoun, W. P., 67, 71, 82, 83, 200
Colt, W. D., 28, 200, 206
Conroy, R.T.W.L., 71, 200
Cook, L., 125, 217
Cook, M. W., 131, 219
Cooper, P. J., 36, 39, 200, 218
Corcoran, D.W.J., 82, 197
Costa, P. T., 19, 200
Costello, C. G., 43, 196
Cox, D. S., 4, 38, 218
Cox, J. L., 19, 207
Cox, T., 18, 61, 80, 178, 209, 221
Coyne, J. C., 21, 43, 198, 200
Cramer, R. E., 43, 200
Cruickshank, P. J., 18, 200
Csikszentmihalyi, M., 43, 208
Cunningham, M. R., 40, 41, 200
Curran, J. P., 16, 200
Czeisler, C. A., 81–82, 221

Dahlgren, K., 72, 195
Daiss, S. R., 98, 200
Darby, B. L., 157, 199
Datar, M., 27, 202
Daubman, K. A., 36, 164–165, 206
Davidson, D., 30, 196
Davidson, R. J., 29, 37, 125, 200, 203, 210
Davis, J. W., 25, 125, 198
DeBusk, R. F., 100, 202, 218
Defour, C. L., 19, 197
Dejonc, R., 30, 200
Dejours, P., 48, 201
Deldin, P. J., 36, 200
Dermer, M., 70, 201
DeRubeis, R. J., 43, 205
Descovich, G. C., 81, 201
deVries, H. A., 49, 119–120, 126, 127, 201
Diener, E., 17, 19, 42, 62, 117, 143, 156, 201, 208
Dillon, K. M., 37, 201
Dodson, L. C., 120, 201
Domino, E. F., 127, 158, 161, 201
Donnerstein, E., 142, 197
Douglas, K., 82, 192, 201
Doyle, C., 21, 22, 213

Droppleman, L. F., 14, 16, 133, 211
Drury, R. L., 85, 204
Dudley, L. M., 46, 201
Duffy, E., 46, 47, 48, 57, 60, 112, 113, 201
Dufty, W. F., 38, 97, 201

Eason, R. G., 46, 201
Eastwood, M. R., 18, 201
Eaves, L. J., 45, 80, 130, 201
Eckenrode, J., 42, 83, 199, 201
Edmondson, H. D., 26, 201
Edwards, A., 40, 217
Eggers, J., 21, 214
Eliasz, A., 42, 201
Elliot, A. L., 71, 200
Ellis, A., 19, 20
Emmons, R. A., 17, 19, 42, 62, 143, 156,
     201, 208
Eneroth, P., 30, 200
Epstein, S., 91, 137, 143, 202
Erbaujh, J. K., 18, 196
Erber, R., 24, 199
Evans, M. D., 43, 205
Ewart, C. K., 100, 202, 218
Eysenck, H. J., 19, 20, 45, 47, 80, 84, 117,
     130–131, 156, 201, 202
Eysenck, M. W., 19, 20, 32, 47, 69, 82,
     130–131, 202
Eysenck, S.B.G., 131, 202

Fahey, T. D., 48, 49, 198
Farley, F., 81, 156, 202
Fenigstein, A., 159, 202
Fibiger, W., 27, 202
Fiebert, M. S., 194
Finesinger, J. F., 115, 211
Floor, E., 37, 210
Fodor, E. M., 102, 202
Fogarty, S. J., 34, 218
Foley, K. M., 28, 202
Folkard, S., 69, 70, 71, 80, 82, 83, 192, 200,
     202, 211
Folkins, C. H., 4, 92, 119, 202
Folkman, S., 63, 208
Folstein, M. F., 18, 203
Ford, J. G., 43, 200
Forgas, J. P., 36, 203
Fort, A., 71, 200, 203
Fowles, D. C., 131, 203
Fox, N. A., 29, 125, 203
Frankenhaeuser, M., 26, 48, 51, 203
Frantz, A., 28, 200
Frazer, A., 26, 211
Fredericks, C., 38, 97, 203
Freeman, G. L., 79, 203
Freeman, L., 114, 218
Freud, S., 46, 191, 203
Friberg, L., 45, 213
Friedman, M., 114, 151, 203
Friel, J., 97, 221
Frith, C. D., 158, 203

Froberg, J. E., 72, 80, 203
Froming, W. J., 19, 220
Frommer, G. P., 37, 95, 197
Frost, R. O., 20, 21, 203
Furnham, A., 131, 203

Gage, D. F., 22, 29, 203
Galanter, E., 64, 132, 211
Galbo, H., 48, 49, 203
Galla, J., 40, 219
Garzino, S., 41, 203
Gaylin, W., 152, 167, 203
Genhart, M. J., 158, 163, 215
Gershon, S., 26, 203
Gertz, J., 86, 204
Gilbert, D. G., 127, 158, 160, 161, 173, 204
Gillberg, M., 98, 204
Gilligan, S. G., 22, 33, 35, 204
Gilliland, K., 24, 69, 82, 131, 159, 204, 214
Gilman, A., 192, 204
Glass, D. C., 102, 204
Glassman, A., 25–26, 204
Globus, G. G., 85, 204
Glusman, M., 28, 206
Golding, J. F., 158, 161, 210
Golub, S., 30, 204
Goodman, H., 38, 97, 203
Goodman, L. S., 192, 204
Goodwin, D. W., 121, 204
Gorgoglione, J. M., 20, 23, 206
Gorsuch, R., 18, 217
Gotlib, I. H., 18, 43, 196, 200, 204
Gottman, J. M., 31, 182, 204, 209
Graeber, R. C., 71, 204
Graef, R., 43, 208
Graf, M., 21, 203
Gray, J. A., 106, 125, 131–132, 191, 204
Green, A. R., 3, 25, 204
Green, D. E., 158, 206
Green, M. L., 20, 203
Greenberg, J., 43, 214
Grinspoon, L., 8, 159, 160, 192, 204
Grover, G. N., 30, 200
Gruen, P. H., 125, 198
Grunberg, N. E., 163, 204
Grzegolowska-Klarkowska, H. J., 178, 205
Guillard, A., 95, 199

Hafer, M. D., 68, 199
Hager, J. L., 192, 205
Halal, M., 21–22, 208
Halberg, F., 67, 81, 87, 201, 205, 216
Halberstadt, L. J., 41, 42, 152, 211
Halperin, A., 106, 215
Hamburg, D. A., 18, 84–85, 198, 211
Hand, E. A., 81, 216
Hanley, G. L., 194, 205
Hargis, K., 22, 215
Harrigan, J. A., 37, 95, 205
Hartmann, E., 26, 38, 97, 205, 217
Hawkinshire, V., F.B.W., 40, 199

Healy, D., 43, 205
Hedges, S. M., 42, 83, 218
Heffernan, M. M., 163, 215
Hefti, F., 38, 97, 222
Hegge, F., 85–86, 212
Heimstra, N. W., 158, 205
Heine, D., 18, 205
Heinze, H. J., 19, 212
Heller, J. F., 43, 213
Hendrick, C., 133, 205
Henschel, A., 55, 97, 118, 122, 123, 207
Hepburn, L., 19, 202
Hernandez, D. E., 28, 209
Hicks, R. A., 97, 205
Hildebrandt, G., 80, 197
Hilgard, E. R., 10, 49, 64, 167–168, 193, 205
Hinz, L. D., 43, 205
Hoban, C., 30, 200
Hockey, R., 32, 205
Hoffman, H., 85, 212
Hoffman, M. S., 40, 206
Hollandsworth, Jr., J. G., 92, 205
Hollon, S. D., 43, 205
Holmes, D. S., 26, 119, 210
Hooe, E. S., 131, 219
Hord, D. J., 98, 209
Horn, D., 158, 206
Horne, J. A., 47, 79, 181, 182, 205
Horton, J. R., 38, 205
Hoskins, C., 87, 205
Houde, R. W., 28, 202
Hovland, C. I., 79, 203
Howarth, E., 40, 206
Huang, Y. H., 126, 214
Hudson, S. M., 30, 211
Hull, J. G., 19, 121, 159, 206, 221
Hume, K. I., 192, 202
Humphrey, L. L., 21, 207
Humphreys, M. S., 24, 47, 69, 82, 131, 206, 214
Hyland, M. E., 43, 206

Ibayashi, H., 81, 206
Ignatowska-Switalska, H., 42, 207
Iguchi, H., 81, 206
Ikard, F. F., 158, 206
Ingram, R. E., 43, 206
Inturrisi, C. E., 28, 202
Iran-Nejad, A., 17, 62, 201
Isen, A. M., 4, 8, 20, 21, 22, 23, 33, 34, 35, 36, 43, 157, 164–165, 193, 199, 206
Iversen, L. L., 8, 26, 43, 120, 121, 126, 206
Iversen, S. D., 8, 26, 43, 120, 121, 126, 206

Jackson, D. N., 83, 206
Jacobsen, F. M., 158, 163, 215
Janal, M. N., 28, 206
Jandorf, L., 4, 38, 218
Janowsky, D. S., 26, 207
Jensen, J., 37, 209

Johnson, E., 35, 207
Johnson, J., 19, 221
Johnson, L. C., 4, 97, 98, 207, 209
Johnson, M. H., 36, 207
Jones, D. M., 18, 210
Jones, G. E., 92, 205
Jones, M. T., 26, 207
Julia, H. L., 8, 9, 24, 159, 216

Kaiko, R. F., 28, 202
Kalat, J. W., 48, 125, 207
Kales, A., 54, 207
Kales, J. D., 54, 207
Karpman, V. L., 48, 207
Kato, K. I., 81, 206
Kavanagh, D. J., 36, 207
Kelly, I. W., 41, 215
Kendell, R. E., 19, 207
Kendrick, D. T., 157, 196, 199
Kerkhof, G. A., 79, 82, 207
Ketai, R., 15, 207
Keys, A., 55, 97, 118, 122, 123, 207
King, D. S., 37, 95, 104, 207
Kirchenbaum, D. S., 21, 207
Kirchler, E., 41, 207
Kirkcaldy, B. D., 19, 207
Kjellberg, A., 18, 72, 178, 197
Kleitman, N., 4, 71, 79, 85, 94–95, 97, 102, 123, 207
Klonowicz, T., 42, 207
Knauth, P., 70, 202
Komaroff, A. L., 37, 95, 198
Kopell, B. S., 84–85, 211
Korving, H. J., 79, 207
Kosturn, C. F., 159, 210
Kourides, I. A., 28, 202
Kramer, P. M., 18, 201
Krantz, S. E., 36, 203
Krieger, D. T., 27, 213
Krietsch, K., 38–39, 141, 191, 199
Kripke, D. F., 85, 208
Kroenke, K., 37, 95, 208
Kues, J. R., 37, 95, 205
Kuhl, J.F.W., 81, 201
Kuhlman, D. M., 131, 222
Kunkel, H., 19, 212
Kurtz, D., 95, 214

Lacey, J. I., 47, 58, 114, 208
Lacey, W. H., 108, 210
Laird, J. D., 21–22, 208
Lamb, D. R., 126, 127, 208
Landgren, B. M., 30, 200
Lane, J. W., 21, 214
Lang, A. R., 159, 210
Lang, P. J., 192, 208
Larsen, R. J., 17, 42, 82, 117, 137, 143, 156, 201, 208
Larson, R., 43, 208
Laser, P. S., 19, 221
Lavie, P., 85, 86, 204, 208

Lazarus, R. S., 43, 63, 103, 133, 193, 208
Lazzarini, A. J., 18, 61, 178, 209
Leak, D., 26, 207
Leask, R., 30, 196
Lebo, M. A., 133, 209
Lefcourt, H. M., 19, 209
Leng, V. C., 70, 211
Levenson, R. W., 31, 46, 209
Leventhal, H., 29, 173, 209
Levin, I. P., 36, 200
Levin, P. F., 23, 206
Levine, A. S., 28, 212
Levine, S., 17, 51, 156, 201, 220
Lewinsohn, P. M., 41, 167, 209
Lewy, A. J., 40, 209
Li, C. H., 28, 202
Libet, J. M., 30, 218
Lieberman, H. R., 158, 209
Lilly, R. S., 133, 205
Lindsley, D. B., 47, 209
Linn, B. S., 37, 209
Linn, M. W., 37, 209
Lipsey, J. R., 29, 214
Lobban, M. C., 70, 80, 202
Lorr, M., 14, 16, 133, 211
Lotts, D. J., 131, 219
Lubin, A., 98, 209
Lubin, B., 18, 222
Lundberg, G. G., 95, 209
Lunde, D. T., 84–85, 211
Luria, R., 18, 203
Lushene, R., 18, 217
Luttinger, D., 28, 209
Lutz, D. J., 43, 200
Lykken, D. T., 45, 219
Lyons, W. E., 10, 209

MacDonald, K. B., 47, 83, 209
Mackay, C. J., 6, 18, 61, 178, 209
Mackenzie, W. E., 19, 207
MacKinnon, R., 19, 199
MacLean, P. D., 125, 210
Madigan, R. J., 36, 210
Magaro, P. A., 36, 207
Magoun, E. W., 125, 212
Malemed, E., 38, 97, 222
Malmo, R. B., 47, 94, 114, 193, 210
Mandler, G., 47, 51, 63, 132–133, 210
Mangan, G. L., 158, 161, 210
Mangelsdorff, A. D., 37, 95, 208
Manucia, G. K., 43, 157, 210
Markoff, R. A., 28, 210
Marks, J., 192, 210
Marlatt, G. A., 159, 210
Martin, E. G., 108, 210
Martin, J. B., 28, 199
Martin, N. G., 45, 80, 130, 201
Mason, S. T., 4, 25, 26, 126, 166, 210
Matheny, K. B., 20, 22, 110
Matthews, G., 18, 210
Matthews, K. A., 53, 102, 151, 198, 210

Maxmen, J. S., 14, 214
McArthur, J. W., 28, 199
McArthur, L. A., 8, 77, 167, 210
McBrearty, E. M., 38, 199
McBride, G., 64, 210
McCann, L. I., 26, 119, 210
McClearn, G. E., 45, 213
McClelland, D. C., 37, 210
McClure, J. N., 126, 213
McCrae, R. R., 19, 200
McDougall, W., 108, 211
McGee, R., 33, 213
McGuinness, D., 29, 125, 211, 214
McGuire, R. J., 19, 207
McKinney, W. T., 43, 221
McMaster, M. R., 43, 200
McNair, D. M., 14, 16, 133, 211
McNeal, E. T., 3, 4, 25, 26, 166, 211
Meares, A., 118, 211
Mehrabian, A., 18, 39, 211, 216
Meier, N. J., 37, 95, 208
Melges, F. T., 84–85, 211
Mendels, J., 25, 26, 194, 211
Mendelsohn, M., 18, 196
Mendelson, W. B., 40, 215
Metalsky, G. I., 41, 42, 152, 166, 211
Metcalf, M. G., 30, 211
Meyer, J. P., 18, 204
Mickelsen, O., 55, 97, 118, 122, 123, 207
Milberg, S., 24, 32, 33, 199
Miles, H.H.W., 115, 211
Miller, A. J., 27, 202
Miller, G. A., 64, 132, 211
Miller, H., 33, 34, 221
Miller, N., 43, 157, 198
Miller, N. H., 100, 218
Miller, R. G., 26, 215
Miller, R. J., 27, 29, 164, 211
Miller, R. S., 19, 209
Mills, J. N., 71, 200
Milner, P., 164, 212
Minors, D. S., 191, 192, 202, 211
Mock, J. E., 18, 196
Moline, M. L., 81–82, 221
Monjan, A. A., 37, 211
Monk, T. H., 70, 71, 80, 202, 211
Montalbetti, N., 81, 201
Mook, D. G., 162, 211
Moore, L. E., 112, 219
Moos, R. H., 84–85, 211
Morgan, W. P., 93, 211
Morley, J. E., 28, 212
Morris, W. N., 157, 212
Moruzzi, G., 125, 212
Mountcastle, V. B., 48, 125, 212
Mullaly, R., 192, 212
Mullens, W. R., 120, 201
Munte, T. F., 19, 212
Murphy, D. L., 33, 34, 36, 199, 221
Murray, E. J., 102, 118, 123, 193, 212

Naber, D., 28, 164, 191, 213–214
Naitoh, P., 98, 212
Natale, M., 20, 22, 212
Natsoulas, T., 10, 212
Neale, J. M., 4, 38, 42, 83, 218
Nehemia, G., 36, 206
Neiss, R., 47, 114, 212
Nemeroff, C. B., 28, 209
Nesselroade, J. R., 133, 209
Nisbett, R. E., 19, 194, 212
Normansell, L. A., 28, 213
Nowicki, G. P., 36, 164–165, 206
Nowlis, H. H., 164, 212
Nowlis, V., 3, 14, 15, 16, 23, 59, 164, 178, 212
Nutt, D. J., 3, 25, 204

Olds, J., 164, 212
Orr, W., 85, 212
Orsulak, P. J., 26, 216
Osmond, H., 192, 212
Östberg, O., 79, 181, 182, 205
Overton, D. A., 33, 78, 212
Owens, H., 14, 212

Panksepp, J., 28, 51, 125, 192, 193, 212, 213
Papez, J. W., 125, 213
Parlee, M. B., 85, 213
Parry, B. L., 40, 215
Patel, U. A., 158, 216
Patel, V., 37, 210
Patkai, P., 72, 84, 195, 213
Patrick, S., 19, 218
Pauker, S., 19, 217
Pauli, J. A., 9, 11, 19, 31, 69, 75, 80, 82, 87, 103, 131, 138, 150, 156, 175, 182, 219
Pauly, J. E., 81, 216
Pearlson, G. D., 29, 214
Pedersen, N. L., 45, 213
Peele, S., 10, 213
Pellegrini, R. J., 97, 205
Pepper, G. M., 27, 213
Perrillo, R., 19, 218
Persinger, M. A., 40, 213
Peters, D. P., 172, 219
Peters, R., 33, 213
Peterson, C., 41, 42, 43, 166, 211, 213
Peto, J., 158, 216
Pettersson, K., 72, 213
Phoebus, E. C., 85, 204
Pickar, D., 28, 36, 164, 191, 199, 213–214
Pignatiello, M. F., 23, 213
Pittman, T. S., 43, 213
Pitts, F. N., 126, 213
Plomin, R., 45, 47, 198, 213
Plutchik, R., 125, 213
Poland, R. E., 26, 215
Polivy, J., 21, 22, 24, 213
Poole, M. F., 40, 219
Posner, J. B., 28, 202

Post, R. M., 3, 28, 30, 43, 160, 164, 191, 200, 213–214
Potkay, C. R., 19, 151, 195
Powell, J. B., 37, 95, 208
Prange, A. J., 28, 209
Pressley, M., 74, 91, 137, 216
Pribram, K. H., 29, 64, 125, 132, 211, 214
Price, T. R., 29, 214
Purcell, A. T., 3, 61, 178, 214
Pyszczynski, T., 43, 214

Quattrone, G. A., 19, 214

Rao, K., 29, 214
Randall, C. L., 30, 218
Ransford, C. P., 26, 214
Rasar, L. A., 23, 213
Ray, O. S., 165, 214
Redmond, D. E., 126, 214
Reed, E. W., 53, 115, 221
Reese, L. B., 100, 202
Rehm, L. P., 36, 215
Reich, T., 194, 221
Reilly, N. P., 157, 212
Reinberg, A., 81, 220
Revelle, W., 24, 47, 69, 82, 131, 206, 214
Rholes, W. S., 21, 214
Rich, S., 45, 219
Ricks, D. F., 37, 95, 205
Ridgeway, D., 133, 216
Rietveld, W. J., 79, 207
Rimm, D. C., 19, 199
Rimondi, S., 81, 201
Riskind, J. H., 21, 22, 214
Rizzuto, A., 40, 198
Robinson, R. G., 29, 214
Robinson, T. E., 47, 114, 191, 220
Robson, J., 80, 221
Rogers, E. J., 104, 214
Rogoff, J. M., 108, 214
Rohmer, F., 95, 214
Roig, C., 81, 216
Romano, J. M., 43, 214
Rooijen, L. V., 23, 215
Rosa, R. R., 98, 218
Roscoe, B., 26, 201
Rosenbaum, A. H., 26, 216
Rosenblatt, M., 28, 199
Rosenhan, D. L., 22, 215
Rosenman, R. H., 114–115, 151, 203, 215
Rosenthal, N. E., 40, 158, 163, 215
Rosenthal, R. H., 83, 121, 215
Ross, G., 37, 210
Ross, J., 24, 32, 33, 199
Rossi, A. S., 42, 83, 215
Rossi, E. L., 85–86, 215
Rossi, P. E., 42, 83, 215
Roth, D., 36, 215
Rotton, J., 41, 215
Routtenberg, A., 124–125, 215
Rowell, L. B., 48, 215

Roy-Byrne, P., 30, 200
Rubadeau, J., 9, 151, 153, 215
Rubin, R. T., 26, 215
Rubinow, D. R., 28, 30, 164, 191, 200, 213–214
Ruderman, A. J., 39, 106, 157, 216
Rushton, J. P., 74, 91, 137, 216
Russell, G. W., 40, 196
Russell, J. A., 18, 133, 164, 216
Russell, M.A.H., 158, 216
Rutenfranz, J., 70, 202
Ryan, P., 28, 210
Ryle, G., 3, 15, 216

Sack, D. A., 40, 215
Safer, M. A., 22, 29, 203
Salovey, P., 22, 35, 215, 217
Saltin, B., 49, 216
Sanders, D., 30, 216
Sanders, J. L., 40, 216
Saron, C., 37, 210
Satin, M. S., 42, 83, 218
Saunders, D., 30, 196
Sawyer, D. A., 8, 9, 24, 159, 216
Schachter, S., 132, 191, 216
Schaff, G., 95, 214
Schalling, D., 82, 216
Schatzberg, A. F., 26, 216
Scheier, M. F., 77, 159, 199, 202
Schein, E. H., 123, 218
Scherer, K. R., 18, 216
Scherson, A., 85, 208
Scheving, L. E., 81, 216
Schildkraut, J. J., 25, 26, 125, 216
Schlosberg, H., 164, 216
Schnore, M. M., 57, 216
Scholz, M., 19, 212
Schwartz, M. F., 23, 43, 206
Schwarz, N., 10, 64, 217
Seligman, M. E. P., 41, 42, 43, 152, 166, 211, 213, 217
Selye, H., 51, 117, 122, 192, 217
Semmel, A., 41, 42, 166, 211
Sepinwall, J., 125, 217
Shacham, S., 18, 217
Shaw, F. H., 26, 203
Shephard, R. J., 49, 126, 217
Sherk, D., 19, 209
Sherrington, C., 58–59, 217
Shurcliff, A., 165, 217
Sime, W. E., 4, 92, 119, 202
Simon, L., 24, 69, 82, 131, 214
Singer, G., 27, 202
Singer, J. A., 35, 217
Siviy, S. M., 28, 213
Skinner, B. F., 191, 217
Skriner, G. S., 28, 199
Skwerer, R. O., 158, 163, 215
Slade, P., 30, 217
Slavney, P. R., 19, 217
Smallberg, S. A., 36, 199

Smith, R., 37, 95, 205
Smoller, J. W., 39, 217, 220
Snyder, S. H., 43, 126, 206
Sonnenschein, D., 85, 208
Soyka, F., 40, 217
Sperry, R. W., 93–94, 217
Spielberger, C. D., 18, 217
Spinweber, C. L., 38, 97, 217
Spring, B., 4, 38, 97, 141, 158, 163, 215, 217
Stagner, B., 38–39, 199
Steele, R. S., 98, 217
Steiner, M., 18, 205
Sternbach, R. A., 48, 113, 217
Stinnett, J. L., 26, 211
Stone, A. A., 4, 38, 42, 83, 218
Stone, J. I., 19, 221
Strack, S., 21, 198
Strassman, H. D., 123, 218
Strelau, J., 43, 117, 156, 218
Strube, M. J., 19, 218
Stukovsky, R., 30, 197
Stunkard, A. J., 39, 217, 220
Sudilovsky, A., 159, 160, 195
Sugarman, D. A., 114, 218
Sullivan, J. L., 37, 95, 198
Surwillo, W. W., 193, 210
Sutker, P. B., 30, 218
Sweeney, P. D., 19, 197
Szegda, M., 21–22, 208

Takahashi, P. J., 9, 11, 19, 31, 69, 75, 80, 82, 87, 103, 131, 138, 150, 156, 175, 182, 219
Tanguay, P. E., 98, 218
Taub, J. M., 4, 18, 98, 218
Taylor, C. B., 100, 202, 218
Taylor, H. L., 55, 97, 118, 122, 123, 207
Taylor, M. J., 36, 218
Taylor, R., 34, 218
Taylor, S. E., 34, 198
Teasdale, J. D., 22, 23, 33, 34, 199, 218
Tellegen, A., 3, 16, 17, 18, 45, 61, 62, 133–134, 164, 178, 219, 221, 222
Teplov, B. M., 42, 219
Thaler, M. B., 123, 218
Thayer, R. E., *passim*
Thompson, D. M., 33, 220
Tiggemann, M., 41, 220
Tom, G., 40, 219
Tomarken, A. J., 21, 29, 207, 209
Tomkins, S. S., 3, 13, 220
Torsvall, L., 80, 195, 220
Touitou, C., 81, 220
Touitou, Y., 81, 220
Tracy, M. L., 98, 209
Troccoli, B. T., 142, 197
Tucker, D. M., 29, 125, 220
Tulving, E., 33, 220
Tune, G. S., 80, 220
Turin, A. C., 8, 9, 24, 159, 216
Turner, C. W., 19, 218

Turner, J. A., 43, 214
Tversky, A., 35, 207

Underwood, B., 19, 220
Underwood, G., 10, 64, 220
Ursin, H., 51, 220

Valdimarsdottir, H., 4, 38, 218
Vanderwolf, C. H., 47, 114, 191, 220
van Praag, H. M., 125, 220
Velten, E. C., 20, 21, 220
Vermillion, M. E., 68, 199
Vestre, N. D., 19, 220
Vickers, M. D., 26, 201
Vilkin, B., 104, 214
Vincent, J. E., 157, 199
Viney, L. L., 42, 220
Vlaander, G.P.J., 23, 215

Wadden, T. A., 39, 217, 220
Wagener, J. J., 21–22, 208
Warburton, D. M., 158, 159, 220, 221
Ward, C. H., 18, 196
Wardlaw, S., 28, 200
Ware, E. E., 19, 209
Warner, P., 30, 196, 216
Waterhouse, J. M., 191, 192, 202, 211
Watson, D., 3, 16, 17, 18, 19, 42, 61, 62,
    133–134, 164, 178, 191, 199, 221
Watson, F. L., 192, 202
Watson, S. J., 27, 164, 195
Watts, B. L., 87, 221
Watts, C., 80, 221
Webb, W. B., 97, 98, 176, 197, 221
Wehr, T. A., 40, 215
Weinberger, J., 98, 221
Weiner, B., 43, 221
Weingartner, H., 33, 34, 36, 199, 221
Weitzman, E. D., 70, 81–82, 211, 221
Werner, M., 80, 197
Wesnes, K., 158, 159, 220, 221
West, C., 19, 207
West, J. B., 48, 221

Wettler, A., 116, 125, 151, 166, 219
Wever, R. A., 192, 221
Wheeler, E. O., 53, 115, 221
White, B., 38–39, 141, 191, 199
White, P. D., 53, 115, 221
Whitton, J. L., 18, 201
Whybrow, P. C., 43, 221
Wilcox, K. J., 45, 219
Willemse-Geest, H.M.M., 79, 207
Williams, D. G., 19, 221
Williams, J. M. G., 43, 205
Williamson, D. A., 43, 205
Williamson, P. A., 29, 125, 220
Wilson, G. T., 106, 216
Wilson, T. D., 19, 194, 212, 221
Winefield, A. H., 41, 220
Winokur, G., 194, 221
Wispe, L., 43, 221
Wocial, B., 43, 207
Wood, D. R., 37, 95, 208
Wright, R. A., 98, 222
Wright, W. F., 36, 222
Wundt, W., 46, 222
Wurtman, J. J., 38, 96, 97, 104, 158, 163,
    209, 215, 222
Wurtman, R. J., 38, 96, 97, 104, 222
Wyer, R. S., 64, 222

Yalom, I. D., 84–85, 211
Yates, A. J., 38, 205
Young, P. T., 164, 222
Young, R. D., 159, 206
Young, T., 28, 210

Zajonc, R. B., 3, 13, 43, 103, 193, 222
Zaroulis, C. G., 28, 202
Zentall, S. S., 83, 222
Zentall, T. R., 83, 222
Zevon, M. A., 16, 222
Zillman, D., 194, 222
Zimmerman, J. C., 81–82, 221
Zuckerman, M., 18, 81, 114, 117, 131, 222
Zwilling, G., 97, 205

Subject Index

Activation. *See* Arousal
AD ACL (Activation-Deactivation
  Adjective Check List), 6, 18, 59–62,
  178–180
Aerobic-anaerobic mediation of mood,
  126–127
Age and mood, 80–82, 152–156. *See also*
  Biological cycles, age
Aggregation value in mood research, 91,
  137–139
Alcohol. *See* Drug influences on mood
Alertness, 70, 72, 180
Anger, 16, 59, 166
Antecedents of mood, 13, 44. *See also*
  Mood
Anxiety
  as a motivator, 114
  neurosis, 115
  chronic, 118
  See also Tense arousal
Apathy. *See* Exhaustion
Applications of mood principles to self,
  168–177
Arousal, general, 31–32, 46–48, 112–114
  alternative models (Eysenck, Gray,
    Mandler, Watson & Tellegen), 129–134
  criticisms of, 47, 114
  dimensions of, 47, 60–62, 178–180
Attention deficit disorder. *See*
  Hyperactivity
Attention to danger, 51–52, 106, 128
Autosuggestion, hypnosis, and mood, 20–
  22

Behavioral inhibition, 106, 131–132
Behaviorists, radical, 13
Biological function of mood, 3–4, 6–7, 10,
  37, 64–66, 128–129, 134–136, 148–150
Biochemical correlates of mood, 4, 5, 25–
  29, 44, 125–126, 166
Biological cycles, 13, 24, 29–30, 33, 67–87,
  148
  age and, 80–82, 191
  circadian (diurnal) rhythms of energy, 9,
    67–87, 116, 138, 152–156, 170, 174–
    175, 181–183

compatibility, social and, 86–87
definition of terms, 67
endogenous energy cycles, 71–72
infradian rhythms of energy and tension
  (menstrual cycles), 83–85
peak of energetic arousal (acrophase),
  68–70
ultradian rhythms, including BRAC
  cycle, 85–86
Blue-Monday phenomenon, 42
Brain
  lateralization and mood, 29, 125
  mechanisms underlying energy-tension
    interactions, 124–126
Breathing response during danger, 107,
  126–127, 192

Caffeine. *See* Drug influences, caffeine
Calm-energy, 7, 53–54, 119–122, 136, 150–
  152
Calm-tiredness, 7, 53–54, 136, 150–152
Carbohydrates. *See* Food and mood
Catecholamine hypothesis of depression,
  26. *See also* Biochemical correlates
Chronobiology. *See* Biological cycles
Clothing and mood, 192
Cognition and mood, 3, 5, 13–14, 22, 32–
  37, 43, 44, 77, 98–101, 104–106
Cognition vs. affect, primacy, 43
Compliance of subjects with experimental
  procedures, 142–144
Congruent memory processes, 32–36
Concentration camp moods, 122–123
Conscious awareness, 9–10, 49–50, 52, 54–
  59, 63–65, 99–101, 103–104, 147, 149,
  167–171
Consequences of mood, 13–14. *See also*
  Mood
Creativity and mood, 36, 164–165
Current status, mood research, 13–45. *See*
  also Mood

Daily cycles of energy. *See* Biological
  rhythms, energy
Danger, effects on mood, 6–8, 50–52, 101–
  104, 106–109, 115, 128–129

Daylight saving time and mood, 71
Demand characteristics. *See* Expectation
    effects
Depression-elation, 18, 20–26, 29, 32–36,
    43, 53–54, 105, 115–116, 148, 151–
    152, 166, 173, 184
Dimensions of mood, 15–20, 44. *See also*
    Arousal, dimensions of
Dispositional character of mood, 15
Definitions: mood, affect, emotion, feeling,
    14–15
Drug influences on mood, 8, 13, 24–25, 33,
    43, 120–121, 191–192
  alcohol, 121, 159, 161–163
  antidepressant agents, 26
  caffeine, 8, 9, 24, 159, 161–163, 188
  cocaine, 8, 159, 160, 165
  cross-substance associations, 163
  heroin, 165
  naloxone, 28–29
  nicotine, 127–128, 158–159, 161–163,
    172–173

Eight State Questionnaire, 16. *See* Mood
    measurement
Emergency reaction, 51–52, 106–109. *See*
    also Tense arousal
Emotional states, 13
Endorphins. *See* Opioids
Energetic arousal, 6–8, 21, 48–50, 68–72,
    110–136, 149–152, 179–180
  age and, 79–82
  morning-evening types and, 79–80, 182–
    183
Energy-tension relationship, 7, 63–65, 110–
    136
Energy-tension effects on behavior, 74–75,
    113–124
Evolution and mood, 5–6, 10, 62–65, 85,
    148. *See also* Biological functions of
    mood
Exercise (and mood), 24, 26, 31–32, 45,
    48–50, 88–93, 119, 148–149, 171–174,
    176
  as an experimental variable, 92, 187–188
  biological bases, 93–95
  compared to circadian cycles, 91
  compared to a sugar snack, 172
  duration of mood enhancement
    following, 90–91, 188
  effect on problem perception and
    optimism, 91–92
  effect on anxiety, 119–120, 188
  and tiredness, 94–95
Exhaustion, 21, 122–124, 156
Expectation effects, 21, 23, 30, 89, 92, 141–
    144, 191
Experimental induction, 13, 20–24
Extraversion, 19–20, 130–131
  and energetic arousal, 82–83, 131
Eysenck Personality Questionnaire (also
    EPI), 19

Fear. *See* Tense arousal
Feeling good, 23. *See also* Good-bad mood
Fight-or-flight reaction, 7, 51–52, 64–65,
    106–109. *See also* Tense arousal
Film effects on mood, 22–23
Food and mood, 38–39, 45, 96–97, 139–
    142, 148–149, 157–158, 160–161, 185
  diet programs, 39
  sugar ingestion, 38, 96–97, 139–142,
    157–158, 161–163, 188
Freeze response. *See* Skeletal-muscular
    inhibition

Genetic bases of mood, 45
Good-bad mood, 3, 15–17, 36, 148, 150–
    151, 163–165, 191. *See also* Positive-
    negative affect

Happiness-sadness, 33–34
Health and energy, 95, 176
Hedonic continuum, 18, 148, 163–165
Helping and mood, 43
Hyperactivity, 121, 191–192
Hypnosis. *See* Autosuggestion

Illness and mood, 37–38, 95–96
  allergic response, 37, 104
  epileptic seizures, 37
  immune system response, 37–38
Individual differences and mood, 19, 42–
    43, 78–83
Inhibitory response. *See* Skeletal-muscular
    inhibition
Insomnia, 54, 116, 153–156, 176
Internal-external control and mood, 19
Introversion. *See* Extraversion
Irrational beliefs and mood, 19
Irritable behavior, 118–119

Jet lag and mood, 71

Lactic acid and anxiety, 126
Laboratory test conditions. *See* Naturalistic
    vs. laboratory
Language of arousal, 59–62. *See also* AD
    ACL
Laughter, 165
Loss of control, 102

Mood
  behavior association, 15, 149
  current status of mood research, 13–45
  disorders, 43. *See also* Depression-elation
  essential features, 147–152
  external events vs. natural processes,
    166–168
  food. *See* Food and mood
  management. *See* Self-regulation of
    mood
  manipulations of, 20–24
  measurement of, 14, 16–19, 137–139,
    178–180, 184–186

and memory, 13, 32–36
effects on behavior, 15, 149–150
effects on cognition, 36. *See also*
Cognition and mood. *See also* other
mood headings
Mood Adjective Check List, 16. *See also*
Mood measurement
Morning-evening types, 79–80, 182–183
Motor activity, gross voluntary, 93–95,
192. *See also* Exercise
Multidimensional arousal model, 110–128,
134–136
Multiple Affect Adjective Check List, 18.
See also Mood measurement
Muscular inhibition. *See* Skeletal-muscular
inhibition
Music effects on mood, 22–23

Naturalistic vs. laboratory test conditions,
139–144
Nervousness. *See* Tense arousal
Network theory of mood and cognition,
35–36
Neuroticism, 130–131
and tense arousal, 131, 156
Neurotransmitters. *See* Biochemical bases
Nomothetic single-occasion research
designs, 137
Nutrition. *See* Food and mood

Opioids and mood, 27–29, 126
Optimism, 9, 31, 73–78
Optimal (poor) periods of the day, 182

Pain and arousal, 104
Peak of energetic arousal (acrophase), 68–
70
Pharmacological agents. *See* Drug
influences
Physical fitness and mood, 93, 95, 176–
177
Physiological bases of mood, 13, 25–32, 44,
48–52, 124–128, 148. *See also*
Biochemical correlates of mood
Physiological vs. self-report correlations,
56–59
Pleasant (unpleasant) events and mood,
41–42
Pleasure dimension and mood. *See*
Hedonic continuum
Positive and negative affect, 16–18, 44,
133–134, 148, 150, 163–165, 167. *See
also* Good-bad mood
orthogonality, 17
PMS (Premenstrual Tension Syndrome),
29–30, 83–85, 105–106
Problem perception and mood, 8–9, 73–78,
116, 184
Procrastination and energy-tension
interactions, 116–117
Profile of Mood States, 16. *See also* Mood
measurement

Reliability of mood measurement, 74, 91,
137–139
Requirements vs. resources as danger, 101–
104. *See also* Tense arousal
Risk-taking and mood, 36

Self-awareness. *See* Conscious awareness
Self-efficacy, 100–101, 106
Self-esteem and mood, 8–9, 151, 153, 185,
193
Self-observation, 9–10, 144–146, 168–171,
181–189. *See also* Conscious
awareness
Self-ratings of mood, 15–19. *See also*
Conscious awareness; Self-observation
Self-regulation of mood, 11–12, 157–163,
171–177
Sexual moods, 16, 166
Shift-work and mood, 72
Skeletal-muscular inhibition, 51–52, 106–
109, 127–128, 154–155
Sleep and mood, 97–98, 176, 188
Sleep deprivation, 94–95, 97, 102–103,
118, 123, 193
Smiling, posture and mood, 21–22
Smoking and arousal states, 172–173, 185.
See also Drug influences on mood,
nicotine
Social compatibility. *See* Biological cycles,
compatibility
Social support and mood, 42
Starvation effects on mood, 55, 97, 118,
122–123
State-dependent memory, 9, 32–36, 78
Stress, 24, 28, 42, 112–113, 122–123, 150,
152–156. *See also* Requirements vs.
resources
Subjective state, mood, 14. *See also* Self-
ratings of mood
Subtle but persistent moods, influence of,
104–106
depression, 105–106
breaking a diet, 104–105
mechanisms of action, 105–106
PMS, 105–106
sugar craving, 162
Sugar effects on mood. *See* Food and mood

Temperament and mood, 14. *See also*
Extraversion; Neuroticism
Tense arousal, 6–8, 50–52, 101–104, 106–
109, 110–136, 149–152, 179–180, 191
Tense-energy, 7, 53–54, 114–115, 136,
150–156
Tense-tiredness, 7, 53–54, 115–117, 136,
150–156, 163
Tension-energy relationship. *See* Energy-
tension relationship
Tension reduction, 176–177, 194
Treadmill walking, energy and tension, 90
Traits of personality and mood, 14, 19–20
Type-A personality, 53, 114–115, 151

Unidimensional arousal model, 112, 132–133
Unemployment and mood, 41, 152–156

Variability of mood, 19–20
Velten procedure, 20–21, 34, 191
Vulnerability to tension, 117–119, 153–156

Walks, brisk, and mood, 88–93, 171–174.
    See also Exercise

Weather, geophysical phenomena and
    mood, 39–41
  humidity, 40
  ionic concentration, 40
  mood cycles, 41
  sunshine, 40
  winter depression, 40–41
Worry and time of day, 73–74